THE
SHADOW
UNIVERSITY

The Betrayal of Liberty on America's Campuses

ALAN CHARLES KORS

HARVEY A. SILVERGLATE

THE FREE PRESS

New York   London   Toronto   Singapore

THE FREE PRESS
A Division of Simon & Schuster Inc.
1230 Avenue of the Americas
New York, NY 10020

THE FREE PRESS and colophon are trademarks
of Simon & Schuster Inc.

Designed by Carla Bolte

Manufactured in the United States of America

10   9   8   7   6   5   4   3   2   1

Library of Congress Cataloging-in-Publication Data

Kors, Alan Charles.
    The shadow university: the betrayal of liberty on America's
campuses / Alan Charles Kors, Harvey A. Silverglate.
        p.   cm.
    Includes bibliographical references (p.   ) and index.
    1. Academic freedom—United States.   2. Freedom of speech—United
States.   3. Education, Higher—Political aspects—United States.
4. Political correctness—United States.   I. Silverglate, Harvey A.   II. Title.
LC72.2.K67   1998
378.1'21—dc21   98–8728
                                                                         CIP

ISBN 0–684–85321–3

TO ELSA AND ERIKA

CONTENTS

PART IV: THE ASSAULT ON DUE PROCESS

PART V: RESTORING LIBERTY

ACKNOWLEDGMENTS

This book is a far from exhaustive account of the betrayal of liberty on America's campuses. Many times, faced with the need to reduce its size and to transform it from an encyclopedia to a humane text, we eliminated the narrative or even summary of several scandals in favor of a closer, longer look at a particularly revealing or representative case. Each of those instances hurt, because we wanted, among other things, to bear witness for the victims of unbearable oppressions and intrusions and to name for public obloquy their unjust tormentors. We hope that what has been lost in detail will be compensated for by an overall revealing and representative picture of unfairness and oppression that illuminates the deeper conditions of our colleges and universities.

The following individuals were extraordinarily kind, and, in some cases, quite courageous in assisting us. Some pointed us in the right directions and toward the right people; others opened their files and private lives to us; yet others provided invaluable assistance, advice, criticism, or welcome candor. If we thanked everyone who aided us, our list would be book-length, and some of those thanked would lose their jobs. Thus, with great admiration and warmth toward those unnamed here, we acknowledge our particular debt in these regards to Eden Jacobowitz, Thor Halvorssen, Greg Pavlik, Tim Monaco, Bob Chatelle, Kelly Mulroney, Debra (Cermele) Ross, Jordana Horn, Michael Cohen, J. Christopher Robbins, Dan Ben-Amos, Jeremy Chiapetta, Dana Gurwitch, Lindsey Kaser, Hal Pashler, Michael Bressler, Peter Chang, Goon Pattanumotana, Eric Tienou, James Aist, Michael Greve, Saul Steinberg, Hans Bader, Francis Randall, Joseph A. Watson, Dan Ritchie, Judith Kleinfeld, Jay Bergman, Norman Fruman, Bob Costrell, Jim D'Entremont, Declan McCullagh, Michael Meyers,

Andrew Good, Linda Seebach, Jeanne Baker, Gia Barresi, David Boaz, Philip Cormier, Jillian Earp Durand, Adam Dershowitz, Alan Dershowitz, Nathan Dershowitz, Sandra Fennell, the late Allen Ginsberg, Mike Godwin, Nat Hentoff, Virginia Postrel, Dorothy Rabinowitz, William Van Alstyne, Lincoln Herbert, Michael Itagaki, Eugene Volokh, Vivek Jain, Will Moynahan, Inati Ntshanga, David Rosenberg, Jolyon Silversmith, Richard Vigilante, Adam Bellow, Chauncey Wood, Devon Hincapie, Wendy Kaminer, Natasha Lisman, Eric Losick, Daffodil Tyminski, Roderick MacLeish, Jr., Gary Brasor, Brian and David LaMacchia, Philip Greenspun, Glenn Ricketts, Leroy and Tatum Young, Kenny Williams, Eric Johnson, Daphne Patai, Steven Shavell, Eric D. Blumenson, Ed Cutting, Leslie E. Jones, and Ryan Hanley.

In addition, we gratefully thank the legion of middle-level administrators at so many universities, who, fed up with the double standards and injustices of their institutions, sent us materials to document the betrayal of liberty that threatens both freedom and decency. We also gratefully thank the legion of students who not only told us their stories (which we would otherwise not likely have learned because of ubiquitous college confidentiality rules), but who went to such great lengths to document their claims. Special thanks are due our agent, Freya Manston, who understood and enthusiastically supported this project long before many others did, and our editor at the Free Press, Paul Golob, who has been a supportive, sensitive, activist editor in the old-fashioned tradition that is fast disappearing elsewhere in publishing. Monica Mehigan has supervised the mechanics of computerized production with efficiency and dedication. Most essentially, Erika Kors superintended and participated in revisions to and preparation of the manuscript through countless versions during several years, a labor that was absolutely vital to us, that comforted us, and that kept us organized at every stage. Elsa Dorfman contributed her numerous skills, spirit, and encouragement.

We of course should mention the fortuity of our having met in Princeton in September of 1960, each of us a freshman coming from New Jersey high schools whose graduates were eligible for a scholarship at Princeton endowed by a donor who had a chance connection to our respective schools. A lifetime friendship of mind and soul, formed then, has flowered into this long-planned collaboration. We are therefore thankful to the Fates as well.

Finally, this book simply could not have been written without the deep support of our wives, Elsa Dorfman and Erika Kors. Their love, their patience, their wisdom, their understanding, their encouragement, and, indeed, their herculean labors on behalf of this project were, again and again, our salvation. We wrote this book, in some significant measure, for the children whom we and our wives love more than life—Isaac Dorfman Silverglate, Samantha Kors, and Brian Kors. May they continue to struggle for the liberty that is their human birthright.

Alan Charles Kors
Wallingford, Pennsylvania

Harvey A. Silverglate
Cambridge, Massachusetts

April 1998

INTRODUCTION

Americans think a great deal about colleges and universities, but they do not examine them very closely. Every spring, most of the nation's high school seniors choose a place for what well might be the most important four years of their lives. They and their parents pore over catalogs, read guidebooks, visit campuses, talk with school counselors, and share advice and impressions with relatives, friends, and neighbors, many of whom knew these institutions decades ago. For most high school seniors, the prospect of attending college, whatever its apprehensions, inspires real enthusiasm. A new world—freer, more interesting, more respectful of their emerging individuality and adulthood—awaits them.

Indeed, colleges and universities are singular institutions in American life. Whatever jokes or complaints one hears about professors or tuition, the fact remains that we place most of our sons and daughters in the care of colleges and universities. We charge these institutions with preparing future citizens for participation in the life of a free and productive society. We offer them special status and protection in that task, indeed, a wall of immunity from excessive scrutiny. We pay them handsomely, and, with breathtaking trust, almost never ask for an accounting of what we receive in return.

During the antiwar and social protests of the late '60s and early '70s, institutions of higher education were frequently in the spotlight, less for anything *they* did than for the demonstrations, culture, and lifestyles of the students who attended them. A generational revolution appeared to touch significant numbers of undergraduates, and, while it lasted, it was a major phenomenon and the stuff of daily news. For most citizens, however, the '60s are long over, and, in their minds, universities have returned to calm and ordinary lives (however "ordinary" one can call places populated by eighteen- to twenty-two-year-olds). Most students of the '60s have gone on to jobs, families, and significant lives in worlds far from the scenes of their undergraduate moments, and they assume that their peers who stayed on at universities have undergone the same evolutions and adaptations.

During the past several years, however, colleges and universities once again have caught the attention of the public at large. People hear about "political correctness," and there is a vague sense that some individuals or groups on campuses may have tried to carry the regulation of others' conduct and speech just a bit too far. A few wonder how the Berkeley Free Speech movement of the '60s ever culminated in *restrictions* of speech. The wackiest of these tales—like the 1993 "water buffalo affair" at the University of Pennsylvania—have received a brief flurry of remarkable media attention, but then were soon forgotten.

Editorialists and occasional readers of literature on the universities are aware of something deeper going on—often characterized as "the culture wars"—but, except to the most committed, the scope of what is happening seems confusing, to be waited out rather than figured out. It is clear that the curriculum in the humanities and the social sciences has changed, and that this has something to do with gender, race, and sexuality, but in what ways, precisely, few are sure. Those with their eyes on the behavior of academics in these fields know that there is something of a shouting match in a very small sauna—lots of noise, heat, and steam, but very little in the way of audience. There seem to be a lot of -isms bandied about—"racism" and "sexism," to be sure, but also "postmodernism" and "multiculturalism." There are lots of different theories about what these arguments truly mean, if, indeed, they mean anything at all. At any rate, for most high school seniors, these developments do not even register on the radar screens of their lives. Most incoming students and their parents have the vague sense that there may be a few crazies set loose on campuses, but that it should be easy enough to sort things out and avoid the worst of it.

Among the most politically focused, however, there is a sharper sense of a growing turmoil at universities. On the Left there is a hope that universities are dealing with problems of power and injustice more explicitly and progressively, and a fear that the "excesses" of political correctness might bring such a good endeavor into disrepute. On the Right there is a belief that whole disciplines have transformed the classroom into a pulpit from which supposed "oppression" is analyzed in wholly partisan fashion, transforming students into willing consumers of a politics of "victimization." Across the spectrum, wherever there are individuals who believe that open minds and

critical inquiry favor their cause, there is a concern that various academic in-
doctrinations and posturings may be replacing critical classroom education.

It is vital that citizens understand the deeper crisis of our colleges and universities. Contrary to the expectations of most applicants, colleges and universities are not freer than the society at large. Indeed, they are less free, and that
diminution is continuing apace. In a nation whose future depends upon an
education in freedom, colleges and universities are teaching the values of censorship, self-censorship, and self-righteous abuse of power. Our institutions of
higher education greet freshmen not as individuals on the threshold of adulthood, but as embodiments of group identity, largely defined in terms of blood
and history, who are to be infantilized at every turn. In a nation whose soul
depends upon the values of individual rights and responsibilities, and upon
equal justice under law, our students are being educated in so-called group
rights and responsibilities, and in double standards to redress partisan definitions of historical wrongs. Universities have become the enemy of a free society, and it is time for the citizens of that society to recognize this scandal of
enormous proportions and to hold these institutions to account.

The '60s may be long past for most Americans, with various and diverse
legacies left behind, but strangely enough, the *best* aspects of that decade's idealistic agenda have died on our campuses—free speech, equality of rights, respect for private conscience and individuation, and a sense of undergraduate
liberties and adult responsibilities. What remain of the '60s on our campuses
are its *worst* sides: intolerance of dissent from regnant political orthodoxy, the
self-appointed power of self-designated "progressives" to set everyone else's
moral agenda, and, saddest of all, the belief that universities not only may but
should suspend the rights of some in order to transform students, the culture,
and the nation according to their ideological vision and desire.

Universities are administered, above all, not by ideological zealots, but
by careerists who have made a Faustian deal. They have preserved the most
prestigious, productive, and administratively visible sides of their institutions—the parts, not coincidentally, that the public and potential donors
see—from almost all of the depredations of ideological fervor. Physics, fund-
raising, athletics, microbiology, the medical schools, mathematics, financial
management, physical plant, alumni relations, business, and metallurgy, for
example, though no doubt caught up in the currents of our age, are not in
the hands of ideological zealots. Rather, whole departments of the liberal
arts have been given to those for whom universities represent, in their own

minds, the revolutionary agency of our culture, walling them off, so to speak, from the parts of universities that trustees, rightly or wrongly, take most seriously.

Far more significantly for the future of liberty, however, and providing the focus of this book, the university in loco parentis—the university standing in the place of parents—has been given over to the self-appointed progressives to do with what they will. The result has been an emerging tyranny over all aspects of student life—a tyranny that is far more dangerous than the relatively innocuous parietal rules of ages past. It is a tyranny that seeks to assert absolute control over the souls, the consciences, and the individuality of our students—in short, a tyranny over the essence of liberty itself.

The real threat to liberty comes from this "shadow university," the structures built, almost without debate or examination, to "educate," or, more precisely, to reeducate, far from the accountability of the classroom. To know the betrayal of liberty on our campuses, one must understand what has become of their divisions of university life and student life, residential advisors, judicial systems, deans of students and their officers, and of their new and profoundly disturbing student rules and regulations. This threat has developed not in the glare of publicity, debate, and criticism, as has been the case with new academic disciplines, courses, and pedagogies, but in the shadows. Indeed, few professors, including those most critical of what they see as ideological zealotry at their institutions, are aware of the transformation of the university in loco parentis that has occurred. The shadow university, with its shadow curriculum, dominates freshman orientation, residential programming, extracurricular student life, the promulgation of codes and regulations, and the administration of what passes, on our campuses, for justice.

The ultimate force of the shadow university is its ability to punish students and, increasingly, faculty behind closed doors, far from public and even campus scrutiny. If professors give biased lectures, grade students down for ideological nonconformity, and favor those who agree with them, these activities ultimately become more broadly known. The shadow university, however, hands students a moral agenda upon arrival, subjects them to mandatory political reeducation, sends them to sensitivity training, submerges their individuality in official group identity, intrudes upon private conscience, treats them with scandalous inequality, and, when it chooses, suspends or expels them. Having grown heady with arbitrary power over students, the shadow university now engages in the systematic intimidation and attempted reeducation of faculty, too. The first imposition, in the classroom, is merely an abuse of a power that generally may be avoided by choice and in any event is not accomplished in secret. The second imposition of the shadow university is inescapable, and is an exercise in something truly chilling: a hidden, systematic assault upon liberty, individualism, dignity, due process, and equality before the law. After reading this book, no one—academic or nonacademic citizen—should be able to doubt the reality and moral urgency of this phenomenon.

Critics of modern trends at our universities have looked above all to multicultural studies, to the new scholarship, to the therapeutic classroom, to affirmative action, or to conferences on the body or sexuality as sources of their unease or outrage. Reasonable individuals, however, may disagree about every one of these phenomena. That, indeed, is precisely the point: Reasonable (and unreasonable) individuals *do* disagree about these things, and debate them openly and vociferously. To the extent that one believes that truth or critical perspective emerges from sustained argument, one should be confident that whatever correctives or refutations the intellectual age requires will or, at least, can emerge from these debates.

In the shadow university, however, that precondition of informed change—free and unfettered debate among free individuals—is precisely what has been replaced by censorship, indoctrination, intimidation, official group identity, and groupthink. The issue of whether we shall have intelligent and thoughtful universities can be addressed only if we have free universities, and the shadow university has suppressed that very freedom itself. Speech codes, prohibiting speech that "offends," protect ideologically or politically favored groups, and, what is more important, insulate these groups' self-appointed spokesmen and spokeswomen from criticism and even from the need to participate in debate. Double standards destroy legal equality and all meaningful accountability, teaching the worst imaginable lessons about the appropriate uses of power. Freshmen orientations and extracurricular "educational" programming offer partisan and intrusive indoctrination that is the opposite of, and incompatible with, a critical liberal education. Crude justice is administered, in secret, in biased fashion and without that due process that teaches lessons about civilization and the rule of law. Administrators, eager to buy peace and avoid scandal, deny the obvious truth of what is occurring, and, when pressed, invoke false doctrines of being legally bound by absolute confidentiality.

The goal of this book is to expose the shadow university, to let the sunlight shine on it, and to shame. It also is to give courage and a sense of common mission to those who know or suspect such things about our colleges and universities but do not know quite how to prove them or quite what to do. Finally, this book aims to remind citizens about the chasm that has emerged between the modern realities characterizing our institutions of higher education and the timeless but fragile values upon which the survival of freedom depends.

Part I

THE ASSAULT ON
LIBERTY

CHAPTER 1

THE WATER BUFFALO AFFAIR

On the night of January 13, 1993, Eden Jacobowitz, a freshman at the University of Pennsylvania, had been writing a paper for an English class when a sorority began celebrating its Founders' Day beneath the windows of his high-rise dormitory apartment. The women were singing very loudly, chanting, and stomping. It had prevented him from writing, and it had awakened his roommate. He shouted out the window, "Please keep quiet," and went back to work. Twenty minutes later, the noise yet louder, he shouted out the window, "Shut up, you water buffalo!" The women were singing about going to a party. "If you want a party," he shouted, "there's a zoo a mile from here." The women were black. Within weeks, the administrative judicial inquiry officer (JIO) in charge of Eden's case, Robin Read, decided to prosecute him for violation of Penn's policy on racial harassment. He could accept a "settlement"—an academic plea bargain—or he could face a judicial hearing whose possible sanctions included suspension and expulsion.[1]

The JIO's finding that there was "reasonable cause" to believe that Eden had violated Penn's racial harassment policy for having shouted "Shut up, you water buffalo!" to late-night noisemakers under his window was outrageous in terms of normal human interactions at a university. Loud and raucous festivities had occurred beneath the windows of students since the Middle Ages. For centuries, would-be scholars, disturbed or awakened in the still hours, had shouted their various and picturesque disapprovals at the celebrants. "Water buffalo" would have been one of the mildest such epithets ever uttered.

The JIO's decision also was unconscionable given the history of the debates over speech codes at Penn. In 1987, over the strenuous objections of a handful of professors, Sheldon Hackney, president of the University of Pennsylvania, promulgated the university's first modern-era restrictions on speech, in the form of prohibitions on "any behavior, verbal or physical, that stigmatizes or victimizes individuals on the basis of race, ethnic or national origin . . . and that has the purpose or effect of interfering with an individual's academic or work performance; and/or creates an intimidating or offensive academic, living, or work environment."[2] In September 1989, to explain the policy to incoming students, the administration gave specific examples of what would constitute the serious crime of "harassment": students who drew a poster to advertise a "South of the Border" party, showing a "lazy" Mexican taking a siesta against a wall; a faculty member who referred to blacks as "ex-slaves"; and students who, in protest of "Gay Jeans Day" (when undergraduates were asked to dress in jeans to show solidarity with gay and lesbian students), held a satiric sign proclaiming "Heterosexual Footwear Day."[3]

There were ironies in this presentation of "incidents of harassment." When Louis Farrakhan spoke at Penn in 1988 over the protests of several Jewish organizations, Hackney issued a statement in which he conceded that Farrakhan's statements were "racist, and anti-Semitic, and amount to scapegoating," but concluded: "In an academic community, open expression is the most important value. We can't have free speech only some of the time, for only some people. Either we have it, or we don't. At Penn, we have it."[4]

Indeed, in the very month that his administration was prohibiting social criticism of Gay Jeans Day and posters of sleeping Mexicans, Hackney was campaigning, to great national applause, against Senator Jesse Helms's efforts to deny federal funding, by the National Endowment for the Arts, of works such as Andres Serrano's "Piss Christ," a crucifix immersed in the artist's urine. According to Hackney, it was impossible "to cleanse public discourse of offensive material" without producing "an Orwellian nightmare" or the horror of "self-censorship." We were not, in Hackney's words, "Beijing" (an argument put to him earlier against his own speech code), but the "Land of Liberty," where efforts "to limit expression" deemed "offensive" violated the essence and spirit of "democracy" and made social "satire" impossible.[5]

The debate over the harassment policy had heated up at Penn in 1989–90, however, because of a federal court decision. Despite the university's private status, which placed it outside the sway of the Bill of Rights, the administration always had insisted that its speech code could pass constitutional muster. In 1989, however, a federal district court declared the University of Michigan's code, which was less restrictive than Penn's, to be unconstitutional. It embarrassed Hackney when his critics now pointed out that students at Pennsylvania State University or at local community colleges had more rights of free expression than students at the University of Pennsylvania. Accepting the advice of a professor of law to change Penn's overbroad, vague, and imprecise restrictions, and declaring that they were interested in prohibiting merely "words used as weapons," Penn's administration promulgated a "narrower" prohibition of "offensive" speech. The new code specified three conditions which, if met simultaneously, would constitute verbal harassment. This was the definition governing Eden Jacobowitz's case:

Any verbal or symbolic behavior that:
1. is directed at an identifiable person or persons; and
2. insults or demeans the person or persons to whom the behavior is directed, or abuses a power relationship with that person, on the basis of his or her race, color, ethnicity, or national origin, such as (but not limited to) by the use of slurs, epithets, hate words, demeaning jokes, or derogatory stereotypes; and
3. is intended by the speaker or actor only to inflict direct injury on the person or persons to whom the behavior is directed, or is sufficiently abusive or demeaning that a reasonable, disinterested observer would conclude that the behavior is so intended; or occurs in a context such that an intent only to inflict direct injury may reasonably be inferred.[6]

It still was a vague speech code, but it now prohibited epithets, jokes, and derogatory stereotypes uttered solely with the intention "to inflict direct injury." At a meeting of the Faculty Senate, a critic of both speech codes and selective enforcement asked Hackney if it would be racial harassment "if someone called a black with white friends an 'Uncle Tom' or an 'Oreo,'" or "if someone called a white person a 'fucking fascist white male pig'"? Hackney answered, "No."[7]

Eden, however, had not called anyone the officially protected "fucking fascist Uncle Tom." According to Eden, his first adviser, Director of Student Life Fran Walker—whom he had randomly selected from a list of judicial advisors presented to him by the Judicial Office—advised him to accept the settlement now offered by Robin Read:

1. Write a letter of apology to the complainants, in which you acknowledge your inappropriate behavior. . . .

2. Plan, develop and present a program for residents of High Rise East regarding some aspect of living in a diverse community environment by the end of the Spring 1993 term . . . under the supervision of . . . [the] Program Director, High Rise East;

3. Be on residential probation for as long as you live in a University residence. Should you be found guilty of violating any Residential Living policy, rule, etc., you will be immediately evicted from all University housing;

4. Receive a notation on your transcript, stating "Violation of the Code of Conduct and Racial Harassment Policy," to be removed at the beginning of your junior year.[8]

The reason that Eden had been singled out for persecution was particularly distressing. There had been fifteen sorority members celebrating under the high-rise's windows, and in the twenty minutes that passed between Eden's "Keep quiet!" and his "Shut up, you water buffalo!" a large number of students had shouted down to the women to leave them in peace. From all accounts, some few students had shouted apparently racial epithets, from "black asses" to "black bitches." Nonetheless, Eden had uttered nothing but "water buffalo."[9]

Five of the fifteen women now believed themselves, as Penn encouraged through its orientations and diversity programming on racism, to be the victims of "racial harassment." Within short order, the five women, with the university police in tow, were sweeping the dormitory looking for offenders. Only Eden Jacobowitz, it turned out, of the many students who had expressed their late-night annoyance, chose to come forward into the corridor, and he freely identified himself to the university police as the student who had shouted "water buffalo"; other students were identified by third parties. The next day, all students suspected of shouting were summoned one by one to the university police headquarters and asked if they had known the race of the celebrants. Street-smart Penn students, with one guileless exception, all said the equivalent of, "No, it was dark." Eden said, "Of course. It was bright as day out there. But their race had nothing to do with what I said."[10] The university now had its scapegoat.

Although the other students involved in the case initially claimed that Eden had used racial epithets, they soon recanted. As a result, Robin Read stipulated, in the presence of Eden's advisor, that the only "offensive" comments he had made had been "water buffalo" and "zoo."

To be considered "racial harassment" under Penn's policy, Eden's words had to be either clear racial epithets or clear derogatory stereotypes, and they had to be uttered "only" with the intention to inflict direct injury. How could "water buffalo" be a racial stereotype, and how could his motive have been other than to express his anger at the noise? When Read first informed Eden that the women had taken the phrase "water buffalo" as a specifically racial term of abuse, he was appalled, and he offered to explain to the young women that he had meant nothing racial whatsoever and to apologize for any rudeness. The JIO replied, "That is not good enough." When Eden said that "water buffalo" had no relation to race, Read said that water buffalo were "primitive, dark animals that lived in Africa." Eden Jacobowitz is a deeply religious Orthodox Jew, the descendant of Holocaust survivors, and a graduate of a leading yeshiva, a religious Jewish school. When he protested vehemently that everything in his being, his upbringing, and his religious commitments forbade racism, Read inquired, "Weren't you having racist thoughts when you said 'water buffalo'?"[11]

Eden refused to accept any settlement. He wrote a courageous letter to Read, given that she would be his prosecutor at a hearing. He accused her of putting her "political standing" above "the rights of students" and issues of "innocence," because "you simply . . . did not want to deal with the pressures of vindicating someone of racial harassment charges." He reminded her that both he and his roommate originally had been charged with shouting "non-racial comments at some members of the Delta Sigma Theta sorority on January 13," but that only he had been charged with harassment, because "my roommate claimed not to know the race of the people involved while I was totally and categorically indifferent to the race of the people involved." His words, he reiterated, "referred solely and only to the noise level outside my dormitory window." He characterized her interpretation of "water buffalo" as "the farthest meaning from my mind . . . your words not mine." He had simply objected to "the noise level produced by sporadic stomping and shouting right outside my window at midnight while I was trying to write a paper." If the noisemakers had been "Orthodox Jews," he assured her, "I would have said the same thing." He challenged Read's claim "that it was important to take the women's interpretation of my words and the pain that they inflicted upon them into account," reminding her that "As you know, I have asked from the very first day . . . to meet with the women to apologize for shouting in response to their noise and to make it clear that my words had no racial meaning." He accused her of ignoring all the evidence of eyewitnesses, raising in his mind "the terrifying possibility that this has become a show trial for a new policy." He understood the possible dangers of a hearing in the current climate, but, he wrote, "Your conclusion of guilt leaves me no choice but to pursue justice, the most precious of human conditions." He would risk anything to clear his name, because "I would die before shouting racist comments at anybody." He copied his letter to President Hackney, Provost Michael Aiken, Vice Provost for University Life Kim Morrisson, Assistant to the President Steve Steinberg, and the general counsel.[12] No one replied. Read eventually wrote back, a month later, disagreeing with his characterization of their discussions and her motives.[13] The entire weight of the university was coming down on a frightened freshman. Shortly after refusing the settlement, Eden called history professor Alan Charles Kors, who became his new advisor.

In preparing for a hearing, Eden secured a long list of black and white eye-witnesses from the high-rise eager to testify that he was the very opposite of a racist, and that on the night in question, he had merely said "water buffalo" (as the JIO already had stipulated). Because it seemed obvious that Eden was responding to noise, not seeking to inflict injury, Kors spoke to a former general counsel of the university, Professor of Law Stephen Burbank. Burbank termed the case "ludicrous" and "open and shut" (because the charges did not even touch the categories of the university's own definition of harassment) and agreed to testify on Eden's behalf.

Encyclopedias and dictionaries revealed the obvious: that "water buffalo" had no racial connotation. The animals were the "Indian Buffalo . . . domesticated in Asia" *(Britannica),* "domesticated Asian buffalo" *(Merriam Webster's Collegiate Dictionary),* "the common Indian buffalo" *(Webster's Unabridged New International Dictionary),* and limited "to southern Asia" *(Grolier's Academic American Encyclopedia).*

The issue now was not the speech code itself, but Eden's innocence even assuming the speech code's legitimacy. Many offered discreet help. Dan Hoffman, a Pulitzer Prize–winning literary critic and poet, spoke to the curator of mammals at the Philadelphia Academy of Natural Sciences, who had consulted *Walker's Mammals of the World* (the Bible, it turns out, of mammalian zoology). Authorities, Hoffman wrote, gave "the range of the 75 million domesticated water buffaloes as from Nepal to Vietnam." The African buffalo, it turned out, was not a water buffalo, but a Cape buffalo, and "confusing the African Cape Buffalo with the Asian water buffalo is clearly an error." [14] A brilliant black ethnographer at Penn, a scholar who had walked the streets of racial tension, confirmed that he "never" had heard the term "water buffalo" used as a racial epithet or derogatory stereotype of blacks. He provided both a written and a taped deposition for Eden. He also referred Kors to several eminent scholars who worked in black linguistics, African-American studies, African-American folklore, and African folklore. None, a phone call to each revealed, ever had heard of the term "water buffalo" used either as a racial epithet or as a derogatory (or any other form of) stereotype of blacks.

A professor of linguistics at Penn sent an inquiry to an international linguistics listserve: "Have you ever heard 'water buffalo' used as a racial epithet?" The replies revealed that in one Asian country it indicated an overeater and in another a fool. A senior professor in African history further confirmed that "water buffalo" had no African or racial connotation whatsoever, and he agreed to testify at any hearing. Acquaintances provided a bevy of innocuous "water buffalo" references: the humorist Dave Barry, in *Dave Barry Does Japan,* referred to himself several times as a "water buffalo" when he did something clumsy or out of place; the white cavemen of *The Flintstones* used "water buffalo" as a friendly term; in the classic film *His Girl Friday* (1939), Cary Grant called Rosalind Russell "a water buffalo."

The whole case took on a new light, however, when the world-renowned Israeli scholar, Dan Ben-Amos, whose field is African folklore, replied. "What would water buffalo have to do with Africans or African-Americans?" he asked. Informed about the facts of the case, Ben-Amos asked if the student were Israeli or spoke modern Hebrew. Learning that Eden's parents were both Israeli and that he had attended a Hebrew-language high school, Ben-Amos explained that "*Behema* is Hebrew slang for a thoughtless or rowdy person, and, literally, can best be translated as 'water buffalo.' It has absolutely no racial connotation." When Kors asked Jacobowitz, "What's the first thing that comes into your mind if I say '*behema,*'" Eden said, "Wow . . . that's amazing. In my yeshiva, we called each other *behema* all the time, and the teachers and rabbi would call us that if we misbehaved." He supplied a list of students and teachers from his school who would be glad to testify about it.

Through Ben-Amos, Penn's speech code now occasioned a sustained scholarship on the term *behema.* Jastrow's *Dictionary of the Targumim, The Talmud Babli and Yerushalmi, and the Midrashic Literature* offered, as the first definition of the term, "water-ox." Brown's *Hebrew and English Lexicon of the Old Testament* translated *behema* as "ox of water." Dahn Ben-Amotz's (no relation) *World Dictionary of Hebrew Slang* defined the term *behemott* in the plural of biblical Hebrew as "water-cows and cattle" and, from modern Hebrew, as people of thoughtless behavior.

Michael Meyers, the visionary black leader of the New York Civil Rights Coalition and a member of the National Board of the ACLU, had worked on race relations for twenty-five years—in particular, black-Jewish tension. Asked about "water buffalo" as a racial epithet, he said (and wrote), "I have *never* heard the term 'water buffalo' used as a racial epithet." He also agreed to testify to this. Crucially, he suggested that Kors call Deborah Leavy, the executive director of the Pennsylvania ACLU, who agreed that she and Stefan Presser, the general counsel of the Pennsylvania ACLU, would join the case pro bono on Eden's behalf. Leavy added, "My father-in-law calls people *behema* all the time." Eden now had two legal teams behind him. After hearing the details of the case, Arnold and Sonya Silverstein, two attorneys of Kors's acquaintance, had offered to represent Eden pro bono, providing the first ray of hope that Penn might be forced by the rule of law to honor its own policies in this case. A similar offer came from the lawyer in charge of the Civil Rights Committee of the Eastern Pennsylvania Anti-Defamation League of B'nai B'rith after an exchange of letters with Penn.

At this point, no one in the mainstream media was familiar with the case, but a growing number of professors were responding with outrage. Kenny Williams, a renowned scholar of American literature at Duke University, had replied to an inquiry about "water buffalo" that if Eden had wanted to use a racial epithet, there was, sadly, a vast lexicon from which to choose. "Water buffalo," she noted, was not one of them. "How in the world," she asked, "can anyone find racism or racial intent in that term?" She put it perfectly: "What is perhaps most disturbing about this matter is the assumption . . . that a word . . . will mean whatever a particular thought-control officer will deem language to mean. . . . Language will cease to have any communicative value." Williams, who is black, saw another dimension to the case:

> On a personal level, what is more disturbing . . . is the ability of some administrator . . . to define (in effect) an entire race and to introduce another racial term into language. . . . This is the real racism. . . . The student did nothing wrong, and if the students who were called "water buffalo" didn't like it, they should have merely stated that fact and in the process taken their noise making activities elsewhere! Young people have a marvelous ability to solve their own problems. Issues of racism are too serious to be treated frivolously by administrators.[15]

By the first week of April, Eden and Kors were doing everything possible to settle the case quietly within the university. The provost, Michael Aiken, though bemused by the thought that "water buffalo" could be considered racial harassment, referred the case to the vice-provost for university life, Kim Morrisson, who referred it to Larry Moneta, the associate vice-provost for university life, to whom the judicial system reported. President Hackney referred the case to his assistant, Stephen Steinberg, who e-mailed Kors about "your wholly appropriate concerns" about Read's decision, emphasizing that "If after talking with Larry [Moneta], you feel things are not satisfactorily resolved, please let me know, and I'd be happy to talk further . . . thanks for your patience." On April 13, another assistant to Sheldon Hackney, explaining that the news had broken of Hackney's impending nomination as chairman of the National Endowment for the Humanities (NEH), and apologizing for the delay in communication that this had caused, wrote: "Sheldon had also been occupied with the latest breaking news, although I have briefed him on our latest conversation. . . . He did ask me to convey his appreciation for your concern about the University's potential to become embroiled in a controversy that appears to offer little gain for anyone." She added, "I would also like to thank you most sincerely for the deep concern and willingness to act upon it that you have demonstrated throughout Eden's case. . . . Eden and others will remember you with gratitude and respect." The next day, however, Moneta telephoned Kors not about "the possibility of progress," but in order to quote from the second college edition of the *American Heritage Dictionary,* which listed "Asia and Africa" as places where water buffalo might be found. That evening, Steinberg called and said that guilt or innocence was for a hearing to decide. With racial anger on one side of the balance and, on the other, one frightened freshman and one eccentric professor, the administration had now decided to prosecute Eden for shouting "water buffalo."

Two months later, testifying before the U.S. Senate during his confirmation hearings for the chairmanship of the NEH, Sheldon Hackney proclaimed himself an enemy of speech codes: They were "counterproductive," he told Senator Harris Wofford of Pennsylvania. One could not get to civility by the wrong means, which he now described as "a speech code backed up by penalties." Pressed about Penn's own code, Hackney said that, although he now opposed such a code, it was nonetheless meant only to cover face-to-face confrontations. Senator Edward Kennedy asked him directly if under Penn's code the water buffalo case, by then dismissed, should have occurred. Hackney, discussing the case for the first time under oath, replied:

No. I think that this was a misapplication of that policy in the circumstances, and, I think, a great mistake to try to pursue it, for several reasons. One, it was not really a face-to-face encounter. The other is a matter of equity, if you will. Eden Jacobowitz was only one of a group of people en-gaged in this activity, and maybe the least culpable one.[16]

Senator Kennedy asked Hackney to give the committee the "facts" of the water buffalo case. On the issue of why Jacobowitz had been singled out, the nominee was quite eloquent:

> The only student who would admit to saying anything was Eden Ja-cobowitz, who said that he had used the term "water buffalo," and had yelled at the sorority sisters, who were singing, "If you want to have a party there is a zoo nearby." There in fact is a zoo within about a mile of the uni-versity. . . . Eden Jacobowitz is an Israeli . . . and there is a Hebrew term, *be-heyma,* which is frequently used among people; it is a mild reproach, but used quite commonly. It sort of means, Oh, you rude person. . . . There is no other explanation that one can think of.[17]

With Penn determined to continue with the prosecution, Eden and Kors called Robin Read and laid out to the JIO their entire defense. No date had been set for a hearing, and Read still had the opportunity to drop the charges in the face of this new evidence. She was asked, "Will you examine it, talk to the witnesses, and see if it wouldn't be a mistake to continue the prosecu-tion?" "Yes," she promised. Two weeks later, Eden was informed that the Ju-dicial Office wished to schedule a hearing, and he discovered that Read had contacted not one of his new witnesses.

The judicial administrator at Penn was John Brobeck, a retired professor of medicine, whose position was described by the Judicial System Charter as wholly "independent" and existing to secure the end of "substantive justice." He set a hearing for Monday, April 26, a date that would force Kors to can-cel a major scholarly meeting. Brobeck, however, was explicit and emphatic: "The hearing will be held on April 26, period. If you can make it, wonder-ful. If you can't, then Eden will have to be there without his advisor. There is no possible change of the April 26 date."[18] When Hackney was advised that Eden now would take his case to the deeper court of public opinion, he replied, "Do what you have to do."[19]

What Eden "had to do," simply put, was to prevent Penn's administra-tion from continuing the travesty, and to secure some modicum of equal jus-tice. At Penn, however, there was no equality before the law. One incident caught the double standard in all of its hypocrisy. In 1990, several black members of a racially integrated campus fraternity had tried to teach a lesson to a white student in another fraternity, a student named Sheffield, whom they believed to be a bigot. By mistake, they kidnapped a student named O'Flanagan. In Municipal Court that spring the following charges and underlying facts were admitted, uncontested, in connection with the accused kidnappers' plea bargains:

> [The kidnappers] played a tape of a Malcolm X speech containing references to violence directed at whites. . . . O'Flanagan believed that no one would be able to hear any possible cries for help. . . . [They] drove [him] to a secluded playground/park area. . . . They encircled [him], whispering to him again the phrase "Sheffield Deathfield!" . . . They also taunted him by referring to lynchings in the South, in Alabama. [He] remained handcuffed to the metal structure [in an inner-city playground] for a period of time . . . barefoot and only minimally clothed, and the night was cold and rainy. . . . They then conducted a mock "trial" which consisted in part of [his] being subjected to physical discomfort, emotional distress, and repeated and intense verbal abuse. . . . [They] talked about lynchings . . . and they shouted obscenities and abusive language at him. Among the phrases used were statements such as (a) "Fuck you!"; (b) "racist"; (c) "You're a neo-Nazi racist fuck!" . . . [They] then shoved [him] back in the car, recuffed him and drove him to the intersection of 34th and Chestnut Streets. During this 10 to 15 minute ride, they again played the same Malcolm X tape. At the intersection, they pulled [him] from the car, blindfolded. [He] believed he was being left in the middle of a highway or a busy street.[20]

Now, if that was not racial harassment, it was hard to see what might be, yet Penn simply suspended the integrated fraternity from having an active chapter on the campus. No individual punishment. No sensitivity seminars. No stamped transcripts.[21] Reverse the races, and the date of the kidnapping would have become an annual day of shame at Penn.

———————

Eden, in fact, seemed a pawn in a larger game of campus racial politics. In that spring of 1993, Penn was being sued over the number of "Mayor's Scholarships" it awarded. These provided a significant number of Philadelphia high school graduates—disproportionately black—with the means to attend the university—and Hackney was accused of racism. It was the tenth year of his presidency, and he obsessed throughout on racial relations. If some half-wit—whether racist or provocateur—scribbled an epithet on a stairwell, the campus would gratify the miscreant by acting as if a fascist night had descended. During freshmen orientations, students were taught at "diversity education" seminars to perceive the campus as a hotbed of racism.

Hackney was a captive of the very perception of endemic racism that Penn had encouraged and of the expectation that had been created that all "disadvantaged" groups had the right not to be "offended." Penn's policies invited students, including the women who had disturbed Eden, to react to ordinary abrasions and, indeed, to disagreeable opinions, as intolerable racism. Hackney's attempt to guide his administration across the dangerous terrain created by those policies severely limited his ability to respond soberly to such reactions. Nothing illustrated this better than the case of Gregory Pavlik, which preceded, and, in the end, energized the water buffalo affair.

The independent undergraduate campus newspaper, the *Daily Pennsylvanian (DP)*, had about fourteen opinion columnists, and it always was hard-pressed to find even one conservative to mix among them. It was not easy being the token *DP* conservative, who always elicited a flood of accusations of racism, sexism, homophobia, ignorance, and malice, often from administrators as well as from students. For the spring semester of 1993, the *DP* had found its lone conservative columnist in a transfer student from Rensselaer Polytechnic Institute, Greg Pavlik, soft-spoken and retiring in private, but a blunt and outspoken "paleoconservative" in his columns.

Pavlik, in fact, was much more critical of neoconservatives than of the Left. The real Right, for Pavlik, opposed centralized big government, nondefensive wars, and foreign intervention. Pavlik indeed exposed most students to an unfamiliar political point of view. In a February column, "The Price of Intervention," he described neoconservatives as "traitors," and he warned against the New World Order, "the globalists' desire for empire," the loss of sovereignty in foreign affairs to the UN, and young Americans returning "in body bags" during our interventions from Korea to the Balkans.[22] Whatever neoconservatives there might have been at Penn read his columns in peace. Others read some of his opinions with great anger.

Two columns, in particular, elicited a firestorm. In "Rethinking the King Holiday," Pavlik described the civil rights movement as an assault against property and individual liberty, and he attacked King's political and personal ethics, seeing the latter, in particular, as a betrayal of the obligation of Christian clerics to "set a moral standard as consecrated ministers of God."[23] In "Not as Clear as Black and White," Pavlik attacked what he saw as Penn's double standard on matters of race. He claimed that the Onyx Society, an exclusively black honors organization, had hazed its blindfolded initiates in the residential Quadrangle at 2:30 A.M. and had thrown eggs at Quad windows. In response, some residents of the Quad had thrown water at the egg throwers. Members of Onyx, Pavlik claimed, now hurled threats, more eggs, and antiwhite slogans at the awakened residents of the Quad. The university, Pavlik charged, had treated the event as an outrageous act of bigotry against blacks, instead of punishing the Onyx Society for hazing and for violations of the code of conduct—standards to which white fraternities were held. Indeed, the Judicial Office had punished the water throwers of the Quad, sentencing them to a written apology, fifteen hours of community service, and residential expulsion. He claimed that when Quad residents asked the university's chief JIO, Catherine Schifter, whether they could press charges against members of the Onyx Society for their behavior, she had replied that "the Onyx Society would find out their identity and things could get nasty." According to Pavlik, when he phoned Schifter to confirm the facts, she denied nothing, but she said, "If that shows up in the *DP*, you're dead."[24]

If the goal of having a controversial columnist was to set the campus into debate, then the *DP* had succeeded. Pavlik's columns elicited an outpouring of both substantive criticism and assaults upon his character. The most remarkable letter, however, appeared in the *DP* on March 19, signed by "202 African-American Students and Faculty," with the banner headline: AFRICAN-AMERICAN COMMUNITY RESPONDS TO PAVLIK. The authors denounced Pavlik as "racist," and they pronounced "his written attempts to discriminate" intolerable. "Hiding beyond the delicate laws of freedom of speech" gave him no right "to slander, demean, harass, and incite violence in those who don't share a Eurocentric upbringing." The words were carefully chosen, because "harassment" and "demeaning" individuals on grounds of race constituted violations of Penn's judicial code. The *DP*, the 202 signers of the letter declared, was also culpable, because to publish Pavlik was to accept his design "to demean and discredit": "If the *DP* prints it, then we must infer that they agree with, and condone it."[25]

Scores of the authors and signatories of the letter knew something that the campus did not know. On March 2, the JIO, the target of his critical editorial of February 25, had awakened Greg at 9:00 A.M. by telephone, to inform him that he was under investigation for thirty-four student-initiated charges of "racial harassment" by means of his editorial columns. After a week of seeking help, Pavlik found Kors, who immediately left an urgent message for Sheldon Hackney. Hackney knew about the charges, and assured Kors that they "aren't going anywhere." Hackney's name already was in the media as a likely Clinton nominee to head the NEH, and Kors suggested to him that "if someone is threatened officially at your University for the expression of views that some find offensive, you will have no credibility whatsoever. The phone call from the JIO was threatening and chilling." Hackney agreed, and the next day Pavlik was informed that the case was over. On April 1, Schifter finally wrote to Pavlik, "to inform you officially that, in light of my investigation of thirty-four complaints of possible racial harassment against you, the circumstances do not indicate that there was violation of any policy of the University. Accordingly, the investigation of the complaints against you is concluded and subsequently dismissed."[26]

It was in the midst of such tensions and official hesitations that the water buffalo case developed. In March 1993, just after the charges against Pavlik had to be dropped, Hackney wrote a lengthy piece for the university's official *Almanac,* explaining that Penn was paying a fearsome price for the fact that "the Civil Rights movement of the 1960s never completed its task." He described a meeting in January 1993 with "a group of Penn faculty and staff of color." He was shocked, he wrote, because he had learned that "students, faculty, and staff members of the University community still feel frustrated and oppressed by what they experience as a hostile environment, where demeaning incidents continue to occur—in our classrooms by faculty, on our campus by public safety officers, and in our residences by fellow students." He did not specify the incidents—despite requests—but by "in our residences" they certainly appeared to include the Onyx Society episode discussed by Pavlik and the Jacobowitz case. Hackney explained what he had ordered his administration to do:

> This is the time to tell all members of our community again, but this time in a way that must be heard, that we will not tolerate acts that demean students, faculty, and staff—not in the classroom, not in support offices, not on the campus, and not in our residences. We will find means to ensure that such acts have important consequences. . . . Those who believe they can, with impunity, damage important members of our community have no place.[27]

Hackney's letter appeared on March 18. Four days later, Read charged Eden Jacobowitz with racial harassment. With Pavlik off the hook, Eden was now the only trophy fish.

Neither Eden nor Kors knew how to bring the water buffalo case to public attention, but on April 15, Hackney did that himself. On that day, when

Pavlik's final column was going to appear (his topic was the lack of substantive debate at Penn), a group of black students "confiscated" the *DP*'s full press run, fourteen thousand copies, from campus distribution points. When *DP* distributors and staff who tried to prevent the confiscation were threatened and reviled with racial epithets, they complained to Robin Read, who did not pursue any case of violence, threat, or abuse, let alone of racial harassment, by blacks against the *DP* staff.[28] The national media, however, always notice the unpunished silencing of the press, and they asked the university if and when charges might be brought against the individuals responsible for suppressing the *DP*. Penn responded that these would come in due time. In fact, however, not one of the students charged with the theft was punished. Indeed, the only person penalized was a University Museum officer who had attempted to stop individuals from running, a trash bag in hand, from a security-conscious museum. He was suspended from his job for overreaction and for a failure to intuit a larger, "political" protest.[29]

The Penn administration's equivocal response to the *DP* theft caught the national eye. Associate Vice-Provost Moneta, on April 16, explained that "both the behavior *and the grounds for the behavior* are among the most serious issues the University can face."[30] [emphasis added] Hackney issued a statement on the confiscation, reaffirming the right of the *DP* to express its views, but noting that the theft had been "precipitated by the pain and anger that many members of the minority community have felt in response to the *DP*'s exercise of its First Amendment rights to freedom of the press." In Hackney's assessment: "This is an instance in which two groups important to the University community, valued members of Penn's minority community and students exercising their rights to freedom of expression, and two important University values, diversity and open expression, seem to be in conflict." By the conclusion of his statement, Hackney had dropped the word "seem": "As I indicated above, two important University values now stand in conflict . . . the First Amendment right of an independent publication . . . [and] a comfortable and permanent minority presence in a diverse and civil University community."[31] By comparison, Hackney's sense of "conflict" had been quite different on the day after the attempted assassination of President Reagan in 1981, when a left-wing *DP* editorial columnist, Dominic Manno, wrote: "Too bad he missed . . . I hope [Reagan] dies." As the Secret Service descended upon Penn and the media focused on the editorial column, Hackney issued a statement to the press on Thursday, April 2. He noted, unambiguously, that freedom of expression at Penn was categorical: "He has a right in our society, and especially on a university campus, to speak his mind, no matter how abhorrent his ideas."[32]

On Sunday, April 18, the *Philadelphia Inquirer's* editorial on the *DP* incident noted Hackney's implication that there was "no room for the 'peaceful coexistence' at Penn between the imperatives of diversity and free expression," and advised him to solve that problem "before heading off to his new job" at the NEH.[33] In the *Village Voice,* the progressive civil libertarian Nat Hentoff castigated Hackney's "patronizing paternalism," terming the belief that blacks could not live with the First Amendment "yet another prejudicial stereotype."[34] The liberal president of the *DP* alumni association, Howard Gensler, then working at the *Philadelphia Daily News,* wrote to all *DP* alumni (many of whom worked in the media) expressing outrage over Hackney's failure to understand that "diversity must also include the opinions of white male conservatives."[35] The story was picked up widely. Eden did not know it, but the theft of the *DP* and Hackney's feeble response had created a new moment. Now there was genuine curiosity about Hackney as a presidential nominee and about issues of liberty at Penn. When the water buffalo story went public, it was received with interest. Once received, it fascinated the nation more than anyone would have imagined.

When Eden took his case public, he was exercising his clear right under Penn's Judicial Charter, which guaranteed that a respondent could disclose otherwise confidential information about his experience, in which case, "any person whose character or integrity might reasonably be questioned as a result of such disclosure shall have a right to respond in an appropriate forum."[36] If Eden Jacobowitz had chosen Read's deal, then his parents, the campus, and the world would have known nothing of the charges against him. In similar circumstances, almost every student accepts settlement offers. Admitting guilt and undergoing "thought reform," protected by the confidentiality of records, is an easy way to end an ordeal. Eden would not do it. He knew that he never had directed a word of racial hatred at anyone, and he refused to say that he had, whatever the consequences. He was candid, thoughtful, and kind, and these qualities were obvious to virtually every journalist who interviewed him during the next few months. From the *Village Voice* and *Rolling Stone,* to the major television networks, to *Newsday* and the *Washington Post,* to the *Wall Street Journal,* those who investigated the truth of this absurd case caught Eden's spirit and innocence.

Eden's story entered the world by chance. One of Kors's New York friends, hearing of the case during a social phone call on April 20, mentioned the story to an acquaintance at the *Forward,* the former Yiddish-language New York daily that was now a widely respected English-language weekly with a special interest in cultural, political, and Jewish affairs. The story broke in the *Forward*'s April 23 issue, a few days before Eden's hearing. The *Forward* ran the story above the masthead, under the ineffable headline PENNSYLVA-NIA PREPARING TO BUFFALO A YESHIVA BOY. The former Yiddish newspa-per explained that "water buffalo" was a reasonable translation of "a non-sectarian Hebrew put-down often heard at his Long Island yeshiva—'be-hema,' a word that means 'livestock' or 'buffalo' but whose slang meaning is idiot." The *Forward* linked the story to Hackney's nomination to the NEH and to the theft of the *DP*, and included elements of Eden's story (later con-firmed by Hackney in his Senate testimony) that were essential to under-standing the injustice of the case: "'I just described the noise and not anything that would do with their race. . . . I decided to help the police, so I volun-teered myself. I told the police what I said and they wrote it down." The *For-ward* concluded its lengthy story by a reference to Monday's upcoming trial: "A Penn spokeswoman, Carol Farnsworth, declined to comment on the case, citing confidentiality. 'This is not like a regular court system,' she says." [37]

That same morning, the editor of the *Wall Street Journal* brought the *Forward* into an editorial board meeting, and columnist Dorothy Rabi-nowitz decided to pursue the matter. An investigative journalist and edito-rialist with courage and a will of steel, Rabinowitz has one overriding public passion: She hates abuse of power, by governments, by businesses, by prosecutors, and by educators. She long had been one of the few editorial voices in the country to understand the abuses of "political correctness" at the universities, and she has written powerful pieces against the new impo-sition of intolerant orthodoxies. When she called Hackney, she pressed him for serious answers about what was going on at Penn. Apparently thinking that she was some inconsequential staffer, he said, "I don't need to take this from some reporter," and hung up the phone on her. Indeed, several other reporters and editorialists had called the university, which now knew that the story was fully in the open.[38]

On Friday, April 23, Brobeck called Kors to announce that the Monday hearing had been postponed, citing "too much publicity," but then correcting himself: "The real reason is that the women no longer have an advisor." The advisor had been Zoila Airall of the Division of Residential Living. "She doesn't want to appear in the case," Brobeck admitted, "and we can't have the hearing without their advisor." When reminded of his insistence that the hearing would be held on April 26 even if Eden had to be completely on his own (while the women's case would be presented by the JIO) and of the fact that Eden would lose his witnesses when the semester ended, Brobeck replied, "It's my judgment call. The case is postponed indefinitely . . . until, at earliest, in the fall." When Eden was informed, he asked, "Are they going to have this hang over my head all summer?" Indeed, they were.

No one had thought to notify the media about the postponement of the hearing. Consequently, on the morning of April 26, the *Wall Street Journal* ran Dorothy Rabinowitz's lead editorial "Buffaloed at Penn." It described Eden as "the latest victim of the ideological fever known as political correctness," and it referred the case to the attention of "anyone concerned with the state of reason and sanity on the campuses today." It labeled "Kafkaesque" the fact that someone who had not shouted any racial slurs, and who had told the police what he had said, "would pay a price for his forthrightness." It drew the deeper lesson: "He had yet to learn what they don't teach at freshman orientation; namely he had now entered a world where a charge of racism or sexism is as good as a conviction." Pointing out the obvious facts that a zoo, animals, or even, indeed, *Animal House* were universal references to noise on college campuses, it described Robin Read's discovery of racism in Eden's innocuous phrase as "theater of the absurd." It also noted clearly the "settlement" that Eden had been offered, and the courage it had taken to turn that down.[39] The effect of the *Forward*'s article and the *Wall Street Journal*'s editorial—in the wake of Hackney's nomination and his equivocation on the theft of the *DP*—was electric. Eden was interviewed on television by Tom Snyder and John McLaughlin. George Will devoted his syndicated column in the *Washington Post* to Eden and to the theft of the *DP*s.[40] Within short order, the international media settled in at Penn.

Although, in the final analysis, the University of Pennsylvania took a beating in public opinion because it had, as its leading press officer said the next year "a stupid case to defend,"[41] Penn repeatedly revealed an arrogance that the media scarcely could believe. Hackney's slamming the phone on Dorothy Rabinowitz could have been a metaphor for Penn's entire handling of the case. Reporters were reconciled to hearing the university say that it did not want to discuss the specifics of the Jacobowitz case, but Penn refused to discuss even its speech code, its past practices, its history of enforcement, or its violations of procedure. Reporters, editorialists, cartoonists, and broadcast journalists understood freedom of speech. They understood double standards, due process, and decency. Reporters live by the First Amendment, and many pretty much live by it absolutely. On *NBC Nightly News*, Sara James asked Larry Moneta, "Have you ever heard of 'water buffalo' being used as a racial slur?" He replied: "The issue is not whether I have or not. The issue is also, you know, language in my mind is neutral. It's a question of the context in which language is used."[42] (Two years later, when Penn abolished its speech code, the same Larry Moneta would dutifully go before the media to declare that "at Penn, all speech is free.") The reporters were doing their jobs remarkably—probing, investigating, and developing sources. Within the administration, a growing loathing of the cruelty and utter stupidity of this case led important officials to channel information to the press. Thus, the *Washington Times* reported on April 27 that the postponement of Eden's trial had "prompted speculation that university President Sheldon Hackney ordered the delay to protect his pending nomination to head the National Endowment for the Humanities," to which the reporter added: "School officials, who asked not to be identified, echoed [this] sentiment and speculation about the trial's postponement."[43] The case had turned over a rock at Penn, and it was not just outsiders who did not like what they saw underneath it. On that same day, the *Philadelphia Daily News* lectured Penn that "it's hard to justify breathtaking tuition hikes when acting like a herd of dik-diks."[44]

In the course of the next month, Eden's plight was front page news not only in the Philadelphia newspapers, but, on repeated occasions, in the *Los Angeles Times,* the *International Herald-Tribune,* the *Washington Post,* the *Washington Times,* the (New Jersey) *Record,* and even the *Sacramento Bee,* not to mention hundreds of newspapers that were picking up syndicated reports. Foreign publications such as the *Financial Times* (London), the *Times* (London), the *Toronto Star,* and the *Spectator* (UK) independently treated the story as an example of America gone insane. As the *Financial Times* noted on May 8, "In Europe it is unlikely that one would be caught up in a semi-judicial enquiry as a result of shouting the names of Asian oxen at one's colleagues."[45] It praised American press coverage of the affair. Important journals—the *Village Voice, Rolling Stone, The New Republic, Newsweek, Time,* and *U.S. News and World Report*—devoted much space to the case, all of them understanding full well the gulf between liberal opinion and Penn's cultural radicalism. The story prompted a major piece in the *New York Times,* even evincing an unexpected defense of free speech from Duke's Stanley Fish, otherwise a star of political correctness and the author of a book called *There's No Such Thing As Free Speech . . . And It's a Good Thing Too.*[46]

The water buffalo case had become a sensation. It was not merely news, but the occasion for often multiple major substantive editorials in the nation's leading newspapers. It also was covered on all major television news programs. On *NBC Nightly News,* John Chancellor explained the broader implications of the event, offering, on May 13, a commentary on Eden's prosecution:

Eden Jacobowitz is a student at the University of Pennsylvania. His studies were interrupted by a noisy crowd of students, many black and female. He yelled out his window, "Shut up, you water buffalo." He is now charged with racial harassment under the university's Code of Conduct. The school offered to dismiss the charge if he would apologize, attend a racial sensitivity seminar, agree to dormitory probation, and accept a temporary mark on his record which would brand him as guilty. He was told the term "water buffalo" could be interpreted as racist because a water buffalo is a dark primitive animal that lives in Africa. That is questionable semantics, dubious zoology, and incorrect geography. Water buffalo live in Asia, not in Africa. This from the University of Pennsylvania. Mr. Jacobowitz is fighting back. The rest of us, however, are still in trouble. The language police are at work on the campuses of our better schools. The word cops are marching under the banner of political correctness. The culture of victimization is hunting for quarry. American English is in danger of losing its muscle and energy. That's what these bozos are doing to us.[47]

Talk radio also was exploring the case, with equal scorn being displayed by conservative hosts, such as Rush Limbaugh, particularly mordant on the affair, and by a bemused but outraged array of National Public Radio outlets. Eden had brought the networks, conservative radio, and NPR into agreement. Editorial cartoonists had a particular field day lampooning Penn's language and thought police. Garry Trudeau devoted a full-color Sunday *Doonesbury* to Penn, focusing on the inanity of speech codes in general and on the particular absurdity of taking "water buffalo" as a racial insult.[48] The University of Pennsylvania had become an international laughingstock. Eden, however, still faced a potential catastrophe.

———

From the moment that the April 26 hearing was canceled, Eden appealed to Brobeck, Hackney, and Aiken to drop the charges. Brobeck, a decent man caught up in an absurd situation, conceded the error of postponing the "unalterable" hearing, but he refused to rescue Eden from a continuation of the ordeal. Hackney and Aiken proclaimed themselves incapable of intervening in any judicial matter. In early May, however, as media attention (and ridicule) intensified, the "independent" Brobeck knocked, uninvited, on the door of Kors's home to announce that "we have to have a dispositive hearing on May 14; I've been told to put this behind us." In response to protests that almost all of Eden's essential witnesses were gone for the summer, Brobeck relented, and promised that the hearing would involve only a request to drop the charges. He added that Eden himself need not even come to Penn for the session. At 10:30 P.M. on the night of Wednesday, May 12, however, just one full day before the scheduled hearing, Brobeck called Kors at home: "I have terrible news for you and for me," he said. "I have been instructed by my superiors that I cannot keep my agreement with you. . . . I've been ordered to hold a hearing on guilt or innocence on the 14th." Reminded that he had given his word, that Eden's witnesses were gone, and that his only conceivable "superiors," Aiken and Hackney, had proclaimed him categorically independent, he replied: "Until today, I would have said that I was independent too, but I have bosses, and they've ordered me to do this. . . . I have no choice. I have superiors. Please be gentle with me."

On Thursday morning, Sonya Silverstein, Arnie Silverstein, and the ACLU's Stefan Presser cleared their calendars, Eden came to Philadelphia from New York, and, with the media notified about the astonishing turn of events, the water buffalo defense team worked to seek an injunction in federal court against the May 14 Penn hearing. The Silversteins' office was a beehive, fueled by controlled fury. Surrounded by computers, typewriters, ACLU staff, the Silversteins and their employees, Eden, Kors, and a growing body of Penn students, including the editor of the *DP*, Stefan Presser was like the conductor of an unruly, barely-in-control symphony orchestra. Never ruffled, Presser brought order out of chaos, assigning everyone parts, sending his staff for forms and opinions, keeping his eye on the clock, and occasionally letting the General Counsel's Office at Penn know what he was doing. Stefan Presser was Justice in a suit, and he was in command. With about a half an hour to go before the federal courts closed, and with runners standing by, Presser faxed the ACLU/Silverstein brief to Shelley Green, general counsel of the University of Pennsylvania. The suit was not directed at the university as a corporation, but, rather, at Hackney, Aiken, Morrisson, Brobeck, and Read, as individuals. Fifteen minutes later, the university, over Shelley Green's signature, faxed Presser, with a copy to Brobeck, that the university would honor its earlier agreement that the May 14 hearing would consider only dismissal of the charges.[49]

Penn had told Eden not even to try to assemble his scattered witnesses, but it had not told the JIO to cease preparing her case. The five plaintiffs, their two advisors, the JIO, and the JIO's fifteen witnesses—brought to Penn at Penn's expense—arrived at a May 14 hearing that they fully believed would resolve the issue of innocence or guilt. The JIO had brought two pieces of evidence: an *American Heritage Dictionary* listing "Africa" as a home of water buffalo and—the most shocking—a two-page university police report from the night of the incident that contradicted the very stipulation that Robin Read had made about Eden's words after her own extensive investigation. According to this report, written on the morning of January 14, 1993, when the police went to one room from which insults supposedly issued, every resident had said that every overheard epithet was shouted "by Eden."

What had happened? The truth would emerge after the summer, when a resident of the dorm wrote an op-ed in the *DP,* explaining that on the night of January 13–14, 1993, the students who had shouted epithets panicked, and that because Eden had stepped forward, they falsely attributed everything to him in their dealings with the university police.[50] On May 14, 1993, however, something far more dramatic happened. The university knowingly suppressed the second police report in the apparent hope of gaining a conviction against Eden Jacobowitz. In fact, the university police, at the request of the JIO, had conducted a two-week investigation starting on January 14, 1993, and had written a long, 12–14 page, report about what actually had occurred. This time, the residents of Eden's dormitory told the truth to the university police, who filed their report wholly corroborating Eden's own true story. That report was presumably the basis of Read's initial stipulation about "water buffalo" and "zoo." At the May 14 hearing, Eden knew nothing of that longer report, his witnesses were not there, and he was apparently meant to be railroaded into a conviction that would transform the case and salvage Penn's reputation. (One year later, a university officer saw Kors walking across campus. He ran over to thank him for having "defended the water buffalo kid," and asked what Eden had thought of "the long report" that proved his innocence. Shocked to learn that neither Eden nor his defense even knew of the existence of such a report—let alone had seen it—he explained that "we did a very long report that showed that Eden was telling the truth about everything." A few weeks later, a campus reporter asked the then chief of university police, John Kuprevich, if he had a copy of the fourteen-page police report on Jacobowitz." "Yeah, I have it," Kuprevich replied, "but it's confidential." It was bad enough that the university was scapegoating a wholly innocent student who happened to admit that he had said "water buffalo." When the May 14 hearing actually came, Penn stood ready to accuse him of saying still other things that it had been told he absolutely had not said.)

The May 14 hearing was surreal. Outside, there were sound trucks, an army of reporters, and Eden's pro bono lawyers, Sonya, Arnie, and Stefan, who were excluded from the proceedings. Inside, Eden and Kors faced an intensely hostile panel of three professors, one graduate student, and one undergraduate, false evidence in hand, who had come to decide Eden's guilt or innocence. When Robin Read began the presentation of her evidence, Kors interrupted and read the letter from Green to Presser. The panel, Read, and the plaintiffs were dumbfounded to learn that this was not to be a dispositive hearing.

The panel heard Eden out on the procedural grounds for dismissal. It then asked the plaintiffs to talk about their experience of that year. The plaintiffs discussed how they had suffered; Robin Read cried as they spoke; and the panel convened in private. When they returned, they announced that they had ten days by which to present a procedural report to the vice-provost for university life, and, they warned Eden and Kors, that if, in the interim, they "so much as read one word" in the media about this hearing or this preliminary judgment, then, in the words of a professor on the panel, "It will go very hard on Eden Jacobowitz. Do you understand that, Professor Kors? If you speak one word of this to the media, it will go very hard on Eden." They imposed, in their own phrase, "a gag order." They refused to dismiss the charges, and ruled that the trial should be carried over until next fall.

Eden left the building to face a crush of media. News of Brobeck's broken promise and of the general counsel's retreat was in newspapers and on radio and television. The media, having waited for hours on a narrow street, seemed annoyed by the gag order. Arnie Silverstein got off the deepest line of the affair: "I can't wait to get off Penn's campus," he told the reporters, "and get back to the United States of America." At an ACLU press conference, Stefan and Sonya explained the events of the past week, and the ACLU spoke about free speech and due process, but whenever they were asked about the hearing, they said that they couldn't talk. When Kors returned to his office, there were scores of calls from the media, but he told everyone that he could not discuss the hearing. When Dorothy Rabinowitz called, Kors said the same thing, received an awesome three-minute lecture on a free country, a free press, and his own lack of testosterone, and broke his silence and told her everything.

By mid-afternoon, in response to intense media inquiry, Penn simply lied to all inquirers and said that no gag order ever had been issued by the panel. The panel's report was due on May 24, and with each day, media coverage intensified. Eden's picture was on every newsstand, and the ACLU of Pennsylvania was giving lessons to the country about why freedom and due process matter. There was ever louder discussion of the likely effect on Hackney's NEH nomination. Indeed, a member of Clinton's transition team politely and affably requested copies of coverage of the affair by "the Jewish press." Shortly after, Hackney telephoned Kors from Washington, D.C., and proposed a deal: if Eden apologized for rudeness, he believed that the women would drop the case, and the university would dismiss all charges. He laid out a scenario: "At noon on the twenty-fourth, [Vice-Provost] Kim [Morrisson] will hold a press conference, saying that the panel has met and has decided that the case should be heard on its merits, if not right away, then at the beginning of the fall term. The women will hold a press conference on the campus and drop the charges. Would Eden be willing to apologize after that?" When he heard the proposal, Eden, who repeatedly had offered to apologize for saying "water buffalo," instantly agreed, glad that this whole nightmare would end. On May 24, 1993, the final act of the farce was played out. The hearing panel delivered its verdict, and Kim Morrisson held a press conference announcing that the hearing would occur in the fall. Almost immediately, the women, flanked by a trustee and eminent professors, held a press conference, and claiming that media attention had denied them the possibility of a fair hearing at Penn, they dropped their charges. They said they now would take their case to public opinion (which they never did). On the heels of that, the university announced that there were no charges pending against Eden Jacobowitz. The ACLU and the Silversteins held a press conference immediately after, and Eden once again expressed his regrets. The ACLU again explained that no humane good could be accomplished by such speech codes or such malicious prosecutions.

Just before that press conference, Eden and his attorneys had discussed whether or not to play a particular answering machine tape to the reporters. They decided, in the spirit of the moment, not to do so. The message was from Eden's first judicial advisor, Fran Walker, director of student life, whom he had chosen in January 1993 from the list of "good and well-trained advisors" presented to him by the Judicial Office. On the Tuesday after the May 14 hearing, alarmed by the aberrant university police report that the JIO had been planning to introduce as the compelling document of the case, Kors had called Walker to confirm, once again, that she had been present when Robin Read had stipulated that her investigation showed that Eden had said merely "water buffalo" and "zoo," and not any epithets. She confirmed that. Asked if she would put that in writing or testify to it at a hearing, she said that she would have to get the permission of the general counsel to do so. Reminded that she was a critical witness in a judicial system that promised "substantive justice" to "the University community," she replied, candidly, "I am not just a member of the university community. I am an administrator, and my attorney in this instance is the general counsel. I must get the permission of the university's general counsel."[51] The next day, she left a message on Kors's answering machine: "The general counsel's office has instructed me that I am not permitted to testify about that meeting."

The aftermath? The administration appointed a university commission to investigate what went wrong in the water buffalo case. In April 1994, it concluded that there had been two main sets of villains: first, Jacobowitz and Kors, for talking to the press and taking the case outside the university; and second, the Pennsylvania ACLU, for "interfering" in a purely internal university matter, and even threatening to take the university to the nation's courts. Penn's judicial system, it reported formally, "could not withstand the stress of intense publicity and international attention."[52] That is indeed true at most universities. It is why we are writing this book. Penn's report was reminiscent of those Southern sheriffs in the early '60s talking about "outside agitators" stirring up trouble in their counties, where justice was fine, thank you. Well, academic justice is not fine, as we shall discover.

CHAPTER 2

FREE SPEECH IN A
FREE SOCIETY

Constitutional protections do not establish clear norms for campus speech. For one thing, constitutional free speech doctrine applies directly only to public institutions, not to private ones. For another, even when constitutional doctrine applies, it does so differently at public universities than at other public institutions or agencies. (Indeed, the First Amendment even imposes differing constraints on elementary schools, secondary schools, and public universities.) Additionally, most nonsectarian campuses (and many sectarian ones) promise that academic life will be governed by academic freedom, which differs from constitutional doctrine.

Nonetheless, it is important to examine the extent to which free speech is protected and valued by civil society at large. After all, while universities are communities unto themselves, they are also part of the larger society. They derive their independence from the willingness of the larger society to tolerate—even protect and nurture—a level of freedom beyond what society is willing to tolerate in its neighborhoods, elementary and high schools, and workplaces.

Exceptions Plague the Rule

"Congress shall make no law . . . abridging the freedom of speech, or of the press." The meaning of the First Amendment to the United States Constitution would appear to be beyond doubt. The vast majority of American citizens hold close to their hearts the idea that they can say whatever

34

they please. As some First Amendment absolutists ask rhetorically: "Which part of 'no' don't you understand?"

However, the current legal status of the First Amendment did not even begin to emerge until early in the twentieth century. The United States Supreme Court did not find occasion to enforce the First Amendment's free speech and press provisions until the American Civil Liberties Union (ACLU), under the influential leadership of its founder, Roger Baldwin, sought to safeguard the rights of protesters against American involvement in World War I.

In 1925, the ACLU won a Pyrrhic victory for free speech in the case of one of the founders of the U.S. Communist party in *Gitlow v. New York*.[1] Benjamin Gitlow had been convicted under the 1902 *New York Criminal Anarchy Law* for publishing a pamphlet that advocated proletarian revolution but did not seek any immediate breach of the peace. The ACLU argued that punishment of the author of the pamphlet violated the First Amendment. This now may seem a simple case, but in 1925 it was not clear that the federal guarantees of speech and press protection restricted state and municipal authorities. Nevertheless, the U.S. Supreme Court held that because the First Amendment embodied fundamental rights, those rights were also protected by the Fourteenth Amendment, which required that state and local governments accord citizens "due process of law." Although it did proceed to apply free speech principles, however, the Court nonetheless affirmed Gitlow's conviction on the ground that his particular expression presented a danger to the public welfare and was therefore unprotected.

Despite Gitlow's loss, the incorporation of First Amendment rights into Fourteenth Amendment "due process" proved vital to the development of free speech jurisprudence. In 1936, the ACLU was assisting labor unions to assert free speech and assembly rights against local governments. In *Hague v. Committee for Industrial Organization*,[2] the ACLU challenged an ordinance that allowed the municipal government of Jersey City, New Jersey, to forbid any public assemblies that, in the view of the director of safety, might lead to "riots, disturbances or disorderly assemblage." The CIO was denied the right to distribute leaflets, and the Socialist party's requests to conduct meetings were rejected. Using *Gitlow*, the ACLU was able to challenge the city.

In an opinion that broke new ground for the First Amendment but was animated by tradition and common sense, Justice Owen Roberts held that the parks and streets where the CIO and others were speaking were held "in trust" for the public as a forum in which to exercise the rights of speech. Local governments no longer could restrict speech because they controlled the land upon which a speaker stood. This decision marked the origin of the "public forum" doctrine.

Such decisions laid the foundations of a later explosion of cases that explored the substantive meaning of freedom of speech and press. With time, the amendment was interpreted to cover a range of expressive activity well beyond conventional political speech. Art and entertainment came to be protected, along with sexually suggestive or even explicit material that did not reach the level of what the Court called "obscenity." Certain types of nonverbal but expressive conduct were brought under the shelter of the amendment. Protection continues to be extended to new media as they develop, such as telephone systems and the Internet.

While freedom of speech is constantly shifting and frequently expanding, it is also true that "no law" does not come even close to meaning "*no law.*" Scholars, lawyers, and government officials have built careers by seeking to find the loopholes by which to censor free citizens. The broad range of protected speech, while substantial, can be misleading. The hortatory language with which Supreme Court majorities wax poetic about the virtues of a free "marketplace" of ideas can induce a false sense of security in the citizen who enrages governmental officials or a large mass of citizens. Much First Amendment litigation has involved not efforts to *expand* the amendment's reach, but, rather, to ward off repeated official attempts to punish unpopular ideas. The history of First Amendment jurisprudence has been written by the efforts of those who have sought to whittle away free speech rights by positing one exception after another, and by those who have resisted, confirming the insight of Philip Kerby, former editorial writer for the *Los Angeles Times,* that "censorship is the strongest drive in human nature; sex is a weak second."[3] The very existence of such repeated efforts has acted, in some degree, as a deterrent to the exercise of free speech, because the defense of freedom can be expensive and risky. The very refusal of the Supreme Court to be absolutist has exerted a modest chilling effect on robust speech.

The Court has established four primary exceptions to free speech: (1) Speech posing a "clear and present danger" of imminent violence or lawlessness; (2) disclosures threatening "national security"; (3) "obscenity"; and (4) so-called "fighting words" that would provoke a "reasonable person" to an imminent, violent response.

The first exception to the First Amendment was the "clear and present danger" test, announced in the 1919 case of *Schenck v. United States.*[4] Justice Oliver Wendell Holmes, who wrote the opinion, construed the exception very narrowly. The First Amendment did not protect words when they were "used in such circumstances and are of such a nature as to create a clear and present danger that they will bring about" some evil that government has the right to deter. Justice Holmes sought to limit this speech restriction by giving his famous example of when violence-provoking speech presents such an imminent danger that the speech itself, not just the resulting conduct, could be outlawed: "The most stringent protection of free speech would not protect a man in falsely shouting fire in a theatre and causing a panic." This concept was invoked in the 1969 decision of *Brandenburg v. Ohio*,[5] which, citing some McCarthy-era Supreme Court cases protecting the advocacy of revolutionary belief and rhetoric, held that legislation could restrict "advocacy [that] is directed to inciting or producing imminent lawless action and is likely to incite or produce such action." *Brandenburg* involved a rally and speeches by members of the Ku Klux Klan suggesting that violence against blacks and Jews might be appropriate to protect white Christian society.

While the "clear and present danger" test might seem like a minor or even sensible exception to the First Amendment, it has given would-be censors the wedge they need to seek broader exceptions. The very existence of such an exception to the First Amendment emboldened the authorities in Ohio to prosecute Clarence Brandenberg for merely *advocating* violence. The Supreme Court repeatedly had to reinforce the limits on this exception before mere advocacy ceased being the repeated target of censors.

Perhaps the most instructive example of this process by which seemingly narrow exceptions to free speech encourage would-be censors is the "national security" exception, created in the 1931 Supreme Court case of *Near v. Minnesota*.[6] J. M. Near and his cohorts published a newspaper, the *Saturday Press*, which in an ongoing series charged that various political and law enforcement officials and power brokers in Minneapolis were part of a conspiracy to protect, rather than to investigate and prosecute, a Jewish racketeer. The state charged that the allegations were "malicious, scandalous and defamatory," and it sought to stop, "perpetually," the publication of future issues of the paper. Minnesota sought this result by enforcement of a state statute that established a procedure to prohibit, as a "public nuisance," the publication of a "malicious, scandalous and defamatory newspaper, magazine or other periodical."

The Supreme Court established in *Near* a heavy presumption of unconstitutionality against any governmental effort to prohibit speech in advance of publication. If the material being published was in fact not protected, then the state might attempt to punish it after it was uttered. However, prohibiting publication in advance is "to put the publisher under an effective censorship," what came to be known as a "prior restraint" on speech. Unwilling, however, to pronounce an absolute rule against prior restraints, the Court noted that the doctrine "is not absolutely unlimited" and might not apply "in exceptional cases." It gave as an example that in time of war "a government might prevent actual obstruction of its recruiting service or the publication of the sailing dates of transports or the number and location of troops." This so-called "troop ship exception" has had an infamous subsequent history. On the basis of this flexibility (in reality more of a loophole) in the law against prior restraints, governments have acted repeatedly to prevent disclosure of purportedly classified (but, in fact, simply embarrassing) materials.

The federal government, for example, sought in March 1979 to enjoin *The Progressive* magazine from publishing an article entitled "The H-Bomb Secret: How We Got It, Why We're Telling It." This formula for supposedly producing a hydrogen weapon had been gathered by the magazine from public library sources and was hardly a secret, but the government tied up the effort to publish it for seven months with a temporary court injunction, until a local Madison, Wisconsin, newspaper published a letter (from a self-described conservative) detailing the critical information that the government was seeking to suppress. Faced with the horse out of the barn, the government dismissed its own case as "moot." The result of the inconclusive litigation was that the seven-month prior restraint—the longest in American history—never was finally adjudicated as either constitutional or unconstitutional.

The "troop ship exception" has been invoked to attempt to block publication of other materials of public importance where "national security" seems to have been little more than a cover to avoid embarrassment to the government. In 1971, President Richard Nixon and his attorney general, John N. Mitchell, sought to stop publication by the *New York Times,* the *Washington Post,* and the *Boston Globe* of the "Pentagon Papers," the military's history of the nation's involvement in the Vietnam War. The purported justification for this prior restraint was that publication would injure national security. *Near* was cited as precedent. Publication was delayed twelve days until the Supreme Court ruled against the government.

In 1980, the CIA successfully enforced a provision in its employment contract against a former agent, Frank W. Snepp III, that required clearance of any information relating to intelligence activities with the agency before publication.[7] Snepp had published a book regarding CIA activities in South Vietnam; an injunction issued by the Supreme Court prevented further publication without authorization as required under the contract. This was an idiosyncratic case, because the government's power to enforce a prior restraint rested on a contract willingly entered into by Snepp. However, it gave would-be government censors new hope that perhaps they could force public employees to sign away their speech rights.

In yet other areas of First Amendment jurisprudence, consistently broad protection for speech has been clouded by the hint of a possible exception. For example, the Supreme Court's notoriously vague definition of "obscenity" has resulted in a chill for many serious writers and artists. The Court announced the modern definition of obscenity in the 1973 case of *Miller v. California*: "(a) whether 'the average person, applying contemporary community standards' would find that the work, taken as a whole, appeals to the prurient interest; (b) whether the work depicts or describes, in a patently offensive way, sexual conduct specifically defined by the applicable state law; and (c) whether the work, taken as a whole, lacks serious literary, artistic, political or scientific value." [8] Thus, the Court left the determination of standards by which prurient appeal would be judged up to jurors who would determine the standards in the local community.

However, the Court was forced to backtrack almost immediately when, in 1972, Georgia brought a prosecution against exhibitors of the popular and award-winning movie *Carnal Knowledge*. A visibly disturbed Supreme Court warned in *Jenkins v. Georgia*[9] that notwithstanding the *Miller* local standard, obscenity laws, no matter how puritanical the local community, simply could not apply to a movie like *Carnal Knowledge*. A jury's discretion to apply "community standards" was not unlimited. The Court recognized that by giving local communities leeway in *Miller*, so that New York City could adopt a different standard from Salt Lake City, it inadvertently had sent a message that great movies and classic literature could be outlawed. The Court had learned a lesson in how, in the area of free speech, a small exception could overrun the rule.

Confusion over obscenity continues. In April 1990, a Cincinnati museum and its director were charged with violating state obscenity laws for showing the photography exhibition *Robert Mapplethorpe: The Perfect Moment*, which contained depictions of sadomasochism, homosexuality, and partially nude minors. (The exhibition, ironically, had opened at the University of Pennsylvania.) In this case, however, the jury acquitted, and the campaign against Mapplethorpe's work was blunted.

First Amendment jurisprudence is littered with people who uttered speech unpopular to some and who paid a price, even if ultimately vindicated. There is no way of knowing how many citizens have been harassed simply because the words "Congress shall make *no* law" (emphasis added) are interpreted as having exceptions. Nor is there any way to measure the amount of self-censorship that results from the uncertainty caused by such exceptions, however few they are.

The exception most frequently invoked by supporters of campus speech codes is for "fighting words," a doctrine honored in constitutional law more in theory than in practice. It gained life in the 1942 case *Chaplinsky v. New Hampshire.*[10] The Supreme Court unanimously upheld the criminal conviction of Walter Chaplinsky, who, proselytizing on the street in Rochester, New Hampshire, denounced organized religion as a "racket." When Chaplinsky would not moderate his attacks, and when the crowd got angry and restive, a police officer took Chaplinsky toward the police station (but did not yet arrest him). During this trip, Chaplinsky accused the city marshal of being "a goddamned racketeer" and "a damned Fascist," and went on to charge that "the whole government of Rochester are Fascists or agents of Fascists." For this, Chaplinsky was arrested and charged under a statute prohibiting anyone from addressing "any offensive, derisive or annoying word to any other person who is lawfully in any street or other public place, nor call[ing] him by any offensive or derisive name." The Supreme Court upheld the conviction on the ground that Chaplinsky had used "fighting words" likely to provoke an immediate violent response from the listener. In a statement that is famous both for its support of the prohibition against "fighting words" and its later citation by those, across the spectrum, seeking to outlaw offensive language, the Court majority wrote that "there are certain well-defined and narrowly limited classes of speech" that could be banned. "These," the Court intoned, "include . . . insulting or 'fighting' words—those which by their very utterance inflict injury or tend to incite an immediate breach of the peace." "Such utterances are no essential part of any exposition of ideas," the Court ruled, and could be banned in "the social interest in order and morality."

The Court, thus, took into account the value of offensive speech in accomplishing what speech was, in theory, supposed to accomplish, a *reasoned search for truth.* Justice Holmes previously had addressed this issue in his dissent in the notorious 1919 case of *Abrams v. United States,*[11] where seven justices upheld the espionage conviction of five Russian-born Jewish radicals for publishing a pamphlet seeking to provoke resistance to the American war effort as well as to American efforts to undermine the Russian Revolution. Holmes concluded that in all but the most dire situations, the interest in public order and morality must be subordinated to the interest in free speech, and he posited the basis of what later came to be accepted as the "free marketplace of ideas" approach—the notion that no belief is so clearly certain or correct that it justifies suppressing those who question it. "When men have realized that time has upset many fighting faiths," Holmes wrote, "they may come to believe even more than they believe the very foundations of their own conduct that the ultimate good desired is better reached by free trade in ideas—that the best test of truth is the power of the thought to get itself accepted in the competition of the market." Holmes noted the importance of protecting "the expression of opinions that we loathe and believe to be fraught with death, unless they so imminently threaten immediate interference with the lawful and pressing purposes of the law that an immediate check is required to save the country."[12]

However, Holmes's notion of the primacy of free speech and of the narrowness of any exceptions, laid out in *Schenk*'s "clear and present danger" test, was not sufficiently deeply etched when, in the *Chaplinsky* decision, the Court gave a last gasp to the doctrine that offensive speech could be outlawed in the name of public safety and morality because it supposedly did not contribute to reasoned dialogue as defined by those in power. Later, Holmes's view, shared by Justice Brandeis, led to the important *Brandenburg* "incitement to imminent lawlessness" test. The claim by some that *Chaplinsky* survived *Brandenburg* rests on an assumption that those to whom such language is addressed might be so beset by uncontrollable impulses that violence is imminent.

The "fighting words" doctrine existed alongside the related concept of "group defamation," another phrase often invoked by proponents of speech restrictions on campus. The group defamation concept first appeared in 1952 in a controversial 5 to 4 opinion, *Beauharnais v. Illinois*.[13] At issue was a statute forbidding anyone from making, selling, publishing, or exhibiting "in any public place . . . any [writing or picture] which . . . exposes the citizens of any race, color, creed or religion to contempt, derision, or obloquy or which is productive of breach of the peace or riots."

A leaflet had petitioned the city government of Chicago "to halt the further encroachment, harassment and invasion of white people . . . by the negro." It went on: "If persuasion and the need to prevent the white race from becoming mongrelized by the negro will not unite us, then the aggressions . . . rapes, robberies, knives, guns and marijuana of the negro, surely will." The leaflet's author was prosecuted under the statute. A bare majority of the Court, in an opinion by Justice Felix Frankfurter, upheld this legislative effort to deal with "wilful purveyors of falsehood concerning racial and religious groups [that] promote strife and tend powerfully to obstruct the manifold adjustments required for free, ordered life in a metropolitan, polyglot community." In doing so, it cited a history resulting in "exacerbated tension between races, often flaring into violence and destruction" in the Chicago area. The Cicero race riots of 1951 had occurred just months before the case was decided.

Each of the four justices who did not join the majority wrote a separate vigorous dissent. Interestingly, one common theme running through three of the four dissents was the extent to which minority groups, temporarily thrilled at their victory over bigots, should beware. The dissenting justices, no enemies of racial equality, warned:

> JUSTICE HUGO BLACK: Today Beauharnais is punished for publicly expressing strong views in favor of segregation. . . . The same kind of state law that makes Beauharnais a criminal for advocating segregation in Illinois can be utilized to send people to jail in other states for advocating equality and nonsegregation. . . . If there be minority groups who hail this holding as their victory, they might consider the possible relevancy of this ancient remark: "Another such victory and I am undone."

> JUSTICE WILLIAM O. DOUGLAS: Today a white man stands convicted for protesting in unseemly language against our decisions invalidating restrictive covenants. Tomorrow a negro will be hailed before a court for denouncing lynch law in heated terms. . . . [This decision] is notice to the legislatures that they have the power to control unpopular blocs. It is a warning to every minority that when the Constitution guarantees free speech it does not mean what it says.

> JUSTICE ROBERT JACKSON: No group interest in any particular prosecution should forget that the shoe may be on the other foot in some prosecution tomorrow.

Justice Douglas may have been the most prescient of the dissenters. Noting the possibility that group libel statutes so readily could—and likely would—be turned against any group or individual, he hinted that the decision was likely never to be followed and would die a well-deserved death, "that this is only one decision which may later be distinguished or confined to narrow limits." This indeed is precisely what happened.

By the time *Beauharnais* was announced, the Court already had begun to undermine one of *Chaplinsky*'s two rationales—namely, that the state had a valid interest in protecting the sensibilities of citizens confronted by vilifying language. Indeed, the Court had second thoughts about part of its *Chaplinsky* rationale only one year after the case was decided. In 1943, the Court decided *Cafeteria Employees Local 302 v. Angelos,*[14] in which it said that use of the word "Fascist"—the precise "fighting word" used by Chaplinsky—is "part of the conventional give-and-take in our economic and political controversies" and, thus, that it was protected under federal labor laws.

In 1949, the Court further undermined the idea that offensive speech is not protected. In *Terminiello v. Chicago,*[15] it reversed the disturbing-the-peace conviction of a suspended Catholic priest and follower of the notorious anti-Semite Gerald L. K. Smith. Father Arthur Terminiello gave a speech in Chicago attacking "Communistic Zionistic Jews," moving an unsympathetic crowd to violence against him. Justice Douglas wrote that the "function of free speech under our system of government is to invite dispute. It may indeed best serve its high purpose when it induces a condition of unrest, creates dissatisfaction with conditions as they are, or even stirs people to anger." Thus, the Court sent a message that the First Amendment prohibits the punishment of words merely because they might produce an angry reaction. *Terminiello* was particularly important, because the offensive language there, even though it in fact produced a violent reaction, was not viewed as "fighting words."

However, the more substantial move toward protection of offensive, even enraging language came with both opposition to the Vietnam War and the battle for racial equality in the 1960s. Late in the decade, Sidney Street, a black bus driver, torched his American flag upon learning that civil rights leader James Meredith had been shot in Mississippi. Street accompanied the incendiary act with the words "We don't need no damn flag." He was convicted under a state law criminalizing flag desecration. Even though a five-member majority of the Court gave lip service to *Chaplinsky*'s dual rationales of punishing language that would either produce a violent reaction or injure sensibilities, it reversed Street's conviction.[16] Street's offense, however, clearly would have injured the sensibilities of passersby. The Court's seeming self-contradiction on the question of whether "protection of sensibilities" was a viable rationale for punishment of speech confused the lower courts.

Two years later, *Street*'s ambiguity was resoundingly resolved. Paul Cohen was arrested in Los Angeles County Courthouse for wearing a jacket on which were emblazoned the words "Fuck the Draft." He was convicted for "offensive conduct" because, the state court ruled, "offensive conduct" meant "behavior which has a tendency to provoke others to acts of violence." Even though no one actually threatened Cohen, an attack was "reasonably foreseeable."

The Supreme Court, in an opinion written by the great conservative jurist John Marshall Harlan, reversed Cohen's conviction in 1971. Harlan said in *Cohen v. California*[17] that "Fuck the Draft" was not "obscene," because it was not at all erotic, and that its offensiveness did not render it unprotected. Furthermore, in an important holding relevant to the issue of current campus speech codes, the Court said that Cohen's slogan did not constitute "fighting words" because it was not *directed to any particular individual.* Ultrasensitive passersby, Harlan noted, could protect their sensibilities by "averting their eyes."

Cohen made its most important statement by its severe limitation of the doctrine that *Chaplinsky* had established. For the first time, the Court accorded explicit constitutional protection to the "emotive function" of speech, noting that expression of emotion was as much a function of speech as was the "cognitive" role previously singled out by Holmes and others for protection. It noted, further, that the emotive function "may often be the more important element of the overall message sought to be communicated." Emotion joined logical argument as worthy of protection.

The implications of this development for the constitutional protection of offensive language cannot be overstated. In *Cohen,* because we find a confluence—indeed, a synergy—between the use of offensive language and the goal of political protest, Cohen's statement should be viewed as core political speech. However, *Cohen* hinted at a willingness to protect speech for reasons beyond its utility for the expression of political opinion. It spoke of the value, in a free society, of allowing the individual to choose how to express himself. This recognition of the value of self-expression was coupled, in the Court's view, with an inability of the state to make a principled distinction between "offensive" language and other language, because it is "often true that one man's vulgarity is another's lyric." The Court expressed the fear that the state, given broad powers to distinguish "vulgarity" from "lyric," would utilize the twilight zone between them to "seize upon the censorship of particular words as a convenient guise for banning the expression of unpopular views." Under this formulation, the most dissident speech, expressed in the most vehement and emotional style, is both worthy and needful of a high level of protection. This innovation would have implications years later, when the Free Speech movement occasioned by campus antiwar and civil rights protests of the '60s and '70s evolved, astonishingly, into the speech code movement of the '80s and '90s.

Cohen remains intact and is invoked by the Court when it faces expression that offends contemporary sensibilities. In the 1990 case of *United States v. Eichman,* for example, the Court invalidated the Flag Protection Act of 1989 (outlawing flag-burning and desecration), declaring that while "desecration of the flag is deeply offensive to many . . . the same might be said, for example, of virulent ethnic and religious epithets, . . . vulgar repudiations of the draft, . . . and scurrilous caricatures."[18] All are protected.

Cohen undermined *Chaplinsky* in yet another respect with implications for speech codes. *Chaplinsky* had assumed that a vile epithet was likely to provoke a violent response. This had allowed the Court to approve punishment of "fighting words" given the supposed *link* between such speech and violent *conduct,* because the prevention of violence has always been deemed a proper role of government. The approach in *Chaplinsky,* however, had put any controversial speaker at the mercy of the so-called "heckler's veto"—the power of even a small number of individuals to prevent a speech. The Court in *Cohen* voiced doubt that many would react violently to offensive speech not directed to them personally and ruled that the presence of a few people with "lawless and violent proclivities . . . is an insufficient base upon which to erect" a regime of censorship.

The "heckler's veto" had long been a problem in First Amendment law. In an infamous 1951 case, *Feiner v. New York,*[19] a member of the Young Progressives of America had been successfully prosecuted for denouncing President Truman, among others, on a city street. The Supreme Court upheld the conviction on the ground that the opinion of the arresting policeman— that the speech was about to cause a violent reaction—had to be credited. Free speech absolutist Justice Hugo Black suggested in dissent that the peace be kept by applying the constraints of the law directly to the violent listener, rather than to the offensive speaker. *Cohen* moved in precisely this direction. This left *Chaplinsky's* "fighting words" doctrine intact only in situations where offensive speech was used in face-to-face confrontation. It obliterated *Chaplinsky's* willingness to allow prosecution of offensive language to protect listeners' sensibilities. In the atmosphere of escalating antiwar and civil rights protests in the late 1960s and '70s, the Court was allowing for more robust discourse.

The conditions under which an anticipated violent response could justify censorship, even in a face-to-face confrontation, were further narrowed in *Gooding v. Wilson.*[20] Wilson had been arrested because he told a police officer, at an antiwar protest at an army induction center: "White son of a bitch, I'll kill you." By a lopsided 5 to 2 vote, the Supreme Court invalidated the Georgia statute making it a misdemeanor to engage in the use "to another [and] without provocation . . . [of] opprobrious words or abusive language tending to cause a breach of the peace." The Court acted because the statute was so broad as to outlaw, indiscriminately, *both* protected and unprotected speech—an example of a traditional First Amendment doctrine forbidding "overbreadth" in the regulation of speech. However, in an important development, the Court here began to make distinctions between different types of audiences, noting that speech that might provoke an immediate violent reaction from one listener under one set of circumstances might not do so with respect to other listeners in other situations. Offensive language directed to a police officer "who, on account of circumstances or by virtue of the obligation of office, cannot actually then and there resent the same by a breach of the peace" could not be banned. Put another way, speech, independent of context, cannot be determined to be "fighting words"; to fall within that exception to the First Amendment, the Court suggested, the words must be directed at a person who would be likely to respond violently. Such an approach would have serious philosophical and legal implications for the debate, which raged (and still rages) in the following decades, over whether college students who were minority group members or women should be considered patronizingly to have a threshold of self-control lower than that of the average citizen.

Even if a statute is drafted to conform to the narrow definition of "fighting words," First Amendment jurisprudence may still make it unconstitutional. In the immediate aftermath of *Cohen* and *Gooding,* the Court reversed a spate of convictions for use of offensive language, mostly in the context of antiwar and—note well—campus protests. One case decided in 1973 presaged the speech code controversies of the following decade. In *Papish v. Board of Curators of the University of Missouri,*[21] the Court ordered reinstatement of a graduate journalism student at the University of Missouri. The student had distributed a newspaper containing a cartoon depicting policemen raping the Statue of Liberty and the Goddess of Justice, as well as a headline reading MOTHERFUCKER ACQUITTED (referring to a member of the radical group Up Against the Wall, Motherfuckers). The Court held that "the mere dissemination of ideas—no matter how offensive to good taste—on a state university campus may not be shut off in the name alone of 'conventions of decency.'" Importantly, the Court continued: "Since the First Amendment leaves no room for the operation of a dual standard in the academic community with respect to the content of speech, and because the state University's action here cannot be justified as a nondiscriminatory application of reasonable rules governing conduct, the judgments of the courts below must be reversed."

At today's universities, of course, Papish might be charged with "sexual harassment" for using expression that trivializes rape. The Court in *Papish,* however, applied to offensive speech in the public university the governing principle of the First Amendment—that regulation of speech, even where allowed, must be content neutral. Papish had been penalized for *what* he was saying. This, the Court ruled, is what the Constitution forbids.

"Content neutrality" was not an entirely new idea. As far back as 1929, Justice Holmes, dissenting in *United States v. Schwimmer,*[22] penned one of the most often-quoted phrases in American constitutional law when he called for "the principle of free thought—not free thought for those who agree with us, but freedom for the thought that we hate." Harvard Law School constitutional scholar Laurence Tribe wrote in the 1988 edition of his acclaimed constitutional law treatise that "if the Constitution forces government to allow people to march, speak and write in favor of peace, brotherhood, and justice, then it must also require government to allow them to advocate hatred, racism, and even genocide."[23]

A statute would be deemed content specific as opposed to content neutral in one of two ways. First, it may focus on the message which is delivered, as opposed to the time, place, and manner in which that message is presented. For example, the punishment in *Papish* was based on what the graduate student wrote; however, an ordinance prohibiting the use of a sound truck at 3:00 A.M. would be neutral with respect to content and, thus, constitutional. Second, it may penalize a specific *viewpoint.* For example, a statute prohibiting political candidates from speaking in the library is neutral with respect to viewpoint, but it would not be if it prohibited only Republicans or Socialists from speaking in the location.

In 1992, the Supreme Court addressed the application of the principle of content neutrality to the "fighting words" doctrine in *R.A.V. v. City of St. Paul,*[24] a decision with particular relevance if a public campus speech code ever should reach our highest court. This case involved a cross-burning by white youngsters on the property of a black family. The defendant was prosecuted under a city ordinance making it a crime to place "on public or private property a symbol . . . which one knows or has reasonable grounds to know arouses anger, alarm or resentment in others on the basis of race, color, creed, religion or gender." Every member of the Court agreed that the ordinance was unconstitutional. Five of them, however, based their reasoning on a theory with profound implications for the future direction of First Amendment law and for legislation such as the group defamation statute in *Beauharnais* and even the "fighting words" doctrine of *Chaplinsky*. The Court assumed that the ordinance was aimed *only* at the supposedly unprotected category of "fighting words," and yet it still invalidated it on its face. The Court noted that even fighting words have expressive purpose, and that the First Amendment limits the restriction of otherwise unprotected speech when that restriction is based on content. The Court concluded that the fundamental flaw of the ordinance was that it was not *content* neutral, because it restricted only those fighting words addressed to particular subjects, namely race, creed, and color. Furthermore, the Court held that the ordinance was not *viewpoint* neutral, because in practice it would punish fighting words from only one side of the fence. Justice Antonin Scalia, writing for the Court, gave an example:

> One could [under St. Paul's ordinance] hold up a sign saying, for example, that all "anti-Catholic bigots" are misbegotten; but not that all "papists" are, for that would insult and provoke violence "on the basis of religion." St. Paul has no such authority to license one side of a debate to fight freestyle, while requiring the other to follow Marquis of Queensbury rules.

This opinion was a straightforward application of the principle of neutrality, which prevented St. Paul from forbidding communication—in this case, "fighting words" symbolized by the burning cross or swastika—by adherents of an officially disfavored viewpoint, without similarly limiting the good guys. In *R.A.V.,* the Court found a mechanism for discouraging authoritarian excess by groups that are temporarily in control and can dictate what is "correct." The mechanism was implicit in the dissenting opinions in *Beauharnais,* particularly Justice Black's admonition that "another such victory and I am undone." Members of "protected" racial minorities should not celebrate a repressive victory over racists, because the prosecution of segregationist speech today can pave the way for the prosecution of integrationist speech tomorrow.

Viewed from a more ancient perspective, the Supreme Court has established a "golden rule" of constitutional doctrine, according to which we are all forced to treat others as we would insist upon being treated. "Equal protection under the law" means that we are all either protected by, or potential victims of, the same laws. No better mechanism to achieve fairness is likely ever to be developed than that of forcing us all to live under the rules that we impose upon others.

Indeed, even before *R.A.V.,* the "fighting words" doctrine was largely defunct, enjoying some lip service but little vitality. Its recent history does not give proponents of censorship more cause for optimism than did the cases decided in *Chaplinsky*'s immediate aftermath. A review of Supreme Court cases in the past two decades demonstrates that in not a single case has the Court upheld a conviction for speech on the basis of *Chaplinsky*'s "fighting words." Nadine Strossen, law professor at New York Law School and president of the ACLU, went so far as to suggest in a 1990 article that the "fighting words" doctrine simply is no longer the law.[25]

However, *R.A.V.* goes further and likely has fatal implications for attempts to adopt a double standard—applying punishments to speech to "protect" some groups but not others, restricting "hate" speech but not other speech. Because this is the very essence of speech codes—they outlaw "incorrect" but not "correct" speech—such codes are not likely to survive where constitutional protections come into play, such as on public campuses or on private campuses where state or local laws apply free speech protections. The First Amendment runs head-on into a chief justification offered by proponents of codes—that they are reasonable and even necessary because they are aimed at protecting "historically disadvantaged" groups. The only "disadvantaged" person, in the eyes of that First Amendment upon which everyone's liberty depends, is one reduced to silence.

CHAPTER 3

WHAT IS ACADEMIC FREEDOM?

The American Association of University Professors (AAUP) has provided the most authoritative and widely accepted definition of the contours of academic freedom in the United States. After having been enlisted to mediate several high-profile disputes between university administrators and individual professors, the AAUP, in 1915, appointed a committee to draft guidelines that would define more concretely the precepts that long had enjoyed wide currency in the United States and Europe, but which had proven difficult to specify and implement. The resulting document, *General Report of the Committee on Academic Freedom and Tenure*,[1] was heavily influenced by the notion that truth was not a fixed absolute, but, rather, a goal continually pursued in an open and contentious intellectual marketplace. The 1915 report was less intent on bestowing specific rights on professors (and it did not deal at all with the rights of students) than on assuring that the pursuit of knowledge and truth be allowed to proceed, unhindered, by the professoriate in general.

Central to the 1915 report was the committee's definition of "the function of the academic institution," which included "to promote inquiry and advance the sum of human knowledge." The committee noted that fields of modern academic and scientific endeavor were only in their infancy, and that "in the spirit life, and in the interpretation of the general meaning and ends of human existence and its relation to the universe, we are still far from a comprehension of the final truths, and from a universal agreement among all sincere and earnest men." Therefore, the committee reasoned, it was essential to protect, as "the first condition of progress, [a] complete and unlimited

50

freedom to pursue inquiry and publish its results."[2] The university was to be a refuge from *all* tyrannies over men's minds—those of the state, university trustees and administrators, and public opinion.

In addition to faculty members' having the freedom of unfettered inquiry, the report also recognized their freedom to teach their particular fields without interference as to content, except when the execution of their teaching duties could fairly be classified as incompetent or neglectful.

Yet there was a notable exception to the teacher's freedom to teach whatever he, in his sound professional judgment, wished when dealing with young students. The teacher was admonished to avoid "taking unfair advantage of the student's immaturity by indoctrinating him with the teacher's own opinions before the student has had an opportunity fairly to examine other opinions upon the matters in question, and before he has sufficient knowledge and ripeness of judgment to be entitled to form any definitive opinion of his own."[3] That was about as close as the 1915 report came to championing anything that could be viewed as a student's right to be free from the *coercive* shaping of his or her mind.

The report acknowledged that not all institutions were suited for academic freedom. There were "proprietary" institutions "designed for the propagation of specific doctrines," such as church-supported, religious, and denominational institutions. These were so named because they do not owe devotion to any notion of "public trust," but, instead, owe fealty to the orthodoxies they were created to serve. Such institutions "do not . . . accept the principles of freedom of inquiry, of opinion, and of teaching" that make up the concept of academic freedom. The report noted the special obligation of such institutions—a corollary of their right to impose orthodoxies—honestly and accurately to disclose their special missions. They "should not be permitted to sail under false colors [because] genuine boldness and thoroughness of inquiry, and freedom of speech, are scarcely reconcilable with the prescribed inculcation of a particular opinion upon a controverted question."[4] Thus, the AAUP made provision for academic institutions that necessarily (and, one should add, constitutionally) had to be free to impose their particular orthodoxies, while at the same time insisting that they were morally obligated to adhere to what one today would call "truth in advertising."

In order to effectuate the 1915 report, the AAUP recommended that academic peer committees be established to review attempts to discipline or dismiss faculty members. It established the notion that after a trial period professors be granted tenure, making dismissal for improper motives difficult. Further, the report set out procedural rights essential to the protection of substantive individual academic freedom. Charges against a professor had to be stated clearly and in writing, and a fair hearing accorded before a "judicial committee" chosen by the faculty. The accused "should have full opportunity to present evidence," and charges of "professional incompetency" should be adjudicated by his peers within his university or, at his option, "by a committee of his fellow specialists from other institutions."[5]

Columbia University history professor Walter P. Metzger, in his article "The 1940 Statement of Principles on Academic Freedom and Tenure,"[6] noted an important early addition to the arsenal of protections in the 1915 report. In 1916, Harvard's president, A. Lawrence Lowell, in a high-profile case, refused to discipline a faculty member who expressed pro-German sentiments during World War I, not only because of the personal academic freedom of faculty, but because the university could not monitor the political views of faculty without being forced either to discipline those with whom it differed, or, by inference, to be seen as lending its imprimatur to the views of those *not* disciplined. By what Metzger terms "mutual dissociation"[7] the AAUP asserted that the professor does not speak for the institution, nor the institution for the professor. This institutional neutrality has proven useful to all and has survived, only occasionally tattered, the test of time.

The 1915 report was updated by the AAUP's 1940 Statement of Principles.[8] The 1940 statement served as an antidote to the public's tendency to see the 1915 report as a declaration of special rights and privileges for teachers alone. The AAUP now declared its purpose "to promote public understanding and support of academic freedom, for such institutions are not meant to promote the welfare of either teachers or the universities themselves but rather to advance the common good." Such advancement, the 1940 statement posited, "depends upon the free search for truth and its free exposition." Thus, in order to secure public support for a special degree of liberty on campuses, the drafters emphasized not only "the rights of the teacher in teaching" but also the rights "of the student to freedom in learning," and the public benefit in allowing the conditions that would advance human knowledge.[9]

The next major advance in the definition of academic freedom was the AAUP's 1967 *Joint Statement on Rights and Freedoms of Students.*[10] The joint statement posited the inseparability of the "freedom to teach and freedom to learn." Thus, it brought to the fore the student's right to seek his or her own truth. The joint statement advised professors to "encourage free discussion, inquiry, and expression" in the classroom. This was followed by a plea for the "protection of freedom of expression." In exchange for paying attention to their prescribed studies, "students should be free to take reasoned exception to the data or views offered in any course of study and to reserve judgment about matters of opinion."[11] The section on student affairs sought to protect individual and organized student activity and expressions of opinion as long as students did not cause disruption of the functioning of the university, an admonition not unexpected given the campus turbulence of the times. A section on student publications insisted "the student press should be free of censorship."[12]

The 1967 joint statement specified rights and responsibilities for both students and institutions, including the procedures to be followed when a student was accused of violating a university's standards of conduct. Those standards should be limited to what the institution "considers essential to its educational mission and its community life." The standards, the AAUP insisted, should leave the student "as free as possible from imposed limitations that have no direct relevance to his education." Offenses must be "clearly defined" and should be published and publicized so that students are aware of expectations in advance. Students should be free from any "form of harassment" or efforts by administrators "to coerce admissions of guilt or information about conduct of other suspected persons."[13] Punishment should not be inflicted, nor a student's status changed, pending resolution.

The AAUP called for due process hearings, urging more *formal* procedures in more *serious* cases, if the accused student requested such a hearing. Hearing committees should be composed of disinterested faculty members and, at the accused's request, students. The student should be informed, in writing, of the charges "with sufficient particularity, and in sufficient time, to ensure opportunity to prepare for the hearing." The student "should have the right to be assisted in his defense by an adviser of his choice," and the prosecution should have "the burden of proof. . . . The student should be given an opportunity to testify and to present evidence and witnesses [and] to hear and question adverse witnesses." The verdict "should be based solely" upon evidence introduced at the hearing. "In the absence of a transcript," the student had the right to "a digest and a verbatim record, such as a tape recording, of the hearing." The student should have a "right of appeal to the president or ultimately to the governing board of the institution."[14]

In chapters to follow, we shall consider the extent to which these procedural guarantees for students, bequeathed by the 1960s as an essential part of "academic freedom," are still honored by academic institutions, and the extent to which courts have felt the need to impose minimum levels of procedural fairness where lacking. Let us turn now to a brief consideration of the extent to which courts have come to join substantive principles of academic freedom with First Amendment doctrines of free speech.

————————

When a court intervenes in a university's refusal to accord free speech rights to a student, it does so under the legal rubric of enforcing a constitutional or statutory right to free speech rather than a precept of academic freedom. Courts, after all, interpret and enforce constitutions and statutes, not AAUP policies, unless a professor or student sues the university for a breach of a contract that promised academic freedom. Nonetheless, the two concepts have become intertwined. Courts, in effect, have come to enforce certain principles of academic freedom as defined in civil society by the academic profession, in the guise of judicial enforcement of constitutional rights.

Duke University law professor William W. Van Alstyne, a respected scholar in the area of academic freedom and the First Amendment, observes in his essay "Academic Freedom and the First Amendment in the Supreme Court of the United States" that the phrase "academic freedom" made its debut in American constitutional law in a dissent by Justice William O. Douglas in the 1952 case of *Adler v. Board of Education.*[15] New York had adopted a statute ordering the Board of Regents to enact regulations denying public school employment to "subversives," defined as those who advocated force or violence to overthrow the federal government. The statute established a legal presumption that membership in certain "subversive" groups was proof of such advocacy (the regents were to hold hearings to formulate a complete list), and it mandated both loyalty oaths and loyalty hearings. The court majority ruled that this did not impose upon conscience and speech, because "if [teachers] do not choose to work on such terms, they are at liberty to retain their beliefs and associations and go elsewhere." Justice Douglas, with only Justice Hugo Black agreeing, argued that such a statute would "raise havoc with academic freedom." Specifically, he complained that the "system of spying and surveillance with its accompanying reports and trials cannot go hand in hand with academic freedom." He lamented the production of "standardized thought, not the pursuit of truth." Douglas argued the statute also would violate the First Amendment, because it would preclude adherents of a particular school of thought from engaging in the teaching profession in any public school in the state. "Indeed," Douglas warned, "the impact of this kind of censorship on the public school system illustrates the high purpose of the First Amendment in freeing speech and thought from censorship." The statute, for him, was "typical of what happens in a police state." Thus, the first mention of "academic freedom" in constitutional jurisprudence relates it explicitly to First Amendment concerns.

The invocation of academic freedom by Justice Douglas, a former professor himself, appears to have inspired another scholar-turned-jurist, Justice Felix Frankfurter, to take the analysis further later that year. In *Wieman v. Updegraff*,[16] the U.S. Supreme Court again dealt with a state statute that required a loyalty oath by public employees. The Court held the statute unconstitutional because it operated in an "arbitrary or discriminatory" manner. However, several justices wished explicitly to link the First Amendment and academic freedom. Justice Frankfurter added that the First Amendment protected teachers in particular because intimidation was incompatible with the profession. Such intimidation not only silences the teacher, Frankfurter warned, but also "has an unmistakable tendency to chill that free play of the spirit which all teachers ought especially to cultivate and practice." Frankfurter's language, discussing the role of teachers and of educational institutions, echoed the AAUP's 1915 and 1940 statements:

> To regard teachers—in our entire educational system, from the primary grades to the university—as the priests of our democracy is . . . not to indulge in hyperbole. It is the special task of teachers to foster those habits of open-mindedness and critical inquiry which alone make for responsible citizens. . . . Teachers must . . . be exemplars of open-mindedness and free inquiry. They cannot carry out their noble task if the conditions for the practice of a responsible and critical mind are denied to them.

This approach—that academic freedom was essential to a teacher's performing his or her role—if accepted by a majority of the justices, would reverse earlier Supreme Court decisions that protected a teacher's right to hold and express opinions but not his or her right to a public job. To hold such a job, the Court had reasoned in case after case, was a "privilege" and not a "right." Soon, however, the First Amendment analysis of Black and Frankfurter would come to obliterate the distinction between "privilege" and "right," and the linkage of academic freedom and the First Amendment would reign.

This alliance between the First Amendment and academic freedom took a further step in 1957, with *Sweezy v. New Hampshire*.[17] Not satisfied with the efforts of Senator Joseph McCarthy and the federal government, New Hampshire enacted its own Subversive Activities Act. At legislative hearings convened under the authority of the statute, Professor Paul Sweezy of the University of New Hampshire was subpoenaed and questioned about certain lectures he had given at UNH. Sweezy, a self-styled "classical Marxist" and "socialist," denied advocating the use of violence, but he had coauthored an article that criticized the use of violence by capitalist nations seeking to preserve a social order that he felt should, and would, eventually collapse. This collapse, he predicted, would be met by violence on the part of those seeking to create a "truly human society."

Sweezy answered some questions, but he drew the line when asked about the content of his lectures. He was cited for contempt of the legislature and jailed. Sweezy's conviction was reversed by the U.S. Supreme Court on a technicality. In the course of doing so, however, the Court spoke in terms that made clear the majority's displeasure with the whole business of inquisitions into loyalty. It spoke of the "essentiality of freedom in the community of American universities" as being "almost self-evident." "To impose any straitjacket upon the intellectual leaders in our colleges and universities," warned the justices, "would imperil the future of our Nation." Justice Frankfurter took advantage of the opportunity to write a "concurring opinion" in which he criticized the then–politically correct justification that the state had asserted for wielding powers of inquiry and intimidation over academics—the notion that interference with academic freedom could occur "in a limited area in which the legislative committee may reasonably believe that the overthrow of existing government by force and violence is being or has been taught, advocated or planned." This "governmental intrusion into the intellectual life of a university" created such "grave harm," Frankfurter wrote, that this purported justification for repression was inadequate. He stressed "the dependence of a free society on free universities" and decried the state's "intervention . . . that inevitably tends to check the ardor and fearlessness of scholars."

A number of loyalty cases followed, and while the Court overturned convictions with regularity and sent the message that ideological inquisitions would not be tolerated, a majority of the justices had not yet settled upon a rationale combining the First Amendment and academic freedom. That situation changed with the landmark 1967 case of *Keyishian v. Board of Regents of the University of the State of New York*.[18] Here the Court once again faced New York's teacher loyalty laws, which had figured in the 1952 *Adler* case in which the teacher lost his challenge. This time, however, the Court, by a vote of 5 to 4, overturned the statute on the ground that its vagueness violated the Constitution. It ignored the reality, warned the Court, that "our Nation is deeply committed to safeguarding academic freedom, [a] transcendent value to all of us and not merely to the teachers concerned." This being so, the Court declared these values part and parcel of the First Amendment, "which does not tolerate laws that cast a pall of orthodoxy over the class-room . . . [which is] peculiarly the marketplace of ideas." For the first time, the Court blended academic freedom and the First Amendment. There was a dissent by four justices, but even they did not question the right of a university teacher to study, write, and teach about subversive doctrines. They drew the line, however, at granting job protection to one who not only taught *about* such an idea but also "advocated such doctrine himself."

By the late 1960s, as the nation's obsession with loyalty, subversion, and political conformity waned, new academic freedom and First Amendment cases arose. In *Tinker v. Des Moines Independant Community School District,*[19] John F. Tinker, aged fifteen, brought a lawsuit to contest a high school prohibition against the wearing of black armbands in protest against the Vietnam War. They had been suspended for violating this rule. This time the Supreme Court was more unified, with a majority of seven declaring the ban an unconstitutional prior restraint on the students' free speech:

> First Amendment rights, applied in light of the special characteristics of the school environment, are available to teachers and students. It can hardly be argued that either students or teachers shed their constitutional rights to freedom of speech or expression at the schoolhouse gate. . . . In our system, state operated schools may not be enclaves of totalitarianism. . . . Students may not . . . be confined to the expression of those sentiments that are officially approved.

The crux of *Tinker v. Des Moines Independent Community School District* was that as long as expressional activity was not disruptive to the educational mission, it could not be banned. Reasonable time, place, and manner restrictions were permissible, but a "place" restriction could not effect a total ban on expressional activity everywhere on the premises, and a "time" restriction did not mean all day. The Court observed that public school administrators, even on the junior high and high school level (that is, below "higher education"), could not invoke a general fear of "disorder or disturbance" as an excuse for repression. Speech unpleasant to some obviously has the potential to cause disturbance, but a free society entails a certain amount of risk, and "our history says that it is this sort of hazardous freedom—this kind of openness—that is the basis of our national strength and of the independence and vigor of Americans who grow up and live in this relatively permissive, often disputatious, society." "In our system," the Court concluded, "state-operated schools may not be enclaves of totalitarianism."

Later, the Court took modest steps to limit the sweep of the *Tinker* doctrine, but these cases did not alter the fundamentals. For example, in one 1986 case, *Bethel School District No. 403 v. Fraser,*[20] the Court allowed a public high school assistant principal to discipline Matthew Fraser for sexually oriented comments in a speech to the student assembly. It said that although "the First Amendment guarantees wide freedom in matters of adult public discourse," this does not mean "that simply because the use of an offensive form of expression may not be prohibited to adults making what the speaker considers a political point, the same latitude must be permitted to children in a public school." The majority noted that there is a state interest "in protecting minors from exposure to vulgar and offensive spoken language." (Minors, of course, would exclude college students.)

Similarly, in the 1988 case of *Hazelwood School District v. Kuhlmeier,*[21] the Court allowed a high school principal to censor the school newspaper. Pointing out that the rights of high school students are not necessarily the same as those of adults, the Court observed that allowing controversial speech in a school-sponsored and -financed newspaper was different from allowing students to express themselves as in *Tinker.*

Principles of free speech and academic freedom have remained strong in public secondary education and, by implication, nearly absolute in public higher education, because whatever degree of control school administrators might reasonably be given over young children and adolescents, the courts logically have recognized less justification for exercising such control over college students and professors. This was evident in the 1972 case of *Healy v. James,*[22] where the campus chapter of Students for a Democratic Society (SDS) sought official administrative recognition at Central Connecticut State College. Without such recognition, the SDS chapter would have been unable to post notices on campus bulletin boards and use college facilities to hold meetings. Mainline political groups, such as Young Republicans and Young Democrats, had official recognition. The college's president denied recognition, claiming that since SDS "openly repudiates" the College's dedication to academic freedom, it was not entitled to invoke academic freedom in order to obtain official recognition, and in any event its rhetoric (though not its conduct) was violent. In effect, the college president sought to force SDS to live with the consequences of its own ideology. The Supreme Court, however, turned the tables on the president, insisting that the college live with the consequences of its own ideology and with the First Amendment.

This time the Court unanimously upheld the speech and associational rights of students, observing that "state colleges and universities are not enclaves immune from the sweep of the First Amendment." "We break no new constitutional ground," said the Court, "in reaffirming this Nation's dedication to safeguarding academic freedom." Since the mere advocacy of violence was constitutionally protected, SDS's violent words, in the absence of violent actions, could not justify a ban. An educational institution's use of its academic freedom to *curtail rather than promote* the ends of higher education did not sit well with the U.S. Supreme Court in *Healy.* Academia, at least in the public sector, was being held to its own advertised ideals. The courts were now embracing the view that promises were made to be kept, even by academic administrators.

First Amendment and academic freedom doctrines were further clarified the following decade, when the Court decided *Regents of the University of Michigan v. Ewing*[23] in 1985, leaving the right of appropriate and professional academic judgments intact. Scott Ewing was dismissed from the University of Michigan Medical School after failing an important national exam and was refused readmission on academic grounds. He claimed that because some others who failed the exam had been allowed to retake it, procedural fairness required that he have the same opportunity. The Supreme Court unanimously ruled *against* the student: "When judges are asked to review the substance of a genuinely academic decision," wrote the Court, "they may not override it unless it is such a substantial departure from accepted academic norms as to demonstrate that the person or committee responsible did not actually exercise professional judgment." The justices expressed "a reluctance to trench on the prerogatives of . . . educational institutions and our responsibility to safeguard their academic freedom, a special concern of the First Amendment." Thus, as long as a public school exercises its academic authority in good faith, it may invoke institutional academic freedom to avoid state intervention on subjective issues like assessment of academic competence.

Subsequent decisions have reiterated these themes. Yet, oddly, even though the Court has dealt with issues of institutional academic freedom and of personal academic freedom, it has not dealt with balancing the two in any single case. But an unlikely case from New Jersey gave the U.S. Supreme Court the opportunity to resolve this vital question.

———————

On April 5, 1978, a man named Chris Schmid was arrested for trespass while distributing United States Labor Party political literature on the campus of Princeton University. At the time, it seemed an unlikely scenario for a major test case of the extent to which the Constitution protects academic freedom. It was an even less likely test of the curious dual nature of academic freedom—the dichotomy and tension between the institutional academic freedom that protects private (and, to some extent, public) universities from interference by the state, on the one hand, and the personal academic freedom that protects students and faculty from tyrannical university administrators, on the other.

Had Schmid been an undergraduate, the case would have raised the question of whether academic freedom—as woven into free speech law—protected Princeton from being told by a court what to permit its students, or protected its students from being forbidden by Princeton from distributing political literature on campus. However, Schmid was not a Princeton student, the Labor Party was not a university-approved organization, and neither Schmid nor the party had been invited onto the campus by a student or faculty member.

Furthermore, the prosecution was brought in a *state* court, not in the federal system that had led the way in resolving issues on the frontier of legal analysis. That frontier was visited here, however, in the conflict between a private college administration's right to control its own campus and the arguable right of others to use that campus, traditionally kept open to the public, as a forum to express their views—even when the college had not approved of this guest.

Schmid defended himself against the criminal trespass charges pressed by the university (with the cooperation of the local prosecutor) by claiming a violation of his rights to free speech and assembly under both the First Amendment to the U.S. Constitution and the free speech and association provisions of the Constitution of New Jersey. Schmid faced a monumental obstacle, because Princeton was not a "state actor," but, rather, a private entity. Nevertheless, even though Princeton owned the campus, Schmid claimed a right to distribute political literature and state his views, in a nondisruptive manner, to willing students. The campus, Schmid argued, was not like any ordinary piece of private property, such as a home or even a place of business. It was, instead, private property dedicated to a public purpose entirely consistent with political proselytization.

Princeton took the unusual step of intervening in a criminal case. It argued that state and federal free speech provisions, and principles of academic freedom, protected not Schmid, but, rather, the university from being told by an arm of the state—the court—that it had to admit Schmid and his views to its campus. The New Jersey Supreme Court was facing a complex issue—one that the U.S. Supreme Court never had faced directly. Although there were precedents addressing related questions, none had squarely resolved the conflict between the private institution's freedom from state interference and the individual's asserted right to free speech in certain possibly "public" forums.

Lacking guidance from the U.S. Supreme Court, the New Jersey court declined to decide the *Schmid* case on federal constitutional grounds. Instead, it relied on the state Constitution, over which that court had primary interpretive authority. Thus, for the first time, a court set out to interpret the applicability of these state-assigned rights to an individual censored, in his view, by a private liberal arts university. Although a state cannot offer its citizens *fewer* rights than are ensured by the federal Bill of Rights, it can offer *more* without federal interference—provided that, in the process, it does nothing to trample any federal constitutional provision such as, in this case, Princeton's right to control its campus.

The state court ruled in favor of Schmid and reversed his trespass conviction.[24] The court's opinion was and remains controversial. The case, after all, pitted those who viewed institutional academic freedom, as well as property rights, as the bulwark of liberty against those who viewed individual academic freedom as paramount. Part of the academic freedom accorded students and professors, in that latter view, consisted of their right to hear outsiders on the campus, which was the obverse side of the speaker's right to access.

The Court's method for resolving these tensions was ingenious, or perhaps devious, depending upon one's point of view. It observed that although it did not have power to insist that the university dedicate its campus to a use dictated by the state or by the court, it did have power to insist that the university be bound by its own characterization of its purpose and educational mission. In essence, the Court said that in view of the primacy of free speech under the state Constitution, when a university advertises itself as an "open" or "public forum," truth in advertising dictates that it abide by its promise. (Such a forum, in legal terminology, is a place, public or private, where people, including members of the public, traditionally gather to exchange, offer, or listen to views on various topics.) In this manner, the Court claimed that it was *honoring,* rather than countermanding, Princeton's autonomous right to define and carry out its own educational mission (protected by the First Amendment) and to control access to and uses of its private property (protected by the Fifth Amendment), at the same time that the Court was protecting Schmid's right of free speech.

To alleviate criticism that it was interfering with a private party's property rights, and to give weight to its own concession that a court "must give substantial deference to the importance of institutional integrity and independence" and to the "academic freedom" that requires that "an educational institution [control] those who seek to enter its domain," the Court looked to Princeton's own published description as evidence of its goals and purposes. "Princeton University," enthused the Court, "itself has furnished the answer to this inquiry in expansively expressing its overriding educational goals." The Court quoted Princeton's own regulations:

> The central purposes of a University are the pursuit of truth, the discovery of new knowledge through scholarship and research, the teaching and general development of students, and the transmission of knowledge and learning to society at large. Free inquiry and free expression within the academic community are indispensable to the achievement of these goals. The freedom to teach and to learn depends upon the creation of appropriate conditions and opportunities on the campus as a whole as well as in classrooms and lecture halls. . . . Free speech and peaceable assembly are basic requirements of the University as a center for free inquiry and the search for knowledge and insight.

These words, the Court reasoned, expressed a willing dedication to individual academic freedom: "No one questions that Princeton has honored this grand ideal and has in fact dedicated its facilities and property to achieve the educational goals expounded in this compelling statement."

Not content merely to cite the university's regulations, the Court went on to quote Princeton's president, William G. Bowen, who, in a 1978 essay entitled "The Role of the University as an Institution in Confronting External Issues,"[25] wrote that Princeton, in keeping with its "philosophy of education," is obligated "to expose students . . . to a wide variety of views on controversial questions." "We are not talking here about something that is merely desirable; we are talking about something that is essential," Bowen concluded.

Scouring Princeton's own published documents, the Court even found a regulation that demonstrated that "the University itself has endorsed the educational value of an open campus and the full exposure of the college community to the 'outside world.'" In short, Princeton had on numerous occasions pronounced itself an open campus, and Schmid and the Court were seeking merely to hold the university to its word. Noting that "private colleges and universities must be accorded a generous measure of autonomy and self-governance if they are to fulfill their paramount role as vehicles of education and enlightenment," the Court ruled that because Schmid's activities coincided with Princeton's educational mission, the university's decision to exclude him was unconstitutional.

The New Jersey Supreme Court's resolution of *State v. Schmid* left Princeton appearing to be hoist by its own petard. Although the Court's opinion applied specifically only to Princeton and any other public or private campus in New Jersey that similarly advertised itself as "open," the principles at stake were important enough, and Princeton's assertion that its own federal constitutional rights were violated was sufficiently serious, that, when Princeton appealed, the U.S. Supreme Court agreed to review the case. Whereas the New Jersey Supreme Court relied upon that state's free speech provision, Princeton's countervailing property rights were based on the Fifth Amendment to the U.S. Constitution. The U.S. Supreme Court would consider Princeton's federal constitutional right to own and control its own property and would determine whether that right overcame Schmid's state constitutional right of access as defined by the New Jersey Supreme Court. Further, the state court's resolution, notwithstanding its delicate balancing act, necessarily restricted Princeton's First Amendment right to control the content and execution of its educational mission as conceived by its own leaders. The decision not to allow Labor party activists onto campus and give them access to Princeton's students was, arguably, a right that the First Amendment reserved for the university and its administration.

The direct clash of liberty interests in *Schmid* has its disturbing side. Ideally, institutional and personal academic freedom should be complementary, mutually reinforcing concepts. The university's freedom from state interference in its academic governance, and the professor's and student's individual freedom from both state and university administrative interference, should work together to give teachers and students not one, but two layers of protection. However, when a university infringes the academic freedom of its students and faculty, and when it then uses the *shield* of institutional academic freedom, and of First and Fifth Amendment rights, to defend itself against judicial review of the university's own infringements, these rights clash with rather than complement each other. The question was whether the Schmid case was an example of a real clash. This was a hard case for some, and friends of academic freedom, while excited over the prospect of adding the state constitution to liberty's arsenal, were likewise fearful of the legal adage that "hard cases sometimes make bad law."

The *Schmid* case presented the U.S. Supreme Court with an opportunity to delineate the contours of institutional and personal academic freedom, and to relate these concepts to First Amendment (free speech and assembly) and Fifth Amendment (property) doctrines. It therefore must have disturbed the Princeton administration that now that the sides were lining up on these pivotal issues, the American Association of University Professors (AAUP), considered one of the staunchest supporters of academic freedom in the country, entered the fray by filing a "friend of the court" brief on behalf of Schmid rather than of the university. In some respects, the AAUP's brief echoed the protests of some dissident Princeton faculty members who also now criticized the Bowen administration for using academic freedom as a shield to protect itself rather than as a sword to promote liberty. Thus, by this time, Schmid could not be said to be unwelcome by everybody on the campus. The AAUP pointed out that the university's claims of institutional autonomy were not necessarily consonant with other aspects of academic freedom. The AAUP further charged that Princeton's efforts to close its campus to Schmid in no way protected or advanced the university's academic mission. The state court, noted the AAUP, had been very careful to abide by the university's own description of its academic mission and campus. There was no undue outside imposition here. The AAUP was clear that one of its primary interests was in preventing a court decision that would insulate the administration from the rule of law with respect to the university's incursions into the academic freedom and the contract rights of members of the faculty.

The university, of course, was correct in its argument about the dangers of the expanded role asserted by the New Jersey Supreme Court. Yet, the dissident faculty members and the AAUP likewise had a basis for their concern over the specter of a major university going before the highest court in the land to defend its administration's decision to *limit* the diversity of speech on its campus. Princeton, by banning Schmid's distribution of political literature from campus, had provoked a clash of fundamental constitutional principles. No resolution could possibly please all advocates of academic freedom, who were deeply split over the case. To those who supported Schmid, the university administration seemed arrogant, hypocritical, and reckless in its abuse of its own institutional academic freedom, and it had gotten the judicial comeuppance it deserved. To those who supported Princeton's position, state intervention seemed an intolerably serious incursion into the institutional autonomy essential to both the preservation of academic freedom and the indispensable role of the private university in American life.

The U.S. Supreme Court never resolved this conundrum in the *Schmid* case, nor since. For better or worse, when the Court learned that Princeton, even before the New Jersey Supreme Court ruled, had modified its regulations in such a way so as to render the specific controversy—though not the controversial questions—between Schmid and Princeton moot, it dismissed Princeton's appeal without deciding the competing legal claims. This left the New Jersey Supreme Court's decision intact, even though it did not have the imprimatur of the U.S. Supreme Court and thus was not binding outside of that state.

While to some the Supreme Court's action seemed disappointing and anticlimactic, to others it was just as well that the issues remained unresolved. At least for the time being, leaving the issues open arguably gave universities and lower courts more time to arrive at a sensible modus vivendi between the academic freedom of educational institutions and the academic freedom of individuals from restrictions upon liberty inflicted either by the state or by their own university administrators.

To this day, the U.S. Supreme Court has not resolved a direct conflict between assertions of individual versus institutional academic freedom, just as it has not yet decided a case where a campus speech code has been challenged under the First Amendment. When, however, these issues do face the high court directly, it is certain that not only the First Amendment, but, also, values of academic freedom will figure in determining the result.

College and university administrators have learned little since the *Schmid* controversy, as, indeed, they have learned little from the U.S. Supreme Court's rescue of academic leftists and suspected leftists during the McCarthy era. The nature of politically incorrect speech is different today from the 1960s, '70s, and even '80s, but the reaction of repressive college administrators remains depressingly the same.

Indeed, in a virtual repeat of the situation that led to the *Schmid* litigation, the *Harvard Crimson* reported in November 1996 that a filming crew from *The 700 Club*, a Christian conservative television network, came to Harvard to interview some undergraduates about their religious attitudes and was promptly escorted off campus by university security officers. A Harvard official, who "requested anonymity," was quoted as explaining:

> "They interviewed students in [Harvard] Yard? That's definitely something that's not allowed," the official said. "If they have permission, they could

shoot [scenery] in the Yard to establish they are at Harvard. But students are absolutely not to be interviewed."[26]

One of the undergraduates who had been approached before the camera crew was stopped told the *Crimson* that he was "impressed" with the interviewer and had no problem with being interviewed. Nonetheless, the camera crew, Harvard's news office explained, had failed to discuss its plans with the university and, in any event, the press was rarely allowed in Harvard Yard. *The 700 Club,* as was reported by the *Crimson,* "is hosted by televangelist Pat Robertson, the founder of the Christian Coalition," a conservative Christian organization. The attempted interviews were to be on the subject of "the meaning of Christmas."

Twenty years ago it was an unpopular Labor party that was kept off of the Princeton campus and not allowed to distribute political literature to students. More recently, academically unpopular televangelist interviewers were kept out of Harvard Yard. The music may change, but the melody of selective academic freedom lingers on. Given what we shall see are modern campus incursions on liberty and conscience—restrictive speech codes, mandatory "sensitivity training," and other forms of attitudinal indoctrination—it is only a matter of time before higher education, both public and private, once again forces or tempts the courts to intrude. The judicial resolution of the competing interests and principles, regardless of which party wins, could well damage the cause of liberty and academic freedom, even while trying to vindicate these values. This can be the result when complex cases involving competing values must be resolved in court. In a constitutional democracy, after all, voluntary restraint and private good faith in civil society are, in the long run, more important than courts and constitutions. As the jurist Learned Hand observed: "Liberty lies in the hearts of men and women; when it dies there, no constitution, no law, no court can save it."[27] That is true for everyone, including our colleges and universities.

CHAPTER 4

MARCUSE'S REVENGE

It seems surprising, at first glance, that the most potent and far-ranging assault on the First Amendment's central principle—content neutrality—has come not from politicians protecting power or reputations, nor from government agencies protecting their notions of decency or security, but, rather, from America's universities, where academic freedom has been thought to require more liberty and tolerance than in "the real world," not less. More startling yet, this assault comes above all from the political and cultural Left, which, since World War I, has been the prime beneficiary of the move toward near-absolute constitutional protection for speech. Indeed, the legal doctrine of free speech has focused crucially on the rights of revolutionaries, counterculturalists, antiwar protesters, visionaries, prophets of doom, progressives, and, generally, dissidents from the dominant Western capitalist system. How is it, then, that today's most vocal critics of the First Amendment are in the academy and on the Left, the heirs, in fact, of the generation that, thirty-five years ago, gave us the Free Speech movement?

Free speech, of course, has enemies everywhere along the political spectrum. The desire to silence others remains a powerful human instinct. Indeed, the modern age has witnessed the occasional alliance of groups (as in the antipornography community) that agree on little other than the need to suppress certain forms of speech. Nonetheless, on college campuses the drive for speech codes, for double standards in their applications, for the mechanisms of indoctrination in their rationales, and for the disciplinary systems to enforce their strictures, comes from the Left. From what intellectual antecedents does this arise?

The contemporary movement that seeks to restrict liberty on campus arose specifically in the provocative work of the late Marxist political and social philosopher Herbert Marcuse, a brilliant polemicist, social critic, and philosopher who gained a following in the New Left student movement of the '60s. Marcuse developed a theory of civil liberty that would challenge the essence and legitimacy of free speech. Although he repeatedly declared his belief in freedom and tolerance, Marcuse built on the work of Rousseau, Marx, and Gramsci to articulate an alternative conception of liberty, placing him at odds with the Berkeley Free Speech movement, the U.S. Supreme Court's First Amendment doctrines, academic freedom, and the values of most liberal democrats. Indeed, this alternative framework for liberty, which used some traditional terms but assigned them new meanings, became the foundation of academic speech codes.

In a 1965 essay entitled "Repressive Tolerance," Marcuse concluded that the supposedly neutral tolerance for ideas in the America of the 1960s was in reality a highly *selective* tolerance that benefitted only the prevailing attitudes and opinions of those who held wealth and power.[1] Such "indiscriminate" or "pure" tolerance, he argued, effectively served "the cause of oppression" and the "established machinery of discrimination." For Marcuse, as long as society was held captive by institutionalized and pervasive social and economic inequality, and by militarism—what he characterized as "regressive" practices—"indiscriminate tolerance" necessarily would serve the highly discriminatory interests of regression.

The holders of power, Marcuse argued, maintained their control by keeping the population "manipulated and indoctrinated," so that ordinary people "parrot, as their own, the opinion of their masters." In such circumstances, "the indiscriminate guaranty of political rights and liberties" is actually "repressive." The "class structure of society," Marcuse wrote, creates "background limitations of tolerance" that necessarily limit true democratic tolerance even before the courts create whatever explicit limitations they devise (such as "'clear and present danger,' threat to national security, heresy"). He believed that "within the framework of such a social structure, tolerance can be safely practiced and proclaimed" by those in power because dissenting—even radical—voices were powerless to change that structure.

Marcuse did not directly assail Holmes's and Brandeis's notion that ideas for societal change should be, in Marcuse's words, "prepared, defined, and tested in free and equal discussion, on the open marketplace of ideas and goods." Rather, he asserted that the current "marketplace" was rigged because of its "background limitations." Before a *true* marketplace of ideas could be established, where genuine democracy could flourish, current inequities would have to be eliminated, and this could not be done while equating the rights of dominant regressive expression and of marginalized progressive words and ideas. For Marcuse, true equality included equality of circumstances, but the playing fields were so far from being socially, economically, or culturally level that equality in contemporary society was a myth. If the powerful and the weak were required to play by the same rules, he argued, the powerful always would win, and this would have dire consequences since the powerful supported an agenda of war, cruelty, and repression.

According to Marcuse, the indoctrinated had to be given the tools with which to see the truth. How were people to be freed from the bonds that keep them prisoners under a purely illusory tolerance? Marcuse responded that "they would have to get information slanted in the opposite direction, [which] cannot be accomplished within the established framework of abstract tolerance and spurious objectivity." Marcuse posited that there was a true and superior species of "tolerance which enlarged the range and content of freedom." This tolerance, however, "was always partisan," because it was "intolerant toward the protagonists of the repressive status quo." For Marcuse, tolerance was moral and real only when harnessed to the cause of "liberation." Given the current structure of society, a nominal freedom that allowed the expression of "false words and wrong deeds" to work against the attainment of "liberation" and of true "freedom and happiness" became "an instrument for the continuation of servitude."

For a revolutionary theorist, Marcuse was refreshingly frank. The "reopening" of the channels of true toleration and liberation, now "blocked by organized repression and indoctrination," must be accomplished, sometimes, by "apparently undemocratic means." Marcuse suggested that these would include "the withdrawal of toleration of speech and assembly from groups and movements which promote aggressive policies, armament, chauvinism, discrimination on the grounds of race and religion, or which oppose the extension of public services, social security, medical care, etc."

Marcuse was untroubled by his double standards. His framework was coherent and consistent, provided one's assumptions were correct. Correct assumptions, he believed, could readily be determined by "everyone" who is "in the maturity of his faculties as a human being, everyone who has learned to think rationally and autonomously." Such people naturally would pursue "the historical calculus of progress," which, for Marcuse, "is actually the calculus of the prospective reduction of cruelty, misery, suppression."

"Liberating tolerance," Marcuse wrote, in contrast to "indiscriminate tolerance" or "repressive tolerance," would be "intolerance against movements from the Right, and toleration of movements from the Left." This duality "would extend to the stage of action as well as of discussion of propaganda, of deed as well as of word." It was important that intolerance apply to regressive words as well as to regressive deeds, because, for Marcuse, words had real consequences, and if the consequences were to be avoided, the words must be silenced.

Marcuse's premise, which separated his political philosophy fundamentally from First Amendment jurisprudence, was that liberty, in the current stage of historical and social development, was a zero sum game: "The exercise of civil rights by those who don't have them presupposes the withdrawal of civil rights from those who prevent their exercise." For Marcuse, the application of these "anti-democratic notions" would foster a society that promoted universal tolerance and true freedom. To achieve a society of universal tolerance, one could not tolerate reactionary ideas.

Marcuse focused on the education of the young: "The restoration of freedom of thought may necessitate new and rigid restrictions on teaching and practices in the educational institutions which, by their very methods and concepts, serve to enclose the mind within the established universe of discourse and behavior." Because students already were so heavily brainwashed to think in the manner that established power had ordained, true "autonomous thinking" was virtually impossible, and one had to take steps to wrench students from the regressive channels into which society had cast their minds. "The pre-empting of the mind vitiates impartiality and objectivity," he wrote; "unless the student learns to think in the opposite direction, he will be inclined to place the facts into the predominant framework of values." Marcuse mocked the "sacred liberalistic principle of equality for 'the other side,'" because "there are issues where . . . there is no 'other side' in any more than a formalistic sense."

Indeed, Marcuse confidently posited that it would not be difficult to determine "the question as to who is to decide on the distinction between liberating and repressing, human and inhuman teachings and practices." The distinction between these two poles, he assured his readers and students, "is not a matter of value-preference but of rational criteria." Once the rational criteria were identified, truth was easy to determine. With this certainty, Marcuse believed that he could describe the means by which the academy should bring about this "reversal of the trend in the educational enterprise." Ultimately, such a reversal should "be enforced by the students and teachers themselves, and thus be self-imposed, the systematic withdrawal of tolerance toward regressive and repressive opinions and movements." In the short term, Marcuse proposed that the academic shock troops of this revolution undertake to "prepare the ground" for effecting such changes, even if that might involve a resort to violence. Marcuse was not troubled by this, because "there is a difference between revolutionary and reactionary violence, between violence practiced by the oppressed and by the oppressors."

Once such a reversal had begun, students and faculty could become engaged in the struggle. To free the minds of students, Marcuse prescribed that they not be exposed to that "spurious neutrality" which was part of the problem because it "serves to reproduce acceptance of the dominion of the victors in the consciousness of man." Thus, for example, history would be taught so that the student understands "the frightening extent to which history was made and recorded by and for the victors, that is, the extent to which history was the development of oppression."

In short, to produce conditions in which freedom could flourish first on campus and then in the greater society, reeducation in a progressive university was essential. Revolutionary thinking then could break the stranglehold of the powerful on the minds of students and citizens. This reeducation alone could create a "progressive" society, where true freedom and democracy would reign. Once this had been achieved, Marcuse promised, there would be no further need for such "anti-democratic" expedients that were, after all, aimed simply to redress the imbalance between "oppressor" and "oppressed." Censorship, during this "reversal," was essential, because ubiquitous, dangerous, and regressive notions were too quickly translated into practice. Indeed, censorship, for Marcuse, must be deeply pervasive, although historically temporary. The result, he promised, would be to restore *real* freedom, and the words "freedom" and "liberty" once again could attain their "true meanings."

Marcuse's prescriptions for a progressive society have not noticeably taken root in the "real world" outside the academy. Most of the trends toward greater free speech for all—trends that he so abhorred—have accelerated in the three decades since he published his essay. Nevertheless, Marcuse's prescriptions are the model for the assaults on free speech in today's academic world.

Where Marcuse addressed all social inequality, Richard Delgado, Charles R. Lawrence III, Mari Matsuda, Catherine MacKinnon, and Stanley Fish focus on race and gender bias. These theorists take issue with the modern Supreme Court's insistence on content-neutral protection of *all* speech. Some proponents of "progressively" intolerant speech codes (such as Delgado, Lawrence, and Matsuda) try to reconcile their views with a surface support for First Amendment values. Others (including MacKinnon and Fish) are more openly hostile to the neutral equality before the law upon which First Amendment jurisprudence insists.

Lawrence, Delgado, and Matsuda trace their intellectual endeavors to a 1981 incident at Harvard Law School. When Harvard selected a white male to teach a course, "Race, Racism and American Law," that had been taught by departing Professor Derrick Bell, Harvard Law School's first tenured black professor, students organized a boycott and rallied in favor of an alternative course. Professors Lawrence and Delgado were invited to give guest lectures; Matsuda participated as a student.

After their experience at Harvard, Lawrence, Delgado, and Matsuda each contributed key law review articles essential to the emergence, visibility, momentum, and intellectual respectability of a movement called "Critical Race Theory." Delgado's 1982 article "Words That Wound: A Tort Action for Racial Insults, Epithets, and Name Calling" was published in the *Harvard Civil Rights–Civil Liberties Law Review.*[2] Matsuda's "Public Response to Racist Speech: Considering the Victim's Story" appeared in the 1989 *Michigan Law Review.*[3] Lawrence's "If He Hollers Let Him Go: Regulating Racist Speech on Campus" saw light in a slightly different form in the *Duke Law Journal* in 1990.[4] These three highly influential essays were collected and republished, with a joint introduction, in 1993.

In the introduction to this volume, the authors, self-described as a "motley band of progressive legal scholars of color," echoed Marcuse's critical theory. They focused on "how areas of law ostensibly designed to advance the cause of racial equality often benefit powerful whites more than those who are racially oppressed." They shared Marcuse's prescription for preventing destructive conduct by censoring the words that precede conduct: "This is a book about assaultive speech, about words that are used as weapons to ambush, terrorize, wound, humiliate, and degrade."[5] The attempt to identify words as "weapons" indicates that the authors did not consider themselves to be dealing with speech protected by the First Amendment. Rather, they attempt to avoid the First Amendment's near-absolute protection of offensive language by *redefining* "repressive" words as "weapons," breaching the distinction between speech and action. Lawrence, now a professor at Stanford, argued that racist speech conveys a message of white supremacy, and that by "construct[ing] social reality" in this manner, such speech limits the "life opportunities" of nonwhites. "This act of constructing meaning," he concluded, "makes racist speech conduct." Nonetheless, mirroring the language of Supreme Court speech decisions that had carved out exceptions, he argued that since being called a racial epithet "is like receiving a slap in the face," the "injury is instantaneous," the harm is "clear and present," and the invective leads to neither reflection nor discussion of any idea.[6]

Richard Delgado's essay explicitly claimed conformity with the First Amendment. The University of Colorado professor was proposing legislation that would enable victims of racial epithets to bring civil lawsuits for monetary damages in the courts, a governmental action that is by definition subject to First Amendment limitations. Delgado thus argued that racial epithets are "fighting words" deprived of protection by *Chaplinsky v. New Hampshire*. However, faced with the argument that the First Amendment is meant to protect, in part, "the values of individual self-fulfillment to be furthered through free expression," he wrote that since racism "stifles rather than furthers the moral and social growth of the individual who harbors it," the tolerance of racist speech actually *retards* the personal growth of the hater as well as of the victim. Racial insults could not be part of any "marketplace of ideas" because they "are not intended to inform or convince the listener" and "invite no discourse," but merely to inflict harm. Finally, Delgado argued, "racism, in part through racial slurs, furthers all the evils caused by the suppression of speech," because it disables both speaker and listener from participating in meaningful discourse.[7]

Mari Matsuda also sought to demonstrate, in fact, that hate speech codes are consistent with the First Amendment, arguing that racist speech should not be limited as narrowly as the definition of ordinary "fighting words." A modification of *Chaplinsky* was required for racist and sexist speech, she argued, because only white men were truly able "to fight." Thus, "under existing law, insults of such dimension that they bring men—this is a male-centered standard—to blows are subject to a first amendment exception. The problem is that racist speech is so common that it is seen as part of the ordinary jostling and conflict people are expected to tolerate, rather than as fighting words." However, she continued, "the effect of dehumanizing racist language on the target is often flight rather than fight. Targets choose to avoid racist encounters whenever possible, internalizing the harm rather than escalating the conflict. Lack of a fight and admirable self-restraint then defines the words as nonactionable." Thus, using her analysis of human behavior, Matsuda insisted "that an explicit and narrow definition of racist hate messages will allow restriction consistent with first amendment values." Her theory seemed to assume that victims of such speech—namely, people of color, whom she described as "classes of human beings who are least equipped to respond"—were somehow more vulnerable than others. Consequently, hate speech is "outside the realm of protected discourse." [8] As with Marcuse, the lack of a level playing field makes equal access to "free" speech neither truly equal nor truly free.

Matsuda likewise mirrors Marcuse in her argument that there is *less* justification for absolute free speech on college campuses than in the outside world. Matsuda, however, wrote more with the "human potential" language of the '90s than with the "revolutionary" language of the '60s. In her view, "universities are special places, charged with pedagogy and duty bound to a constituency with special vulnerabilities." College is "a major life-stress event" and a "period of experimentation" that could have profound effects on the student's life, and on his or her "ability to remain open, creative, and risk taking." For Matsuda, content neutrality can inflict psychological harm on vulnerable students "who perceive the university as taking sides through inaction and who are left to their own resources in coping with the damage wrought." Damage is likewise done "to the goals of inclusion, education, development of knowledge, and ethics that universities exist and stand for. Lessons of cynicism and hate replace lessons in critical thought and inquiry." Hence, censorship is more consonant with the goals of higher education than is unfettered speech.

Matsuda acknowledged that in the Vietnam era, free speech enabled students to pit themselves "against university administrators, multinational corporations, the U.S. military, and established governments." She did not argue that speech rights in that context were wrong. Indeed, she noted, "In the context of that kind of power imbalance, the free speech rights of students deserve particular deference." However, for Matsuda, the free speech precedent of the Vietnam era did not apply to "racist speech" by students. In her formulation, precedent gives way to "context": "Racist speech on campus occurs in a vastly different power context. Campus racism targets vulnerable students and faculty. Students of color often come to the university at risk academically, socially, and psychologically." [9]

Matsuda's position requires a mechanism for determining who is empowered and who is oppressed, and which categories of speech may be suppressed. She made a confident distinction, for example, between Jews as victims of the Holocaust (protected) and Jews as Zionists (subject to repression). Marcuse firmly believed that this process was capable of "objective" and "rational" determination. There was no danger, in their view, that the differential assignment of rights would backfire, since they were wholly confident that any rational being, once freed from the dominant group's indoctrination, would agree with their own values.

It is intriguing that these three theoreticians dance so cautiously around the First Amendment, because, in reality, the three attack the underpinnings of modern First Amendment theory as fundamentally as did Marcuse's "Repressive Tolerance." Above all, the authors diverge from current First Amendment values by positing a goal or end result for free speech, when free speech, in constitutional theory, is a right in and of itself. As Matsuda put it, her "confrontation [with] the contradiction between first amendment absolutism and the goals of liberty and equality" led to her current position. Lawrence, too, "placed race at the center of his analysis."

Nonetheless, Delgado's, Lawrence's, and Matsuda's objections to robust and equal free speech indeed echo Marcuse. In their joint introduction, they object to "arguments for absolutist protection of speech made without reference to historical context or uneven power relations." "Racism," they complain, then becomes "just another idea deserving of constitutional protection like all ideas."[10] Individuals are *not,* in their world, equal before the law. The practical effect of this two-tiered system for protecting speech becomes evident in some of Matsuda's examples. The use of the epithet "nigger" by a white toward a black would be outlawed as racist, whereas Malcolm X's famous characterization of Caucasians as the "white devil" would not. For Matsuda, Malcolm's "assault" does not fall into the proscribed category "because the attack is not tied to the perpetuation of racist vertical relationships." Even though the white might be "hurt by conflict with the angry nationalist," the white "is more likely to have access to a safe harbor of exclusive dominant-group interactions." Similarly, "an angry, hateful poem by a person from a historically subjugated group," to Matsuda, is "a victim's struggle for self-identity in response to racism," whereas a similar poem by a member of an advantaged group is proscribed because it is "tied to . . . structural domination." Spike Lee's use of "a rapid-fire sequence of racial epithets spoken by characters from different racial groups" in his movie *Do the Right Thing* "offers an incisive antiracist critique of racist speech" and is therefore permitted, whereas the "racist dialogue" used by the white writer Mark Twain "to portray a racist land" exposes young black children to "racist language . . . in a white-majority setting" and hence constitutes an "assault" and results in real harm.[11]

Any tension with the First Amendment experienced by Lawrence, Delgado, and Matsuda, however, is considerably diminished in the work of Catherine MacKinnon and Stanley Fish. They are explicit in their disdain for the First Amendment's absolutist and noncontextual approach. In her influential book *Only Words*,[12] MacKinnon, a feminist legal scholar at the University of Michigan, introduced her chapter "Equality and Speech" with the blunt statement that "the law of equality and the law of freedom of speech are on a collision course in this country." In her analysis, "the constitutional doctrine of free speech has developed without taking equality seriously— either the problem of social inequality or the mandate of substantive legal equality."[13] The main target of MacKinnon's attack is the Supreme Court's increasingly content-neutral protection for offensive and unpopular speech for all people in virtually all circumstances. Her theory echoes Marcuse's view that the dominant school of constitutional interpretation fosters "inequality" by insisting upon the *equal* allocation of speech rights to people *unequally* situated. MacKinnon challenged the concept of equality before the law, dubbing it a legal fiction that perpetuates social inequality. She argues that "the more the speech of the dominant is protected, the more dominant they become and the less the subordinated are heard from."

MacKinnon's rhetoric is unmistakably Marcusean, especially the notion that liberty is a zero-sum game, and that giving it simultaneously to "dominant" and "subordinated" groups inevitably reinforces the power of the dominant group. The implementation of campus speech restrictions "formally predicated on federal laws that require equal access to an education on the basis of race and sex," she argued, is necessary for redressing this imbalance.

One of MacKinnon's most provocative examples of the undesirable results of equal speech rights is also one of the most revealing. She assails the notion of the evenhanded application of the First Amendment by comparing two influential Supreme Court decisions, the 1969 case of *Brandenburg v. Ohio*[14] and the 1982 *Claiborne Hardware Company v. National Association for the Advancement of Colored People*.[15] As discussed in chapter 2, the Court in *Brandenburg* had extended the First Amendment's protections to the hate speech of the Ku Klux Klan, while allowing criminal prosecution of specific *actions* carrying out the organization's racist agenda. *Claiborne Hardware* grew out of the state of Mississippi's efforts to destroy the NAACP, which had led protests against employment discrimination, especially an economically devastating boycott of local merchants in Claiborne County. Local businesses brought suit against the national organization and its local leaders, claiming that the boycott was an illegal economic conspiracy, and that associated acts of violence, vandalism, and arson resulted in damage to property. The white merchants obtained a verdict from a local white judge and jury, which, if upheld, would have crippled the NAACP. The U.S. Supreme Court reversed largely on the basis of *Brandenburg,* holding that the local leaders and the national organization had not incited the crowd to imminent lawlessness, even if a few violent individuals were inspired by the heated rhetoric of the boycott's leadership. The Court thus distinguished the *speech* of the boycott leaders from the violent *actions* taken.

MacKinnon noted that, unlike *Brandenburg,* which protected the KKK, *Claiborne Hardware* brought the dichotomy between speech and action into the service of saving the nation's oldest and best known civil rights organization. She claimed that it was unjust to accord the two groups the same protection under the First Amendment, as *properly* interpreted. For MacKinnon, it was not problematic to define a principled basis for treating the NAACP and the Klan differently under the law: "Suppressed entirely in the piously evenhanded treatment of the Klan and the boycotters—the studied inability to tell the difference between oppressor and oppressed that passes for principled neutrality in this area as well as others—was the fact that the Klan was promoting inequality and the civil rights leaders were resisting it, in a country that is supposedly not constitutionally neutral on the subject."[16] As with Marcuse, the crucial distinction was between the "regressive" and the "progressive."

Stanley Fish's attitude toward the current judicial interpretation of the First Amendment is refreshingly overt in the title of his 1994 book *There's No Such Thing As Free Speech . . . And It's a Good Thing Too.*[17] Fish attacked the notion that there is now, ever has been, or ever could be anything in the law that might be described as "reason, merit, fairness, neutrality, free speech, color blind[ness], [a] level playing field, [or] tolerance." Reliance on such terms, he argued, "is almost always as part of an effort to deprive moral and legal problems of their histories." He decried what he termed "the game [of] 'moral algebra,' a game that is played by fixing on an abstract quality and declaring all practices that display or fail to display that quality equivalent."[18] This "willful disregard of history," for Fish, is the primary difficulty with a legal system in which the First Amendment is central. He equates the "equal" and "neutral" distribution of speech rights to the critique of "the supposed impartiality of French law" as expressed in the famous quip by Anatole France, "Yes, the law of France is impartial; it forbids the rich as well as the poor from sleeping under bridges."[19]

Fish criticized the notion that we should endure the pain inflicted by hate speech merely because of some vague hope that there is a greater good to be achieved by equal tolerance of all ideas. In Fish's analysis, "Nothing can provide us with a principle for deciding which risk in the long run is the best to take." For this reason, he suggested that "right now, the risk of not attending to hate speech is greater than the risk that by regulating it we will deprive ourselves of valuable voices and insights." He claimed that "to put our faith in apolitical abstractions" such as "the marketplace of ideas" is merely a political "guise," not at all superior to more outright political value judgments that propose restricting the speech of dominant groups in favor of disadvantaged groups.[20] Fish, of all major proponents of hate speech codes on campus, perhaps came closest to Marcuse when he wrote with admirable directness:

> To the student reporter who complains that in the wake of the promulgation of a speech code at the University of Wisconsin there is now something in the back of his mind as he writes, one could reply, "There was always something in the back of your mind, and perhaps it might be better to have this code in the back of your mind than whatever was in there before." [21]

Fish openly suggested that he was receptive to the prospect of both ideological indoctrination and ideological intimidation of students. He was equally blunt in responding to the classic claim of free speech absolutists that the beginning of censorship is a perilous "slippery slope" that would result in pervasive and unpredictable restrictions on freedom. "Some form of speech is always being restricted, else there could be no meaningful assertion," he wrote: "We have always and already slid down the slippery slope; someone is always going to be restricted next, and it is your job to make sure that the someone is not you." For Fish, the content neutrality of the First Amendment represents an unreachable utopia that ignores political considerations and cannot provide guidance for dealing with society as it really functions. Fish suggested that those who adhere to this utopian concept of tolerance for hateful speech are, in a very real sense, responsible for that speech and for its results. "Tolerating may be different from endorsing from the point of view of the tolerator, who can then disclaim responsibility for the effects of what he has not endorsed," wrote Fish, "but, if the effects are real and consequential, as I argue they are, the difference may be cold comfort." [22]

The debate over freedom of speech is a constitutional, political, and moral contest of profound dimensions. It is a battle that proponents of speech codes have been able to wage with remarkable success on many campuses, in spite of what may seem to be the inviolable restrictions by the First Amendment on public universities and the demands of academic freedom on private campuses. It is deeply ironic, of course, that the concept of racial and gender equality that drives the desire for speech codes is the very result of the exercise of free speech rights by civil rights activists, whose own ability to express themselves usually depended on equal protection before the law, and on the tolerance of speech uttered by some of society's most despised groups. Nonetheless, as we now shall see, the proponents of "progressive" intolerance have had great success on our campuses.

———

Drafters of college speech codes almost invariably begin by setting out the core principle of any self-proclaimed liberal arts institution of higher learning—that the essential goal of the pursuit of teaching, learning, and research relies upon academic freedom and upon freedom of speech and inquiry. They posit the necessity of including all members of the academic community in this pursuit and proceed to take steps purportedly aimed at making these social and educational opportunities available to all. To ensure these benefits to groups of students perceived to be "historically underrepresented" or "historically disadvantaged," the codes severely limit the speech rights of individual students by prohibiting the utterance of certain unkind and, they claim, destructive words.

We have studied several hundred of these codes. While some definitions of banned speech are extremely broad and others substantially narrower, differences from one code to another are matters of degree rather than of kind. The codes require a suspension of belief in the ordinary meaning of words in order to accept the contradictions so often contained within the same code, frequently within the same paragraph, and sometimes within the same sentence. On the one hand, the codes claim to cherish free speech and academic freedom, including the freedom to express even the most challenging and offensive ideas; on the other, certain categories of "offensive" speech are banned in order to create a "comfortable" and "inclusive" learning atmosphere.

The ability of a university to endorse two contradictory policies is perhaps explained as simple hypocrisy. Indeed, this does appear to be part of the answer on many campuses, where administrators have agendas far removed from the common pursuit of knowledge. However, whether hypocritical or sincere, the drafters of these codes still feel a need to justify the seemingly contradictory goals of free speech and free inquiry, on the one hand, and limitations on speech in order to achieve equal access to educational opportunity, on the other. Reconciliation of these opposing concepts is achieved primarily by Marcusean logic.

A window into the thinking of some crafters of speech codes is found at Stanford University. The initial drafting effort of Stanford's code was strongly influenced by Professor Thomas Grey of the law school, who has posited that, under certain circumstances, constitutional commitments to freedom of expression, and to civil liberties in general, conflict with the nation's commitment to providing equal access to educational opportunities, and to civil rights in general. In a 1991 article in the *Harvard Journal of Law and Public Policy*, Grey expressed discomfort at the collision, but considered the conflict "inescapable."[23] In his view, the tension between academic freedom and equal educational opportunity arises from an inherent conflict between civil liberties and civil rights, between liberty and social equality.

This premise is problematical. Freedom of speech is a "liberty interest," and it deals solely with an individual's ability to express himself or herself as he or she desires. In contrast, civil rights legislation is largely protective and egalitarian, expressing the broader societal concern with how citizens are faring in comparison to other citizens. Put another way, the First Amendment protects the individual from the oppressive exercise of governmental power, whereas civil rights jurisprudence offers the individual recourse to the government for assistance in obtaining the necessary tools and opportunities to reap the benefits of equal participation in economic, social, and cultural life.

How do the drafters of speech codes attempt to bridge this perceived gap between libertarian and egalitarian interests? They accept the dramatic thesis that individual speakers express not only their own individual views, but also those of their entire gender or ethnic group. In Grey's Stanford speech code, banned epithets reflect "a widely shared, deeply felt, and historically rooted social prejudice against people with that [insulting] trait."[24] Because the speaker of such epithets is expressing a "widely shared prejudice," he or she has ceased to speak as an individual or to express merely his or her own thoughts, and has become a living symptom and symbol of societal oppression. In Grey's view, such statements "make the atmosphere more difficult for [members of targeted groups] on a campus and hence deny them a level educational playing field with students not so stigmatized."[25] A "difficult atmosphere" is, thus, the deprivation of rights and opportunities. It is therefore appropriate, by this theory, to halt the speech of individuals (and to deny their status as discrete, autonomous beings), in order to combat this cumulative effect. The traditional formula—that free speech is allocated equally to all and is not to be limited in terms of content and viewpoint—perpetuates majority dominance. Individual equality before the law must be sacrificed in the name of equal opportunity for the members of groups.

Further, Grey justified the unequal application of speech restrictions by making an analogy between problems of racism and sexism on the campus, on the one hand, and at the commercial workplace, on the other. Grey recognized that traditional First Amendment jurisprudence prohibits governmental restrictions on speech on the basis of content and viewpoint, except in very limited and long-recognized narrow areas, such as defamation, obscenity, and threats. In Grey's mind, however, special circumstances created by unequal power relationships between management and labor justified differential allocation of speech rights in the workplace, including constraints upon certain categories of speech and viewpoints. Thus, he found that American labor laws could sanction an employer for stating, during a union organizing election: "If I have to pay union rates, I doubt I'll be able to keep this plant open." That, argued Grey, is treated as a threat to the workers and prohibited as an unfair labor practice directed at discouraging union organizing. On the other hand, the government would not be able to punish an employee for saying, in the same context: "Employers who resist unionization often find a less cooperative work force afterwards."[26] The reason for such different treatment is based, he concluded, on the power differential between employer and employee. From this, Grey moved to the proposition that the insults "nigger" and "whitey" are not equivalent because "American society and its history have created the asymmetry [between the black and white races]; a regulation cannot attempt to redress that asymmetry without taking it into account." Grey denies that it is "patronizing to students of color" to restrict insults hurled at them without restricting insults hurled at others. The vulnerability of black students and their lesser ability to "take care of themselves in verbal rough-and-tumble"—in short, their status as a "'protected group'" that is "in need of official protection"—is a product of history.[27]

Grey and those in his camp ultimately must take issue with the historic dissent penned in 1896 by Supreme Court Justice John Marshall Harlan in the case of *Plessy v. Ferguson*,[28] in which the majority established the constitutionality of the "separate but equal" doctrine in public facilities. Harlan's words remain vital today to those who believe that equality before the law must be accorded to all, regardless of "context." He wrote: "In respect of civil rights, common to all citizens, the constitution of the United States does not, I think, permit any public authority to know the race of those entitled to be protected in the enjoyment of such rights." All citizens, said Harlan, are "equals before the law," and equal treatment under and by the law is a hallmark of "the personal liberty enjoyed by every one within the United States." Harlan proceeded to analyze the philosophical and legal issue now at the heart of the debate between Marcuseans and classical liberals—the meaning of legal equality in a society characterized by many kinds of social inequality, including inequalities of deep historic dimension. After analyzing (sympathetically, alas) white claims of dominance, he claimed that the law could not grant them special status:

> The white race deems itself to be the dominant race in this country. And so it is, in prestige, in achievements, in education, in wealth, and in power. So, I doubt not, it will continue to be for all time, if it remains true to its great heritage, and holds fast to the principles of constitutional liberty. But in view of the constitution, in the eye of the law, there is in this country no superior, dominant, ruling class of citizens. There is no caste here. Our constitution is colorblind, and neither knows nor tolerates classes among citizens. In respect of civil rights, all citizens are equal before the law. The humblest is the peer of the most powerful.[29]

Justice Harlan thus tried to reconcile the obvious fact of social inequality with the need, nonetheless, for legal equality. His warnings were ignored, and Jim Crow segregation flourished. By contrast, Grey argued that in some settings, including American college campuses, administrative power had to assure affirmative social equality, even at the expense of liberty from coercive power unequally applied.

———

The attempt of speech codes to balance the right of free speech with the "right" to be free from harassment deeply reflects Marcuse's notion of "freedom" and "tolerance." It is a fundamentally Marcusean idea that tolerance must be redefined so as to advance a positive social and moral agenda. The codes express a deep commitment, in general, to freedom of speech and inquiry, but when they express an equal commitment to a group member's right to be free from verbal harassment, it leads, in the name of positive freedom, to the broad and open wholesale banning, not only of speech and other traditional modes of expression, but even of looks, body language, and, in some cases, laughter. It leads, in short, to progressive intolerance.

University administrators seem unconcerned by the double standards and differential allocation of rights fostered by these policies. Speech codes mandate a redefined notion of "freedom" and are based on the belief that the infliction of a prescribed moral agenda on a community is justified by, in Marcuse's words, "the historical calculus of progress" in which every enlightened and rational person naturally strives to "[reduce] cruelty, misery and suppression." [30] Since the reduction of "cruelty, misery and suppression," in this view, requires less of an emphasis on rights and more on assuring "historically oppressed" persons the means of achieving equal rights, liberty must, for now, take a back seat. The whole notion of individual liberty becomes subordinated to redressing historical wrongs against groups. Codes dismiss free speech rights in favor of a predetermined notion of historical moral responsibility, commanding students and faculty to censor themselves and one another in the paramount interests of the educational community and of historical justice. Restrictions on speech are justified by the assertion of a compelling need to promote freedom for some by limiting freedom for others. To the code writers, as to Marcuse, freedom is a zero-sum game.

Consider the carefully worded policy of Carnegie Mellon University (CMU) in Pittsburgh.[31] In CMU's "Policy on Free Speech and Assembly," originally adopted in 1988 and republished periodically in the faculty handbook and the student handbook, the university advises its members that CMU "encourages freedom of speech, assembly and exchange of ideas. This includes the distribution of leaflets and petitions, as well as demonstrations or protests involving speaking, discussion or the distribution of information." CMU's policy statement then defines content-neutral "limits" to this policy of academic freedom, restrictions on the time, place, and manner of speech, applied equally: "The enforcement of these restrictions will not depend in any way on any subject matter involved in a protest or demonstration."

Going even further, CMU's "Statement Concerning Controversial Speakers," issued by its trustees at the height of the Vietnam War protests in 1967, reaffirmed in 1979, and republished annually, offers a ringing endorsement of academic freedom and free speech:

> The assumptions of freedom are that men and women will more often than not choose wisely from among the alternatives available to them and that the range of alternatives and their implications can be known fully only if men and women can express their thoughts freely.

Indeed, the CMU statement, reminding us of how the academic Left sounded in the 1960s, warns that the exercise of academic freedom, essential to the university's mission, will not always be pleasant to experience, but that such unpleasantness does not change the need to protect it:

It is inevitable that such an environment will from time to time appear to threaten the larger community in which it exists. When, as they will, speakers from within or from outside the campus challenge the moral, spiritual, economic or political consensus of the community, people are uneasy, disturbed and at times outraged. In times of crisis, this is particularly true. But freedom of thought and freedom of expression cannot be influenced by circumstances. They exist only if they are inviolable. They are not matters of convenience but of necessity. This is a part of the price of freedom.

That was then. This is now. In 1991 CMU promulgated its "Policy Against Sexual Harassment." While reiterating in the first paragraph the university's dedication "to the free exchange of ideas and the intellectual development of all members of the community," suddenly, with barely a transition, CMU proceeded to outlaw, among other things, "verbal conduct of a sexual nature [when it] has the purpose or effect of unreasonably interfering with an individual's work performance or creating an intimidating, hostile or offensive work environment." Now, CMU places the need for "the free exchange of ideas" in the same sentence as the need to promote "the intellectual development of all members of the community." Because the truly unfettered exercise of free speech can create a "hostile environment" that deprives a category of "historically disadvantaged" students (in this case, women) of being able to participate in the life of the university, such speech must suffer restrictions. One kind of freedom has to give way to another; one student's freedom has to be restricted in order to assure another's. For CMU, such a balancing of interests assures freedom for *all* students. Nobody's "work performance" may be impeded by a "hostile environment."

On one level of abstraction, the notion that one person's freedom must be restricted to protect another's is hardly controversial. "Your right to throw your fist ends at the tip of my nose" is a common formulation in law and ordinary life. Yet the notion that *speech* may be restricted, particularly on an academic campus, is new and very different. The notion that the tip of one's nose defines the limit of a physical assault becomes transformed into the notion that the tip of one's ego defines the limit of a verbal "assault." Equally significant, this "protection" against "hostile environment" and certain other consequences of speech is assigned unequally, by the explicit terms of codes, for enjoyment by certain categories of "disadvantaged" students identified by sex, race, sexual orientation, and disability. For CMU, one kind of freedom does not really give way to another; rather, liberty is reinterpreted so as not to conflict with equality. CMU thus can impose restrictions on speech in the face of its ringing endorsement of open expression, and do so without any apparent self-consciousness or contradiction.

Just as CMU insists that, freedom being a zero-sum game, it has no choice but to sacrifice some individuals' "inviolable" liberties, the Massachusetts Institute of Technology (MIT) believes that speech restrictions are necessary to ensure balanced freedoms:

> Freedom of expression is essential to the mission of a university. So is freedom from unreasonable and disruptive offense. Members of this educational community are encouraged to avoid putting these essential elements of our university to a balancing test. . . . It is usually easier to deal with issues of free expression and harassment when members of the community think in terms of interests rather than rights. It may be "legal" to do many things that are not in one's interests or in the interests of the members of a diverse community. Most people intuitively recognize that there may be some difference between their rights and their interests.

This seemingly balanced request to students to respect one another's rights and avoid open conflict is in truth a call to self-censorship. The code requests that students not exercise rights that, although perfectly legal, might be found offensive. The code, however, does *not* suggest that students who are offended by someone's exercise of "freedom of expression" consider whether it is really in their interest to file a complaint. Most important, however, is the fact that in the final analysis, the MIT code, as with most speech restrictions that encourage self-censorship, does not rely *only* upon voluntary censorship, but also upon the coercive and punitive power of the institution. Self-censorship is not merely encouraged; it is *required*. The MIT code, after it defines "harassment" as "any conduct, verbal or physical, on or off campus . . . which creates an intimidating, hostile or offensive educational, work or living environment," goes on to warn that "harassment may . . . lead to sanctions up to and including termination of . . . student status."

Harassment codes have proliferated on campuses all across the country. They are found on campuses large and small, public and private, the great public universities and the small liberal arts colleges, the experimental and avant-garde campuses as well as the traditional and even the parochial institutions. However, on campuses with specified missions, whether a seminary or a Swarthmore, the existence of official orthodoxies is clearly disclosed to potential students, so that there is sufficient "truth in advertising" to make the restrictions voluntary and, thus, fair. At most institutions there is a "bait and switch" where students are promised academic freedom but are given speech codes and double standards instead.

———————

The common conflict between libertarian and egalitarian principles takes different forms at our universities. There are codes that prohibit the use of "fighting words" and those that ban speech that "creates a hostile educational environment." (Many codes include both.) The fighting words code is typified by University of California Berkeley's definition:

> "Fighting words" are those personally abusive epithets which, when directly addressed to an ordinary person, are, in the context used and as a matter of common knowledge, inherently likely to provoke a violent reaction whether or not they actually do so. Such words include, but are not limited to, those terms widely recognized to be derogatory references to race, ethnicity, religion, sex, sexual orientation, disability, and other personal characteristics. "Fighting words" constitute "harassment" when the circumstances of their utterance create a hostile and intimidating environment which the student uttering them should reasonably know will interfere with the victim's ability to pursue effectively his or her education or otherwise to participate fully in University programs or activities.

Because the fighting words exception to the First Amendment has been largely abandoned in practice by the Supreme Court, speech codes based upon it have fared badly in the lower courts (though none has yet reached the Supreme Court). When a federal district court in 1991 invalidated the University of Wisconsin code,[32] and when a state Superior Court in California four years later invalidated the Stanford code,[33] they noted that the fighting words concept had been so narrowed by the Supreme Court that it was useless.

Far more common are the hostile environment codes, which echo the language of guidelines promulgated for the workplace by the Equal Employment Opportunity Commission (EEOC) and apply them, essentially unchanged, to educational settings, equating students and workplace employees. The Supreme Court has not yet spoken definitively on the question of whether the hostile environment concept underlying speech restrictions in the workplace may be applied to institutions of higher education. Hence, campus administrators appear to favor this formulation as a basis for restricting speech and probably will continue to do so until the Supreme

Court says otherwise, as it likely will at some point. The language in these codes varies little. Typical is the University of Nevada–Reno:

> Sexual harassment of employees or students includes any unwelcome sexual advances, requests for sexual favors, or *verbal* or physical conduct of a sexual nature when: (1) submission to such conduct is made either explicitly or implicitly a term or condition of an individual's employment or status in a course, program, or activity; or (2) submission to or rejection of such conduct is used as the basis for employment or educational decisions affecting that individual; or (3) such conduct has the purpose or effect of unreasonably interfering with an individual's work performance or educational experience, or *creates an intimidating, hostile, or offensive environment* for working or learning [emphasis added].

The first two restrictions, already present in most codes of professional conduct, seem perfectly reasonable policies to protect students from extortion and invidious discrimination. The third destroys the freedom of students and faculty to speak their minds.

It is instructive to consider how legal concepts applicable to the workplace are now widely applied to institutions of higher learning, and even to the "clients"—the students—of those universities. (Sears, after all, cannot summon its customers to company hearings and educational panels on sexual harassment.) Almost invariably, when administrators and faculty members who promulgate these codes are challenged on grounds of academic freedom, they assert that such codes are required by federal laws. This claim is extraordinarily shaky.

At the height of the battle for civil rights in the Jim Crow South, Congress passed the landmark Civil Rights Act of 1964.[34] Section 703(a) of Title VII deemed certain practices unlawful when engaged in by employers. It outlawed discrimination in the hiring, firing, and treatment of employees "because of such individual's race, color, religion, sex, or national origin." In its reference to "sex," this statute aimed at discrimination on the basis of gender, and harassment of a sexual nature was considered one species of gender-based discrimination. It was left to the EEOC to issue regulations to enforce these provisions.

The EEOC issued guidelines in 1985, identifying harassment of employees based on sex and terming it employment discrimination under Title VII. After discussing "unwelcome sexual advances and requests for sexual favors" tied to the retaining or advancing in one's job status, the guidelines turned to "hostile environment":

Unwelcome sexual advances, requests for sexual favors, and other verbal and physical conduct of a sexual nature constitute "hostile environment" sexual harassment when such conduct has the purpose or effect of unreasonably interfering with an individual's work performance or creating an intimidating, hostile, or offensive working environment.[35]

This formulation is familiar to anyone who has read university sexual, racial, and other harassment codes. However, even in the workplace, the outlawing of "verbal conduct of a sexual nature" marked a stark departure from the traditional dichotomy between conduct (subject to being banned and punished) and speech (subject to far more limited regulation, especially when not demanding sex as a condition of employment or advancement). Other than this blurring of speech and conduct, however, the EEOC guidelines on sexual harassment represented a fairly routine exercise of long-standing employer/employee legal concepts. If someone with *supervisory* authority engaged in discrimination by means of sexual harassment, the company could be held liable, just as any employer is responsible for the actions of its executives. If a lower-echelon employee harassed a peer and the company failed to take remedial steps, then the company would be liable on the ground that it allowed unlawful workplace conditions to fester.

These EEOC guidelines were the focus of the 1986 U.S. Supreme Court case of *Meritor Savings Bank, FSB v. Vinson,*[36] where they received the Court's imprimatur. However, that case did not involve a challenge under First Amendment free speech principles. The Supreme Court merely decided that the EEOC had the power to devise this formulation, including the workplace "hostile environment" concept. Further, the Court suggested that the "hostile environment" test would likely apply to other categories of workplace discrimination, such as race and religion.

Eight years after the Civil Rights Act of 1964, in the same year that it enacted the Equal Employment Opportunity Act, Congress passed the Education Amendments of 1972.[37] Title IX of that statute mandated nondiscrimination on the basis of sex in any educational "program or activity receiving Federal financial assistance." This nondiscrimination section further defined prohibited activity as the exclusion of a person "from participation in," and denial to a person of "the benefits of," any federally subsidized program. Since virtually every institution of higher learning receives federal money, these provisions apply broadly to private and public schools.

In a 1992 case, *Franklin v. Gwinnett County Public Schools,*[38] the Supreme Court upheld the liability of the public schools in Gwinnett County, Georgia, for sex discrimination under Title IX. A male teacher had coerced a high school student into having intercourse, and, she alleged, the school authorities took no action to halt this conduct and even discouraged her from pressing charges. Upon the teacher's resignation, the school closed the matter. The Supreme Court held that the student could sue the school district for allowing such sexual harassment—a form of sex discrimination under Title IX—to continue. In doing so, the Court casually mentioned the standard for sex harassment in an earlier Title VII workplace case, *Meritor,* where the EEOC's "hostile environment" formulation had been approved for the workplace:

> Unquestionably, Title IX placed on the Gwinnett County Public Schools the duty not to discriminate on the basis of sex, and "when a supervisor sexually harasses a subordinate because of the subordinate's sex, that supervisor 'discriminates' on the basis of sex." *Meritor Sav. Bank, FSB v. Vinson.* We believe the same rule should apply when a teacher sexually harasses and abuses a student.[39]

From this kernel has grown the unsupported but influential notion that the EEOC's "hostile environment" standard defining sexual, racial, and other harassment *in the workplace* could be applied as well by the Department of Education or individual complainants to purely *verbal* "harassment" *in academic institutions of higher learning.* Because the EEOC's definition of Title VII workplace harassment includes a proscription of offensive language directed to employees, the assumption developed that offensive language directed *to students,* and even when used *by* students, may, and indeed must be banned on campus pursuant to Title IX. However, *Franklin v. Gwinnett* involved not merely speech, but speech followed by coerced sex. Further, Franklin was a high school student, not a young adult in college. This Supreme Court case hardly seems a precedent for "hostile environment" speech codes in colleges and universities.

This assumption of the applicability of workplace concepts to the world of higher education has virtually no underpinning, and in fact authoritative First Amendment case law (discussed in chapter 2) makes it highly unlikely that Title VII proscriptions of offensive speech would be applied to college and university students under Title IX. (It might, of course, apply to administrative personnel or even faculty members in certain circumstances in their role as employees.)

One notable lower court decision hints at how the U.S. Supreme Court, given its fairly solid defense of the First Amendment in recent decades, might resolve a contest between verbal sexual harassment and hostile environment doctrine versus free speech claims. In *UWM Post v. Board of Regents of the University of Wisconsin,* the U.S. District Court for the Eastern District of Wisconsin, in declaring the University of Wisconsin's speech code unconstitutional under the First Amendment, said:

> The Board of Regents argues that this Court should find the UW Rule constitutional because its prohibition of discriminatory speech which creates a hostile environment has parallels in the employment setting. . . . First, Title VII addresses employment, not educational settings. Second, . . . [the law] would generally not hold a school liable for its students' actions since students normally are not agents of the school. Finally, even if the legal duties set forth in *Meritor* applied to this case, they would not make the UW Rule constitutional. Since Title VII is only a statute, it cannot supersede the requirements of the First Amendment.[40]

Further, the court made clear that since the prohibited speech was constitutionally protected, the fact of its being uttered on a university campus not only did not strip the speech of constitutional protection, but in fact added to it. So convincing was the court's logic that the university chose not to appeal.

Universities' protestations that "the government makes me do it" have become more common since an infamous incident at Santa Rosa Junior College in California. Three undergraduate women complained to the federal San Francisco regional Office of Civil Rights (OCR) that the school, at student request, had established separate all-male and all-female Internet bulletin boards and that the women had been discussed on the male board in sexually derogatory terms. They asserted, among other things, that the men's discussion constituted "hostile environment" sexual harassment that the college had a duty to remedy. After lengthy negotiations between the college and OCR, a settlement was reached in which the college agreed to adopt a computer network "hostile environment" speech code. In a memorandum sent on September 20, 1994, by the college's attorney to the OCR's San Francisco office, the college noted that federal district courts in Michigan and Wisconsin had declared state university speech codes unconstitutional, but the college capitulated nonetheless. Santa Rosa's settlement entailed, among other provisions, the college's adoption of speech restrictions on its Internet bulletin boards. Had the college fought the regional OCR office, however, it likely would have prevailed for the reasons set forth in its attorney's memo to that office. Indeed, when *New York Times* columnist Anthony Lewis criticized the University of Massachusetts for proposing a speech code purportedly to comply with "Federal Department of Education regulations," Norma V. Cantu, Assistant Secretary for Civil Rights at the Department of Education in Washington wrote to the *Times* "to reassure Mr. Lewis and school officials that there are no Department of Education regulations that endorse or prescribe speech codes." [41]

The speech deemed "sexual harassment" or "racial harassment" by the EEOC (in the workplace setting) or the Department of Education (in the academic setting) is constitutionally protected speech anywhere else. As noted, uttering "offensive" speech is at the very core of First Amendment protected activity, as the Supreme Court made clear in *Cohen v. California*[42] (the 1971 "Fuck the Draft" case) and *R.A.V. v. City of St. Paul*[43] (the 1992 cross-burning case). Were a test case on this issue to reach the Supreme Court, it is likely that the First Amendment would trump the "hostile environment" regulations applied to the speech of college students. Private universities, which enjoy First Amendment protection from government pressure but are *not* required by the First Amendment to respect the speech rights of students, would remain free to enforce properly advertised speech restrictions, but they no longer would be able to hide behind governmental edicts. Further, in a test case of Title IX, the Supreme Court likely would rule that students' using offensive speech to other students, or the college's failure to ban such speech, does not constitute discrimination by the college itself, any more than a company's failure to restrict the bigoted speech of its customers would be interpreted as discrimination by the company. Thus, a college without a speech code restricting students' speech would not risk loss of Title IX federal funds.

Until the Supreme Court steps in, however, public and private universities, citing government requirements, will continue to enforce codes that take the current self-contradictory approach to free speech and academic freedom, proclaiming them proudly while demolishing them utterly. One essential aspect of that self-contradiction is the equation of speech and action. The codes do not call themselves "speech codes," but place bans on offensive "verbal behavior" alongside prohibitions of physical conduct, such as unwanted sexual touching and more heinous actions such as rape, indecent assault, or battery. These physical behaviors, of course, have been crimes and civil violations (so-called "torts") for centuries, and their prohibition by a university, like a prohibition of murder, is redundant. Thus, after its obligatory proclamation of being "committed to the open exchange of ideas where all views, popular and unpopular, can be freely advocated," the Mills College code warns that "offensive *conduct*" is punishable, and proceeds to ban "forms of *communication* . . . of a sexual nature . . . when such *conduct* has the effect of creating an intimidating, hostile, or offensive . . . educational environment." [emphasis added]

The traditional dichotomy between speech and action is blurred almost everywhere in higher education. Oregon State University widely distributes a pamphlet entitled *Sticks and Stones Can Break My Bones but Words Can Never Hurt Me*. The import of the pamphlet is that words indeed can wound, and that a prohibition of offensive speech is not in conflict with academic freedom. It is no news that words can be hurtful. What is remarkable, however, is how the wound inflicted by mere words, regardless of how offensive, is not differentiated from a *physical* wound inflicted by a weapon. The theologian who tells us that we are going to hell (which is profoundly "hurtful") is quite different from the theologian who has us stoned (which is assault). The law offers us no protection against the former, except our right to ignore or respond, but it offers a great deal of protection against the latter. This distinction is rejected by speech codes.

The line between speech and action thus blurred, there is no discernible limit to what kinds of speech may be banned. The University of Southern California adopted one of the broader definitions of "verbal sexual harassment," which includes:

> written or spoken epithets; derogatory or sexually suggestive comments or slurs about an individual's body or dress; questions or statements about sexual activity, other than in an appropriate context such as academic study of such activity; sexual jokes and innuendo; whistling or suggestive sounds.

Such "conduct . . . need not be directed at a particular individual" and includes language offensive both "intentionally or unintentionally" as long as it creates a "hostile academic environment."

Many codes explicitly encourage charging a student with sexual harassment even if his intent is innocent. At the University of Puget Sound in Washington state the danger is particularly acute, because there is no obligation even to hint to a speaker that his speech is unwelcome, for "whether conduct is unwelcome depends on the point of view of the person to whom the conduct is directed. [While] it is generally better for the person harassed to make it clear that the conduct is unwelcome," nonetheless the conduct may be found to be unwelcome even if the person did not manifestly object to it. The City University of New York warns that "sexual harassment is not defined by intentions, but by impact on the subject." As Herbert London, a dean and a professor of humanities of New York University, notes, since "accusations are based on 'impact,' not intention, therefore, the accused is guilty, if the accuser believes him to be guilty."

Bowdoin College has a broad definition of harassing speech, which includes "telling stories of sexual assault which minimize or glorify the act." (So much for reading the epics aloud!) This formulation would appear to bar a male from stating to a female that there are worse things in life than "date rape"—a view that might irritate some but that clearly is core political opinion. Should a man be held liable for expressing such views to a woman who might "experience" it as harassing? Also proscribed are "leering, staring, catcalls; vulgar jokes, language, photographs or cartoons with sexual overtones," and even "terms of familiarity." Despite the extraordinarily broad range of prohibited speech, the speaker at Bowdoin is obligated to discern when speech will be subjectively perceived by the listener as harassing. "No one," warns the code, "is entitled to engage in behavior that is *experienced by others as harassing*," regardless of the speaker's intentions or the unreasonableness of the victim's assumptions. This creates a world where speakers must walk, in a fog, on the edge of a cliff.

Furthermore, Bowdoin's rules against "sexual assault" forbid sexual relations under "circumstances in which a person is compelled or *induced* to engage in a sexual act." Since one is normally "induced" (as opposed to "coerced") to have sex by means of a mating ritual that is at least partially verbal, this guideline would appear to make the whole process of courtship and flirtation risky—subject to being understood as normal and innocent by one partner but as harassment by the other. After all, one person's "compulsion" is another's "inducement," and one's "inducement" might be another's "seduction."

At the University of Connecticut, on the other hand, responding subjectively can be prohibited overreaction, for the code bans "treating people differently solely because they are in some way different from the majority, . . . imitating stereotypes in speech or mannerisms, . . . [or] attributing objections to any of the above actions to 'hypersensitivity' of the targeted individual or group." Henry Louis Gates, Jr., has labeled this hypersensitivity provision "especially cunning" because "it meant that even if you believed that a complainant was overreacting to an innocuous remark, the attempt to defend yourself in this way would serve only as proof of your guilt."[44]

The University of South Carolina, in its 1995 sexual harassment policy, on the one hand warns those overly sensitive to offense that the institution is "committed to freedom of speech and to the liberty of academics to teach, publish, and profess matters that others may find offensive." Members of the university community adhere to standards of "acceptable behavior," including "civility, mutual respect, and tolerance," the policy suggests, "not because we are required to do so, but because conscience dictates it." In the next section, however, South Carolina's sexual harassment policy ignores the appeal to freedom, conscience, and voluntary self-restraint and imposes a ban on "verbal or other expressive behaviors . . . commonly understood to be of a sexual nature." Whether a "hostile environment" has been created is judged "from the perspective of a reasonable person of the complainant's gender." Thus, conscience governs nothing; instead, a male is governed, in matters of freedom, by standards set by generic women.

Syracuse University's sexual harassment code explains why sexual harassment, which includes "leering, ogling, . . . sexual innuendoes, [and] sexually-derogatory jokes," is such a serious violation: "What these behaviors have in common is that they focus on men and women's sexuality, rather than on their contributions as students . . . in the University." This provision would limit students' self-governance to intellectual pursuits alone, while excluding from freedom emotional, let alone sexual, aspects of their lives. Syracuse's admonition—that "sexual harassment is not about voicing unpopular ideas" but, rather, is "a form of intimidation," and therefore that some types of speech are forbidden—is contained not in the code's definition section, but, rather, in its section on "academic freedom." The Orwellian justification for this placement is that since harassing speech "can silence some members of the University community," banning offensive speech actually promotes rather than limits academic freedom.

The conflict between the highly individualistic nature of academic freedom and the anti-individualism of group protection figures prominently in Columbia University's "Policy Statement on Discrimination and Harassment." Adopted by the University Senate in 1990, the policy blurs the concepts of individual and group identity. It begins by proclaiming that "Columbia University prides itself on being a community committed to free and open discourse and to tolerance of differing views." This being so, as "a community, we are committed to the principle that individuals are to be treated as human beings rather than dehumanized by treatment as members of a category that represents only one aspect of their identity." Yet the policy then allocates special treatment to individuals precisely on the basis of a single aspect of their identity. Columbia's policy proceeds with standard "hostile environment" definitions purportedly to enhance individualism. Students considered, because of their group identities, to be "most vulnerable to discrimination and harassment," however, are given more protection than others to allow them to be individuals. As the pigs said in Orwell's *Animal Farm*, "All animals are equal, but some animals are more equal than others."[45]

Brown University, until recently, was headed by Vartan Gregorian, a widely reputed free speech advocate (and someone who, as a faculty member at San Francisco State in the '60s, represented the radical group Students for a Democratic Society, not because he agreed with them, but because he pleaded for their freedom of expression). However, behind the high-minded exhortations in defense of academic freedom published in the student handbook, there lurk dramatic speech restrictions. One university publication quotes from a 1991 *Rolling Stone* magazine interview of Gregorian. Talking about the perceived tension between academic freedom and community values, Gregorian expressed his "worry [that] people don't speak their mind." "It is far more dangerous," he said, "for people to be 'politically correct' but intellectually dishonest." He said that the choice is "whether you enforce behavior or whether you enforce intellectual liberation." Referring to college speech codes, he asked: "Where does the harassment begin and where does freedom of speech end?" His position on the effect of campus speech restrictions, for public consumption, was clear:

> There's not been a dialogue, because everybody is worried about not saying the "politically correct" thing or doing the "correct" thing, because people hate to be called racist or sexist. But I think it's myopic, it's historic retrogression. People have come here—we want to know what they think. I don't want people who come here to take their prejudices away with them. It will be far more strident prejudice if people are not allowed to discuss it. We should not allow people to discuss their prejudices only with their psychiatrists.[46]

These inspirational themes in Brown's promotional literature contrast sharply with the "Harassment and Free Speech" section of Brown's actual student handbook. "Brown University," begins the body of the policy, "through its policies and procedures, seeks to provide an environment that is free from sexual harassment [because] such conduct seriously undermines the atmosphere of trust and respect that is essential to a healthy work and academic environment." As do so many schools, Brown offers a stunningly broad definition of sexual harassment, which includes "unwelcome sexual propositions, invitations, solicitations, and flirtations." Its definition also criminalizes precisely the sort of expression that Gregorian claimed it would be "myopic," "retrogressive," and counterproductive to seek to suppress, including:

> unwelcome verbal expressions of a sexual nature, including graphic sexual commentaries about a person's body, dress, appearance, or sexual activities; the unwelcome use of sexually degrading language, jokes or innuendoes; unwelcome suggestions or insulting sounds or whistles.

The student also learns that Brown's Equal Employment Opportunity/Affirmative Action office has developed "a course designed to inform those who *inadvertently* violate this Policy of the problems they create by their insensitive and/or illegal conduct. The course shall be *mandated* for those in violation of this policy." [emphasis added]

Is it possible, one must ask, to have the kind of honest dialogue envisioned by President Gregorian at Brown under a censorship regime such as his administration put into place?

These codes share a common premise that to effectuate true freedom on campus, in which "disadvantaged" students participate in the campus community equally with "advantaged" students—all defined by blood and history—certain restrictions on speech must be imposed by official power upon individual lives. Freedom is, in theory, highly valued, but to provide equal access to it, it first must be destroyed. It has proven politic, or perhaps nostalgic and comforting, to treat academic freedom and the free-speech doctrines of the '60s as quaint but rhetorically exhilarating holdovers, still technically in force but now virtually meaningless. Perhaps Marcuse's ability to reconcile liberty and dictatorship has come of age, and Orwell's characterization of such thinking as "doublethink" does not bring the flash of recognition that it once did.

CHAPTER 5

THE MORAL REALITY OF POLITICAL CORRECTNESS

Many in the academy insist that the entire phenomenon labeled "political correctness" is the mythical fabrication of opponents of "progressive" change. They argue that political correctness does not exist as a systematic, coercive, repressive force on American campuses. They claim that critics of universities have questionable motives and offer merely recycled anecdotes, not hard evidence, of abuses of power. For example, the authors of an American Association of University Professors' (AAUP) special committee report, "Statement on the 'Political Correctness' Controversy," insisted, without irony, that claims of "political correctness" were merely smokescreens to hide the true agenda of such critics—a racist and sexist desire to thwart the aspirations of minorities and women in the academic enterprise.[1]

Such views seem so very odd to those—students, faculty, and close observers—who dissent from prevailing campus orthodoxies, and who experience the unremitting reality of speech codes (or, more precisely, of the "verbal behavior" provisions of "harassment" policies), of ideological litmus tests, and of sensitivity or diversity "training" that undertakes the involuntary thought reform of free, young minds. It is almost inconceivable that anyone of good faith could live on a college campus unaware of the repression, legal inequality, intrusions into private conscience, and malignant double standards that hold sway there. One charge of verbal harassment casts a pall over everyone's "thought crimes," producing systemic self-censorship, but defenders of the current academic regimes list that merely as "one" instance of (in many of their views, quite justifiable) constraint.

However, when those who deny the power of political correctness think about the McCarthy period, when repression came from the Right, they understand fully and unambiguously how a climate of repression achieves its results without producing a massive body count (to match the massive spirit count) on every campus. In the Left's history of the McCarthy period, the firing or dismissal of one professor or student, the inquisition into the private beliefs of one individual, let alone the demands for a demonstration of fealty to community standards—in that case, a partisan notion of "Americanism" (as now it is a partisan notion of "multiculturalism")—stand out as intolerable oppressions that coerced people into silence, hypocrisy, betrayal, and the withering or numbing of individual freedom. The claim that McCarthyism was a myth, and that a small number of anecdotes had been recycled to create the appearance of systematic repression, would be met with incredulous (and justifiable) outrage by the Left.

In fact, in today's assault on liberty on college campuses, there are not a small number of cases, nor a small number of speech codes, nor a small number of apparatuses of repression and thought reform. Number aside, however, it is nonetheless true that a climate of repression succeeds not by statistical frequency, but by sapping the courage, autonomy, and conscience of individuals who otherwise might remember or revive what liberty could be.

Human history teaches that those who wield power rarely see their own abuse of it. This failing pervades the entire ideological, political, cultural, and historical spectrum. It is not an issue of left and right, but of human ethical incapacity. In Montesquieu's eighteenth-century classic of social commentary *The Persian Letters,* the traveler Uzbek is exquisitely aware of every injustice that he encounters in the world—except the ruthless injustice of his own vile despotism over his harem and his dependents. There is much of Uzbek in all of us.

Those who exercise power, in any domain, tend to compare their actual power to their ultimate goals, usually concluding from this that they barely have any power at all, and, certainly, that they are not abusing what little they have. Further, most of us sadly develop the capacity to treat the suffering, oppression, or legal inequality of individuals or groups whom we see as obstacles to our own goals or visions—or even with whom we merely feel little affinity—as abstractions or exaggerations without concrete human immediacy. By the same token, most of us experience the suffering, oppression, or legal inequality of individuals or groups with whom we identify, or to whom our own causes are linked, as vivid, intolerable, personal realities. It is precisely to neutralize this grievous tendency of human nature that societies establish formal law, equal justice, and the prohibition of double standards.

Open-minded readers should study the chapters that follow not only for their scope, but also to put themselves with human empathy in the place of those who now dissent sincerely, as is their right, from regnant beliefs and values. Our colleges and universities do not offer the protection of fair rules, equal justice, and standards for all seasons to the generation that finds itself on our campuses. No one who denies such protections to others has any honest claim upon them in the future.

Most students respect disagreement and difference, and they do not bring charges of harassment against those whose opinions or expressions "offend" them. The universities themselves, however, encourage such charges to be brought. At almost every college and university, students deemed members of "historically oppressed groups"—above all, women, blacks, gays, and Hispanics—are informed during orientations that their campuses are teeming with illegal or intolerable violations of their "right" not to be offended. To believe many new-student orientations would be to believe that there was a racial or sexual bigot, to borrow the mocking phrase of McCarthy's critics, "under every bed." At almost every college and university, students are presented with lists of a vast array of places to which they should submit charges of such verbal "harassment," and they are promised "victim support," "confidentiality," and sympathetic understanding when they file such complaints.

What an astonishing expectation (and power) to give to students: the belief that, if they belong to a protected category, they have a right to four years of never being offended. What an extraordinary power to give to administrators and tribunals: the prerogative to punish the free speech and expression of people to whom they choose to assign the stains and guilt of historical oppression, while being free, themselves, to use whatever rhetoric they wish against the bearers of such stains. While the world looks at issues of curriculum and scholarship, above all, to analyze and evaluate American colleges and universities, it is, in fact, the silencing and punishment of belief, expression, and individuality that ought to concern yet more deeply those who care about what universities are and could be. The assault on free expression has proceeded dramatically, largely hidden from public view. Most cases never reach the public, because most individuals accused of "verbal" harassment sadly (but understandably) accept plea bargains that diminish their freedom but spare them Draconian penalties, including expulsion. Even so, the files on prosecutions under speech codes are, alas, overflowing.

Freedom is a fragile and composite thing, and people assail any part of it at their peril. It surprised no civil libertarian that the first victims of Ontario's feminist-inspired antipornography legislation were the writings and book-stores of lesbian feminists.[2] If you tear down laws protecting freedom, they will not be there to protect you. The alternative to the rule of law is the use of force. What people sow, they eventually reap.

Speech codes, with all of their formal clauses, are in fact a parody of the rule of law. This is seen best when these seemingly legalistic codes are sub-jected to the actual rule of law, which occurs when the speech restrictions of harassment policies at public universities are summoned to the bar of legal scrutiny. Speech, in fact, is freest at public universities because admin-istrators of state universities are aware, at some level, that they are state agen-cies, bound by the restrictions on state power over individual liberty set out in federal and state constitutions. If a public university violates one's consti-tutional rights, one can go to court. By contrast, professors and students at private universities are far less likely to take their cases public. They lack re-course to any "appellate" tribunal location capable of commanding an ad-ministration to honor freedom. Though more cases are brought against public universities (because of this appellate jurisdiction), their speech codes are certainly not stronger than those of private universities. In their more open record, one sees the nature and mechanisms of the current assault on liberty.

Despite the profound importance, symbolic and substantive, of speech codes, we should not view their presence or absence as the yardstick of free-dom. Freedom dies in the heart and will before it dies in the law. Speech codes merely formalize the will to censor and to devalue liberty of thought and speech. Even without invoking codes, universities have found ways to si-lence or to chill freedom of opinion and expression. Defenders of free speech at colleges and universities become tarred by the sorts of speech they must defend if they wish to defend freedom in general. No one who defends trial by jury over popular justice in a murder trial is called a defender of mur-der; such a person is seen, by all, as a defender of trial by jury. The defender of free speech, however, is forever being told, on American campuses, that he or she is seeking, specifically, to make the campus safe for "racism," "sex-ism," or "homophobia." That is true if what one means is that the defender of free speech seeks to make the campus safe for the expression of all views, and for the clash of visions, ideas, and passions. At the time of Senator Mc-Carthy, many were intimidated into silence by the question "Why would you want to protect the speech of a Red if you are not a Red?" The issue, then and now, is not the protection of this or that person's rights by our sub-jective criteria of who deserves freedom, but the protection of freedom itself.

Protection of free speech is not needed for inoffensive, popular speech with which all or most members of a community agree. Such speech is not threatened. Freedom is required precisely for unpopular speech, the toleration of which is one of the marks of a free society. At some point, and in some location, of course, what is popular speech in one place becomes unpopular speech elsewhere. That is why, morally and practically, none of us enjoys more freedom of speech than is accorded the least popular speaker. At a university, of course, no one has an inherent right to be a professor. Universities have ample time, at the moments of hiring, promotion, and tenure, to review a teacher's and a scholar's work, and to decide if it meets their standards. Such power of review should be exercised with tolerant respect for honest differences of opinion—universities depend on that—but it should be exercised. Once in a classroom, however, or conducting research, professors should be free, indeed encouraged, to teach without penalty what they believe to be the truth about their fields of inquiry. Such a system is indeed as messy as human freedom itself. Each of us can name professors whose appointment and subsequent tenure by a university are, for us, objects of wonderment and despair. The lists, however, will not be the same. One's objection to such cases, if one values academic freedom, must be to the act of appointment and tenure (as having been made on inappropriate or inadequately critical academic grounds), and not to the freedom bestowed.

The speech-code provisions of harassment policies are merely symptoms of the willful assault on liberty on our campuses: the suppression and punishment of controversial and unpopular ideas; the banning of terms that offend listeners invested with special rights; and the outlawing of discourse that, in the eyes of the defenders of the new orthodoxies, "creates a hostile environment." The essential purpose of a speech code is to repress speech. It may serve other ends, such as making its framers feel moral, powerful, or simply safe from the attacks of those who would criticize them. It also demonstrates, for all to observe, who controls the symbolic environment of a place—a heady feeling for the wielders of power, and a demonstration, of course, that also succeeds in silencing others.

If colleges and universities were beset not by the current "political orthodoxy" but by some other claim for the unequal assignment of protections and rights—"religious orthodoxy" or "patriotic orthodoxy," for example—victims of those calls for repression and double standards would find the evil obvious. Imagine secular, skeptical, or leftist faculty and students confronted by a religious harassment code that prohibited "denigration" of evangelical or Catholic beliefs, or that made the classroom or campus a space where evangelical or Catholic students must be protected against feeling "intimidated," "offended," or, by their own subjective experience, victims of "a hostile environment." Imagine a university of patriotic "loyalty oaths" where leftists were deemed responsible for the tens of millions of victims of communism, and where free minds were prohibited from creating a hostile environment for patriots, or from offending that "minority" of individuals who are descended from Korean War or Vietnam War veterans. Imagine, as well, that for every "case" that became public, there were scores or hundreds of cases in which the "offender" or "victimizer," desperate to preserve a job or gain a degree, accepted a confidential plea bargain that included a semester's or a year's reeducation in "religious sensitivity" or "patriotic sensitivity" seminars run by the university's "Evangelical Center," "Patriotic Center," or "Office of Religious and Patriotic Compliance." Living daily in such a climate—and climates do change—would the same defenders of current codes and repressions call for quantitative studies of the effects of such speech codes on the general academic population?

Speech codes, to the very extent that they are successful, repress by the fear they inspire, not by the number of public cases they produce, and not by the frequency with which a teacher or student risks everything to fight their provisions in a campus trial. Imagine a campus on which being denounced for "irreligious bigotry" or "un-Americanism" carried the same stigma that being denounced for "racism," "sexism," and "homophobia" now carries in the academic world, so that in such hearings or trials, the burden of proof invariably fell upon the "offender." A common sign at prochoice rallies— "Keep your rosaries off our ovaries"—would be prima facie evidence of language used as a weapon to degrade and marginalize, and the common term of abuse—"born-again bigot"—would be compelling evidence of the choice to create a hostile environment for evangelicals. What panegyrics to liberty and free expression we would hear in opposition to any proposed code to protect the "religious" or the "patriotic" from "offense" and "incivility." Yet what deafening silence we have heard, in these times, in the campus acceptance of the speech provisions of so-called harassment codes.

The goal of a speech code, then, is to suppress speech one doesn't like. The goal of liberty and equal justice is to permit us to live in a complex but peaceful world of difference, disagreement, debate, moral witness, and efforts of persuasion without coercion and violence. Liberty and legal equality are hard-won, precious, and, indeed, because the social world is often discomforting, profoundly complex and troublesome ways of being human. They require, for their sustenance, men and women who would abhor their own power of censorship and their own special legal privileges as much as they abhor those of others. In enacting and enforcing speech codes, universities, for their own partisan reasons, have chosen to betray the human vision of freedom and legal equality. It was malignant to impose or permit such speech codes; to deny their oppressive effects while living in the midst of those effects is beyond the moral pale.

On virtually any college campus, for all of its rules of "civility" and all of its prohibitions of "hostile environment," assimilationist black men and women live daily with the terms "Uncle Tom" and "Oreo" said with impunity, while their tormenters live with special protections from offense. White students daily hear themselves, their friends, and their parents denounced as "racists" and "oppressors," while their tormenters live with special protections from offense. Believing Christians hear their beliefs ridiculed and see their sacred symbols traduced—virtually nothing, in the name of freedom, may not be said against them in the classroom, at rallies, and in personal encounters—while their tormenters live with special protection from offense. Men hear their sex abused, find themselves blamed for all the evils of the world, and enter classrooms whose very goal is to make them feel discomfort, while their tormenters live with special protections from "a hostile environment." The purpose of speech codes—patriotically orthodox or politically orthodox—is to suppress speech, and to privilege one partisan, ideological view of the world. Ideally, for the purposes of oppression, the very threat of the code suffices. When that does not suffice, those codes are, indeed, invoked.

The social goal of speech codes is to protect specific individuals—defined by group—from, among other things, ideas, expressions, and even private, consensual behaviors that offend them. These group identities may be purely historical ("historically oppressed" or "underrepresented" minorities); defined by blood ("race" or "ethnicity"); or sexuality ("gender" or "sexual preference"). The way to know the goals of such codes is not only to consult their use in actual practice, but also to consult those universities that have sought to explain "harassment" to their students, until those very explanations exposed their either unconstitutional or hypocritical agendas to public judgment. In chapter 1, we saw Penn's definitions and explanations of "harassment" at freshmen orientations. At the University of Michigan, the Office of Affirmative Action issued a guide entitled *What Students Should Know about Discrimination and Discriminatory Harassment by Students in the Uni-*

versity Environment, precisely to specify prohibited conduct. The Michigan guide cited examples such as "a male student makes remarks in class like 'Women just aren't as good in this field as men,' thus creating a hostile learning environment for female classmates." What it actually creates, of course, as a federal court saw with clarity when it declared the Michigan code manifestly unconstitutional, is an environment in which a student may not utter a particular empirical proposition (whose truth or falsity could be a matter of debate). The guide wished to make clear what kinds of expressions or verbal behaviors were illegal at the university, leaving students adequately forewarned. Thus, it had a section of examples, under the heading: "You are a harasser when . . ." These included: "You tell jokes about gay men and lesbians, [or] you display a confederate flag on the door of your room in the residence hall" and "You comment in a derogatory way about a particular person [sic] or group's physical appearance or sexual orientation, or their cultural origins, or religion."[3]

Two cases will serve as good introductions to the problems facing free speech (and freedom of thought) at our colleges and universities: that of Anthony Martin of Wellesley College, and that of Edward M. Miller of the University of New Orleans. By academic year 1993–94, Anthony Martin, professor of Africana studies, had been teaching at Wellesley College for twenty-one years. Wellesley had weighed his intellect and research when hiring him, promoting him, and granting him tenure. Martin believed and taught that Jews had been particular enemies of Africans and black Americans, teaching this for years, during which time he had received frequent positive assessments and merit raises. If Wellesley thought that Martin was an inadequate scholar and teacher, it had had adequate time to address that issue. Martin's views were well known and controversial. Indeed, in the mid-1980s, in the midst of public controversy about his beliefs, Martin had been denied a merit raise by the president of the college at that time, Nannerl Keohane, and, using the prior assessments of his work and his prior merit increases as evidence, Martin had sued Wellesley and achieved a favorable settlement.

In 1993–94, Martin assigned a notoriously anti-Semitic book, *The Secret Relationship Between Blacks and Jews,* as required reading in his courses. News of this caused an uproar both on and off campus. A significant number of faculty members, including the chair of the Africana Studies department, found the book, and Martin, intellectually absurd, and they criticized him severely, more than half the faculty denouncing him in writing. His work was well received, however, by several journals of black studies, and he had strong student evaluations of his teachings (though, as with all controversial professors, the process of self-selection may have predetermined that). He then wrote a book, *The Jewish Onslaught: Dispatches from the Wellesley Battlefront,* which sought to portray a Jewish conspiracy against him and other blacks, including "unprincipled attacks, defamatory statements, assault on my livelihood, and physical threats." Wellesley responded with an announcement that Martin would not be given any merit raise at all, which was rare at the college. Wellesley certainly had the right to make judgments about "merit," and it stated, in writing, that "the decision not to grant a merit increase to Professor Martin reflects the judgment of his peers, who concur that the book he continues to teach as truth . . . is devoid of scholarly credibility, and his own book, *The Jewish Onslaught,* is intellectually flawed and unbalanced."[4]

The evaluation of the text he assigned—as a means of determining merit—was dangerous in general principle, but perhaps unavoidable as a means of assessing his pedagogical value. There was, after all, no question of revoking his tenure or faculty status, and no one has an inherent right to a "merit" increase. Wellesley also evaluated, however, as part of its determination of his salary, the polemical work that he wrote about his dispute with the college. This seems, to say the least, inappropriate to the college's determination of his "merit." Unsurprisingly, Wellesley found his criticism of itself "flawed and unbalanced." The president of Wellesley, Diana Chapman Walsh, sent a letter in December 1993 to forty thousand alumnae, parents, and friends of Wellesley. She defended Martin's right to freedom of expression "without fear of reprisals," but she denounced both Martin's "recurrent and gratuitous use of racial or religious identification of individuals," and, with reference to his book criticizing actions that he believed had been taken against him, his "attempt to portray Wellesley College as a repressive institution bent on silencing him."[5] The letter, by the person ultimately responsible for granting or withholding promotions and merit increases, not only criticized Martin's mode of scholarship, teaching, and criticism of Wellesley, but also established criteria by which Martin was to be judged institutionally. If those criteria were applied literally and universally, what would become of everyone's ability to speak "without fear of reprisals," including that of scholars who were poles apart from Martin's beliefs and style?

The reason that there never is a consensus for the liberty to be singular and controversial is that so many say, "Yes, I believe in freedom of speech, but, . . ." with mutually exclusive "buts" that carve out exceptions which, taken together, would add up to a profound disbelief in freedom of speech.

These "buts" are particularly prodigal at times of public anger and contro-versy, which are, of course, the very moments when commitment to unfet-tered free expression is put most harshly to the test. For decades, Wellesley had judged Martin favorably. In the midst of a great public outcry, however, it decided to punish him for his beliefs. Conservatives, liberals, and libertari-ans, who almost universally praised Wellesley's handling of the Martin case, should ponder, long and hard, the criteria articulated in President Walsh's letter, and ask themselves to whom such criteria, generally accepted, might not be applied. The book, she reasoned, was "so offensive that we had a re-sponsibility to counter it." It "crossed the line [between] simply unpopular argument" and "unnecessarily disrespectful and deeply divisive speech." For Walsh, Martin's book "violates the basic principles that nourish and sustain this college community and that enable us to achieve our educational goals: norms of civil discourse; standards of scholarly integrity; and aspirations for freedom and justice."[6] Does any of this sound familiar to critics of "political correctness"?

Wellesley, at least, was a private college, albeit one nominally committed to full academic freedom. The University of New Orleans (UNO), how-ever, is a public university, bound, as such, by the First Amendment. Edward M. Miller is a research professor of economics at UNO. He has won a Mensa Education and Research Award for Excellence for his research on intelli-gence, and he is the author of several professional articles on intelligence and racial differences. He is a statistician. Professors of psychology at major uni-versities attested repeatedly to his credentials in psychometrics. On July 23, 1996, he published a letter—in response to an article in a New Orleans weekly, the *Gambit*—in which he took exception to what he claimed were factual errors in that journal's discussion of debates concerning race and in-telligence. His letter was on his personal stationery, but in a cover letter he identified his university position, stating explicitly that he did so "for pur-poses of identification only," that he was "expressing his own opinion," and that "the University of New Orleans need not agree with the opinions ex-pressed above." In his letter to the editor, he expressed his belief that evi-dence showed a positive correlation between brain size and intelligence, that there are racial differences in brain weight, and that racial differences in IQ scores are of statistical significance.[7]

Within days, the provost of UNO wrote to Miller, advising him that he had violated Administrative Procedure 47.5 (AP) which states that "the pri-vate use of official University insignia, stationery, envelopes, etc., by mem-bers of the UNO faculty or staff is prohibited for the following uses: . . . the expression of personal opinion or endorsements in letters to the news media, elected officials, etc., except in areas of one's professional competence." The procedure further explained that individuals, beyond their areas of professional competence, had no right "to use their association with the University to lend unwarranted weight to their views."[8]

The chancellor of UNO, Gregory O'Brien, wrote a letter to the *Times-Picayune,* among other newspapers, stating that "the university will not tolerate anyone's use of the classroom as a forum to promote racial disharmony." UNO indeed should be a center "where ideas can be exchanged and debated," but, yet "more importantly, . . . where equality and diversity are valued."[9] In the campus publication, *Driftwood,* Associate Dean for Multicultural Affairs Janet Caldwell wrote that Miller was "a colleague who readily voices racist views on behalf of the University." She added that "there is no way that a professor who holds such beliefs can teach African Americans. I hope that Black students are steered away from Miller's classes." Indeed, she emphasized, "We must ensure that all students are taught by professors who are free from beliefs and behaviors which preclude effective teaching and learning." Dean Caldwell used her official title, wrote on letterhead stationery, and said "we," all of which indicated that she was both within the guidelines of the administrative procedure, and, indeed, speaking for UNO.[10]

Miller attempted to place several of his related works on the IQ controversies on reserve in the UNO library, including, ironically, an article that was solicited in 1997 as part of an anthology, *Leading Essays in African-American Studies,* edited by Nikongo BaNikongo, professor at Howard University (a historically black university) and assigned in courses at, among other universities, Howard itself. What "will not be tolerated" at the public university, UNO, was part of discussions and debates at Howard. More dramatically, of course, Miller's "beliefs" officially had been judged disqualifications for teaching at UNO.

On September 30, 1996, Robert D. Chatelle, the cochair of the Political Issues Committee of the National Writers Union (NWU)—a union that is part of the UAW/AFL-CIO—came to Miller's defense. He wrote to Allan A. Copping, president of the Louisiana State University system, and then, in response to Chancellor O'Brien's reply to that letter, wrote to O'Brien himself. Chatelle ardently called them to task for supporting the manifestly unconstitutional AP, and he defended Miller's freedom of expression. Robert Chatelle is, by his own self-definition, a "democratic socialist," "a queer," and "a labor organizer," and he has fought tirelessly for the rights of all individuals across the political, ideological, and personal spectrum in America.

He is the embodiment of the antithesis to double standards. While struggling, always, for the rights of those he deems marginalized by American society, he also has saved conservative journals on American campuses and has rushed to the assistance of victims of political correctness. Chatelle's letter to the powers at UNO, copied, as always, to the media and to important civil libertarians, reminds us all of how the genuine voice of liberty sounds. The NWU, Chatelle noted, with its forty-three hundred members, was committed by its constitution to "'freedom of the press, freedom of speech, and freedom of expression.'" Chatelle informed UNO: "We oppose all actions at colleges and universities, both private and public, that limit or punish the speech of students, faculty, or other employees." He expressed the NWU's "grave concerns about an ongoing incident . . . involving Professor Edward M. Miller . . . not as advocates for Dr. Miller, but rather as advocates for freedom of speech and intellectual and academic freedom." The procedure that Miller was accused of violating was obviously unconstitutional, vague in its notion of expertise, and never could withstand a court challenge. The official letters from administrators about the intolerability of Miller's "beliefs" were unbearably chilling of free speech. Chancellor O'Brien's official letter to the *Times-Picayune,* stating that "the university will not tolerate anyone's use of the classroom as a forum to promote racial disharmony" was an invitation to double standards, Chatelle warned:

> In our experience, we have yet to encounter such a rule that was not selectively enforced. Had Dr. Miller written the *Gambit* contending that there are no racial differences in intelligence, no one would have threatened him under AP 47.5. . . . Courses in Black Studies are offered at the University of New Orleans. In presenting the history of American racism, African-American students may become justifiably angry, and this anger could be said to promote "racial disharmony.". . . Those who expose students to the Afro-Centric positions are probably the most vulnerable. But even teachers who were to show the excellent documentary, "Eyes on the Prize," could themselves be dismissed by Chancellor O'Brien were he to follow his publicly stated policy consistently.[11]

Finally, Chatelle went right to the heart of the drama of the current tragedy at our universities:

> Few developments of the past decades have saddened us as much as the erosion of freedom of expression and academic and intellectual freedom at our institutions of higher learning. As campuses diversified, new tensions arose.

Rather than meet these tensions head on and in a responsible manner, college administrators instead took the easy way out and relied upon that old tired tactic, censorship. . . . All censorship is predicated on the assumption that some ideas are so dangerous that they must be suppressed. Some ideas are dangerous because they are true; others, because they are false. But the proper response to false ideas is refutation, not censorship. The protections guaranteed by the First Amendment are by no means limited to the expression of thought and ideas that promote racial harmony. Such speech needs no legal protection [at UNO]. The whole intent of the First Amendment is to protect the speech of people, such as Dr. Miller, whose ideas are controversial. Those who disagree with him should refute him, but not attempt to silence him.[12]

Down the margin of Chatelle's letter ran the names of the Advisory Board of the NWU: among others, Isabel Allende, Anne Bernays, Ariel Dorfman, Barbara Ehrenreich, Erica Jong, Barbara Kingsolver, Maxine Kumin, Jessica Mitford, William Novak, Grace Paley, Marge Piercy, Adrienne Rich, and Milton Viorst. An admonition from a labor union with such a list of advisors gives Chatelle's letters a special impact when directed to ideologues of the Left.

In July 1997, Chatelle, who completed his term as chair of the NWU Political Issues Committee in June 1997, came again to the defense of rights at UNO. The official UNO newsletter, *Now Notes,* had proclaimed an official "redefinition" of its editorial policy in March 1997. *Now Notes* informed UNO: "Information contrary to university policies, or that is offensive or derisive will be excluded."[13] This definition, of course, allowed *Now Notes* to avoid having to publish Miller's self-defense (his views had earned him death threats, official statements that his beliefs were legally intolerable at UNO, and pressures by local politicians to recant or leave). As Chatelle wrote to the UNO administration:

> This policy is facially illegal viewpoint discrimination. "Offensive" and "derisive" are purely subjective terms with no objective or legal meanings. The notion that published information must be consistent with "university policies" is downright frightening. Consider the consequences of such a policy were it in effect years ago at a racially segregated public university![14]

John Stuart Mill said it best, in *On Liberty* (1859), and we hope that our readers will keep in mind the force of his observation as they encounter the themes and details of this book. Everyone, Mill noted, claims to believe in freedom of expression, but everyone draws his or her own boundaries at the obviously worthless, dangerous, and wrong. Why should we tolerate speech that offends our sense of essential value, security, and truth? To that question, Mill answered, on behalf of both "freedom of opinion, and freedom of the expression of opinion," that there were four compelling grounds: (1) the opinion might be true, and "to deny this is to assume our own infallibility"; (2) the opinion, though erroneous, might, indeed, most probably would "contain a portion of truth," and because "prevailing opinion" is rarely, if ever, "the whole truth," censorship denies us that possible "remainder of the truth" that only might be gained by "the collision of adverse opinions"; (3) even if prevailing opinion were the whole truth, if it were not permitted to be contested—indeed, if it were not, in actual fact, "vigorously and earnestly contested," it will be believed by most not because of "its rational grounds," but only "in the manner of a prejudice"; and (4) if we were not obliged to defend our belief, it would stand "in danger of being lost, or enfeebled, and deprived of its vital effect on the character and conduct," becoming a formula repeated by rote, "inefficacious for good, . . . and preventing the growth of any real and heartfelt conviction, from reason or personal experience."

Mill also addressed the argument that even if one conceded that view of things, one could fairly insist, nonetheless, that such discussion "be temperate, and . . . not pass the bounds of fair discussion." As Mill noted, such "boundaries" are impossible to define, and would be drawn by all in a manner favorable to themselves. If one took the notion of "temperate" and "fair discussion" truly seriously, Mill observed, what ought to be banned would be arguments that stigmatized one's opponents "as bad and immoral men." Indeed, Mill argued presciently: "With regard to what is commonly meant by intemperate discussion, namely invective, sarcasm, personality, and the like, the denunciation of those weapons would deserve more sympathy if it were ever proposed to interdict them equally to both sides; but it is only desired to restrain the employment of them against the prevailing opinion."

Ultimately, Mill concluded, it should be left to public opinion, not to "law and authority," to determine "in whose mode of advocacy either want of candor, or malignity, bigotry, or intolerance of feeling manifest themselves." In short, it was "imperative that human beings should be free to form opinions, and to express their opinions without reserve." The struggle for liberty on American campuses is, in its essence, the struggle between Herbert Marcuse and John Stuart Mill.

PART II

THE ASSAULT ON

FREE SPEECH

CHAPTER 6

THE ASSAULT ON
FACULTY SPEECH

For all members of a campus community, the persecution of faculty speech is the most awesome display of oppressive power. If universities and colleges can silence and punish professors, overturning protections hard-won over generations, it sends a signal that students have no protection at all. Some of that persecution of faculty occurs in decisions about hiring, tenure, and promotion, where the exclusion of politically incorrect views may be hidden from public scrutiny. Such votes are almost always by secret ballot, and no one is required to state formally his or her reason for a particular vote for or against a colleague (or a potential colleague). Who, after all, can see into people's souls?

Hampshire College, however, does offer a window onto souls. Founded in the 1960s as a progressive center of debate and diversity, it embodies the paradox of that legacy. In its procedures, it is nontraditional: There is no tenure; rehiring occurs, in theory, on the basis of excellent teaching; faculty personnel files are open to scrutiny; and all opinions on rehiring must be recorded. In its substance, it has become intolerant and oppressive.

Jeffrey Wallen, whom the *Boston Globe* described as "a left-leaning iconoclast," learned directly what it meant to think independently of campus orthodoxy. In 1989, he was a popular assistant professor of comparative literature who believed that he had no right to use his classroom for political advocacy. When he came up for reappointment, Hampshire's president, Gregory Prince, who usually rubber-stamped favorable votes, expressed concern about seven negative votes against him and forwarded his case to the College Committee on Faculty Reappointments and Promotions. The committee questioned Wallen about whether he had difficulty teaching Third World authors—he answered, "No"—and voted against his reappointment.[1] Although he eventually was rehired, after a long, acrimonious struggle, Wallen learned some remarkable things from the written faculty comments in his file:

—Jeff Wallen does not demonstrate the independence of mind nor the willingness to go beyond pre-conceived attitudes. . . . Upon arrival, he voiced attitudes and opinions in Humanities and Arts meetings about matters he hadn't been here long enough to comprehend.

—I had hoped for someone more dynamic, and less prone to polarizing issues in our school meetings in ways that suggest to me no independent thinking about the issues.

—I found Jeff's views and opinions at school meeting [sic] not only offensive but uninformed and presumptuous.

—On the basis of his course work and his response to a question raised during his reappointment meeting, I seriously question his understanding of the Third World Expectation except on the most superficial, perfunctory basis. His is a conventional attitude of privelege [sic], inappropriate in a faculty member at a time when Hampshire is moving in such a different direction.

—a virtual absence of Third World texts, or any Third World challenge to the canon or to the theoretical priorities in his teaching.[2]

Indeed, the faculty of Hampshire College made the nature of their commitment to free expression abundantly clear. On December 7, 1993, a professor introduced a motion on behalf of freedom of expression to the full faculty, affirming "the right of all members of the College community to the free expression of views in speech or in art, and the right of all members of the community to hear the expression of any views or to view art without censorship, and without regard to the positions or perspectives embodied in that speech or art." In short, "this precludes the censorship or prohibition of non-criminal speech . . . [and] art."[3]

The minutes of that faculty meeting noted vociferous objections. The proposal "appears to only take into account only one side of the argument [and] does not deal with the harassment issue." The proposal was "too broad," "too specific," and "reactionary." According to the notes of several faculty members in attendance, one professor (now a dean) reminded her colleagues that "the First Amendment was written by a rich, white, male slaveowner." Another "could support" free expression, but not when it was qualified by the phrase "without regard to the content or the views expressed" because such freedom should be reserved for views that were "unobjectionable" and not "hurtful" to others. By a vote of 26 against, 21 for, and 1 abstention, the Hampshire faculty voted down the motion for free expression.[4]

The minutes also recorded that after the vote, "One faculty member cautioned it would not be helpful to relay the notion that the faculty had voted down freedom of expression." According to witnesses, that speaker was the president of the college.[5] Hampshire's motto, by the way, on its 1990 catalogue, the year of Wallen's travail, was "Hampshire College: Where it's OK to go outside the lines!"

The details of the Wallen case are a rare glimpse into faculty standards, however, because one almost never knows with certainty the motives underlying decisions about tenure and promotion. What is dramatically visible at our colleges and universities is the explicit punishment of faculty speech. This suppression of faculty freedom of expression is a decapitation of liberty in higher education, and it has occurred, above all, in the areas of sexuality and race.

Sexuality

Much of the cultural Left in the humanities simultaneously has demanded a classroom without "offense" and a freedom to teach new fields that relate to sexuality, pornography, eroticism, and the human body. These are dangerous bedmates, but the unspoken assumption appears to be that when taught from "progressive" perspectives, such courses somehow cannot be the occasions of charges of "harassment." If sexual themes are addressed by anyone deemed, rightly or wrongly, unprogressive, even the pretense of a protective wall of academic freedom quickly can collapse.

Consider the case of Professor Dean Cohen, of San Bernardino Valley College in California.[6] Cohen taught remedial English, and he took full pedagogical advantage of the current vogue for sexual topics. His course, consistent with the "cultural studies" of the paradoxical 1990s, assigned work that focused on such themes as (to quote the court that finally heard the case) "obscenity, cannibalism, and consensual sex with children." A student was "offended," and, in the spring of 1992, she filed a sexual harassment grievance.

The college's Grievance Committee ruled that Cohen "had violated the College's policy against sexual harassment by creating a hostile learning environment." He appealed unsuccessfully within the college, which ultimately ruled that he must provide his students and department chair, each semester, with "a syllabus concerning his teaching style, purpose, [and] content." Further, the college ordered him to "attend a sexual harassment seminar . . . become sensitive to the particular needs and backgrounds of his students . . . [and avoid] techniques [that] create a climate which impedes the students' ability to learn." Finally, the tenured Cohen was informed that any "further violation of the [harassment] policy" would lead to further discipline, "'up to and including suspension or termination.'" The college placed its finding in his permanent personnel file.

Cohen, teaching at a public college, filed suit, and the United States Court of Appeals for the Ninth Circuit, in a ruling of August 1996, saw the issues quite differently. For the circuit court, the college's "hostile environment" policies had violated Cohen's First Amendment rights by their unconstitutional vagueness ("they trap the innocent" by making it impossible to know what was and what was not prohibited, which "discourages the exercise of first amendment freedoms") and by their lack of due process ("they impermissibly delegate" core issues of academic freedom to "low level officials for resolution on an ad hoc and subjective basis," creating "the attendant dangers of arbitrary and discriminatory application").

The court understood not only academic freedom better than the college, but also pedagogy, noting that Cohen "played the 'devil's advocate' by asserting controversial viewpoints," and understanding the relationship of "cannibalism" to Cohen's assignment of Jonathan Swift's "A Modest Proposal," a sardonic, hyperbolic, and profoundly significant eighteenth-century work that made use of the same theme. The court, not the college or its faculty, found it intolerable that "officials of the College, on an entirely ad hoc basis, applied the Policy's nebulous outer reaches to punish teaching methods that Cohen had used for many years [in what] can best be described as a legalistic ambush." The college appealed, but the U.S. Supreme Court declined to hear the case, letting the ninth circuit's decision stand.

Similarly, at the University of New Hampshire (UNH), a federal court had to teach academic citizens the meaning of freedom.[7] In February 1992, Donald Silva, a tenured member of the faculty at UNH since the early '70s, was teaching technical writing. His two major problems were explaining the difference between "focus" and "being diffuse" and making students see that a good definition always offered either concrete or metaphorical examples.

He had evolved two lessons that seemed to work, and he employed them for years. The first utilized a discussion of focus by Hemingway, and the second involved a famous quotation from the most celebrated belly dancer of a prior generation, Little Egypt. As stipulated in court both by UNH and Silva, he explained "focus" as follows: "I will put it in terms of sex, so you can better understand it. Focus is like sex. You seek a target. You zero in on your subject. You move from side to side. You close in on the subject. You bracket the subject and center on it. Focus connects experience and language. You and the subject become one." Further, as mutually stipulated, Silva shared, as he had for decades, a quotation from Little Egypt to illustrate definition by metaphor. How might one define something so foreign to most people's experience as belly dancing? Silva told his class how Little Egypt had done so: "Belly dancing is like jello on a plate with a vibrator under the plate." In the days of Little Egypt, of course, as in the days of Silva's own youth and adolescence, a "vibrator" referred to a handheld scalp vibrator, such as barbers and hairdressers commonly used.

UNH, however, had a standard hostile or offensive verbal conduct harassment policy. Although the preface to that policy specified that UNH's intent was "not to create a climate of fear," it warned that "derogatory gender-based humor," regardless of intent, was potentially actionable, up to dismissal. Six of Silva's female students now formally complained against him, encouraged by Professor Jerilee A. Zezula, to whom they had said (according to her own deposition) that Silva "had described a 'belly dancer' as being like a bowl of jello being stimulated by a vibrator, and how he used a vivid description of intercourse as an example of a type of writing." According to Zezula, "They all expressed a fear of going to speak to him directly because they would never wish to be alone with him." Zezula told the students that "I agreed with them and . . . that they had a very legitimate complaint," and she talked to Silva by telephone. Zezula testified: "I explained that using the word mechanical 'vibrator' . . . would be offensive to women students [and that] the use of sexual intercourse as an example of anything in a technical writing course was very offensive and crude." Zezula advised him to "read the university literature on sexual harassment very carefully."

By March 2, 1992, the six students had filed written sexual harassment charges against Silva with the university, made public by the U.S. District Court for New Hampshire, which also provided the appropriate "*sics.*" One complaint stated: "[W]e were discussing focusing on our target for our report. When Mr. Silva started talking in a sexual manner which I thought was very inappropriated [*sic*] and also very affending [*sic*]. . . . So he said it's like going in and out, side to side, and loosening up so you could find the best target area. I really think that was uncalled for. . . ." The second described the following "occurrances [sic]": "[H]e made a vulgar, inappropriate description of a 'bowl of jello and a vibrator,' to describe the belly dancer . . . [T]trying to explain another subject . . . he used the analogy of intercourse, 'Find the target, loosen up, back and forth, side to side.'" The third stated: "I felt degraded in his class on Wednesday, 26 Feb., and disgusted on 24 Feb. I had questions about our assignment, . . . but due to his use of sex as a 'focus,' I walked away rather than asked [sic] him to clarify again. I didn't want any more strange ex-plainations [sic]." The fourth complained: "I am appalled at the statement made by Don Silva. . . . He insinuated that every student present had first-hand knowledge of his illustration." The fifth charged: "I find Don Silva's constant referrals to sex offensive. . . . I was shocked. I felt demeaned and em-barassed [sic]." The sixth noted: "I was very offended by his sexual refferals [sic]. I was brought up in a house where sex was not something to be discussed openly and freely and it certainly was not something to be taken lightly." These were calls for official charges of actionable harassment.

From the court record, we know what UNH did about these charges. Zezula complained to Professor Neil Lubow, associate vice president of aca-demic affairs at UNH. On February 28, Lubow, Zezula, and the six students met, and later that day, Lubow told Brian Giles, director of the Thompson School of Applied Sciences (in which Silva taught), to seek a replacement for Silva. They further agreed "that we can't leave him in the classroom." In a deposition, Giles was asked, "Had you talked to Don Silva to get his side of it at that time?" He answered, under oath, "No, I had not." He was asked, "Were you looking for replacements at that time?" He answered, "That's correct."

On March 3, 1992, Silva met with Lubow, Giles, and a UNH rape and harassment counselor for one half hour, and was asked, on the spot, to re-spond to the students' written complaints. On that same day, UNH created "shadow classes" for students who wished a different teacher in technical writing. On April 1, Silva received a formal letter of reprimand: "Your be-havior is in violation of University policy prohibiting sexual harassment and will not be tolerated." Silva, remaining suspended, unsuccessfully appealed these findings and penalties within the administration, and then to the Fac-ulty Grievance Committee. On February 2, 1993, the committee commu-nicated its "findings of fact" to UNH President Dale Nitzschke, concluding that Silva indeed "used two sexually explicit examples in his technical writ-ing class." It reported that Silva was unrepentant: "When asked if he would use the same examples to illustrate technical writing in the future, he replied he would do it again 'tomorrow.'" The panel added (failing to disclose that this event had resulted in no charges) that in 1990, Silva had been told by his director that he had erred in discussing a "Dear Abby" column on sexual matters. It concluded, therefore, that not only had Silva "violated the UNH Sexual Harassment Policy," but that "this is the second time in a two-year period that Professor Silva had been formally notified about his use of inappropriate and sexually explicit remarks in the classroom." The committee recommended the following sanctions: 1) suspension for one year without pay; 2) reimbursement by Silva to the University for all costs associated with his behavior, including the creation of alternative sections; 3) participation in "counseling sessions . . . selected by the University of New Hampshire, for a minimum of one year at his own expense"; 4) no "attempts to retaliate" against the complaining students; and 5) a written apology to the complainants "for creating a hostile and offensive environment." (In short, his job, his pay, his soul, his rights of legal redress, and his conscience.) Silva appealed this decision to the UNH Appeals Board (three professors and two students), which, on April 14, 1993, upheld the conviction and the sentence, minus the reimbursement and the letter of apology. Silva asked for injunctive relief from the U.S. District Court.

On September 15, 1994, Senior District Judge Shane Devine ruled that UNH immediately must restore Silva to his rightful classroom place. The court resolved a number of factual matters, above all, that "claims based on 'the age and sophistication' of students" did not apply, "because the students . . . are exclusively adult college students" and that "Silva's statements advanced his valid educational objective of conveying certain principles related to the subject matter of his course [and] were made in a professionally appropriate manner as part of a college class lecture." The deepest part of the court's decision, however, touched upon fundamental First Amendment questions. It applied the U.S. Supreme Court's doctrine that the fact that some individuals find the speech of others "offensive" may not abrogate a First Amendment "which does not tolerate laws that cast a pall of orthodoxy over the classroom." UNH's policy "employs an impermissibly subjective standard that fails to take into account the nation's interest in academic freedom." Citing the Supreme Court in *Keyishian* (see chapter 2), the district court chastised all who have tolerated "verbal conduct" bans at almost all of our colleges and universities: "The essentiality of freedom in the community of American universities is almost self-evident. . . . Scholarship cannot flourish in an atmosphere of suspicion and distrust. Teachers and students must always remain free to inquire, to study, and to evaluate, to gain new maturity and understanding; otherwise our civilization will stagnate and die." In the light of that fundamental doctrine of jurisprudence and freedom, "the court finds and rules that the application of the UNH Sexual Harassment Policy to Silva's classroom statements violates the First Amendment." Speaking for Silva's "liberty interests" and for his "good name, reputation, honor, [and] integrity," the court vacated UNH's suspension, creation of shadow classes, letter of reprimand, and conditions of return, including counseling. In early December 1994, UNH reinstated him permanently, restored his $60,000 in back salary, paid his $170,000 in legal fees, removed all reference to sexual harassment from his file, and decided not to risk filing an appeal.[8]

Three aspects of this case are worth pondering. First, there was Silva's rare decision to fight against the injustice done to him, where most professors would have accepted, in silence, a university's private censure and coerced counseling. Silva underwent two and a half years of public embarrassment and anxiety. If he had not won his case, he would have faced $170,000 in legal expenses for his defiance and certain termination for his refusal to accept penitently the condition of his reemployment. Second, there is UNH's conviction of Silva. Before being judged in a federal court, Silva had been tried by his peers at the University of New Hampshire. The gap between those two decisions is the gap between what now passes for academic justice and the decent rule of law. Thomas Carnicelli, professor of English at UNH, commenting upon the moral significance of Silva's conviction by two hearing boards of faculty and students, noted that it was not some conspiracy of zealots who had packed the campus judicial boards. Quoted in the *New York Review of Books,* he observed that, rather, "a perfectly decent group of people, because of the climate, or the way they were trained, or something, made this incredibly unjust decision. Even the good people can't see clearly anymore."[9] Third, there are the people who create that climate, in which even the good can't see clearly anymore. That same *New York Review of Books* article, discussing the debate at UNH about the harassment policy, quoted Barbara White, professor of women's studies, who gave honest voice to the view of free speech so widely influential on our campuses. In a letter to several groups at UNH, she wrote:

Academia . . . has traditionally been dominated by white heterosexual men, and the First Amendment and Academic Freedom (FAF) traditionally have protected the rights of white heterosexual men. Most of us are silenced by existing social conditions before we get the power to speak out in any way where FAF might protect us. So forgive us if we don't get all teary-eyed about FAF. Perhaps to you it's as sacrosanct as the flag or the national anthem; to us strict construction of the First Amendment is just another yoke around our necks.[10]

———————

Occasionally, the cultural Left reaps what it sows and learns a lesson about the importance of equal protections. Toni Blake, a female graduate student at the University of Nebraska–Lincoln, was an instructor teaching a course on human sexuality in 1993.[11] As Professor David Moshman, president of the Academic Freedom Coalition of Nebraska, reported to the university's Academic Senate, Blake, while teaching about contraception, "used a banana for a standard demonstration on condom application." Further, to make a point about the dangers of impregnation even prior to ejaculation, Blake "joked that men, like basketball players, 'dribble before they shoot.'" A male student accused Blake of "sexual harassment," charging "that she 'objectified' the penis" and created "a hostile environment for him as a man."

For his *Village Voice* column of January 18, 1994, Nat Hentoff interviewed Blake, who told him how this charge, placed in her record, would harm her professionally. Blake had consulted with her department head, and they decided that while the charges were active, she should delete material on human sexuality from her courses. As Blake explained to Hentoff, the silencing of her went well beyond that: "I'm not going to teach human sexuality again. Not in the state of Nebraska. I'm not going through that again."

Such acts of self-censorship are rarely discussed, and do not become "quantifiable," so individuals who care about liberty have to weigh the qualitative issues. Nebraska's encouragement of self-censorship could not have been made any clearer than by the opinion of the university general counsel, Richard Wood, which Moshman reported to the Academic Senate with dismay: "University administrators have broad authority to censor the [faculty's] expression of offensive ideas in or out of the classroom." Moshman warned that such views already had taken their toll: "I have heard report of three cases in which [UN] faculty apparently deleted units from their regular courses that they feared might include or elicit statements offensive to some students. The deleted topics were race, gender, and rape." As Moshman concluded, these might "represent just the tip of the iceberg of chilled expression at the University of Nebraska."[12]

The Achilles' heel of abusive power, however, is that it always goes too far. When drunk with power, censors state their claims honestly, and to justify them they call upon their lawyers to put the patina of legality on those claims, as General Counsel Wood did. Only then do faculty sometimes understand that all of their individual rights are at risk. Rick Duncan, professor of law at Nebraska, appreciated that Wood's statement made clear, at last, the full implications of a repressive university. Introducing a resolution to the Academic Senate, he said: "events culminating in the Wood memo curtailing faculty freedom of speech seem to me by far the most serious threat to intellectual freedom that the University has faced in my 16 years on its faculty." On December 14, 1993, the Academic Senate unanimously passed a declaration of concern about "violations of free speech and academic freedom on campus," rejected Wood's view of the university's regulation of free expression, and urged the administration and faculty to "refrain from censorship and promote a marketplace of ideas on campus for the entire University community." When Wood stated his case frankly, Moshman and Duncan— defenders of liberty, a rarity these days—had their tactical moment, and they took advantage of it.[13]

Repression occurs along the whole spectrum of American higher education. David Ayers was, until May 1992, assistant professor of sociology at Dallas Baptist University (DBU), a conservative Christian University.[14] Ayers, a conservative Christian thinker, had written an essay critical of modern feminism that had been published in a collection named Book of the Year by the journal *Christianity Today*. The article argued that patriarchy was the condition of every well-documented society, that its roots are biological, that women gravitate naturally toward domestic life, and that the feminist call for a gender-neutral organization of society both is unnatural and flies in the face of all social evidence.

Each semester, DBU held a faculty colloquium on matters of scholarly or public interest. In the fall of 1991, the vice president of academic affairs at DBU, Edward Pauley, asked Ayers to present a summary of his article on feminism and a response to the sorts of criticisms it had received. Ayers agreed, copied his talk, and circulated it among the faculty. Feminists at DBU organized a boycott of the colloquium, where attendance was sparse. Pauley introduced Ayers and asked explicitly, "If faculty can't talk forthrightly to each other [here], where can anyone talk forthrightly to each other?" In the course of his talk, Ayers picked up on that theme, lamenting the "aggressive censorship" he found in studies of gender, and calling for an academic world in which "disagreement was welcome."

In response to ongoing anger over Ayers's talk, President Gary Cook and Vice President Pauley announced the organization of an unprecedented second faculty colloquium that semester, for purposes of criticism of Ayers's presentation. This meeting was open to all and well attended by over one hundred faculty members, administrators, and students. The speaker criticized Ayers severely and circulated her paper after the talk, but this was insufficient for Ayers's severest enemies. When Ayers learned from students in his own sociology class that he was the subject of personal attacks in various algebra, English, and physical education classes, he offered his students copies of his critic's paper, which she herself had distributed without restriction at the colloquium, and he put the tape recordings of his and his critic's talks—both of which already were on sale at DBU's media center—on reserve at the DBU library. Shortly after this, Pam Moore, the "Director of Intercessory Prayer" at DBU, formally charged Ayers with defaming a faculty member and with disclosing the confidential materials of a faculty colloquium.

President Cook appointed an ad hoc committee to discuss these charges with Ayers, who immediately requested to have his case heard on the basis of established procedures, written notification, specification of the charges against him, and knowledge of the identity of his accusers. He had not even been told the names of the members of the ad hoc committee, which, in fact, included Cook himself, Pauley (as chair), Moore (the complaining director of intercessory prayer), several vociferous critics of Ayers's paper, and various administrators. Pauley eventually sent Ayers a memo specifying the charges against him: distribution of his critic's (already circulated) paper to his students; placing of the (publicly sold) tapes on library reserve; discussion of the faculty colloquium during class time; and making "harsh" references to his critic's criticisms in his class.

Ayers's courageous dean, John Jeffrey, professor of psychology, sent a memo to all college deans at DBU, informing them of the irregular charges and proceedings, and inviting them to consider the "serious questions regarding academic protocol, academic due process, and academic freedom." In response, Pauley canceled the scheduled meeting of the ad hoc committee and directed Dean Jeffrey himself both to investigate the charges against Ayers and to reach a specific conclusion: "As far as an outcome of this inquiry is concerned, I believe an apology . . . from Professor Ayers is in order." Dean Jeffrey, refusing to participate, replied: "Even if all the charges President Cook has made against Dave Ayers were true, none would represent any perceivable wrongdoing in light of our Faculty Handbook, and the AAUP guidelines. . . . For me to investigate charges in which there is no hint of impropriety would in itself constitute a violation of academic freedom. . . . I am recommending that Dave Ayers seek legal counsel at this juncture." One week later, DBU's administration delivered by hand letters of termination, signed by Vice President Pauley, who had invited Ayers to speak in the first place, to David Ayers, and to Dean John Jeffrey. No reasons for the firings were specified. They both were given one working day to vacate their offices. In short, six weeks after expressing his beliefs about feminism as the invited speaker at a faculty colloquium, David Ayers was fired, and his dean, who had sought to defend his academic freedom, was fired with him. Joseph Salemi, of the University Center for Rational Alternatives, invited academics and others to examine the memos, letters, papers, and tape recordings in which this frightful case is chronicled. These events were covered locally and in Baptist circles, discussed in the *Dallas Morning News,* the *Fort Worth Star-Telegram,* the *Baptist Press,* and the *Baptist Standard,* in the spring and summer of 1992. The case, however, received no significant national attention. Most academics on the Left still can recite the names of McCarthy's victims. They have not heard of Ayers, nor of the principled John Jeffrey.

Suppression of speech is nonsectarian, however. One of the most revealing cases occurred at the opposite pole of Protestant theology from DBU, at the doctrinally and politically liberal Chicago Theological Seminary, closely tied to the United Church of Christ. By February 1992, Graydon Snyder, sixty-one, a biblical scholar, tenured professor of New Testament theology and former dean at the seminary, had been teaching religion for thirty-four years, the last eight at Chicago.[15] To teach the crucial distinction between motive and act, Snyder referred his class on religion to the two textual examples he had cited for thirty-four years. The first was from the Sermon on the Mount, in which the commission by a man of adultery "in his heart" was morally indistinguishable from the act of adultery itself. The second example was from the Talmud, the body of Jewish law supplementary to the Torah. Snyder cited, for his class, the well-known Talmudic example of an unwilled act. A man is fixing his roof. It is an extremely hot day, so the man is naked. Below his roof, a woman, also naked, is lying in the sun. An unexpected gust of wind blows the man off the roof and, in landing on the woman, he penetrates her sexually. According to the Talmud, Snyder noted, the roofer's responsibility was very limited, because his offense was wholly unwilled and unpremeditated. As Snyder explained to his class, "The New Testament says that if you think about doing the act, you've done it. The Talmud says that if you do the act, but didn't think about it, you didn't do it." As Snyder later would tell the *Washington Post,* "I was trying to deal with the Sermon on the Mount and Judaism, not modern problems."[16]

A female student in Snyder's class accused him of exonerating rapists by his distinction, formally complaining that "men are always saying that they don't intend to do any harm and in fact they do." Snyder, she judged, "gave support to men who abused women." The case was taken up by the Seminary's Sexual Harassment Task Force, which charged Snyder with having created an "intimidating, hostile, or offensive . . . working environment," and with "verbal conduct of a sexual nature [that] unreasonably interfered with" a student's work. After meeting with the task force, Snyder wrote a letter to the student—whom he has refused to identify—saying that he regretted any pain he might have caused her, but that his discussion had been appropriate. The seminary reached its verdict in March 1993. It placed Snyder on probation, ordered him to undergo psychotherapy, advised him not to be alone with any students or staff, prohibited him from teaching introductory Bible courses, and sent a letter to all 250 students and faculty, informing them that Snyder was being punished for sexual harassment. Snyder spent one year attempting to have the finding reversed. Then he filed a lawsuit for defamation against the seminary, not the student. Snyder's suit was dismissed, for lack of judicial power to intervene in a religious seminary. The final verdict, however, is in the court of public opinion. The *Boston Globe* editorialized on March 24, 1994: "It is not the ecumenical professor who needs therapy. The ones who need to understand the harm they have done are the inquisitors who sit on the seminary's sexual harassment panel." [17] One of Snyder's attorneys, however, explained the limited impact of only an occasional newspaper editorial on the potentially powerful court of public opinion. He told the *Washington Post,* "For every professor who fights these things, there are literally hundreds who are having their speech chilled." [18]

The ultimate freedom of expression that we all possess—and an essential means of fighting back—is to criticize those whom we believe to be our unfair persecutors, loudly and publicly. One of the potential dilemmas of being charged with harassment, however, is that most codes prohibit "reprisal" or "retaliation," usually undefined, against one's accusers. Too often, the prohibition against "retaliation" means that someone may not even speak vigorously in his or her own defense. Consider, in this light, the case of Richard Osborne, a tenured faculty member at Mesabi Community College, a part of the Minnesota Community College System.[19] In academic year 1992–93, Osborne was accused of sexual harassment by five college counselors with whom he had vigorously disagreed about matters of curriculum and academic policy. Typical of the complaints, as revealed by court records, was the following:

CURRICULUM MEETING 2/19/92: At this meeting Pat Sterle and Beth Wagner presented a proposal for a 2-credit summer college orientation course. . . . Osborne argued in a very attacking manner against approval of the course with statements like, "this course has no academic legitimacy." . . . He also made a motion to table the proposal indefinitely, even though the course was proposed for that academic year. The tone and content of Osborne's remarks were combative and had the effect of questioning the professionalism, integrity and competence of Sterle and Wagner. . . . Both Wagner and Sterle felt "shell shocked" and humiliated as a result of the meeting.

Indeed, because it is important to know what passes for sexual harassment on campuses these days, one charge complained that after Osborne questioned the academic value of a course at a faculty meeting, "Sterle felt both isolated and demeaned in this meeting with her co-workers," and that, indeed, "when the vote was taken on a motion to disapprove the course, Sterle's was the only dissenting vote heard."

Remarkably, Mesabi hired an outside attorney to investigate the charges. The investigator, Penelope Phillips, examined every single incident described by the complainants and concluded that no incident constituted sexual harassment or gender bias. However, she cited Osborne for "reprisal" against the complainants. As punishment of the forbidden "reprisal," Greg Braxton-Brown, president of the community college of which Mesabi was a part, issued a formal letter of reprimand, which became a part of Osborne's official file. What were the illegal acts of "reprisal"? Osborne, knowing that the charges had arisen from intellectual disagreements over academic policy, read a summary of the complaint against him to a meeting of the Faculty Association on March 22, 1993, expressing his concern about the use of the college's harassment policy to silence free discussion of curricular and other academic matters. On March 23, Osborne had circulated a memo to faculty members, expressing his belief that the filing and serious reception of the complaint against him had threatened all of their academic freedoms by using "the System's sexual harassment complaint process" as a "politically-motivated attempt to silence my opposition to what I (and many of you) have regarded as ill-considered policy." If this "act of academic terrorism" were successful, Osborne warned his colleagues, they all would be deprived of "the most cherished freedom of you and every other educator at Mesabi and elsewhere: the right freely and in good faith to dispute among ourselves any and all issues of political, social, and educational policy." Finally, he was reprimanded for having made "a joke" about one of the complainants. In short, the harassment charges against him were judged baseless, but his false accusers were home free, and he was reprimanded for having spoken in his own defense. Indeed, his official personnel file now contained this letter from Braxton-Brown:

> The following actions on your part constitute reprisal: 1. Making a mean-spirited joke about one of the complainants after you received notice that a complaint of sexual harassment had been filed. 2. Reading a summary of the complaint to the entire Faculty Association after being advised to keep the matter confidential. 3. Preparing and distributing a memorandum about the issues raised in the complaint and further embarrassing the complainants. The effect of your actions was to intimidate, embarrass, and harass the complainants. This conduct constitutes reprisal . . . [and] any future violations of college or System policies . . . may result in more serious disciplinary action.[20]

After Osborne's academic appeal was denied on August 9 by Bernardine Bryant, chancellor of the Minnesota Community College system, he filed suit in the U.S. District Court of Minnesota for injunctive and declaratory relief from the reprimand. Faced with a genuine lawsuit and an untenable case, the Minnesota Community College system quickly reached a settlement with Osborne. Most of its terms are confidential, but the public part was telling enough: the letter of reprimand was revoked; all references to the incident were removed from his file; and he received full attorneys' fees and court costs. Meanwhile, legal discovery revealed the "mean-spirited joke" that Osborne had told: "Mr. Osborne . . . made a joke about Ms. Delich [one of the complainants] saying that Ms. Delich allegedly threw a pen at [a] former employee." That's it, in toto. Things are not light on American campuses.

Ethnicity and Race

Judith Kleinfeld, professor of psychology at the University of Alaska–Fairbanks, had dedicated a great part of her life and research to the education of indigenous Alaskans. In September 1991, invited by a university regent and dean to discuss teacher education with a small group of school board members and citizens, she expressed her concern that the educational system often failed native students, not preparing them adequately for teaching positions in the job market. In her opinion, there were "equity pressures on professors to graduate native students" prematurely. When her

comments reached campus, there were public rallies against her "racism."
The University of Alaska–Fairbanks opened an investigation of her statements and forbade her from teaching classes in the education department.
Although the university's investigation eventually concluded, months later,
that there were no grounds for disciplinary action, the harm to Professor
Kleinfeld was done then and there by the very opening of an investigation
and by barring her from classes she had taught for years.

Some members of the university, however, decided to file charges with
the Office of Civil Rights (OCR) of the U.S. Department of Education,
which in April 1992 commenced an investigation of a complaint that she had
made discriminatory statements against "Native American students."[21] President Bush was fond of denouncing "political correctness," but perhaps he
should have looked a bit closer to home. On April 9, 1992, his OCR informed the university and Kleinfeld that it had opened a formal investigation.
Even though the OCR's exonerative decision of August 7, 1992, observed in
the first paragraph that the complaint concerned "remarks in a public meeting regarding grading practices," it claimed that "OCR is required by law to
investigate complaints whenever a complaint is filed [alleging] a possible failure to comply with Title VI." Thus, even Kleinfeld's patently proper exercise
of her academic expertise and judgment—ruled by the OCR to constitute
"legitimate business dialogue, discourse, and exchange of views"—resulted
not only in a university proceeding, but in a four-month government investigation that cost her, by her own calculation, "thousands of dollars in lawyer's
fees." Professor Kleinfeld's words speak volumes about the effects of such pressures against "incorrect" speech: "I am afraid that if I say or write anything remotely controversial, OCR will use my speech against me in subsequent
investigations." Kleinfeld remains "concerned that the university . . . will endeavor to prevent me from speaking in the future in my area of expertise,
teacher education and the education of Native students." She notes that "the
pressures on me to censor my speech come both from OCR and the university," and that, in response, she now has "declined to address in even the
broadest of terms the educational issues that affect Native students." On campus, "I constantly worry about what I can say in the classroom and how I
should respond when students express controversial views."[22]

Gerald Gee was a white assistant professor of public relations at Florida
A&M University, a historically (and predominantly) black university.[23] On
September 20, 1993, the students in his public relations class were discussing
whether or not the university gave them adequate practical experience for
their careers. Gee was saddened by a sense of fatalism that he heard. An or-

dained Methodist priest, Gee had taught students at A&M for seventeen years, and he thought he knew both their concerns and their slang. According to his sworn, uncontested testimony, he told his students that what he was about to say wasn't "directed at any of you, or all of you as a class," but was offered as food for thought. One cannot, he implored, "in this day and age . . . sit around waiting" for a break. Anyone who didn't "take advantage of the opportunities that are there, or who doesn't make opportunities . . . may be guilty of having what some would call a 'nigger mentality'—the sort of thinking that can keep us all on the back of the bus forever."

The phrase, "nigger mentality," of course, however unfortunate, is a term of some currency among black students, often used by militants (and, indeed, rap singers) to deride any perceived fatalism or submission among other blacks. Six of the students in Gee's class, however, complained to the administration. Richard Hogg, provost and vice president for academic affairs, with no investigation, immediately wrote to Gee's dean that "we do not need nor can we tolerate professor[s] in the classroom who are insensitive to the demands of the racially and culturally diverse social environment that we have on our campus." He declared Gee's remark to be "almost beyond comprehension." After an investigation, the university's president, Frederick S. Humphries, wrote to Gee that his contract would not be renewed. Humphries explained that Gee had violated, among other things, A&M's harassment and nondiscrimination policies. Gee filed a grievance, and the Office of Human Resources of the Florida Board of Regents ruled that Gee had been denied due process in the procedures that had led to his termination. In fall 1994, Carrie Gavin, an equal opportunity officer at the university, conducted an investigation. She reported to Humphries that Gee had engaged in "premeditated use of racial slurs that were directed against students in his class." Humphries agreed, and in April 1995, after seventeen years of devoted service and professional honors, Gee was fired, effective after his final year of contract, 1995–96.

Aided by the Center for Individual Rights, Gee sued for relief. Before the U.S. District Court for the Northern District of Florida, the university administration claimed, in March 1995, that "a different standard was not applied to plaintiff because he is white." Documents produced by subpoena, however, revealed that in his October 26, 1993, report to President Humphries, Provost Hogg wrote that Gee's belief that he was close enough to his students to say what he had said, reflected, in Hogg's view, "Gee's lack of understanding of the dynamics of race relations." Humphries's official letter had explained that his nonrenewal resulted primarily from the statement "which [Gee] as a white professor" had made. Further, according to an interview that Humphries gave to Dorothy J. Gaiter of the *Wall Street Journal,* he conceded, in Gaiter's paraphrase, that "Mr. Gee wouldn't be under threat of firing had he been black." In President Humphries's words: "If he had been black, the reaction would not have been the same. . . . There are words in the white community that are used and white people don't react to them, but they would be extremely offensive if someone else uses them."[24] As Gee told *Jet* magazine, he truly was sorry that anyone had been hurt by this, but "I'm not admitting any guilt over misuse of language. I've got a right to use terms that other people use."[25] That phrase, however, "a right to use terms that other people use," is morally, if not always legally correct. In November 1996, U.S. District Court Judge Robert Hinkle granted summary judgment to the university. Gee's speech about state of mind and black success, the judge ruled, was not entitled to First Amendment protection because it addressed no matter of "public concern." In 1997, a panel of the Eleventh Circuit Court of Appeals upheld that puzzling finding, which now is under further appeal by Gee and the Center for Individual Rights.

In September 1997, the University of North Texas meted out a lesser penalty to Professor Don Staples, a tenured professor of film. At a university forum on ways to improve the experience of minority students, a black undergraduate complained that courses contained inadequate materials by minorities. Staples replied that his own course incorporated a large number of contributions by black filmmakers, but that minority students in his class still had poor attendance. For that remark, the university suspended Staples for one week. Chancellor Alfred F. Hurley wrote a memo explaining that while free speech would be protected, "racism will not be tolerated."[26]

By contrast, in the fall of 1997, the white but politically correct president of the University of Florida, John Lombardi, called Adam Herbert, the incoming moderate black chancellor of the entire Florida state university system (of which Florida A&M University is a part), an "oreo," explaining that this meant a black person who acts like a white person. When a few trustees expressed their outrage and their doubts about Lombardi's fitness for his presidency, black students rallied to the progressive Lombardi's support. Lombardi issued a public apology in December 1997, describing his remarks as an "inexcusable error." He was excused, and he remains the president of Florida's flagship university.[27] Gee has not been excused, and he remains fired.

Race, of course, is one of the profoundest and most disturbing issues in American life, which is precisely why we so desperately need to hear each other's honest opinions. If at colleges and universities—dedicated, in theory, to unfettered inquiry and discussion—we seek to silence both curiosity and expression about race, we are in difficulty, indeed. In this regard, few cases have been more disturbing than those of Professors Michael Levin, Leonard Jeffries, and Linda Gottfredson.

Levin and Jeffries both taught at City College of New York (CCNY), part of the City University of New York. They are individuals of categorically different styles and minds. Both men were (and are) tenured professors at a public university. Both expressed views—outside of the classroom—that offended others. Both became the objects, from opposite sides of the spectrum, of attempts to punish thought with which one does not agree.

Michael Levin had been teaching philosophy at CCNY since 1969.[28] Between 1987 and 1990, he stated three beliefs that made his status at the college intensely controversial. In a letter to the *New York Times* (January 11, 1987), he asserted that, from crime statistics, it was rational and ethical for New York shopkeepers to use buzzers to admit or bar individuals on the basis of race. In an article in the Australian scholarly journal *Quadrant* (January–February, 1989), he claimed that whites as a group were inherently more intelligent than blacks as a group. In a letter to *American Philosophical Association Proceedings* (January 1990), he argued that the disproportionately low number of blacks in philosophy was not the result of discrimination but, rather, of significant average differences in IQ.

In response to uproars occasioned by news of those remarks, CCNY took a series of steps involving Levin's faculty status. In the fall of 1988, Dean Paul Sherwin and philosophy chairman Martin Tamney forbade Levin from teaching his introductory philosophy courses. At almost the same time, the Faculty Senate voted 61 to 3 to censure Levin formally for his expressed beliefs. Levin filed a grievance about his teaching status, and the Professional Staff Congress found in his favor, ruling that departmental chairs must make teaching assignments solely on academic grounds. In the fall of 1989, thus, the new chairman of philosophy, Charles Evans, assigned Levin to teach Introduction to Philosophy in the spring. Dean Sherwin, however, wrote a letter on February 1, 1990, to all of Levin's thirty-eight students, characterizing Levin as holding "controversial views on such issues as race, feminism, and homosexuality," informing them that "the Faculty Senate of the College registered its opposition to written statements by Professor Levin," and announcing the creation of "a second . . . section" in which students now could register, "taking into consideration the rights and sensitivities of all concerned" (thirty out of Levin's thirty-eight students chose to remain in his class). On May 4, 1990, Bernard Harleston, president of CCNY, appointed a special committee of six faculty members and one dean "to review the question of when speech both in and outside the classroom may go beyond the protection of academic freedom or become conduct unbecoming a member of the faculty [an offense for which one may lose tenure and be fired], or some other form of misconduct." He instructed the committee "to review information concerning Professor Michael Levin . . . and Professor Leonard Jeffries . . . and to [make] recommendations concerning . . . the response of the College." Michael Levin's fairness as a teacher was not at issue. Indeed, the letter to Levin's students explicitly stated: "I am aware of no evidence suggesting that Professor Levin's views on controversial matters have compromised his performance as an able teacher of Philosophy who is fair in his treatment of students." The only question was CCNY's response to Levin's beliefs as expressed in major journals of opinion.

When CCNY (and CUNY) rejected Levin's argument that the formation of a committee to investigate his views on public issues itself impinged upon his academic freedom, he turned to the U.S. District Court for injunctive relief, raising, in addition, the issue of the special treatment of his teaching. CCNY argued that there was nothing "chilling" of Levin's free speech in a committee to investigate his statements of his beliefs and to advise the president about when such beliefs might or might not rise to grounds for dismissal. The college also argued that its unprecedented "shadow class" for Levin's students encouraged more not less free speech.

District Court Judge Kenneth Conboy disagreed with CCNY, and on September 12, 1991, he granted Levin preliminary injunctive relief. He found that Levin's First and Fourteenth Amendment rights had been violated. He permanently prohibited CCNY "from creating . . . 'shadow or parallel' sections [and] from commencing or threatening to commence any disciplinary proceedings . . . or other investigation predicated solely upon Professor Levin's protected expression of ideas." CCNY appealed, and on June 8, 1992, the U.S. Court of Appeals for the Second Circuit unanimously upheld the heart of Conboy's view of Levin's constitutional rights. The court agreed that "the shadow classes 'were established with the intent and consequence of stigmatizing Professor Levin solely because of his expression of ideas.'" It noted that CCNY's "encouragement of the continued erosion in the size of Professor Levin's class if he does not mend his extracurricular ways is the antithesis of freedom of expression" and produced a "chilling effect on Professor Levin's activities."

Both courts stressed what had been learned factually about CCNY's formation of the committee to investigate Levin. President Harleston had charged it, from the start, "to determine whether Professor Levin's views affected his teaching ability." Writing that "the process of removing a tenured professor is a difficult one," he had observed that Levin's "views are offensive to the basic values of human equality and decency and simply have no place here at City College." As both courts noted, Harleston's language—"when speech both in and outside the classroom may go beyond the protection of academic freedom or become conduct unbecoming a member of the faculty"—formally invited the punishment of the expression of protected opinions.

The defense of Levin's rights involved a broad legal coalition: the Center for Individual Rights, which provided Levin's primary attorney; the AAUP, which filed a brief on Levin's behalf; the ACLU and the Thomas Jefferson Center for the Protection of Free Expression, which both filed friend-of-the-court briefs on Levin's behalf. Again, a college had to be taught how far removed it was from the larger society's commitment to liberty and legal equality.

The case of Professor Leonard Jeffries, chairman of black studies at CCNY, was similar to the Levin case in form, though radically different in content.[29] Jeffries simultaneously suffered and benefitted from the prior uproar over the Levin affair. On the one hand, having moved against the Jewish Levin for expressions of belief about blacks, CCNY clearly felt obliged to move against the black Jeffries for expressions of beliefs about, among others, Jews. Thus does one persecution logically require yet another. On the other hand, the success of Levin's appeals to the federal courts made CCNY more wary about how far it could go.

Leonard Jeffries, like Michael Levin, had begun teaching at CCNY in 1969. His career had been meteoric, and by 1972, he was chairman of black studies, a post that he maintained for two decades. Jeffries was a leading "Afrocentric" scholar, a fact of which CCNY had been fully aware. In his classes, he taught that the descendants of Europeans were materialistic, greedy, and domineering "ice people," while descendants of Africans were humane and communal "sun people." He also taught that an abundance of melanin made blacks intellectually and physically superior to whites, and that AIDS was created by whites as part of a conspiracy to annihilate blacks. CCNY was well aware of the nature of his courses, and none of this had prevented him from frequent reappointments as chairman of black studies. If CCNY found such teaching incompatible with intellectual merit, it had had a very long period of time in which to act on that judgment.

In May 1990, Harleston had paired Levin and Jeffries in his request for advice about the limits of free speech, indicating that he already was well aware of Jeffries's controversial classroom style and content. In March 1991, the committee, with the district court in Levin's case now watching, reported to the president, rebuking Levin and Jeffries for "outrageous and possibly offensive" statements, but recommending that CCNY take no disciplinary action against them. Less than four months later, Harleston reappointed Jeffries to a new three-year term as chairman of black studies. On July 1, 1991, Harleston wrote to Jeffries: "I am confident that with your assistance and guidance . . . we will continue to serve the students . . . of the City College as an educational institution of the highest quality." When Jeffries's persecution began, thus, the work of the investigative committee was done, and CCNY already had decided that his qualifications merited further service as departmental chairman.

In the summer of 1991, however, Jeffries spoke in Albany, at the Empire State Black Arts and Cultural Festival. He asserted that the Russian Jews, in collaboration with the Mafia, "their financial partners," dominated Hollywood and encouraged the nation to hate blacks. He argued that Jews had been major participants in the slave trade. He referred to his CCNY colleague Bernard Sohmer as "the head Jew." News of the speech caused outrage among politicians, in the media, and on campus. In September 1991, the Faculty Senate voted not to censure Jeffries, but it did pass a motion to "disavow and reject" what it termed his "abhorrent anti-Semitic and anti-Italian sentiments." In that same week, President Harleston asked the provost of CCNY to explore whether Jeffries should remain chairman. In March 1992, the public and, above all, media controversy still unabated, Harleston announced that he would advise the trustees to limit Jeffries's term to just one year instead of the usual three. On March 23, the trustees appointed a new chairman to begin in July. In June, Jeffries sued in federal court for violation of his constitutional rights.

CCNY had learned a great deal from Levin's case. Instead of initiating a new inquiry into Jeffries's fitness as faculty member, it merely sought to limit the term of his chairmanship. Rather than suggesting that the exercise of his free speech raised questions about "conduct unbecoming," it argued that it wholly respected his unfettered freedom of expression and had acted solely from a concern that his chairmanship "hampered the effective and efficient operation of the School." The federal district court jury that heard the case in 1993 did not believe CCNY. It found that Jeffries's speech of July 30, 1991, was "a substantial or motivating factor" in the removal of his chairmanship, and that he never would have been denied a full term if he had not made his highly publicized speech. On an issue that would become the grounds for CCNY's ultimately successful appeal of this verdict, however, the jury, as a finding of fact, ruled that although CCNY had not demonstrated that Jeffries's speech "hampered the effective and efficient operation" of any academic unit, it nonetheless had been motivated by such a belief.

CCNY asked District Court Judge Conboy, who had decided the Levin case, to vacate the jury's verdict. On August 4, 1993, Conboy upheld the heart of the decision and ordered Jeffries reinstated as chairman of black studies. CCNY appealed to the United States Court of Appeals for the Second Circuit, which on April 19, 1994, upheld the reinstatement on constitutional grounds. Indeed, the circuit court explicitly noted that, given the Levin case, CCNY surely should have known that it could not punish Jeffries for speech on matters of public concern. In the interim, however, early in 1994, the U.S. Supreme Court, in a controversial ruling destined to have unintended consequences, decided *Waters v. Churchill*, holding that "public employers," toward the goal of "effective and efficient administration," could demote or discipline "public employees" if the employers reasonably believed that the employees' speech would disrupt the efficient functioning of the public workplace. CCNY appealed the Jeffries case to the U.S. Supreme Court, arguing that *Waters v. Churchill* supported its right to remove Jeffries from the chairmanship. In November 1994, the Supreme Court noncommitally ordered the Court of Appeals to reevaluate the Jeffries case in light of *Waters v. Churchill*. When the Court of Appeals did that, it found that the jury's earlier finding—that CCNY had a reasonable expectation that Jeffries's chairmanship would disrupt "the effective and efficient administration" of CCNY—made the demotion of Jeffries constitutional.[30] Because the Supreme Court did not revisit the case itself, it never had the occasion to rule on whether or not the Court of Appeals had extended *Waters* inappropriately to an academic setting, an issue that still remains unsettled.

The Jeffries case should serve as a corrective to three dangerous misperceptions: the claim of the cultural Right that universities and courts constitute a uniform system forever privileging the cultural Left (Jeffries, not Levin, was punished for his beliefs); the claim of many on the cultural Left that their own protections lie in local power and case-by-case subjective adjudications, not in a general commitment to free expression; and the claim that Left and Right cannot unite in defense of freedom itself. Just as the liberal ACLU had filed a friend-of-the-court brief on behalf of Levin, so had the conservative Center for Individual Rights and the conservative Individual Rights Foundation filed friend-of-the-court briefs on behalf of Jeffries.

No case is more instructive about the assault on academic freedom, however, than the attempt to silence and punish Professor Linda Gottfredson at the University of Delaware for her scientific inquiries.[31] Gottfredson, a psychological and sociological researcher in the school of education, promoted to full professor by her university, works on intelligence, aptitude testing, and the uses of testing in employment. On the basis of that specific work, she was named a Fellow of the Society of Industrial and Organizational Psychology, and, for the significance of her work in general, she was named a Fellow of the American Psychological Association. Given the minefield surrounding all research into intelligence and testing, because it always threatens to intersect agendas touching upon aggregate racial differences, there are few sources of funding in the field. One of the major sources is the Pioneer Fund, which in current times has underwritten the significant work of Thomas Bouchard, at the University of Minnesota, on identical twins; of Richard Lynn, at the University of Ulster, on worldwide increases in intelligence; of Robert Gordon, at Johns Hopkins, on the demography of crime rates; and of Seymour Itzkoff, at Smith College, on the evolution of human intelligence. At Delaware, the Pioneer Fund supported Linda Gottfredson's research into the implications of differences in ability for employment policy.

What makes Gottfredson particularly controversial in academic circles is her conclusion that public policy should ignore racial classifications, make meritocratic judgments of individuals as individuals, and end the practice of "race-norming," whereby tested individuals are admitted to educational or employment positions by their rank within a racial group rather than within the overall applicant pool. The policy implications that she derives from her research certainly are shared by significant elements of American opinion, and, what is more important, are clear instances of freedom of expression on matters of intellectual interest and, of course, of public concern. The Pioneer Fund, Gottfredson's work, and her opposition to race-norming all became controversial at Delaware, which is how things ought to be on matters of intense public debate. Some of that controversy, however, starting in 1989, culminated in official complaints and investigations. In 1990, the university sought to prevent her from doing her Pioneer Fund–sponsored research at the university.

The Pioneer Fund had been founded in the 1930s, and U.S. Supreme Court Justice John Marshall Harlan sat on its first board of trustees. It was created to support "research and teaching," and its name was derived from its initial charter on teaching (later amended to remove the word "white"), which stated that "in selecting [recipients of scholarships], unless the directors deem it inadvisable, consideration shall be given to children who are deemed to be descended predominantly from white persons who settled in the original thirteen states." In fact, the Pioneer Fund had awarded scholarships only once, at the time of World War II, and had done so on a nondiscriminatory basis. Delaware knew that fact, but official intrauniversity memos and reports wrote of the Pioneer Fund as "white only" and as devoted to the "reproduction of whites." In fact, of course, it was the University of Delaware itself that had been a segregated, whites only institution in the 1930s and beyond.

Looking at the history of the Pioneer Fund, however, and seeing that some of its grantees did research on IQ, some on race, and a handful on both, critics of Gottfredson sought to deny her the use of her grant. The fund, like most research foundations, does not assign research funds to individuals directly, but grants them to the researcher's nonprofit institution, which administers the grant for the grantee. A university decision not to accept Pioneer Fund support for Gottfredson would have cut off her actual means of scientific investigation. In October 1989, William Frawley, professor of linguistics, wrote to President E. A. Trabant, claiming that the university should accept no research monies from the Pioneer Fund, because it was racist, discriminatory, and anti-Semitic (the claim of anti-Semitism dissolved when it was learned that several of the Pioneer Fund's grantees were Jewish). After intense coverage of these charges in campus and local publications, President Trabant, at the end of 1989, asked the Faculty Senate Committee on Research, chaired by Lawrence Nees, an art historian, to investigate the matter and to make recommendations to him.

In January 1990, Linda Gottfredson had a telephone conversation with a member of that faculty committee, Barbara Settles. Gottfredson took notes as she talked, and she presented those notes and testified under oath about that conversation during later federal arbitration. Neither the university nor Professor Settles rebutted that testimony, objected to the notes, or claimed that Gottfredson had not represented the conversation accurately. Settles warned Gottfredson that the university "was viewed with high suspicion [and] resentment" in the black community, for which Linda Gottfredson was now "the lightning rod." In response to Gottfredson's appeal to academic freedom, Settles replied that it was "difficult to turn people to academic freedom," given that they were "very interested in symbolic vocabulary." As if being metaphorically hit by lightning were not awful enough, Settles warned

Gottfredson that she was "in the right place and time to be run over by a freight train [and should] get out of the way." She advised Gottfredson to "get a lawyer" and, ironically, to take notes on all her conversations.

On April 19, 1990, "the Faculty Senate Committee on Research on the Issue of the University of Delaware's Relationship with the Pioneer Fund," including Professor Settles, unanimously issued its report. The committee had summoned the current president of the Pioneer Fund and asked him if he still subscribed to its initial charter, written in the '30s, that had delineated its two enterprises: the education of the descendants of the "Pioneers" and the "study and research into the problems of heredity and eugenics in the human race generally and such research in respect to animals and plants as may throw light upon heredity in man . . . and research into the problems of race betterment [later changed to "human betterment"] with special reference to the people of the United States, and for the advance of knowledge and the dissemination of information with respect to any studies so made or in general with respect to heredity and eugenics." The president replied, according to the committee, that it was not up to him to change the wording of the person who gave the money almost sixty years ago.

Only the second part of the mission—research—applied to Gottfredson's case, and the committee already knew that scholarships had been awarded just once, half a century ago, and without regard to "pioneer" status. Nonetheless, the committee now compared the refusal by the president of the fund to disavow the founder's bequest, on the one hand, and the university's integration and embrace of "affirmative action," on the other, contrasting each institution's respective "change" since the '30s. It concluded that there was "an obligation to recognize that such views [the charter of the '30s] are clearly and unambiguously in conflict with the University's commitment to racial and cultural diversity." The committee, wielding power conferred by the state, had decided that research funded by the Pioneer Fund was un-Delawarean.

Universities, in fact, administer funding from legally incorporated foundations with a wide range of scientific, political, and ideological agendas. By consensus, the criteria governing this are content neutral: Are researchers free to reach independent conclusions? Are financial arrangements reasonable? Is there any conflict of interest? Will the work be published and open to scholarly criticism? In the case of the Pioneer Fund and Linda Gottfredson (and an associate professor of education, Jan Blits, also funded on her grant), the faculty committee applied a new set of criteria, changing the rules and defining what was ideologically "correct" in scientific research: "The University of Delaware should neither seek nor accept any further financial support from the Pioneer Fund so long as the Fund remains committed to the intent of its original charter and to a pattern of activities incompatible with the University's mission." The committee insisted that the university "has a right to set its own priorities for support of scholarly activities." Because it was committed to creating a "climate" promoting "appreciation of individual and cultural differences," it was free, without doing damage to academic freedom and debate, "not . . . to seek or accept financial support from organizations opposed to its policy on and commitment to racial and cultural diversity." Thus, the committee not only ruled on what the Pioneer Fund actually believed, but it decided that certain inquiries and conclusions by Gottfredson (or others) were outside the protection of academic freedom: "If the University agrees to act in partnership with any organization committed to the proposition that people of different racial and cultural backgrounds are inherently unequal, then that partnership restricts the ability of people from all backgrounds to be treated as fully equal participants in the University community." Could such a ban violate "a more fundamental commitment to free and open inquiry"? No, the committee decided, because the "commitment to racial and cultural diversity is an essential part of, not a rival principle in conflict with, [its] commitment to the right of all people to participate in an environment of free and open inquiry." For a paradigmatic moment of the power to repress "politically incorrect" opinion, one need search no further:

> A substantial, even a preponderant portion of the activities supported by the Pioneer Fund either seek to demonstrate or start from the assumption that there are fundamental hereditary differences among people of different racial and cultural backgrounds. On the basis of this premise the Fund seeks to influence public policy according to a eugenic program.[32]

In fact, as disclosed during federal arbitration, this was not even an approximately true description of the Pioneer Fund's activities, of which the committee had almost no accurate knowledge. That, however, was not the essential issue. Of course, there are scholars who conclude that there are fundamental hereditary differences among people of different backgrounds, and some who seek to influence public policy from that assessment. There are also scholars who believe that there are not fundamental hereditary differences among people of different backgrounds, and some of them seek to influence public policy from that assessment. These are known as disagreements, and, in this case, disagreements about data. Free and thoughtful human beings debate such disagreements in terms of evidence, logic, and the analysis of implications. Universities should be centers of such debate. At Delaware, however, the faculty committee took upon itself the right to identify, categorize, and anathematize what it assumed to be the factual claims and the beliefs of recipients of Pioneer Fund grants, as if dissent from the committee's views of group differences was heresy.

The vote of the committee was unanimous. On April 30, 1990, President E. A. Trabant accepted the report fully, promulgating it as official policy and affirming that "the action is in effect so long as the fund remains committed to the intent of its original charter and to a pattern of activities incompatible with the University's mission."[33] The Board of Trustees ratified the decision and, on July 2, 1990, wrote candidly to the president of the Pioneer Fund about the supremacy of political criteria over principles of unfettered inquiry and of perceptions over actual fact. Discussing the committee's finding that work sponsored by the Pioneer Fund accepted "that there are fundamental hereditary differences among people of different racial and cultural backgrounds," the trustees proclaimed:

> No matter whether that is in fact the orientation of the Pioneer Fund or not, that is perceived as the orientation of the Fund by at least a material number of our faculty, staff, and students. Without judging the merits of this perception, the Board's objective of increasing minority presence at the University could in the view of our Executive Committee be hampered if the University chose to seek funds from the Pioneer Fund at this time.[34]

Robert D. Varrin, associate provost for research, informed Gottfredson by telephone, on June 5, 1990, that if she somehow found any independent way to receive support from the Pioneer Fund, the university would have to decide whether her outside research interfered with her academic duties. Further, he instructed her, such research would not count toward fulfilling research requirements, nor toward yearly evaluations, merit raises, nor, in the case of Jan Blits, promotion. Finally, he stipulated that if she spent 20 percent of her time on Pioneer-funded scholarship, then she would have to work "the equivalent of 120 percent time to meet minimum University obligations." Gottfredson recorded Varrin's conditions in a memo of clarification to him, to which he responded, in writing, on June 15, that "you have accurately represented the sense of our June 5 telephone conversation." Among the specifics of Gottfredson's memo that he was confirming was her understanding that "I could do no Pioneer-funded work whatsoever on campus . . . [I would] not be allowed to use campus facilities . . . my office . . . University services such as Quick Copy and Mail Services . . . the mainframe computer . . . my University address . . . my UD phone number . . . nor regularly use my office to confer with individuals who work with me on Pioneer-funded activities." Further, "I could not support a graduate student to do Pioneer-funded research with me, unless it were off campus." Varrin's own reply of June 15, 1990, added yet another condition: "It is important that the university be connected only with work it supports. Therefore, for Pioneer Fund–sponsored research you should refrain from using the Project for the Study of Intelligence and Society letterhead [a joint Johns Hopkins University and Delaware research program of which Gottfredson was co-director]." In addition, "you should not directly exhibit your university affiliation [sic] when presenting Pioneer research." If she published any paper or book "based on work supported by Pioneer," it should list only "your home or business, not your university, address."[35]

In May 1990, the University of Delaware welcomed its new president, David P. Roselle. At a May 1 press conference, on his first day as president, Roselle supported the right of the university to "choose which organizations may be approved or disapproved as funding sources," saying, "Let's look also at how the Pioneer Fund grant was handled. . . . The faculty committee met and made a decision, and I think they handled it well."[36]

That summer, Professors Gottfredson and Blits defiantly applied for a Pioneer Fund grant through the University, which refused to process the application. Gottfredson and Blits decided to fight. Their faculty collective bargaining unit was the campus chapter of the AAUP, whose president was none other than Barbara Settles herself. The longtime chair of the AAUP grievance commission, however, was Professor George Cicala, who believed in academic freedom, and who knew that it had been guaranteed, both in teaching and research, by explicit, formal contractual obligation. Cicala convinced the AAUP board to accept the case. In September 1990, in accordance with the collective bargaining agreement, the AAUP filed a grievance with the American Arbitration Association, and the university asked for its dismissal.

Although Article II of the collective bargaining agreement stated that "the teacher is entitled to full freedom in research and in the publication of results," the university argued that this was "precatory," not "mandatory." In plain language, it was arguing that the words "full freedom in research" created no legal obligation on its part, but were merely a noble exhortation about the kind of freedom that ought to (but need not) govern a university. The arbitrator—no academic—decided that "entitled to full freedom in research" actually meant what it said, and the case proceeded.

The university correctly stipulated that it would have violated academic freedom if the committee's investigation had focused on Gottfredson's own research and beliefs rather than on some peculiar characteristic of the Pioneer Fund. The committee obviously understood that it could not put everyone's academic freedom at risk, so it had specified, at the outset of its report, that "Gottfredson . . . has not been the focus of this investigation." Indeed, the committee had boasted that it "would reject any charge to conduct an ad hoc inquiry into a faculty member's work. That work enjoys the full protection of academic freedom extended to all faculty members of this University." "The work performed under the grant," it assured everyone, "is not at issue." "The committee," its official report proclaimed, "has never directed its attention to the content or method of any faculty member's research or teaching, and would oppose any [such] attempt." [37]

These claims, however, were utterly false. The committee had taped its proceedings. While arbitration offered no subpoena power, each witness possessed a copy of his or her own testimony. Gottfredson's dean, Frank Murray, had the tape of his own interrogation, and he shared it with her, whence it entered the transcript of the arbitration. Murray himself later would assault academic freedom with such ferocity that the faculty would recoil in horror, but at this juncture he wished to demonstrate his goodwill to Gottfredson. His tape caught the committee in its lie:

> *Professor Sylves:* Are you telling us that the Gottfredson proposal in your opinion, when you passed judgment on it and signed it, was inconsistent with the mission of the University in your opinion? . . . Or that it is inimical to the mission of the college that you're dean of? . . . .
>
> *Murray:* Oh, no, no—
>
> *Sylves:* Did you think it was contrary to the mission—the subject matter of what she was proposing to do?
>
> *Murray:* No. Not the subject matter, no. . . . I mean we're talking about a funny subject matter. The subject matter is the implications of IQ test results, right? . . .
>
> *Unidentified Male Professor:* And you're saying that it is consistent with the mission of the College?
>
> *Murray:* I mean, you're asking as though you think it possibly could be inconsistent.
>
> *Unidentified Female Professor:* We have had people suggest that to us. . . .
>
> *Murray:* Who?
>
> *Sylves:* University of Delaware African American Coalition.

Murray: Oh, I see. That [it] would be inconsistent with the University?

Sylves: Most particularly the mission of the College of Education because of its sensitivity to teacher training and of the need to provide multicultural diversity.[38]

The federal arbitrator, Seymour Strongin, drew the obvious conclusions on August 5, 1991, and found for Gottfredson, Blits, and the AAUP. He ruled it an "unavoidable" conclusion "that the Committee examined the content of Professor Gottfredson's work," indeed, of research materials requested from and provided by Gottfredson (on the premise that it needed them to study not her work, but the Pioneer Fund's procedures) and of the work of Johns Hopkins professor Robert Gordon, of which it knew "undisputedly" that she was the coauthor. He ruled that "the Committee necessarily concluded that Professor Gottfredson's work was also incompatible with the University's mission." In its brief, the University of Delaware had argued that whatever the facts of the Pioneer Fund or Gottfredson's work, it had the right to bar Gottfredson's funding through the university because of "public perception." The arbitrator concluded on behalf of the legally obvious: "Academic freedom is a contractually conferred right, and public perceptions alone, no matter how volatile, cannot suffice to overcome that right." Gottfredson and Blits issued a press release saying that the arbitration decision had vindicated their "academic freedom" from illegal assault.

On September 3, 1991, Dean Murray wrote to them that their claim was false, and that there had been no threat to their academic freedom. Without a hint of irony, he closed: "I would like your response to the issues I raise before I consider what, if any, further actions I should take." On September 13, 1991, however, Murray went a step too far. The focus on academic freedom had given the faculty strange ideas, he believed, and he sent a memo to all faculty and staff of the College of Education entitled "Academic Freedom Policy and Related Matters." It opened a lot of eyes, but not quite in the manner that he intended. Dean Murray quoted the following passage from the university's statement on academic freedom— "Both within and outside the classroom, the faculty should exhibit accuracy, restraint, and respect for opinions of others appropriate to educators and persons of learning"—and he drew the following conclusions from it: "Clearly, public utterances and writings that are inaccurate, intemperate, and disrespectful of the opinions of others, however wrong we find them, are a violation of this requirement and cannot be tolerated." "Furthermore," he informed the faculty, "articles and other publication that violate this requirement, in my view, cannot be considered scholarly. They forfeit, as a result, any claim that they meet our criteria for scholarly work and any protection they might otherwise have under the principles of academic freedom."[39]

The implications of Murray's views of academic freedom, for the whole faculty, now were obvious. Indeed, Murray made clear that he *meant* his strictures to apply to the entire faculty. In November 1991, the local chapter of the AAUP filed charges against Murray for threats to academic freedom. On November 15, the executive committee of the campus AAUP chapter formally rebuked him, noting that "irresponsibility" was one of three grounds for firing even tenured professors. It lectured him that controversy was precisely what academic freedom was designed to protect, and it quoted the U.S. Supreme Court on the " 'transcendent value' of academic freedom." It concluded that his pronouncements "cast a pall over academic freedom and violate our Faculty Handbook and the contract between the University and AAUP."[40]

The faculty saw, if only for the moment, that the threat to one easily could become a threat to all. On September 11, 1991, Murray had sent a particularly ominous memorandum to Gottfredson. He wanted to see the papers produced by students in her courses. He acknowledged that she did not think that he had the "right" to make such a request, and declared that he would "prefer not to take a position now on whether such a right exists": "I would like to see the papers before we determined, or had to determine, the questions of right, property, and so forth." All he wanted was for himself, or, perhaps, "your new department chair, to read over the papers to see what beliefs, if any, about race superiority your students express." Just as he was about to declare that what he found to be "untruth" was unprotected by academic freedom, he wrote that while Gottfredson undoubtedly believed merely, "as you have said, that an individual's membership in a particular group is not an important factor in schooling matters and should not be a basis for educational policy," nonetheless, "I am concerned, as I think you should be as well, about the incidental and unintended lessons you may be teaching." Her students' papers were "relevant data . . . perhaps the best we could have on the question, and I ask that you send them to me as soon as possible. This is a formal request."[41]

On October 1, 1991, the executive committee of the campus AAUP, sensitized by all of these events, informed Murray that "it is an infringement of . . . academic freedom for you to request or demand that [Gottfredson] provide her student papers for the purpose to which you wish to put them.

The university may not conduct ideologically—or politically—motivated investigations of the content of faculty research or teaching."[42]

Individuals matter. Initially alone, Gottfredson and Blits had refused to succumb to pressure; George Cicala, chief grievance officer, had borne witness to academic values. Dean Murray had shown the fangs of arbitrary power. Together, they changed attitudes at the University of Delaware, not toward the content of Gottfredson's work, but toward the freedom of the human mind. Gottfredson and Blits filed suit in federal court for the wrongs that had been visited upon them. In April 1992, the university settled. Most of the terms of that settlement were confidential, but, in what was made public, both Gottfredson and Blits received a year's leave of absence with full pay, and Blits's promotion process (which would occur successfully) was removed from his department and school, and overseen by an independent member of another department acceptable both to the university and to Blits. All prior negative reports about Gottfredson and Blits were expunged from Blits's file. Articles on race-norming that they had coauthored would be reclassified as "research," a status previously denied them. Three years of courage bore fruit. The provost, R. Byron Pipes, in a letter to all faculty, expressed the university's regrets about the "unnecessary disruption in the careers of both faculty members," and he urged that we all "remind ourselves that the freedom to investigate, to pursue research, and to teach in areas of legitimate academic interest is . . . an integral right and obligation of each member of the faculty." He insisted that "it is the obligation of the University Community to protect such freedom," and reaffirmed "the University's commitment to the free, open, and collegial pursuit of scholarship."[43]

In the fall of 1992, the national AAUP proclaimed the banning of funding from an agency because of its beliefs or commitments incompatible with academic freedom. In March 1994, however, Dean Frank Murray told a reporter from the *Delaware State News* that the university had every right to ban external funding if the monies came from a politically objectionable source. President Roselle, a late convert to academic freedom, said of that statement: "There's [*sic*] always people who have differing opinions."[44] Indeed.

Let us not forget, however, President E. A. Trabant. Those tempted to make a hero of someone willing to place "the University's mission" of social justice above the abstraction of academic freedom might do well to consider the arbitrary power created by allowing such freedom to be secondary. Trabant's assault on Gottfredson was not the first time he had sought to purify the mission of his university. In an earlier time, November 1975, Richard

Aumiller, university theater director, lecturer, and faculty advisor to the official campus gay organization, was interviewed by the *Wilmington News Journal*. He spoke about gay life at Delaware, and he estimated that there were "600 gay people on this campus alone."[45] E. A. Trabant summarily fired him for "advocating" homosexuality and for making the university "a mecca for homosexuals."[46]

Oppression, like freedom, is a way of life, accessible by different causes. Trabant wrote to the chairman of the Board of Trustees: "Becoming an advocate and evangelist for gays, he will naturally attract others to the campus to be employed, to hang around, or to be students. Therefore I feel that I have no choice but to step in as president and attempt to correct the situation." In that same letter, Trabant conceded that "the chances of the courts upholding any action that I take are minimal."[47] What is the rule of law to a man with a moral mission?

How do we know these things about the E. A. Trabant of the '70s? Aumiller sued in U.S. District Court, which resulted in disclosure of documents; the university contested the suit; and Aumiller prevailed. Judge Murray Schwartz, after the trial, awarded Aumiller a year's back pay, full attorneys' fees, and fifteen thousand dollars of compensatory and punitive damages. Schwartz also assessed Trabant five thousand dollars individually, but the Board of Trustees paid it for him, because he had fired Aumiller with its "full knowledge and approbation."[48]

Issues of race touch raw historical, political, moral, and psychological nerves in American life. The very depth of racial tension, however, should lead us to want to know how individuals think on such matters, the better to deal, in the open, with the realities we face. The very intractability of racial tension should prevent us from closing any door of inquiry into its roots and mechanisms. Repression deprives us of what, intellectually, we need the most: critical thought, candor, unfettered inquiry, knowledge, and plainspoken mutual criticism. Universities could blaze new trails in these regards; they do not. It protects no person's dignity to be sheltered from freedom. One cannot save liberty by destroying it. Liberty is the exception, not the rule, in human history and in the world today, and once lost, in belief or practice, it is simply gone. It is not to be entrusted to the E. A. Trabants, nor, sadly, to their deans or their faculties.

CHAPTER 7

"SHUT UP," THEY REASONED: SILENCING STUDENTS

Atour of the nation's campuses is not encouraging for friends of student rights. Almost *all* colleges and universities, for example, have "verbal behavior" provisions in their codes, and *most* of the cases in this book involve assaults at various levels on student speech. If this chapter were a visit to every landmark of censorship, it would become a numbing encyclopedia of repression. Let us look at some snapshots of America's campuses, then, to understand the landscape.

New England

Sometimes, policies say it all. In New England, "harassment" has included, within recent times, jokes and ways of telling stories "experienced by others as harassing" (Bowdoin College); "verbal behavior" that produces "feelings of impotence," "anger," or "disenfranchisement," whether "intentional or unintentional" (Brown University); speech that causes loss of "self-esteem [or] a vague sense of danger" (Colby College); or even "inappropriately directed laughter," "inconsiderate jokes," and "stereotyping" (University of Connecticut). The student code of the University of Vermont demands that its students not only not offend each other, but that they appreciate each other: "Each of us must assume responsibility for becoming educated about racism, sexism, ageism, homophobia/heterosexism, and other forms of oppression so that we may respond to other community members in an understanding and appreciative manner." Its very "Freedom of Expression and Dissent Policy" warns: "Nothing in these regulations shall

147

be construed as authorizing or condoning unpermitted and unprotected speech, such as fighting words."[1]

Sometimes, however, policies tell us nothing. In 1975, Yale University rejected the call for speech codes and adopted a policy of full protection for free expression. Yale embraced "unfettered freedom, the right to think the unthinkable, discuss the unmentionable, and challenge the unchallengeable," and it explicitly rejected the notion that "solidarity," "harmony," "civility," or "mutual respect" could be higher values than "free expression" at a university. Even when individuals "fail to meet their social and ethical responsibilities," Yale guaranteed, "the paramount obligation of the university is to protect their right to free expression."[2]

In 1986, however, Yale sophomore Wayne Dick—a Christian conservative—distributed a handout satirizing Yale's GLAD, Gay and Lesbian Awareness Days. It announced the celebration of "BAD, Bestiality Awareness Days," and listed such lectures as "PAN: the Goat, the God, the Lover" and a discussion of "Rover v. Wade." On May 2, Patricia Pearce, the associate dean of Yale College, informed Dick by letter that both an administrative member of the dean's office's Racial and Ethnic Harassment Board and a gay activist had "submitted . . . a complaint alleging harassment in the form of a 'BAD week 86' poster." The college's Executive Committee Coordinating Group had decided that the charge that Dick's poster violated a ban on "physical restriction, assault, coercion, or intimidation" had merit, and that it should be submitted to the full committee. According to Dick, as reported in the *Village Voice* in July 1986, when he asked Dean Pearce how his satiric flier could be actionable if Yale's policy guaranteed full freedom of expression and the right to "challenge the unchallengeable," she replied that it did not protect "worthless speech." On May 13, the Executive Committee found Dick guilty of harassment and intimidation.[3] His mother told the *Boston Globe*: "Wayne . . . feels very strongly about things. He expresses himself freely." At Yale, that earned him two years of probation.[4]

A code, absent a commitment to freedom, will mean whatever power wants it to mean. Assisting a student at Wesleyan University against violations of the speech code in the spring of 1996, Robert Chatelle, of the National Writers Union, wrote to Wesleyan's president and quoted from the university's official policy: "'Harassment and abuse . . . may include . . . verbal harassment and abuse.' You don't need a Ph.D. in logic to notice that . . . verbal harassment is *anything* [Wesleyan] decides it to be."[5] Dartmouth College even decided that free expression was, literally, garbage. In 1993, some students repeatedly stole the conservative *Dartmouth Review* from dormitory delivery sites. The dean of students announced that the confiscations did not violate the code of student conduct. As an official Dartmouth spokesman explained, *The Dartmouth Review* was "litter." [6]

In Fall 1995, Emerson College barred the college's student radio station from playing "rap music" not on a list of forty officially approved pieces that contained no "trigger words." The administration insisted that rap was sexist and caused crime. Arthur Barron, chairman of the Department of Mass Communication, explained: "We want to make absolutely certain that nothing in the body of rap music inspires, incites, either violence or sexism or hatred."[7] James D'Entremont, director of the Boston Coalition for Freedom of Expression, wrote to Barron: "No amount of brain-dead social engineering through censorship is ever going to give us a safer campus or a kinder and gentler society."[8]

Tufts University, in academic year 1988–89, placed a student on disciplinary probation (and sentenced him to fifty hours of community service, later rescinded) for having sold T-shirts with the motto "Why Beer is Better Than Women at Tufts." It listed such reasons as "Beer Never Has a Headache," "You Can Share a Beer With Your Friends," and "If You Pour a Beer Right You'll Always Get Good Head." These statements, Tufts ruled, created an "offensive" and "sexist" environment. If selling the T-shirt violated the speech provisions of Tufts's harassment policy, however, wearing the T-shirt also did, which created a problem for the administration, because the T-shirt had sold well. President Jean Mayer divided the campus into "free-speech" and "non-free-speech" zones. The speech provisions did not apply to the privacy of one's own room or to campus lawns, but they governed dormitory common areas and classrooms.[9]

Most universities have accepted speech codes passively, but students at Tufts, after seven months of debate and public forums about freedom of expression, formed a broad nonpartisan coalition in defense of their rights. Tufts students marked off the physical boundaries between "free" and "unfree" zones with tape and chalk, and they invited the media in. The campus looked like Berlin in 1946. Embarrassed, President Mayer rescinded the speech code.[10] Tufts's next president, John DiBaggio, in a 1996 op-ed in the *Boston Globe,* wrote that "countering hate speech [and] disciplining the hater . . . [are] worth every effort" in principle, but, alas, "editorial writers and lawyers . . . with an easy-to-construct argument—namely, 'Free Speech is good'—don't understand that," which invariably lets "the bigots against whom the speech codes are directed merely dance on the college quad." Speech codes, he concluded, have brought "ridicule on places where great ideas are born." Also, "one day those codes may be turned against their authors."[11] There are more principled defenses of free speech (and the belief that "Free Speech is good" was not, to say the least, "easy to construct"), but this will do.

Authors of these codes rarely make their full agenda explicit, but sometimes a document sheds real light. In June 1989, the Massachusetts Board of Regents adopted a statewide "Policy Against Racism" for higher education. It "proscribes all conditions and all actions or omissions including all acts of verbal harassment or abuse which deny or have the effects of denying to anyone his or her rights to equality, dignity, and security on the basis of his or her race, color, ethnicity, culture or religion." It mandated both "appreciation for cultural/racial pluralism" and "a unity and cohesion in the diversity which we seek to achieve," outlawing "racism in any form, expressed or implied, intentional or inadvertent, individual or institutional." The regents pledged "to eradicate racism, ethnic and cultural offenses and religious intolerance," and "required," among other things, programs "to enlighten faculty, administrators, staff, and students with regard to . . . ways in which the dominant society manifests and perpetuates racism."[12]

They did not call for any program on political tolerance. At the state's flagship campus, the University of Massachusetts–Amherst, in the spring and summer of 1992, the student newspaper, the *Collegian,* lost all real protection of the rule of law.[13] At an angry rally on the campus after the acquittal of the Los Angeles police officers in the Rodney King affair, protesters turned their hatred against the supposed "racism" of the *Collegian,* which had written of the L.A. "riots," unlike Professor John Bracey, later head of the Faculty Senate, who at the rally termed the rioters "our warriors." Protesters invaded the offices of the *Collegian,* smashing windows, destroying property, and assaulting staff. Northampton police arrested one protester for attacking a *Collegian* photographer with a baseball bat and dragging him to the Student Center (the municipal court sentenced him to counseling). The *Collegian* appealed to the university for protection, but was refused. Editors and staff got a Northampton police escort to another municipality, and published a few editions in hiding, but these were stolen and destroyed. Marc Elliott, editor-in-chief, told the *Boston Globe* that it was "like a Nazi book burning."[14] Undefended by the university, the editors of the *Collegian* surrendered and expanded an editorial structure of separate editors and sections for every "historically oppressed" minority on campus. Managing editor Daniel Wetzel told the *Daily Hampshire Gazette,* "There's 100 people running scared right now, and 100 people intimidating them. . . . I'm not going to put a student organization above my safety."[15] He told the Associated Press, "We gave up our journalistic integrity for the safety of the students."[16]

When the *Collegian* appealed for protection, UMass's chancellor, Richard O'Brien, replied that there was a conflict between two values that "the university holds dear: protection of free expression and the creation of a multicultural community free of harassment and intimidation." Publicly, he proclaimed neutrality and offered help in solving the "dispute."[17] Privately, according to Marc Elliott, "We were told by the administration that the choice was to give in or let the campus break up in a race riot where people would get killed." Chancellor O'Brien denied that, and told the press, "We were there to facilitate discussion, not to take any side on the issue."[18]

In 1994, in response to an inquiry about the actions taken by the administration in 1992, the new chancellor, David K. Scott, replied, in writing: "*Collegian* takeover of May 1, 1992: charges were not brought; Whitmore occupation of May 1, 1992: no disciplinary action was taken; Theft of copies of *Collegian* May 4, 1992: Individuals who may have taken copies of the *Collegian* were never identified. It is difficult to call the action theft because the paper is distributed to the public free of charge." As for the physical assault and the destruction of the newspapers: "I am not aware of any specific statements by the administration in response to the incident with the *Collegian* photographer or the theft of copies of the *Collegian*."[19]

In 1995, Chancellor Scott proposed a new harassment policy that would outlaw not only "epithets" and "slurs," but, in addition, "negative stereotyping."[20] The policy caught the eye of the media. *New York Times* columnist Anthony Lewis illustrated the gulf between liberal and campus views of freedom. UMass's policy, he wrote, would "create a totalitarian atmosphere in which everyone would have to guard his tongue all the time lest he say something that someone finds offensive." Lewis asked: "Do the drafters have no knowledge of history? . . . No understanding that freedom requires . . . 'freedom for the thought that we hate'? And if not, what are they doing at a university?" He concluded that the "elastic concept of a 'hostile environment'" intolerably menaced "freedom of speech, at universities of all places."[21]

Tell that to Harvard Law School, which in October 1995 adopted, by an overwhelming vote of its faculty, "Sexual Harassment Guidelines" that ban "speech . . . of a sexual nature that is unwelcome, . . . abusive, . . . and has the . . . effect of . . . creating an intimidating, demeaning, degrading, hostile or otherwise seriously offensive . . . educational environment."[22] Harvard, though a private institution, prides itself on being a citadel of legal education on liberty, but it adopted these rules years after federal district courts had ruled that similar codes violated the First Amendment.[23] Indeed, the guidelines seem to have been enacted precisely in order to suppress speech on the heels of a great campus controversy involving a law student parody of an expletive-filled *Harvard Law Review* article, "A Postmodern Feminist Legal Manifesto," published as a posthumous gesture toward Mary Jo Frug, a radical feminist legal scholar (and the wife of a member of Harvard Law School's faculty) who had been brutally murdered some months earlier.[24] When the parodists bitingly mocked the decision to publish, there were calls from some outraged students and faculty for their discipline or even expulsion. Professor David Kennedy brought formal charges against the students before Harvard Law School's disciplinary body, but those charges were dismissed—not on the basis of academic freedom, but because there was no code of conduct at the law school that would have forbidden the students' words.[25] A year later, the faculty adopted the guidelines that almost certainly would have supplied a basis for punishment of the authors of what was clearly a political parody.

New York

CCNY was not alone in threatening liberty in higher education in New York, and Harvard was far from the first law school to adopt a speech code. In 1989, the faculty of the University of Buffalo Law School voted unanimously in favor of a policy on "Intellectual Freedom, Tolerance, and Political Harassment." As Nat Hentoff reported in *The Progressive,* the law school ruled that student free speech must be limited by "the responsibility to promote equality and justice."[26] Syracuse University, in the fall of 1993, adopted a harassment code whose target was (and is) "offensive remarks," to which it added "sexually suggestive staring, leering, sounds, or gestures," not to mention "sexual, sexist, or heterosexist remarks or jokes . . . [and] sexually suggestive or degrading images or graffiti (such as T-shirts, posters, calendars, mugs, etc.) [or] the use of such images to advertise events." [27] The State University of New York (SUNY)–Binghamton, in March 1991, charged a student, Graham Firestone, with lewd and indecent behavior when he displayed legally nonobscene nude photographs on his dormitory door on an all-male floor. He claimed First Amendment rights, but a representative of the university's Affirmative Action Office, who testified against him, characterized his behavior to the *New York Times* as "degrading and abusive to women."[28] (If only he'd displayed Mapplethorpe's photographs.) In fall 1996, however, that administration did not prosecute students who trashed a press run of the campus's conservative journal.[29]

The reductio ad absurdum in New York occurred in 1993, when Sarah Lawrence College found a student guilty of harassment for "laughing" when one student called another a "faggot." John Boesky, according to witnesses, had his masculinity impugned by a student with whom he had roomed acrimoniously in his freshman year. Boesky called his former roommate a "faggot." Boesky's friend, Marlin Lask, laughed. The student charged Boesky and Lask with harassment.[30]

The college, without letting them even confront their accuser, convicted them of creating "a hostile and intimidating atmosphere," and sentenced them to one year's social probation and twenty hours of community service. Further, it required them to view the videotape Homophobia, read the text of Homophobia on Campus, and write a paper on "homophobia."

Lask was indignant. According to Francis Randall, who was Lask's faculty advocate, Lask took notes of a conversation with Robert Cameron, associate dean of student life, in which he recorded the following judgment: "We know that you are not guilty of any of the items [in the code] 'a' through 'e,' [but] you tried to make an environment that was uncomfortable and demeaning. . . . Laughter is part of demeaning [the student]." Randall's notes of a later conversation with Marilyn Katz, the dean of studies and student life (who requested and confirmed Randall's notes), reflect that she said to him: "I know it makes a good phrase to say he was convicted of laughing, but the laughing was in a context." The closest that the college's administration came to trying to defend itself in what became an increasingly embarrassing situation was when Barbara Kaplan, dean of the college, told the New York Times that she disputed Lask's claim that he was punished just for laughing, but then Kaplan refused to elaborate, citing confidentiality rules.

Lask admitted no wrongdoing. He refused to write a paper on homophobia and took a year at Hebrew University in Jerusalem. During that time, Randall worked for reconsideration, and the New York chapter of the ACLU (NYCLU) joined the case, which Randall believed worried the college most. Norman Siegel, executive director of NYCLU, told the New York Times that the case was "another situation of political correctness run amok, of political correctness being extended into the twilight zone."[31] Lask was permitted to return for his senior year without having to demonstrate in writing his successful thought reform, but the conviction remained a part of his official record. When, in January 1995, NYCLU was about to file suit on Lask's behalf, Sarah Lawrence removed the letter from Lask's file, and Lask dropped his case.

Randall (in a memorandum for his colleagues) explained that in 1991, organizations of gay, black, and Asian students secured a speech code after one anonymous person had defaced the campus with bigoted graffiti in one incident. By 1993, however, the code never had been invoked, and he believed that "there was a hope for, a search for, a case." Ironically, in publicizing the code, the Lesbian, Gay, Bisexual Union of Sarah Lawrence had distributed fliers all over the campus that said: "Faggot—Spic—Nigger—Chink. Has anyone ever said this to you? . . . Sarah Lawrence College has a policy against harassment? USE IT."[32] Same word, note well—"faggot"—but that was not harassment. What if someone had laughed?

The Mid-Atlantic

Did nearby campuses learn from Penn? In November 1994, at Montclair State University (New Jersey), an entire fraternity, Delta Kappa Psi, was sentenced by the campus judiciary to 150 hours of community service because one of its members hung a Confederate flag for fifteen minutes in a cafeteria.[33] Georgetown University provides students and faculty with two separate statements about freedom of expression. The first proclaims "free speech" essential to the university, declares that "more is better," asserts that "to forbid or limit discourse contradicts everything the university stands for," and promises that the only permissible restrictions are content-neutral "considerations of time, place, and manner." The second, under which students and faculty may be prosecuted, warns that "expression" that is "grossly offensive on matters such as race, ethnicity, religion, gender, or sexual preference is inappropriate in a university community."[34] Rutgers University had a category of "verbal assault," and a separate "heinous act," harassment, which included "communication" that is "in any manner likely to cause annoyance or alarm."[35]

The speech provisions of the sexual harassment policy at the University of Maryland–College Park, however, go well beyond those of Rutgers, and are matched, in their repressive strictures, only by those of its neighbor, West Virginia University (discussed following).[36] The Maryland policy lists among "unacceptable verbal behaviors . . . idle chatter of a sexual nature," "graphic sexual descriptions; sexual slurs, sexual innuendos," "comments about a person's clothing, body, and/or sexual activities," "sexual teasing," "suggestive or insulting sounds such as whistling, wolf-calls, or kissing sounds," "sexually provocative compliments about a person's clothes," "comments of a sexual nature about weight, body shape, size, or figure," "comments or questions about the sensuality of a person, or his/her spouse or significant other," "pseudo-medical advice such as 'you might be feeling bad because you didn't get enough' or 'A little Tender Loving Care (TLC) will cure your ailments,'" "telephone calls of a sexual nature," "'staged whispers' or mimicking of a sexual nature about the way a person walks, talks, [or] sits." Further, these verbal behaviors "do not necessarily have to be specifically directed at an individual to constitute sexual harassment."

Even remaining silent about life, sexuality, private views, fashion, or love is no path to safety at Maryland, however, because the policy also prohibits an array of "gestures" and "other non-verbal behaviors." "Gestures" are "movements of the body, head, hands, and fingers, face and eyes that are expressive of an idea, opinion, or emotion." "Non-verbal behaviors," distinguished from "physical behaviors [which involve touching]," are "actions intended for an effect or as a demonstration." The policy offers specific "examples of unacceptable gestures and nonverbal behaviors," including "sexual looks such as leering and ogling with suggestive overtones; licking lips or teeth; holding or eating food provocatively; [and] lewd gestures, such as hand or sign language to denote sexual activity." As if dry lips or American Sign Language were not trouble enough, the policy identifies specific acts of "sexual discrimination" as actionable "sexual harassment," including "gender-biased communications about women or men [and] course materials that ignore or depreciate a group based on their gender."

The University of Maryland, however, has found no problem with permitting the theft, with virtual impunity, of conservative newspapers. Frustrated by such unpunished or lightly punished trashings, especially of "free" newspapers in Maryland (such newspapers are not "free" to the advertisers), the state government made such theft a criminal offense with a five-hundred-dollar fine and/or imprisonment for up to eighteen months. This seems more likely to aid the circulation of ideas than Dartmouth's policy of treating such dissident papers as "litter."

At Carnegie Mellon University, in Pittsburgh, suppression of speech by charges of harassment, formal censorship, and ever more repressive codes has become a way of life. Fortunately, one of the most outspoken civil libertarians on the Internet, Declan McCullagh, was a student at CMU, so as soon as CMU did it, the world knew it.[37] He also was student body president—demonstrating the deep rift between students and their would-be censors.

McCullagh himself was charged with "harassment" for public criticism of the campaign tactics of a candidate in student government elections (a charge later dropped). His accuser wrote to him that "while this may not be enough to legally win [in court] . . . it is more than enough to win a UCD [University Committee on Discipline hearing] on this campus." That is true of charges of "harassment" on most campuses. The same accuser, Lara Wolfson, when she was president of the Graduate Student Organization, was criticized on the student government newsgroup by a fellow graduate student, Erik Altmann, for trying to create "graduate student ghettos." He called her a "megalomaniac." She accused Altmann of "harassment," and Dean of Students Michael Murphy accepted the charges, initiating a formal hearing. Wolfson argued that calling a woman a megalomaniac constituted sexual harassment, citing a large body of feminist "victim theory" on her behalf. Indeed, Barbara Lazarus, associate provost at CMU, submitted a brief for Wolfson, on March 14, 1994: "I have no doubt that this [political criticism of her role as president of the Graduate Student Organization] has created a hostile environment which impacts Lara's productivity as a student leader and as a graduate student. . . . It must be stopped." Altman was acquitted, but every student knew the risks thereafter of debating feminist political figures.

Freedom of speech, of course, is also the right *not* to make certain statements. In 1991, Patrick Mooney, a residential adviser at CMU, declined to wear a pink triangle, a symbol of gay persecution, during mandatory gay and lesbian sensitivity training. He argued that it violated his Catholic religious conscience and his right to control his speech according to that conscience. For that, he was fired by CMU's Housing Office (which reports to Dean Murphy). He sued, and settled his lawsuit favorably with CMU, in 1994, for an undisclosed sum. Meanwhile, every residential adviser knew the cost of even silent dissidence.

On the MIT Website *Justice on Campus,* McCullagh (no conservative— he worked for Friends of the Earth and for Jerry Brown's 1992 presidential campaign) documented a large number of similar efforts at CMU to suppress dissent. Undeterred, CMU in 1994 strengthened its sexual harassment policy, including its restrictions on "verbal conduct." The policy created "trained advisors" and "strongly urged and encouraged" not only any student, faculty, or staff member who "feels sexually harassed" to contact these advisors, but, also, anyone who "knows of or suspects the occurrence of sexual harassment." In November of that year, CMU barred Internet access by its students and faculty to "sexually explicit or obscene material"—banning eighty-one Internet newsgroups that either were "sexually explicit" or had the words "sex" or "erotica" in their title. This produced a barrage of outraged criticism from the Electronic Frontier Foundation, the ACLU, and individual civil libertarians. On campus, McCullagh forged an alliance with gay and lesbian activists, because CMU had used examples of homosexual erotica as instances of what should be banned. The censorship was covered prominently by *Time,* CBS News, the *Chronicle of Higher Education,* the Associated Press, and local media. CMU, once a pioneer of electronic communication, was now in the forefront of censoring the Internet.

Virginia

Virginians, of course, had been pioneers of freedom of expression, foremost among whom had been George Mason (1725–92), opponent of slavery, passionate advocate of liberty both at the federal and state levels, and drafter of the Virginia Constitution, perhaps the first formal American statement of inalienable rights, among them freedom of speech. The fate of that freedom at the university named in his honor is sobering.

On April 4, 1991, during a week of fund-raising events, the Sigma Chi fraternity at George Mason University performed an "ugly woman" skit at the university cafeteria.[38] Eighteen fraternity brothers, dressed in women's clothes by sorority friends, paraded before an audience of students who had paid to see the performance. One of the eighteen was in blackface, with a wig in curlers and with pillows attached to his chest and backside (the students appearing as white women were equally "ugly," because looking ridiculous was the very point of the skit).

Anyone, of course, could have criticized the skit or raised the issue of fraternity attitudes for campus discussion. Individuals had the same options, in short, as Christian students would have had if the fraternity had displayed Andres Serrano's "Piss Christ" or if someone had dressed as "white trash." Instead, several students filed a complaint with the dean of student services, Kenneth Bumgarner. The fraternity publicly apologized to the campus, but on April 19, the dean announced that Sigma Chi "had created a hostile environment for women and blacks, incompatible with the University's mission." He sentenced the fraternity to two years' social and athletic suspension, and he ordered them to plan and to implement "an educational program addressing cultural differences, diversity, and the concerns of women." He also suspended, for one year, the Gamma Phi Beta sorority, whose members had dressed their fraternity friends.

George Mason is a public university, and Victor Glasberg, an ACLU attorney in northern Virginia, although he found the skit offensive, was not about to see the First Amendment disappear because of it. He sued the university in U.S. District Court, which overturned the suspension on constitutional grounds on August 27, 1991. George Mason had argued that the skit was not "protected speech," and that even if it were, there were "compelling educational interests" that overrode that consideration. As Judge Claude Hilton ruled, however, "The First Amendment does not recognize exceptions for bigotry, racism, and religious intolerance, or ideas or matters some may deem trivial, vulgar, or profane." The university appealed the ruling to the U.S. Court of Appeals for the Fourth Circuit, which, on May 10, 1993, unanimously upheld the district court's judgment. The court noted that the fraternity had been punished precisely for its "evident . . . message." Sigma Chi's "purposefully nonsensical treatment of sexual and racial themes," the court found, "was intended to impart a message that the University's concerns, in the Fraternity's views, should be treated humorously." This, the court concluded, was "expressive conduct," and the harm was not what the fraternity had done, but what George Mason had done, its "punishment of those who scoffed at its goals . . . while permitting, even encouraging, conduct that would further the viewpoint expressed in the University's goals." In our system of law, the court explained, government may not forbid or punish expressive conduct because it disapproves of the ideas expressed by that conduct. It urged the university to pursue its laudable goals through means that do not destroy essential freedoms. George Mason himself had understood that perfectly more than two hundred years earlier.

The Border States and the South

West Virginia broke from Virginia over issues of personal liberty, but West Virginia University (WVU) possesses (as we write) the only speech code that makes the University of Maryland's seem benign. It proscribes a range of common expressions and, if applied equally, it would leave no sex or race safe in its conversations. Sexual harassment includes "insults, humor, jokes and/or anecdotes that belittle or demean an individual's or a group's sexuality or sex"; "unwelcome comments or inquiries of a sexual nature about an individual's or a group's sexuality or sex"; "inappropriate displays of sexually suggestive objects or pictures which may include but not limited to [sic] posters, pin-ups, and calendars." WVU even has its own loyalty oath, "The Mountaineer Creed": "I will practice academic and personal integrity; value wisdom and culture; foster lifetime learning; practice civic responsibility and good stewardship; respect human dignity and cultural diversity."[39]

WVU's policies, however, do not threaten everyone, because only certain groups actually are specially protected as elements of "cultural diversity."

WVU's president's "Executive Officer for Social Justice" (OSJ) was autho-rized "to make clear" both the institutional and her own "personal commit-ment [to] creating an equitable campus." The OSJ issues policies to establish the appropriate beliefs about two areas above all, "homophobia" and "sex-ism," and to encourage reports of harassment—from personal experience or from knowledge of "anyone you know."

Thus, WVU prescribes an official, orthodox, state definition of homo-phobia: "Lesbians and gay men are often portrayed as sick, perverted, and immoral or their existence is denied altogether." It prohibits "feelings" about gays and lesbians from becoming "attitudes": "Regardless of how a person feels about others, negative actions or attitudes based on misconceptions and/or ignorance constitute prejudice, which contradicts everything for which an institution of higher learning stands." Among those prejudices is "heterosexism . . . the assumption that everyone is heterosexual, or, if they aren't, they should be." Because everyone has the right to be free from ha-rassment, there are specific "behaviors to avoid." These prohibitions affect speech and voluntary association based upon beliefs: "DO NOT tolerate 'jokes' which are potentially injurious to gays, lesbians, and bisexuals"; "DO NOT determine whether you will interact with someone by virtue of her or his sexual orientation." Everyone must "value alternate lifestyles . . . chal-lenge homophobic remarks . . . [and] use language that is not gender spe-cific." "Instead of referring to anyone's romantic partner as 'girlfriend' or 'boyfriend,'" the OSJ instructs, "use positive generic terms such a 'friend,' 'lover,' or 'partner.' Speak of your own romantic partner similarly." Finally, "educate yourself about homosexuality."

The policy never specifies which of these homophobic beliefs, attitudes, expressions, or personal choices would lead to charges, but it lists them under a general heading of "harassment, insult, alienation, isolation and physical assault." A WVU student could only refer to the sweeping action-able examples of the harassment policy of which it is a part. Further, the ho-mophobia policy ends precisely with the warning that "harassment" or "discrimination" based on sexual preference is subject to penalties that range "from reprimand . . . to expulsion and termination, and including public ser-vice and educational remediation."

WVU's policy and CMU's insistence that resident advisors wear a pink triangle instruct individuals to affirm things that they might not believe, a profound issue of free expression. At Vanderbilt University, a conservative stu-dent group, the Young Americans for Freedom (YAF), rejected affirmative action and believed it wrong to separate its members into categories of race, religion, ethnicity, or gender.[40] On their official campus registration form of 1994–95, asked to "list those steps planned in recruitment to assure that your organization will strive to be inclusive in its membership," YAF replied: "We will not base recruitment on race, culture, or gender." Asked about "exclusivity," they replied: "Anyone who shares the beliefs of YAF and acts accordingly is welcome to join." Asked to indicate the ethnicity of their members, they answered "not applicable." In the fall of 1995, however, campus orthodoxy hardened. In order to reregister as a student organization with Vanderbilt's Campus Student Services, essential to functioning as an on-campus, student group (they were not asking for university funds), YAF was given the same form. Again, when asked to "count or estimate" its membership by Vanderbilt's ethnic categories, it wrote, on that part of the form, "irrelevant."

On October 24, 1995, YAF chairman Erik Johnson received a letter from Michelle Jerome, of Campus Student Services, informing him that "the Community Affairs Board was unable to approve your student organization's request for re-registration because of failure to report demographic information." YAF, declining to speak in ways contrary to its sincere beliefs about America, refused again to supply the information. On December 8, 1995, therefore, Jerome wrote to them that "because your organization has failed to comply with the rules and regulations stipulated by the Community Affairs Board for re-registration . . . effective immediately . . . you will no longer be able to conduct financial transactions or deposit money to this center's number . . . [or] use University facilities or services for meetings [and] events. . . . Any attempts to conduct organization activities will be . . . subject to disciplinary action."

On the whole, though, it's what you *do* express that gets you in trouble. Emory University has a sweeping Discriminatory Harassment Policy that forbids "speech" that creates "a hostile environment," but it denies that this is a "speech code."[41] In 1994, however, the University Senate debated a resolution that would have added a clause to the policy specifying that "all judgments under this policy related to freedom of expression should be consistent with First Amendment standards." It voted the proposal down. Vice President and General Counsel Joseph Crooks, speaking for the administration, asked, "Do we want technical legal rules to preempt community judgments?"[42] The University of Tennessee makes it particularly difficult to be in college, its speech code forbidding "humor or jokes about sex" that create "a hostile environment."[43] Auburn University defines as harassment not only "slurs, jokes, or other graphic or physical conduct," but "attempts to embarrass."[44]

The University of North Carolina (UNC)–Chapel Hill, in November 1995, revoked the charter of a fraternity, Phi Gamma Delta, for a crude letter that, among other things, invited would-be pledges to watch women at a party "stumble around the dance floor in a drunken stupor." It referred to things that, alas, fraternity members have referred to without gravity for generations: masturbation, female genitalia, and oral sex. It was private mail sent to recipients who had chosen to "rush" the fraternity, one of whom showed it to a feminist group, which circulated it widely around the campus. Circulating the letter in protest, in UNC's eyes, was just fine; sending it privately to a friend was actionable.[45]

At Duke University, Martin Padgett, the student editor of a university humor magazine, *Jabberwocky,* wrote about the incompetence of Duke's food-service employees. Students always complain about food-service employees. At Duke, however, those employees are predominantly black. The Black Student Alliance (and other groups) held rallies calling for Padgett's removal. The administrative University Publications Board first merely *urged* Padgett to resign, noting his First Amendment rights. When the rallies continued, however, Keith Brodie, president of Duke, wrote an open letter condemning the articles, and the publications board now dismissed Padgett, not, it claimed, for the articles, but for a failure to respond to the criticism. Padgett had, in fact, responded, but he had said: "We did not intend the articles to be racist." As the *New York Times* reported with understatement, "Some students believe Mr. Padgett's removal is tantamount to censorship [of] legitimate if satirical issues [on grounds of] racism."[46]

Duke was not consistently harsh, however. In September 1993, a black student, Nico Tynes, carried off three hundred copies of the conservative *Duke Review.* Tony Mecia, the editor of the *Duke Review* told the *Herald Sun* on September 28, "It just shows an intolerance of differing views. He had all other kinds of recourses other than throwing out the papers." President Nannerl Keohane condemned the theft, and the judicial board convicted Tynes—who admitted the act—of larceny, 3 to 2. Early in the spring semester, Janet Dickerson, vice president for student affairs, voided the conviction, arguing that the charge of "theft" was dubious under the judicial code's terms of "any wrongful physical taking and carrying away of the personal property of another without the rightful owner's consent with an intention to deprive the owner of its use." The board had rejected such an argument, ruling explicitly that Tynes's goal had been an attempt to deny others the right to read and judge the newspaper's views. Before the hearing, Tynes had told the official campus paper, the *Chronicle,* "I consider it litter, and when I see litter I throw it out." President Keohane upheld the overturning of Tynes's conviction.[47]

As should be clear by now, the theft of student publications at universities is pandemic. Most often, they are campus newspapers and "alternative" conservative publications condemned for "racism," "sexism," or "homophobia." According to the Student Press Law Center (SPLC), a nonpartisan watchdog of student press freedoms, there were twenty such incidents in 1992–93, and at least thirty-five such incidents in 1993–94, after years that previously had averaged only three or four such thefts. That sad trend continues and even accelerated in 1997. In most instances, the thefts occur with impunity. In its publications up to January 1998, the SPLC has documented most of the successful theft, burning, and trashing of student publications in 1996 and 1997 at the following colleges—most often for the expression of conservative and libertarian points of view—with others documented by the *Chronicle of Higher Education* and the Intercollegiate Studies Institute: University of California–Berkeley, Lamar University (Texas), University of California–Santa Barbara, San Francisco State University, Western Washington University, California State University–Long Beach, Rutgers, Central Oklahoma University, Northern Essex Community College (Massachusetts), University of Kentucky, Portland State University, Clark University, Utah State, College of the Canyons (California), St. Johns University, University of North Texas, Boston College, Amherst College, Louisiana State University, University of Texas–Austin, SUNY–Binghamton, UNC–Chapel Hill, and Cornell. In response to the theft of more than two thousand papers at Northern Essex Community College (because of an article critical of welfare), a bill was introduced into the Massachusetts legislature to criminalize the taking of "free" papers. As the *SPLC Report* of spring 1997 noted with impatience, however, "most existing state theft laws should allow the prosecution of free newspaper theft as well."[48]

The will to censor is almost boundless. In February 1996, according to reports from the Associated Press, Winthrop College, in South Carolina, suspended the Internet accounts of two students, one who had solicited money on his homepage, and one who had placed a picture of a naked woman on his. Both students deleted their Webpages and accepted a two-week suspension, soon reduced to one. The fracas led the college to reexamine its whole Internet policy, however, and the administration now restricted Internet use "to official university business" only: "Using E-mail or system-provided mailing lists as a forum for expressing political, religious, or personal opinions is inappropriate." Further, it gave the administration the right to invade students'—and faculty's—private communications in order to monitor compliance: "No personal or confidential information should be exchanged and all communications are subject to periodic and/or random audit." Glenn Broach, professor of political science, told the Associated Press, "It could be a violation of the free exchange of ideas at the university."[49] Indeed. A professor e-mailed Declan McCullagh about wanting to share with him the university's defenses of its policy, but he noted, "I would have to send them . . . U.S. Mail."[50] Much harm begins by going after nudes.

In the spring of 1996, *Alligator Online,* the electronic student newspaper at the University of Florida, announced that the administration had issued instructions banning any material that was "racist, discriminatory, commercial," or, in general, "inappropriate," from all university private Webpages (which would include both the newspaper's and those of every single student). The Electronic Frontier Foundation used the occasion to explain to all interested parties that "viewpoint-based discrimination" is simply unconstitutional, because of the intolerable power of a government that could control what people can say and read.[51]

Students, however, have done particularly well in using the Internet to bring abuses of power to light, which is precisely why individuals who care about public scrutiny and debate must not let the freedom of e-mail and Websites be sacrificed in the name of mere good taste. The assault on student electronic freedom most often arises from the occasional waves of vulgarity that occur in that ocean of free expression. One simply cannot have one without the other, however, because one person's vulgarity is another person's protest or art. The ultimate value of electronic freedom is nothing less than the critical value of freedom itself.

Consider, with that in mind, the University of Memphis.[52] Like most universities, Memphis has a newsserver with a wide diversity of purely campus newsgroups for the use of its students (and faculty), voluntary associations which students are free to visit or not. One such group, umem.personals, evolved into an often crude, unregulated, unfettered forum for the expression of intimate personal preferences. On March 1, 1995, one student posted a message not at all atypical of the vulgarisms that made the newsgroup what it was: "I find hot, wet, and greasy pussy arousing." (The next Henry Miller or Erica Jong he was not.) This topic, however, had arisen from a message to the student, "Hoop," that had been posted on February 28: "Share with us what you find arousing Hoop." That question was posed because Hoop had objected to "just plain tasteless" things that other posters had discussed in umem.personals, such as, in

Hoop's criticism, "incest, rape, and child molestation [which] . . . are not games or jokes to me. I have seen the damage that they have done." Responding to the question about what he found "arousing," Hoop had replied: "What do I find arousing? I think that a sexual relationship with a single person is arousing . . . [and] I don't like: . . . rape, . . . anything mentioning kids that is meant to arouse adults . . . anything that is not consensual." Accused of censorship and pressed on what aroused him, Hoop replied with his infamous post. On March 5, Hoop and a fellow poster received official notification from the assistant dean of students for judicial affairs, Kathryn Story, that their electronic access was revoked, and that they were charged with violating the Student Code of Conduct by "use of computing facilities to send or receive obscene messages."

As word of this spread, various Websites were established nationally to establish the facts and to monitor the case. The Electronic Frontier Foundation and individual "netizens" (citizens of the Web) shared legal precedents and advice with civil libertarians at Memphis and sent these to Dean Story. On March 13, Hoop and the other student had a preliminary meeting with Story, who offered them a choice between a settlement (permanent revocation of their Internet and e-mail accounts at Memphis) and a full hearing before the Social Discipline Committee, which had a wide array of far more serious punishments at its disposal. The other student accepted the settlement; Hoop chose to fight the charges. The date set for the closed hearing was April 6.

Between early March and early April, Internet defenders of freedom of expression were remarkably active, analyzing and debating the obscenity guidelines of *Miller v. California* and legal glosses upon those guidelines, and communicating these to the university, and, in particular, to Dean Story, who was receiving several hundred e-mails per week concerning Hoop's case. Also, the campus paper was being flooded with electronic letters of support for Hoop. Finally, on April 3, after a veritable electronic seminar for the benefit of the university administration on U.S. Supreme Court guidelines on obscenity, the Judicial Affairs Office dropped the case, and Story notified Hoop.

In an earlier letter of March 9, 1995, denying his request for an "open forum," Dean Story's voice had been this: "Per your request, a copy of the newsgroup posting for which you are being charged is enclosed. . . . I have decided . . . not to allow any other individuals [than an advisor and Hoop's parents] to attend this meeting. . . . I do not believe that turning the meeting into a public forum is appropriate." On April 3, after an intensive month-long encounter with the Internet, Dean Story's voice was this: "The charges against you for posting an allegedly obscene message . . . have been withdrawn by this Office. . . . I determined that the posting, taken as a whole within the context of the ongoing political discussion on the newsgroup, did not meet the three-part test for obscenity as articulated by the United States Supreme Court in the *Miller v. California* case." Speech was legally obscene, she explained to Hoop, only if "to the average person, applying community standards, the work, taken as a whole, appeals to the prurient interest; depicts sexual conduct in a patently offensive way; and lacks serious literary, artistic, political or scientific value." The University of Memphis was an arm of the state, and "no matter how highly offensive material may be," she continued, "the University cannot censor it unless it meets the test for obscenity or is otherwise outside of First Amendment protection." Indeed, she now concluded, the stakes were even higher than the obligations of a public university: "As an institution of higher education, we are committed to . . . free speech and academic freedom, and we recognize our role as a marketplace of ideas." Whatever your view of undergraduate language, don't you prefer the Dean Story who sounded more like the citizen of a free if difficult country?

The Midwest

Here, too, speech codes abound, although midwestern federal courts have been quick to find those of public institutions unconstitutional. At the private University of Chicago, although the *Student Information Manual* insists that "freedom of expression [is] fundamental," this only pertains to "reasoned debate." "Personal abuse," therefore, especially when directed to "expression of opinion," is "irrelevant to participation in the free exchange of ideas." Students are warned explicitly that "the University cannot thrive unless each member . . . is treated civilly."[53] At the public University of Illinois at Chicago, the harassment policy criminalizes, among other things, "any unwanted sexual gesture . . . or statement which is offensive [or] humiliating"; each case will be tried by the affirmative action officer alone; and sanctions "will be imposed . . . in a case-by-case basis."[54]

The freedom to criticize is essential, and radical students often use that freedom to condemn what they see as the "Eurocentric," "racist," or "sexist" bias of specific courses, often in frank and revealing student guides to courses. At Wabash College, however, in spring 1995, a conservative student journal, *The Wabash Commentary,* criticized an African-American history course for adopting a "feel good pedagogy" and encouraging personal rather than historical exploration. It quoted classroom praise of the course for help-ing students see their status as victims. In response, Wabash's president, An-drew T. Ford, in the fall of 1995, told incoming students that nothing said in a classroom could be repeated: "What happens in a classroom stays within the classroom. . . . [This culture of] 'candor . . . rigor . . . and the honesty we need to confront issues' requires us to be insiders. We must never break trust with one another."[55]

As the editors of *The Wabash Commentary* told the *Chronicle of Higher Ed-ucation*, "He's saying that if our magazine continues to publish this investiga-tive kind of story, there's no place for us at Wabash." Morgan Knull, who authored the article, had taken the course and wrote from direct experience. The professor, Peter Frederick, said that he would accept "honest criticism or debate," but not the "nasty misrepresentation of . . . other students . . . and of what I was doing as a teacher." Frederick, however, had no problem telling the *Chronicle* that Morgan Knull had discussed "welfare mothers" in-appropriately in the course.

The nature of the actual respect for "candor . . . rigor . . . and the hon-esty to confront issues" that President Ford had nurtured at Wabash was best revealed by the Student Senate's 21 to 7 vote to deny funding to the *Com-mentary*. Chip Timmons, president of the student government, gladly ex-plained to the *Chronicle* that "people are not very open to what they [the *Commentary*] have to say." One student senator said, "Does the *Commentary* harm the college? . . . Then we must not fund it." Knull's response was: "If the reporting is true, let the chips fall where they may." Wabash, he noted, had succeeded "in silencing the only dissent on campus." The money was reallocated to a new publication, *The Wabash Spectrum,* under the College Democrats.

Revelations about courses, however, can be specifically invited by a uni-versity when the goal is "progressive." In September 1985, the Department of Human Relations of Michigan State University (MSU), an administrative unit, issued a set of guidelines for "Bias-Free Communication." These in-structed the community to avoid, among other things, "words . . . that rein-force stereotypes, such as . . . 'colorful' . . . [or] 'black mood.'" Where Wabash sought to protect progressive thought by securing the absolute con-fidentiality of the classroom, MSU invited "systematic feedback" by students to "[hold] instructors . . . accountable," in their "communications, [for] bias, prejudice, and offensive implications." Even at extracurricular meetings, nothing must "stereotype or demean," and all members of the MSU com-munity must avoid "subtle discrimination" such as "eye contact or lack of it, seating patterns, interrupting, dominating the conversation, and verbal cues that discourage some participants from speaking while encouraging others." Indeed, the MSU Office of Human Relations advised: "Tape recording classes can help instructors to identify subtle and overt discrimination."[56]

In the Midwest, contempt for the Constitution by public universities has been an ongoing scandal. The University of Michigan, recall, was the home of a speech policy overturned by an appalled federal district court. An equally repressive policy (also overturned by a federal court) had been imposed on the University of Wisconsin (UW) by its chancellor, Donna Shalala.

In May 1987, a fraternity at UW–Madison had displayed a caricature of a dark-skinned Fiji Islander as a theme for a party.[57] In October 1988, another fraternity held a mock "slave auction." There were angry outcries against both. Students and faculty were free to protest, of course, or to use the occasions to bring what they saw as racism, insensitivity, or stupidity to public consciousness and debate. Instead, as tensions rose, Wisconsin chose to enact a speech code. On March 29, 1990, the Wisconsin ACLU joined a suit against the university, announcing that the important moral goals of toleration and equal opportunity "can be accomplished through means other than the creation of rules which infringe upon the fundamental freedom to express ideas."[58]

The speech code was drafted with the help of UW–Madison Law School professors Richard Delgado, Gordon Baldwin, and Ted Finman, who expressed confidence that it would withstand constitutional attack. On June 9, 1989, upon recommendation by Chancellor Shalala, it was adopted by the Board of Regents, 22 to 5, for the entire Wisconsin system. It prohibited and promised to discipline "racist or discriminatory comments, epithets or other expressive behavior, [in] non-academic matters," that were "directed at an individual or on separate occasions at different individuals," if these "intentionally demean" their objects "and create an intimidating, hostile or demeaning environment for education, university-related work or . . . activity." The issue of "intent," it explained, "shall be determined by consideration of all relevant circumstances." It gave protection to discussions of group characteristics in the classroom, and it specifically exempted faculty members, stating that the policy "applies only to students."

Twelve student plaintiffs challenged the policy in federal court (only one of whom had been prosecuted under it), arguing that the prohibitions went far beyond the university's stated constitutional justification, the "fighting words" doctrine of *Chaplinsky*. The district court examined the cases of all students who had been sanctioned under it. Every single one related to offenses against nonwhites and women, as if no one in the entire Wisconsin system had said an actionable word about white males. Many of the offenses were already crimes (theft, impersonating an officer, assault, and terroristic threats). Many of the sentences were bizarre, demanding that students take specific courses, and otherwise intruding into matters of private conscience.

The court agreed emphatically with the plaintiffs, noting that no definition of "intimidating" or "demeaning," let alone of "hostile," created the "threat to public peace and tranquility" demanded by *Chaplinsky* although the court refrained from ruling on whether *Chaplinsky* still was viable law. Above all, the court held, the policy was unconstitutional precisely because "the UW rule regulates speech upon its content." It disciplined students "whose comments, epithets or other expressive behavior demeans [*sic*] their addressees' race, sex, religion, etc. . . . [but] leaves unregulated [all other] comments, epithets and other expressive behavior that affirms [*sic*] or does [*sic*] not address [those attributes]." Further, where the university claimed that the speech it prohibited lacked social utility, the court noted that "most students punished under the rule are likely to have employed comments, epithets or other expressive behavior to inform their listeners of their racist or discriminatory views." The university surely could restrain its own official speech to work for the goal of expanded educational opportunity, but the students as students were neither employees nor state actors, and the social goal "is inapplicable to this case."

Further, the court ruled, Wisconsin had ignored the constitutional reality that "the First Amendment protects speech for its emotive function even if it lacks cognitive value." Finally, the policy was "unconstitutionally vague," both in its terms—"discriminatory comments," "epithets," "abusive language," "demean"—and its notion of intent. Three leading lights of Wisconsin's flagship law school may have found the policy constitutional, but the federal court did not, declaring it unconstitutional for overbreadth and vagueness.

Undeterred, the chancellor recommended a new code to the regents in the spring of 1992, which they adopted in March.[59] Under this code, to satisfy *Chaplinsky*, UW added the requirement that an intentional, demeaning epithet not only creates a hostile environment, but "tends to provoke an immediate violent response when addressed to a person of average sensibility who is a member of the group that the word, phrase, or symbol insults or threatens." Faced with another lawsuit, however, the regents reversed themselves in September and repealed the speech code, 10 to 6.

The *Washington Post,* a consistent critic of campus speech codes, editorially observed: "Debate, example, and the social pressure of peers are far more effective tools in creating and upholding civility on campus than quasi-legal procedures that often make martyrs out of fools."[60] America knows that; its universities do not.

When federal courts began striking down codes restricting "verbal behavior" at public universities and colleges, other institutions, even in those jurisdictions, did not seek to abolish their policies. Thus, Central Michigan University, after the University of Michigan code had been declared unconstitutional, maintained a far broader and vaguer policy outlawing "offense" on grounds of race or ethnicity, not to mention "epitaphs [*sic,* we hope] or slogans that infer [*sic*] negative connotations about an individual's racial or ethnic affiliation."[61]

In 1993, this policy was challenged, successfully, in U.S. District Court, in a case that reveals much about the current state of American academic life. The court noted that the code applied to "all possible human conduct" and, citing internal university documents, that Central Michigan intended to apply it to speech "'which a person "feels" has affronted either him or some group, predicated on race or ethnicity.'" Central Michigan had argued to the court that its policy, "benign" on matters of free expression, "was not a 'speech code,'" but the court found that if the policy's words had any meaning, they precisely banned protected speech. If someone's "treatise, term paper or even . . . cafeteria bull session" about the Middle East proposed "some ancient ethnic traditions which give rise to barbarian combativeness or . . . inability to compromise," such speech, the court found, "would seem to be a good fit with the policy language." No claim of sincerity was exculpatory, because the policy itself declared "intent" or "good faith" to be irrelevant. Under the policy, the court concluded, "if the speech gives offense it is prohibited."

On May 4, 1993, after the suit had been filed, the president of Central Michigan assured the university community that the policy was not intended to "interfere impermissibly with individuals' rights to free speech." The court declared itself "emphatically unimpressed" by such a savings clause, and "not willing to entrust . . . the First Amendment to the tender mercies of this institution's discriminatory harassment/affirmative action enforcer."

The origin of the suit was instructive. It had arisen from the plight of Central Michigan's white basketball coach, Keith Dambrot. Most of his players were black and, as several of them testified to the court on Dambrot's behalf when he first (successfully) sought a preliminary injunction, they themselves frequently used the term "nigger" as a positive term on the team, to connote someone who is "fearless, mentally strong, and tough." When Dambrot used the term similarly at a practice, however, and word leaked out, protests erupted. Central Michigan and Dambrot agreed on a summary discipline of five days suspension without pay. Campus activists held demonstrations for harsher punishment, which were publicized by regional and national media. On April 12, 1993, Central Michigan informed Dambrot of his termination at semester's end. After the preliminary injunction and the suit, several blacks now joined the actual suit, claiming that their own constitutional rights were equally threatened, given their use of precisely the same term. At that initial hearing, the court repeatedly corrected the university's attorney, who kept defending the banning of "epitaphs." It is sad enough that courts have to teach universities the difference between "epitaphs" and "epithets," but it is tragic that courts and courageous student athletes now must teach universities about the "bedrock" principles of freedom and equality.

The judicial revocation of the speech code at the University of Wisconsin also did not mean the end of the repression of free speech in that system. In November 1994, after the Republican Party swept the national elections, the College Republicans at UW–River Falls put up posters that showed a college student staring at a dancing elephant. The caption read: "College Republicans . . . We're not the minority anymore. We are the politically incorrect majority."[62]

The poster, as its designer, Dana Criona, explained to the campus newspaper, the *Student Voice*, was created with the easy-to-use software program, Microsoft's Creative Writer, whose generic icon for a college student, as fits the times, has a somewhat "multicultural" look about him.[63] In early March 1995, an outside speaker, Ken Stern, was lecturing about bigotry. Told about the poster, he advised the audience that critics of the poster should have an educated discussion about it, not censor it. A residence director, Karna Baseman Stark, however, was at the meeting, and she raised the general issue with the council of her dormitory, Parker Hall, which wrote to the College Republicans to say that they were removing the posters because they were "racist." One member of the board, Sharon Rodrique, even objected to the slogan. As she told the *Student Voice,* "They are not worried about being politically correct, and here they should have been." Lisa Reavill, coordinator of multicultural Services, agreed that the posters were offensive: "It shows an elephant gleefully dancing with an African-American . . . [which] verges into an unethical stance." Reavill admitted that in her poll of the campus, "even African-American students look at it and say 'so what?'" The affair, however, was not to be controlled by students.[64]

On March 9, 1995, Professor Steven Derfler protested the flier to the president of the Student Senate, arguing, without apparent irony, that "the spirit of the First Amendment" had been "noxiously violated by an image that is clearly racist, tied to the language of the flyer." Free speech was usually the right policy, Derfler wrote, but not in this case, "when a blatantly stereo-typic, racist image is portrayed and is associated with the terms 'minority' and 'politically incorrect.'" For Derfler, "the free speech message of the flyer crosses the line into the realm of bigotry, racism, and xenophobia."

Jose E. Vega, assistant dean of the College of Education, also instructed the Student Senate "to take decisive steps to rectify what I deem to be a manifestation of racist behavior." The issue, Vega wrote, was "whether this political entity [College Republicans] should be recognized and funded." Vega also explained that "whoever is responsible for printing and disseminat-ing this flyer needs to offer an apology . . . for this display of prejudice and in-sensitivity." The ban stood.

The graphics of a flier, of course, are an intersection of politics and artis-tic representation, and, for all the academic hand-wringing over the NEA, art also is besieged on college campuses. People for the American Way (PAW) noted, in its 1994 report, *Artistic Freedom Under Attack,* that "while self-styled 'conservative' groups . . . still account for a substantial number of the incidents we have documented, many issue-focussed attacks on art now come from the left side of the political spectrum."[65] Although the most egre-gious academic cases arose from the Midwest, PAW cited a significant num-ber of cases from a range of American campuses. At Dartmouth College, for example, the administration announced a policy "of covering up campus murals that some students feel are derogatory to Native Americans." At Colby College, an artist displayed diverse images of the Rodney King beat-ing, with the title "As Exciting as Police Brutality." The artist insisted that the posters were to resensitize the public to police violence, but protesters denounced them (and destroyed some) for "promoting racism," and Colby's president formally condemned the exhibit. The artist removed his art.[66]

At the University of Michigan–Ann Arbor, the school of law and *The Michigan Journal of Gender and Law* sponsored a symposium and mixed-media exhibit on prostitution. According to PAW's 1994 report, the guest curator of the exhibit, artist Carol Jacobsen, installed a videotape of her own inter-views with prostitutes and a video by a former prostitute. On the day that the symposium began, organizers removed Jacobsen's videos in response to com-plaints from guest speakers. Jacobsen argued that if they objected to any part of the exhibit, they would have to censor the entire show. The organizers replied, PAW noted, that "we really didn't think of it as a censorship issue, but as a safety issue." The show was canceled. Law professor Catherine MacKinnon defended the removal of the works and denounced "a witch-hunt by First Amendment fundamentalists who are persecuting and black-listing dissidents . . . as art censors."[67]

At the University of Missouri, PAW reported, an artist hung a painting that deliberately parodied racial stereotypes. The painting was denounced by a group of students and faculty as "racist." The campus Equal Employment Opportunity (EEO) director said that the university had "no place for something that doesn't show African Americans in a positive light." The work was temporarily removed. When it was discovered that the artist himself was black, however, the EEO director decided that there was a place at the university for his work after all.[68]

Even librarians, those perennial defenders of free expression, no longer are immune to political correctness. At Iowa State University, librarians in August 1995 decided to remove an antiabortion newsletter from their shelves. Bob Sickles, himself a librarian there, had been donating the *Right to Life News* to the library for four years. According to the *Chronicle of Higher Education,* Cynthia Dobson, another librarian, informed Sickles that the four-year collection of the newsletter was being removed from the library's shelves because the library did not offer a publication with the opposing viewpoint. Sickles offered to provide the library with the publications of Planned Parenthood, a prochoice group. This was insufficient. Nancy L. Eason, who heads library services at Iowa State, told the *Chronicle* that the newsletter was being pulled because it was not scholarly enough.[69]

In July 1989, a conservative newspaper at the University of Iowa, the *Campus Review,* created a display case with a T-shirt that showed two gay men in a homosexual act, inside a circle with a line across it (the universal symbol for "no"). Beneath the circle were the words "Stop AIDS," the message of the shirt being, in the words of the *Review*'s editor, "to stop AIDS you have to stop homosexual intercourse." There were protests and calls for censorship, but as Phillip Jones, the dean of student services, said to the *New York Times,* in a model of appropriate academic governance, "There are procedural rules, but none for content. The *Campus Review* has the right to express its political and social point of view in a forum for ideas." In reaching that decision, however, Jones had to overrule Susan Buckley, director of the Women's Resource and Action Center and a staff member of student services. Buckley told the *Times* that the display violated the university's human rights policy and should not have been allowed: "The policy explicitly states that protection from discrimination is extended to gays and lesbians. In my mind, that display encourages harassment." The tragedy of American colleges and universities is that the Susan Buckleys usually prevail over the Phillip Joneses.[70]

Many people, alas, unlike Phillip Jones, say that they "believe in free speech; however. . . ." The University of Kansas, in 1996, decided, in the words of *U. Magazine*—a journalistic insert in college papers across the country—"to cleanse cyberhate from their systems." Defending such a policy, Craig Paul, of the University of Kansas Office of System Support, told *U.* that "Kansas supports free speech. However, we also support the right not to provide university facilities for it." In Paul's words, "In most cases, we will issue a warning to the student, but we can also take away an account or send it to judicial affairs." That is what can pass as "supporting free speech" these days.[71]

At the University of Oklahoma, in April 1996, the administration censored all access to sexually explicit newsgroups on the Internet. President David Boren, a former U.S. Senator, told the *Chronicle for Higher Education* in May that he was proud that the university had adopted a motto of "When in doubt, do not block." Professor Bill Loving, however, pointed out to the *Chronicle* the invariably indiscriminate nature of censorship. Despite what Boren had termed a "scalpel" policy, the university in fact had denied access to a discussion group among victims of sexual assault.[72] A large number of students at the university, and the *Oklahoma Daily,* the student newspaper, rallied to the cause of free speech and kept up a steady flow of information to groups concerned with liberty on the Internet. The Student Congress of the university risked campus prosecution by making access to the banned groups available via its own homepage. The Electronic Frontier Foundation and the organization Fight-Censorship established Websites devoted to the ban.[73] As the *Oklahoma Daily* reported on May 2, 1996, an artist's exhibit opened at the University Museum, recording, in the words of the artist, his "reaction to censorship." Tom Toperzer, director of the museum, ordered the exhibit closed, claiming that the quality of the exhibit was not worthy of hanging in the museum.[74] A professor filed suit to prevent the censorship of the Internet, but on January 28, 1997, President Boren prevailed in *Loving v. Boren* because the Tenth Circuit Court of Appeals tossed Loving's case out on a technicality without reaching the First Amendment question. Boren told the *Chronicle* that he was proud of his "long record of being very protective of the First Amendment."

Minnesota

Minnesota really should have its own chapter. There, public universities act like partisan political seminaries and have almost no concern for the most fundamental issues of free speech. In a state once known for protecting dissidents, a sorry pall of orthodoxy now prevails. If these cases had not actually occurred, they could be parodies.

Recall Wabash College's concern that conservative discussion of what occurred in a college course might inhibit the free, spontaneous flow of ideas. Similarly, at Penn, in November 1985, Sheldon Hackney warned the Faculty Senate that the conservative Accuracy in Academia, by encouraging students critical of courses to make their objections public, posed one of the most essential threats to academic freedom, namely "trial by accusation, and intimidation."[75]

The University of Minnesota (UM), however, encouraged students (and faculty) to bring the sensitivity police into the classroom itself. On August 30, 1993, Patricia Mullen, the director of the Office of Equal Opportunity and Affirmative Action, and Becky Kroll, the director of the Minnesota Women's Center, sent all faculty a memorandum entitled "Improving Classroom Experience." The memorandum arose, they wrote, because of a student who believed that "fellow students' crude comments [during] a classroom discussion of a cultural diversity 'hot topic' . . . Columbus [were not] adequately handled by the instructor." In response, the memo announced a pilot program, the "Classroom Climate Adviser" project. Any student who found that "a classroom discussion about race or gender was disrespectful and insulting," or any instructor who worried that "some students are having trouble distinguishing between theories I have to teach and my personal beliefs about controversial matters in the area of diversity," could request the presence of "a classroom climate adviser." Prudence might well dictate the use of such advisers, by the way, because one of the University of Minnesota's definitions of sexual harassment is "callous insensitivity to the experience of women."[76]

Campus climate, at Minnesota, is distinctly more important than even the most essential object of First Amendment freedom, political speech. In late August and early September 1993, at the main campus in Minneapolis, the College Republicans were registered to participate as one of forty-six different student organizations in a month-long orientation fair. They distributed fliers that were conservative satires of the Clinton administration—critical of the president's policies and values—and all drawn from either the nationally published *Slick Times* or a tax-form parody criticizing Clinton's views of gays and lesbians (widely circulated on the Internet), an issue of major national discussion and controversy. Presidents Johnson, Nixon, and Reagan gladly would have settled for criticism so mild on college campuses.[77]

On August 30, the Office of New Student Programs ordered the fliers removed. The story was widely covered in the *Minneapolis Star Tribune,* the *Pioneer Press,* and on Minneapolis radio, and monitored by an appalled Minnesota ACLU. Also, the university was unapologetically candid about its actions. The assistant director of the Office of New Student Programs, Dave Gerbitz, explained to the media that the fliers were insensitive to gays and feminists: "One of our guidelines [is] to not allow oppressive material." Michelle Karon, director of the Office of New Student Programs, defended the actions of her office: "They [the College Republicans] have the right to their opinion, but the manner is what we found inappropriate. We feel strongly that it's not appropriate at orientation and registration to mock or make humor at the expense of a group." The College Republicans immediately wrote a letter of protest to President Nils Hasselmo. Two weeks later, on September 15, the administration replied, in a letter from Vice President Marvalene Hughes, vigorously defending the ban. The university strongly supported free speech, she informed the College Republicans, but it required "an atmosphere which is respectful of diversity, [and] some of your group's display materials were not compatible with this purpose." The fliers were not "consistent with the goals of the University" and had violated "the University's non-discrimination policy." They also violated orientation guidelines by which students receive an "appreciation of diversity and multiculturalism."

The matter would have ended there except for public scrutiny and criticism. The *Minneapolis Star Tribune* acerbically covered the story five times between September 16 and 22, and editorialized about free speech. The ACLU publicly supported the College Republicans. KSTP-AM devoted considerable airtime to the events. The *Pioneer Press* issued periodic "Updates." Liberal columnist Doug Grow, of the *Star Tribune,* denounced Minnesota's position as "hogwash" and ridiculed President Hasselmo.

On September 22, Hasselmo backed down, announced that the administration no longer would censor student handouts and, reincarnated, wrote to the *Star Tribune* that "I must, and will, protect freedom of speech as a fundamental right under rules of academic freedom and under our Constitution." However, Hasselmo wrote, he was permitting the fliers not because he had erred previously—the university's general counsel had reiterated that the ban was perfectly constitutional—but simply because the suppression of the fliers had "the potential for" or "the appearance of" suppression of free speech.[78] He permitted the College Republicans to resume offering their material on September 21, which was also the final day of the orientation fair.

David P. Bryden, professor of law, posed a rhetorical question worth pondering: "Would the General Counsel of the University approve guidelines for orientation that prohibited attacks on 'family values'?" T. Baxter Stephenson, a former chairman of the College Republicans, was interviewed by the *Star Tribune* on September 16. He noted that "the university censored our handouts because they did not promote diversity, [but] what the university is forgetting is—diversity of thought." "If you can't have diversity of thought, so that you can criticize the President of the United States," he concluded, "then . . . you don't have a university where you can develop your mind."[79] Almost everyone used to believe that.

The case had an interesting ending. A law student at Minnesota, Peter Swanson, supported by the Individual Rights Foundation, sued the university and its administrators for violations of students' constitutional rights, citing Hasselmo's insistence that the regulations were constitutional and still in force but, at his discretion, would be not be applied. Before the suit went to trial, Minnesota and President Hasselmo settled with Swanson. As reported in the *Chronicle of Higher Education,* the essential terms of the settlement were that top-level administrators would hear a lecture about the protection of free speech by the First Amendment and that the university would issue a new policy. In the words of General Counsel Mark B. Rotenberg, "There will be no review or censorship of student materials."[80] Now, individuals, even administrators, should not be forced to hear a lecture, especially one with which they disagree so forcefully, but, that aside, the policy has been revised consistently with the Constitution.

Censorship, however, is a tide that always is coming in, and freedom of speech knows few periods of safety at Minnesota's public campuses. On April 1, 1996, the student newspaper at UM–Duluth, the *Statesman,* published its satiric April Fool's Day issue. An article about a fictional gay bar joked about gay and lesbian culture (although it was not clear at all whether it was satirizing gays and lesbians or, rather, individuals prejudiced against them). It also included a fake advertisement from the "Duluth White Man's Militia," phone number, "KKK-2435" (and here, it would take a stretch, indeed, to see the parody as attacking nonwhites rather than militias). Members of both the UM–Duluth gay and lesbian student group and the Black Student Association seized fifty-five hundred copies of the *Statesman* and passed them out at a student protest rally. As reported in the *Chronicle of Higher Education,* the chancellor of UM–Duluth, Kathryn A. Martin, addressed a meeting of five hundred students who were protesting the paper, and she called the edition "a despicable and blatant misuse of the responsibility of free speech." She announced that the publication may have crossed the line into obscenity, and that the administration was investigating the possibility of disciplinary action against the editors.[81]

UM–Duluth had been given, temporarily as matters turned out, a virtual free hand at that time—by a startling ruling of a three-judge panel of the U.S. Eighth Circuit Court of Appeals—to engage in censorship.[82] In the spring of 1991, Sandra Featherman, newly appointed vice chancellor at UM–Duluth, received several appalling, terroristic threats against her life; these were under investigation by the campus police and the FBI. In the fall semester of 1991, the undergraduate History Club asked its faculty to pose individually for a photo wall, with each professor garbed in the manner of his or her specialty. The teacher of ancient history posed benignly with laurel and a legionnaire's sword. The teacher of the American West posed impishly with a coonskin cap and a .45-caliber pistol resting on his lap.[83]

A group of faculty, calling the photos a threat to Featherman, demanded that they be removed. Then, a few weeks before the long-planned photographic exhibit was unveiled in late March 1992, history professor Judith Trolander also received death threats similar to those against Featherman. In that context, and in response to complaints about the photographs, Judith Karon, UM–Duluth's affirmative action officer, termed the photos "insensitive and inappropriate," and Chancellor Lawrence Ianni ordered the campus police to remove the two offending photographs. The students (and the two professors) successfully sued UM–Duluth in U.S. District Court, which predictably ruled, in April 1995, that the removal of the photographs was a clear, indeed, an "inconceivable" violation of their constitutional rights.

The university appealed to the Court of Appeals, where an initial three-judge panel reversed the district court, ruling 2 to 1 that UM–Duluth's interests as a public agency overrode any First Amendment rights in this case. The court cited the atmosphere of tension, and it reasoned that the "display case" was a constitutionally unprotected "nonpublic forum." In a dissent, Circuit Judge C. Arlen Beam noted that under this reasoning, the students and historians licitly could have "burned an American flag outside the University history department,[but] cannot advance . . . expressive conduct intended to support and publicize areas of teaching expertise and special interest within the department." In Beam's view, "The Court's opinion is not a demonstration of legitimate First Amendment jurisprudence but . . . an example of the triumph of the political correctness agenda." He pointed out that "the opinion would even permit suppression of . . . advocacy of gender and cultural diversity at UM-Duluth if Chancellor Ianni subjectively felt that such speech contributed to an inefficient and negative working and learning environment on the campus because of [either] unlawful or vehement but protected opposition."

Justice Beam's constitutional reasoning was vindicated in July 1997, when the full membership of the Eighth Circuit Court, on further review, threw out the ruling of the three-judge panel. The court decided, by a decisive 8 to 2 margin, that the university had violated the First Amendment of the U.S. Constitution—indeed, that it had not even come close to meeting criteria by which speech could be curtailed by a public institution. Beam's prior dissent now became the majority opinion. The circuit court sent the case back to the trial court to determine damages for the two professors, one of whom had already been terminated (the other being tenured). According to the *Chronicle of Higher Education*, "Mark Rotenberg, General Counsel to the University of Minnesota System, said the university had not decided whether to appeal to the Supreme Court."[84]

The West

The speech code provisions of most western colleges and universities share the same "verbal behavior" restrictions that are becoming ubiquitous in American academic life. Even Berkeley, of all places, adopted them, banning "fighting words," of all things. Nonetheless, there always are opportunities for creative variation. Montana State University, for example, indeed outlaws "sexually explicit or demeaning comments" that create "an intimidating, hostile, or offensive working or learning environment" (the "or" means that just "hostile" or "offensive" will suffice). Examples of "verbal harassment" include "offensive or derogatory remarks, jokes or comments," "innuendos of a sexual nature," "suggestive or insulting sounds such as whistling," and "remarks about clothing, figure, or sexual activities." Examples of "non-verbal harassment" include "displaying posters or photos of a sexual nature." Montana State has created, however, in addition to such "harassment," the actionable offense of "sexual intimidation." Although the term conjures images of illegal physical threats, the university has other things in mind, defining the "crime" as "any unreasonable behavior that is verbal or non-verbal, which subjects members of either sex to humiliation, embarrassment, or discomfort because of their gender." Montana State's examples include "using sexist cartoons to illustrate concepts" and "making stereotypical remarks about the abilities of men or women."[85]

The University of Southern California had one of the broadest definitions of verbal harassment in the nation, until the 1992 adoption of the state's Leonard Law, which extended First Amendment protections to students at nonsectarian private universities. Until very recently, USC included questions or statements about sexual activity, "jokes" and "innuendos," and "whistling and other sounds, etc." among possible acts of harassment by expression.[86] The Leonard Law might well have its limits, however. In April 1997, the Claremont McKenna College suspended a student for a newsletter in response to charges from three female readers that the publication created "a hostile environment," making his return to the college dependent on successful completion of sexual harassment sensitivity training. The Southern California chapter of the ACLU took the case to the Pomona Superior Court, arguing that the newsletter was obviously protected speech. Judge Wendell Mortimer, Jr., however, ruled ingeniously that the newsletter "had the potential to create a hostile environment," so the final verdict is not yet in.[87]

Undeterred by any sense of constitutional limits, the University of North Dakota has a policy that outlaws harassment defined as anything that intentionally produces "psychological . . . discomfort, embarrassment, or ridicule," a category of no small scope.[88] The University of Texas (UT), meanwhile, has been engaged in a precedent-setting assault on freedom of the Internet and of the student press. At UT–Dallas, as both the Electronic Frontier Foundation and Fight-Censorship reported in March 1996, students are permitted access to only three hundred newsgroups, under the guise that all of the rest are not related to "education."[89]

More dramatically, the entire UT system is undertaking a much deeper effort of censorship. In 1986, in *Hazelwood School District v. Kuhlmeier,*[90] the U.S. Supreme Court gave *high school* administrators greater authority than they had previously enjoyed to censor school-sponsored student publications. In 1992, according to the *Student Press Law Center Report,* the Office of General Counsel of the UT system, under J. Robert Giddings, advised UT campuses that *Hazelwood* gave universities greater latitude in controlling sponsored student publications. In documents cited by the SPLC, Giddings, in May 1994, advised UT's associate executive vice chancellor for academic affairs that "educators do not offend the First Amendment by exercising editorial control over the style and content of student speech in school-sponsored expressive activities," including "the prior review of newspaper articles." If this view should be upheld in court, the free speech of every student at a public university would be in peril. Giddings, as cited by the SPLC, proposed that campuses that had exempted student campus publications from censorship now adopt an alternative policy: "The student faculty adviser . . . shall exercise complete oversight authority for the review of all official publications." According to Robert Rollins, a student publications adviser at UT–Pan American, Giddings's advice already has been acted upon at UT–El Paso, UT–Arlington, and UT–Brownsville, all of which now have prior review.[91] In January 1998, the SPLC reported that UT was explicitly committed to putting its system of prior review in place statewide.[92]

At Washington State University, the student newspaper, the *Daily Evergreen* was repeatedly censored in the summer and fall of 1996. In protest, it published an issue on November 1, 1996, that was empty of news on all pages, printing only advertisements and a front-page editorial that demanded an end to censorship. At a meeting of the Student Publications Board on November 4, Bob Hilliard, general manager of student publications, claimed that he had censored the paper on behalf of the interim provost, Geoff Gamble, and that university policies gave him the right to edit and control the content of the *Daily Evergreen*.[93]

In the West as elsewhere, the struggle for campus First Amendment and academic freedoms requires coalitions across the political spectrum. On May 16, 1989, in Washington, D.C., former attorney general Edwin Meese stood next to the ACLU's Morton Halperin at a press conference to announce the settlement of a lawsuit between their common object of concern, James Taranto, a conservative former college journalist, and California State University–Northridge. In 1987, the University of California–Los Angeles had suspended a student editor for printing a cartoon that, in the words of the national ACLU, "made fun of affirmative action." That penalty should have been unthinkable, but worse was to happen. In March 1987, Taranto, news editor of the *Daily Sundial,* the student newspaper at Northridge, wrote a column criticizing UCLA officials for that suspension, arguing that "a university exists to promote the search for truth, and censorship is always detrimental to that search." For writing that editorial, Taranto was suspended for two weeks from his position. The ACLU of Southern California joined his case. The settlement was, above all else, a matter of principle. Taranto received ninety-three dollars in back pay, and the suspension was stricken from his academic transcript. The *Daily Sundial,* which previously had required administrative permission to write on "controversial" matters, won a new policy: "Students working on the *Sundial* are fully protected by the First Amendment of the Constitution."[94]

At the press conference with Meese, the ACLU's Halperin spoke truths that academics still do not want to hear. Conservative students and opinions, he said, were the victims of bias at American campuses: "There is a double standard, and it's a troubling matter." "There are no cases," he observed, "where universities discipline students for views or opinions of the left, or for racist comments against non-minorities."

What did Northridge learn from all this? Not much. In the fall of 1992, a fraternity at the university, Zeta Beta Tau, advertised a party with a south-of-the-border theme by posting fliers referring to a well-known song about a Mexican prostitute. On October 24, Ron Kopita, vice president for student affairs, suspended the fraternity until a hearing could be held to determine if it had violated campus policy. (In *Alice in Wonderland,* columnist Linda Seebach noted in the *L.A. Daily News,* "sentence first, verdict after" was considered the mark of monumental irrationality.) On November 9, Vice President Kopita suspended the fraternity for more than two years, finding it guilty of violating the campus code prohibiting expressions that "promote degrading or demeaning social stereotypes based on race, ethnicity, national origin, gender, sexual orientation, religion or disability." Future members wishing rerecognition in 1994 would have to "engage in activities that will educate them in multiculturalism."[95]

In 1993, however, the California higher educational system quite literally was taught a lesson about the First Amendment.[96] A fraternity at the University of California–Riverside, Phi Kappa Sigma, advertised its own south-of-the-border party with a T-shirt that pictured a man with a sombrero and a bottle of beer. The caption read: "It doesn't matter where you come from as long as you know where you are going." Riverside administrators faced angry protests by Hispanic student groups, who termed the T-shirt a degrading stereotype. Ironically, the fraternity member who designed the theme party T-shirt was Mexican–American, and almost half of PKS's members were minority students. Kevin Ferguson, Riverside's campus activities director, brought charges against the fraternity. The university found PKS guilty, and sentenced it to, among other things, destruction of the T-shirts, mandatory participation by PKS members in cultural awareness programs, and suspension (as an organization) for three years. Vincent Del Pinzo, assistant vice chancellor for student affairs, imposing the sentence, termed the T-shirt "ignorant, insensitive, and considered racist by many chicano/a and latino/a students."

The fraternity, however, fought back. The Individual Rights Foundation took the case pro bono, and PKS filed suit in state court for violation of its members' free speech rights. Facing the suit, Riverside agreed to a settlement, the final point of which was particularly striking. The university agreed to rerecognize the fraternity immediately, to drop all charges, and to send Vincent Del Pinzo and Kevin Ferguson to education concerning the First Amendment. Here, too, it is unjust to force individuals to study things for which they have contempt, although some voluntarily acquired knowledge of what they have been sworn to uphold might well be useful.

What conclusions were drawn from all this? Ira Glasser, executive director of the ACLU, told the *Wall Street Journal,* "When someone wears a t-shirt that others find offensive, too bad!" For those who endured or wore the T-shirts and slogans of the '60s, that must seem fair enough. Ferguson told the *Journal* that whoever had agreed to that settlement must have been unaware that he once taught U.S. government in high school. The social chairman of PKS said that he decided that the next bash would be on the theme of the '70s, and not the "build-your-own-burrito-night" that he had planned. Roberto Tijerina, cochairman of Movimiento Estudiantil Chicano de Aztlan (MEChA), one of the Hispanic groups that had objected to the T-shirts, told the *Journal* that the T-shirt was protected by the First Amendment, but added: "If it was causing a hostile environment, how can you allow that? I think freedom of speech is being twisted out of proportion." Perhaps he had studied in high school under Ferguson.[97]

By 1994, thus, the atmosphere in California had changed, at least when repression was challenged openly. Scott Smith, however, a student at the University of California–Santa Cruz (UC–SC), a campus celebrated for its tolerance of the cultural Left, was threatened with sanctions for his column, "Smitty on a Hill," in an independent, alternative student publication. In a column entitled, "Where's the Women?" he had lamented political correctness and called for a "Miss Nude UC–SC contest" to lighten things up, requesting that all photos be sent to him.[98]

Instead, he received letters from UC–SC officials, warning him that any "actions . . . which produce complaints [seven women had charged sexual harassment by his column] because they are directed at individuals, or, by virtue of their persistent pattern, create a hostile or intimidating climate, could result in sanctions which could range from administrative warning to . . . suspension or dismissal from the University." David Dodson, college administrative officer, wrote to Smith that "your right to state your own views *responsibly* is certainly not subject to sanction [emphasis added]," but warning him that his column might constitute sexual harassment.

Smith posted news of his plight on the newsgroup alt.censorship, and from there it came to the attention of Robert Chatelle of the National Writers Union. After reading Smith's articles and the administration's warnings, Chatelle wrote to Dodson: Smith's column was "patently not sexual harassment." Over half of the NWU's membership, he explained, were women, many were gays and lesbians, and "we believe that bringing false or frivolous charges of sexual harassment does a great deal of harm." Above all, however, he gave Dodson a lesson on the First Amendment: "We suggest that you re-read the First Amendment to the US constitution. You will not find the word 'responsibly' within it. Our nation's founders understood that speech generally considered responsible needed no special protection." Smith's article was protected, he concluded, and "you lack any authority to abridge his constitutional rights."

When Chatelle asked if this could be settled without the need for the NWU to proceed formally, Dodson replied promptly that there had been a "misunderstanding," that Scott's column was not sexual harassment, that no one would interfere with his First Amendment rights, and that he now had sent Scott a letter clarifying all of these points. Students are not brave, however, having invested so much of their time, hopes, and funds in their education. For each Scott Smith, how many undergraduates are silenced or choose never to express themselves at all?

PART III

THE ASSAULT ON
THE INDIVIDUAL

CHAPTER 8

INDIVIDUAL IDENTITY:
THE HEART OF LIBERTY

One branch of First Amendment jurisprudence—the right to private conscience—is particularly relevant to understanding the true nature of freedom, whether in the academy or in the larger society. The protection of inner autonomy from power is at the heart of liberty and decency. The American legal doctrine of a right to freedom of conscience, and the moral values that inform that right, put into bold relief the intrusions upon inner being imposed by speech codes, official group identities, thought reform, and mandatory sensitivity training.

Coerced conformity in matters of conscience is the fatal enemy of liberty, but it is often difficult to resist during periods of crisis, when a society views dissent from majority beliefs as a threat to what it believes to be a vital unity of purpose. This difficulty—and the courage to overcome it—can be seen in a pair of cases decided by the U.S. Supreme Court during World War II, resulting in one of the most remarkable confessions of error in American constitutional history.

On June 3, 1940, with most of the world at war, the Court decided the case of *Minersville School District v. Gobitis,* which at the time seemed destined to become a landmark case.[1] A Jehovah's Witness challenged a requirement that his children salute the American flag in school, citing his religion's understanding of Exodus, which proscribes worship of any idol or "graven image." The Court, however, ruled that the mandatory salute did not violate the First Amendment, relying heavily upon the principle that a government must protect national cohesion, and viewing the requirement of a pledge of allegiance to the flag as a legitimate means to this goal. The opinion was written by Justice Felix Frankfurter, himself a member of a religious minority. He recognized that the issue in the case reflected the "profoundest problem confronting a democracy—the problem which Lincoln cast in a memorable dilemma: 'Must a government of necessity be too strong for the liberties of its people, or too weak to maintain its own existence?'"[2]

Posing the question that way virtually assured the answer that liberty was going to have to be compromised. Although Frankfurter and his colleagues formally recognized that "the affirmative pursuit of one's convictions about the ultimate mystery of the universe and man's relation to it is placed beyond the reach of the law," they noted nonetheless that "when the conscience of individuals collides with the felt necessities of society," it is conscience that must bend. "The ultimate foundation of a free society," the Court wrote, "is the binding tie of cohesive sentiment. . . . 'We live by symbols' . . . [and] the flag is the symbol of our national unity, transcending all internal differences." Indeed, the Court urged, religious minorities should see the flag as a symbol of their own liberty and safety. The invasion of Gobitis's conscience, in effect, was for his own good, because "the enjoyment of all freedom presuppose[s] the kind of ordered society which is summarized by our flag."

A mere three years after *Gobitis* was decided with only a single dissent, the Court reviewed another flag pledge case, however, and this time, by a vote of 6 to 3, even with America herself at war, the justices disavowed *Gobitis*.[3] The West Virginia legislature had enacted a statute to require all public and private schools to teach, foster, and perpetuate "the ideals, principles and spirit of Americanism." The state Board of Education, inspired by *Gobitis,* ordered a daily flag salute. Refusal subjected the student to dismissal and subjected parents to criminal penalties. In *West Virginia Board of Education v. Barnette* (1943), the Court analyzed the constitutionality of such a requirement not solely in terms of religious liberty but, more broadly, in terms of the right of private conscience against governmental coercion of expressions of belief. Writing for the majority, Justice Robert Jackson had no quarrel with West Virginia's requirement that certain courses be taught, nor with its attempts to inspire patriotism by exposing students to national history and traditions. However, the board's flag salute requirement was different, because it compelled a student "to declare a belief [and] . . . to utter what is not in his mind." In matters of belief, human beings were essentially distinct, and each was free to find "jest and scorn" where another found "comfort and inspiration."

The Court now found that what underlay its decision in *Gobitis*—the supposed conflict between liberty of conscience and the state's ability to survive—was both an exaggeration and a distraction from the core constitutional question. The issue was not weak or strong government, but seeing the strength of America in "individual freedom of mind" rather than in "officially disciplined uniformity for which history indicates a disappointing and disastrous end." Enforced conformity, far from teaching the value of liberty, would "strangle the free mind at its source and teach youth to discount important principles of our government as mere platitudes."

Jackson explained why even men of good intentions should not possess the awesome power to compel belief. Both the good and the evil had attempted "to coerce uniformity of sentiment in support of some end thought essential." Such goals had been variously racial, territorial, and religious, but each such effort, Jackson reasoned, raised the bitter and profoundly divisive question of "whose unity it shall be." Nothing, ultimately, would rend society more than "finding it necessary to choose what doctrine and whose program public educational officials shall compel youth to unite in embracing." Surely all of human history taught the "ultimate futility of such attempts to compel coherence," as seen in Roman efforts to destroy Christianity, the Inquisition's attempt to assure religious unity, and "the Siberian exiles as a means to Russian unity, down to the fast failing efforts of our present totalitarian enemies." In short, Jackson wrote for the majority of the Court, "compulsory unification of opinion achieves only the unanimity of the graveyard." He concluded: "It seems trite but necessary to say that the First Amendment to our Constitution was designed to avoid these ends by avoiding these beginnings."

For the Court, arguments that wartime and patriotism raised singular problems constituted "an unflattering estimate of the appeal of our institutions to free minds." Without the toleration of eccentricity and "abnormal attitudes," we could not have either our treasured "intellectual individualism" or our "rich cultural diversities." It would violate the very spirit of liberty to make an exception for coercion of what society found to be its most important beliefs. The "freedom to differ is not limited to things that do not matter much," the Court wrote: "That would be a mere shadow of freedom. The test of its substance is the right to differ as to things that touch the heart of the existing order."

Jackson concluded with a particularly eloquent refutation of claims for the value of enforced orthodoxy in civic life. His words addressed issues that lie at the heart of the links among the First Amendment, academic freedom, and the right of individuals to define their deepest sense of themselves. "If there is any fixed star in our constitutional constellation," he wrote, "it is that no official, high or petty, can prescribe what shall be orthodox in politics, nationalism, religion, or other matters of opinion or force citizens to confess by word or act their faith" in it. "The purpose of the First Amendment to our Constitution," he concluded, was precisely to protect "from all official control" the domain that was "the sphere of intellect and spirit." *Barnette,* not *Gobitis,* became the landmark, defining the constitutional and moral norms: the primacy of individual conscience over the social benefits of conformity, the need for each individual to enjoy liberty in order for a common liberty to exist, and the intolerability of restricting even one person's liberty in "the sphere of intellect and spirit" in an attempt to create some better world.

The Supreme Court's decision in *Barnette* formed the basis for later opinions concerning freedom of conscience. In the 1969 case of *Stanley v. Georgia,* while upholding state laws against the *production* and *distribution* of constitutionally unprotected obscenity, the Court barred states from prosecuting the mere private *possession* of otherwise unprotected expression.[4] In establishing "conditions favorable to the pursuit of happiness," Justice Thurgood Marshall wrote, the drafters of the Constitution "recognized the significance of man's spiritual nature, of his feelings and of his intellect." The quintessentially human realm of private intellect, whether base or sublime, was beyond the control of the state: "Our whole constitutional heritage rebels at the thought of giving government the power to control men's minds."

Similarly, in 1977, a resident of New Hampshire challenged the obligation of every automobile owner to affix a license plate bearing the state motto, "Live Free or Die."[5] New Hampshire had claimed a public interest in promoting "appreciation" of its "history," "pride," and, ironically, "individualism." In *Wooley v. Maynard,* the Court found in favor of a citizen who disagreed with that motto, ruling that the state did not have the power to "coerce" a citizen to broadcast a point of view "which [he found] morally, ethically, religiously and politically abhorrent." The Court concluded that "the right of freedom of thought protected by the First Amendment . . . includes both the right to speak freely and the right to refrain from speaking at all."

The Supreme Court's rule of the sanctity of inner beliefs has been applied in the lower federal courts by both "liberal" and "conservative" judges. In 1971, for example, Judge Marvin Frankel, a liberal on the U.S. District

Court in New York, invalidated, on First Amendment grounds, a parole board's refusal to permit convicted (and paroled) spy Morton Sobell to travel, a refusal based upon Sobell's intention to lecture and participate in political demonstrations on the road. For the parole board, Sobell was not yet "rehabilitated." Judge Frankel observed: "Totalitarian ideologies we profess to hate have styled as 'rehabilitation' the process of molding the unorthodox mind to the shape of prevailing dogma."[6]

In 1985, Judge Frank Easterbrook, a conservative member of the U.S. Court of Appeals for the Seventh Circuit, wrote the court's opinion in _American Booksellers Association Inc. v. Hudnut._[7] The city of Indianapolis had enacted and enforced an antipornography ordinance that claimed to protect women from "subordination." Easterbrook saw through the ordinance's veneer of a "civil rights" law and described it as an effort to coerce a change in attitudes. Noting that supporters of the ordinance "say that it will play an important role in reducing the tendency of men to view women as sexual objects," he concluded that it faced an insurmountable constitutional obstacle: It not only sought to alter attitudes, but it did so in a manner that discriminated by viewpoint, that is, favoring only "speech treating women in the approved way—in sexual encounters 'premised on equality.'" The First Amendment, he ruled, prohibits the state both from establishing a "preferred viewpoint" for or about a group, and from taking steps to change private attitudes to suit that ideological preference.

In language that seems directly to address the drafters of campus codes, the court concluded that a free society lets individuals freely choose, for themselves, those things that affect "how people see the world, their fellows, and social relations." Responding to the city's argument that pornography poisoned the atmosphere for women, the judge rejected any "answer [that] leaves the government in control of all of the institutions of culture, the great censor and director of which thoughts are good for us." The First Amendment, Judge Easterbrook and his colleagues ruled, permitted neither "thought control" nor an officially "approved view of women, of how they may react to sexual encounters [and] of how the sexes may relate to each other." Further, notions of "low value speech" and "fighting words" did not affect this case. The city did not consider the speech of low value, because it "believes this speech influences social relations and politics on a grand scale," and it had not banned all fighting words, but only those of a particular ideology and viewpoint, a selectivity that itself violated the First Amendment.

The city of Indianapolis appealed to the U.S. Supreme Court, which, after accepting the case for review, found the issues so clear that it affirmed

Judge Easterbrook's judgment summarily—that is, without even calling for briefs and oral arguments.[8] The Court of Appeals's holding now has the imprimatur of the U.S. Supreme Court. Under the First Amendment, clearly, there can be no "approved view of women" and of "how the sexes may relate to each other." There can be no imposition of regimes aimed at changing the attitudes of free citizens by censorship and coercion. Indeed, in the 1985 case of *Wallace v. Jaffree,* the Court held that state-sponsored prayer in schools (far more precious to most Americans than any "-ism" taught at our colleges) violated the First Amendment because it interfered with an "individual's freedom to believe, to worship, and to express himself in accordance with the dictates of his own conscience."[9] Freedom of conscience, in America, is an essential legal and moral value, and it begins with the recognition that we are a nation of free individuals who may define for ourselves the deepest part of our being.

At universities, the betrayal of that freedom of self-definition, a betrayal that extends to dictating speech and inner conscience and, indeed, to thought reform, begins with the fraud of "diversity" and "multiculturalism" as perpetrated by in loco parentis ideologues. There is, of course, an authentic meaning to *diversity,* namely the full variety of human beings in their chosen differences, as there is to *multiculturalism,* namely the realities and interactions of individuals from different backgrounds, sometimes overlapping, sometimes contentious, sometimes heartwarming, sometimes unpredictable. On most campuses, however, diversity and multiculturalism, and the programs to "nurture" them, respect neither real differences nor the individualism that lies at the heart of those differences.

Instead, academic notions and programs of diversity and multiculturalism are marked, almost everywhere, by dogmatic and partisan definitions or models. Despite the talk of "celebrating" diversity, colleges and universities do not, in fact, mean the celebration, deep study, and appreciation of evangelical, fundamentalist, Protestant culture; nor of traditionalist Catholic culture; nor of the gender roles of Orthodox Jewish or of Shiite Islamic culture; nor of black American Pentacostal culture; nor of assimilation; nor of the white, rural South. These are not "multicultural." They also do not mean the serious study of West African Benin culture, nor Confucian culture, both requiring intensive linguistic mastery and scholarly inquiry to achieve understanding. All that the social engineers of diversity mean, in fact, is the appreciation, celebration, and study of those people who think exactly as they do about the nature and causes of oppression, wherever they are found and however nonrepresentative those thinkers might be of the broader groups that they purportedly represent. Academic diversity and multiculturalism have remarkably narrow limits—race, gender, "oppressed" ethnicity, and sexual preference—as articulated by self-proclaimed "progressives." The academic use of the terms "diversity" and "multicultural" has become a politicized perversion of language.

Universities operate with a humanly impoverished notion of "diversity," excluding personality, social class, spirituality, taste, and private passions. Anyone who knows undergraduates knows that in matters of personality alone, the diverse manifestations of the affirmation or fear of life are, in fact, much more striking and essential than the categories of race, gender, and sexual orientation by which universities today almost uniquely, and for partisan purposes, distinguish among the lives lived there. Indeed, when colleges do think about affirmation and vulnerability, they do so from the racist and misogynistic notions that ego strength correlates to externalities, and that whites, men, and heterosexuals have it while blacks, women, and gays do not. A white male student who lost a father in Vietnam is deemed strong enough by racial definition to hear a professor call his late father a "baby killer," whereas a woman or black must be protected from the punch line of a joke.

The imposition of officially designated group identities, coming after the abolition of official segregation and legal inequalities, is a scandal and a betrayal. It is an inherent human right, and an extension of individual freedom, to form voluntary associations by the criteria of one's choice. Individuals have the right to define or not to define themselves primarily by race, sex, ethnicity, religion, moral code, politics, or any other chosen quality. It is every individual's right to join, or not, with others who have made the same voluntary choices. It is no one's right, however, to impose those intimate and private choices.

At the intellectual level, the crudeness of academic group identity links Finns and Sicilians, Basques and Iowans, into one "Eurocentric" culture. At the practical and humane level, the assignment of official group identity has been a dysfunctional approach that has worsened, not bettered, human relations on campuses, creating institutional and personal walls, and failing to take advantage of the open spirit with which most undergraduates enter a university. Our campuses have become ever more segregated and balkanized.

At the moral level, the mania of official group identity has entailed a denial of the only authentic meaning of liberation: the right to be an individual by one's own choices, free of external coercions and impositions. It has intruded upon the sanctity of self-definition and private conscience. What have we done to the individuality of gays, lesbians, blacks, and women by imposing an official group identity upon them? What does it mean to have women's centers that effectively distinguish between real women with appropriate consciousness and ersatz women who have "internalized oppression"?

Universities welcome their first-year classes not as equal individuals joining a community of inquiry, but as historical and genetic embodiments of group identities. Then they wonder why those students have ever greater difficulties in overcoming their differences. Most colleges and universities with significant populations of racial minorities hold separate orientations for them, introducing them, before they have even begun their academic lives, to their official identity, their official advocates, and their official spokesmen and spokeswomen. Minorities in the class of 1999 at Princeton University were invited to a special "minority orientation." At the bottom of that invitation, they were told they also were welcome to attend the university's general orientation. They were invited to request hosts of their own minority group.[10]

Programmatic differentiation by race is now typical in higher education. Half a century after the defeat of Nazism, our universities distinguish by blood and equate blood with culture. Sixty years after the Nuremberg Race Laws, we ask our students to check off their bloodlines and to act accordingly. The justification for this submergence of the individual into the tribe is the same as it was under Fascism: The individual is a function—politically, morally, and historically—of genetic and cultural collectivities. Campus life begins with the sorting out of students into oppressors and victims. This has proven catastrophic in terms of the distances and mutual suspicions of undergraduate relationships.

Administratively, this arrangement creates powerful new fiefdoms and co-opts the militants into the maintenance of order. Ideologically, it imposes, without discussion, one partisan view of American society as reflected in campus life. What makes news now is the rare abandonment of the norm of identity politics in education. In the summer of 1994, the University of Delaware, in response to criticism that it discouraged integration, announced the elimination of its special four-day orientation for black students. President David Roselle explained that Delaware had "incorporated" black student orientation "into the whole orientation," a two-day program that encouraged first-year students to meet professors, get to know the campus, and learn about academic opportunities and expectations.[11] Delaware's black students now were free to accept or reject invitations from any number of voluntary associations to be members or participants, without the university's assignment of official identities.

The University of Delaware has not had many imitators. Higher education explicitly welcomes individuals of specific bloodlines as official "minorities," encouraging them to link to the campus by means of this group identity and to recognize their "leaders." Thus, the "Office of Multicultural Student Affairs" at the University of South Carolina (USC), part of the Department of Student Life, separates races from the start. Its 1996 Webpage announced its Minority Student Welcome: "the annual program for incoming freshmen where the leaders of major student organizations and other ethnic minority oriented organizations welcome the freshmen to USC and solicit their involvement." The Webpage directed minority students to the "Association of African-American Students" and informed them about the "Minority Student Honors Night," which recognized minority students "who have excelled in academic, leadership and campus/community service" and offered "major awards" and "certificates for academic achievement" (as if these were not earned simply as USC students). The multicultural office announced "Workshops of Cultural Sensitivity and Diversity," whose sessions would lead students to address "issues of diversity, moving these issues to the forefront of discussion," with "perspectives . . . challenged and new pathways . . . employed." The "Minority Assistance Peer Program [would] assist minority freshmen to be successful at USC by providing them with a trained peer counselor." The office organized a "Multicultural Outreach," specifically defined as "continued support for all groups of color in community building . . . an ongoing platform for education and learning."[12] It is not "welcome student," but "welcome carrier of blackness." The multicultural office functions to put an end to any thought of, "at last, here, I shall be accepted for my unique individuality."

At Smith College, in the fall of 1990, each freshman received a copy of a handbook prepared by the Office of Student Affairs. Its first item was a "definition" of "ETHNIC IDENTITY: a group of people who share a common identity that may arise from similar geographic origin or shared history." The Office of Student Affairs explained what made individuals who they were: "They have a background, world view, lifestyle, and experience by which they [the 'group of people who share a common identity'] define themselves or are defined." The handbook offered a set of politically charged "Preferred Terms" for ethnic groups. "Puerto Rican," for example, was defined as "one of the major Latino groups recognized in the U.S., who while citizens of this country, are not permitted to vote in this country or have congressional representation" (as if the citizens of Puerto Rico had not voted for such commonwealth status in free elections). The Smith College handout on ethnic identity claimed to introduce students to the names by which people "preferred" to be called, but one wonders how many Smith students actually preferred "European American," or, indeed, "People of Color," defined as "a concept created by various ethnic groups, distinguished by brown, red, yellow, and black skin hues; origins from all over the globe, and most importantly a common history of conquest or subjugation by European nations."[13]

Swarthmore College, on its official 1996–97 "Black at Swarthmore" page, uttered perhaps the single most patronizing statement in all of this sadness on American campuses: "Sometimes, being Black at Swarthmore means getting out to enjoy a ball game on a gorgeous fall day."[14] Under "academic opportunities of special interest to Black students," only one scholarly "opportunity" was named, the "Black Studies Program" (as if majoring in Classics, Chemistry, Psychology, English, Politics, or Economics were not, by race, of "special interest" to them).

Under "Support Systems," "Black at Swarthmore" listed merely two: the "Black Cultural Center" (BCC) and the "Swarthmore African-American Student Society." Swarthmore urged its black students to go there for "support." Why? In Swarthmore's view, they ought to want to socialize above all around race: "Many Black students find the BCC to be one of the more comfortable places on campus to study, socialize, or just hang out." Swarthmore, in fact, has scores of "support systems," vast numbers of "educational, cultural and social" organizations," but "Black at Swarthmore" refers no student to any of these. Similarly, Swarthmore is a rich musical community, indeed, one of the richest of any small college in America. Under "Musical Cultural Groups," however, "Black at Swarthmore" refers students to only three: Gospel Choir ("a spiritual inspiration, cultural identification, and social outlet for several dozen Black students, alumni, and community members"); Sophisticated Gents ("an a cappella group of Black men who sing a wide range of music"); and Sistahs ("the women's a cappella group . . . founded to complement the Gents"). Swarthmore's extraordinary dance groups, string quartets, orchestras, choirs, and choruses? Not a mention. It is one thing, of course, if all of these voluntarily black ethnic groups, among countless other groups, spontaneously arose from the free choices of students. It is quite another that Swarthmore's "Black at Swarthmore" should stamp them as "officially" black at the college and define identity by them. The University of Iowa lists only two "Cultural Centers," the Afro-American Cultural Center and the Latino Native American Cultural Center.[15] Why ever leave then? The first has "private rooms for confidential consultations, study and meetings; typewriters and computers for public use; library and other resource materials; newsletter; employment listings; film series, t.v. lounge, and games; party and social areas; fully-equipped kitchen facilities." The second, with a similar array, exists as a place "where Latino and Native American cultures can be nurtured and enhanced," and it "has become the focal point of a supportive community, cultural expression and diversity." A curious meaning of "diversity."

Franklin and Marshall College has an "Associate Dean for Advisement and Multicultural Affairs" who manages and does programming for the Black Cultural Center; conducts "training programs in Cross-Cultural Awareness"; oversees the Kwanzaa Celebration and the Martin Luther King, Jr., annual observance; contributes to first-year student orientation; is responsible for a separate "Multicultural Student Orientation"; and provides "administrative guidance to multicultural student organizations."[16] At the University of Maryland, two "European" groups actually make it onto the "Student Diversity Resources/Race-Ethnicity" Webpage, which addresses the needs of "African and African American," "Asian and Asian American," "Latin and Latin American," "Native American," "Jewish," and "Irish and Irish American" students.[17] Ancestral linkage joins the foreign student from Malaysia and the child of American professionals of Chinese descent into one common "race" or "ethnicity." These six being the only official "races and ethnicities," the rest of the students are mere undiverse individuals.

At Occidental College, the "Cultural Resource Center" is devoted to "clubs and organizations who value and work toward achieving the goals of multiculturalism on campus." These, it turns out, include only lesbians, gays, Asians and Americans of Asian descent, Hispanics, blacks, Pacific Islanders, and feminists.[18] No Irish need apply.

At the University of Nebraska, the Office of Student Affairs has a division for "Multi-Cultural Affairs," whose mission is to provide "unique support services," "instruction," and "assistance" to those students who "qualify" for its programs. Its Webpage proudly announces that "a combination of Nebraska General Tax dollars, U.S.A. congressional funds, private foundation, and other revenue sources enables the Multi-Cultural Affairs office to address the educational needs of its participants," who are limited to "students whose ethnic background is African, Hispanic/Latino, Native American, Asian American, as well as qualified students who are low income and/or first generation."[19]

At UMass–Amherst, a brochure, *The Multicultural Experience,* introduces newcomers to the meaning of "multicultural" by means of "ALANA . . . an acronym for African, Latino, Asian and Native American." UMass's "multiculturalism" includes seven "cultural centers": Carribean; Native American; Latin American; black (two centers, the Malcolm X Community Center and the Martin Luther King, Jr., Cultural Center); Asian; and the Sylvan Multicultural Center. Under the rubric "Housing Services," the "multicultural" brochure suggests that "you may also wish to explore one of the Special Interest Residential Programs." Indeed, for "multicultural" minorities, UMass offers racially separatist dormitories that provide the chance to avoid unsympathetic white American students, or, for that matter, anyone of a different "culture." These programs speak of "programming" and "community," but UMass equates culture and politics quite explicitly. Thus, *The Multicultural Experience* section invitingly entitled "Welcome to Amherst!" describes the lecturers of interest to "multicultural" students. In its entirety:

> Guest lecturers have included Lani Grenier [*sic*], a professor of law at Yale University [*sic*] who was recently nominated for a civil rights post in the Clinton administration; Yuri Kochiama, a Japanese-American civil rights activist; Leonard Jeffries, a professor from the City University of New York whose provocative theories on race and genetics have garnered him widespread recognition; and Winona LaDuke, a Native American author, ecologist, political scientist, and activist in several causes.[20]

Proponents of the separatist racial residences and support programs that emerged in the 1970s and 1980s, and that have grown in number steadily, argued that "safe" and "supportive" spaces for "minorities" would result in better and more natural relations among all groups. No such improvement has occurred. Indeed, by the fall of 1989, in an extensive survey of students at twenty universities, the *New York Times* reported: "Poor race relations on campus were by far the most frequently mentioned concern of students interviewed." Ironically, in that same issue, a separate article reported on the formation of the NUANCE residence at UMass. Its residence director, Paulette Dalpes, said that although she would conduct an eight-week, one-credit colloquium there "to help white students understand racism," NU-

ANCE existed for nonwhites. Her words revealed how UMass then officially classified students: "'We're not trying to meet the needs of white students in this program. We're trying to meet the needs of people of color.'"[21]
So much for mutual discovery.

Middlebury College calls its multicultural residence PALANA, for
"Pan-African Latino Asian Native American," whose members enjoy a separate "living and learning center." Everyone is invited to "visit, attend programs or just fulfill curiosities about what the center is all about," but, the
PALANA Website explains, membership is limited by ethnicity. The resi-
dency application also stressed that there was a PALANA view of things and,
indeed, a PALANA personality: "All" residents "are required to learn the
history of PALANA and its relevance today . . . [and] must be able to respond
to questions from the college community and prospective students on the
meaning of PALANA. All past residents have been strong individuals."[22]

Why should these students, identified by ethnicity and worldview, have
their own dormitory, while academic multiculturalism most surely would
not give one to southern whites, Jews, evangelicals, or Republicans? More to
the point, why should the college assign categories of personal identity at all?
One alternative—color-blind, apolitical, and respectful of all self-defini-
tions—would be to let students form residential cohorts, groups of two to
twelve students who, for whatever private reason they choose, all receive
rooms in the same dormitory. That both ends the problem of isolation and
gives equal rights to all senses of self. What that cohort should not have,
however, is a veto over the ethnicity, race, politics, religion, ancestry, or
worldview of its neighbors. That ends the problem of residential apartheid.
Students unwilling to forgo that veto over their neighbors always could
choose to live off campus.

Cornell University offers residential living around issues of ethnicity.
Unlike UMass, whose Harambee program is specifically "for students of
African descent," Cornell presents all such residences as organized, in theory,
around "ethnic interest," although, in practice, it plays out to virtually the
same racial end. Michael Meyers, head of the New York Civil Rights Coalition (NYCRC), fought Cornell on its tolerance of segregated dorms. He
failed in an antidiscrimination complaint against Cornell, because the nominally "thematic" composition of the dorms survived legal scrutiny.[23] (Meyers
recalls going from Harlem to Antioch College, and discovering, with delight, the lived reality of interracial friendships and interactions. When Antioch chose to accept racial self-segregation in dormitories, he resigned in
sorrow from its Board of Trustees.)[24]

Cornell's first black dormitory, Ujamaa, was opened in 1971, after negotiations that ended the harrowing armed takeover of the main student union by black students. In 1976, the State Department of Education investigated segregation at Ujamaa, ruled that whites were explicitly excluded on grounds of race, and found that Cornell distributed materials to students saying that the residence was explicitly for blacks. Cornell entered into a consent decree that permitted the dormitory to survive if admission was not based on race. In 1995, when the NYCRC began its unsuccessful effort to end dormitory segregation at Cornell, three of 140 residents of Ujamaa were white. In 1991, Cornell opened a Native American residence; a Hispanic dormitory followed in 1994. Indeed, Cornell's only reported refusal to offer one of the "historically oppressed groups" its own residence occurred when President Frank Rhodes denied a dormitory to gay students because, according to the *Wall Street Journal,* "He was concerned about a Cornell campus that was becoming 'increasingly fragmented.'" Cornell defended all of its other fragmentary dorms against the NYCRC's complaint. As Meyers told the *New York Times,* "Cornell University, . . . in effect, [has] accepted and promoted ethnic and racial separatism in the campus, [which] feeds and reinforces traditional ethnic stereotypes."[25]

At UMass, in 1996, some Asian-American students in the Asian dorm objected to the presence of white students who chose to live there because they were studying East Asian languages and cultures. Although the university denies it, trustworthy sources at UMass assure us that the white students were forced out of the dorm by pressure from the administration.[26] No one, however, denies what happened at Wesleyan University in the spring of 1996. When nine students who were not black were assigned to the campus's Malcolm X House (there were nine vacant singles in "X House," and the nine nonblacks had requested singles), protests by black students led the administration to preserve the house as all black. Wesleyan's president, Douglas J. Bennet, told the *Chronicle of Higher Education* that he favored having a house where black students could explore their racial identity, but, remembering the university's "antidiscrimination policy," that this need not preclude "the possibility that people of another cultural affinity or ethnicity can be a part of it." Wesleyan's Housing Office certainly gave the protesting students grounds for feeling betrayed. Its brochure described Malcolm X House as "a place where African and African American students could explore and sustain their cultural heritage." Indeed, the prior spring, two nonblack students assigned to Malcolm X House had been told that they could not move in because university policy prohibited it.[27]

Colleges and universities have accepted a new "compensatory" version of separate but unequal. Whites obviously could not veto the presence of nonwhites in a college dormitory. Such inequality arises from the universities' belief that its students are not individuals, but instances of blood and history, and from the universities' fear of angering militants who name themselves the heirs of that blood and history. At the College of the Holy Cross (Massachusetts), an antidiscrimination policy explicitly prohibits discrimination on the grounds of race. No discriminatory organization may receive funds or official recognition. The Black Students' Union (BSU), however, has a charter, in place since 1990, that specifically states that elected officers must be "of African descent." In November 1995, the Student Government Association voted to strike the racial restriction from the BSU's rules as a condition of official recognition. On November 16, the administration overruled the student government. The president of Holy Cross, Father Gerard Reedy, told the *New York Times:* "We rely on the Black Students' Union as a bridge. There is a need to have black kids oriented by kids who are also in the minority." The BSU, which had either forty (the *New York Times*) or ten (the *Chronicle of Higher Education*) members who were nonblacks concerned with black life on campus, thus became the only one of some eighty recognized campus organizations to have a racial qualification for office.[28]

In April 1996, the Black Law Student Association (BLSA) at the University of Iowa amended its charter to bar nonblacks from membership. The administration informed the BLSA that it would lose its recognition—a campus office and funding from student fees—if it did not rescind that rule. As the dean of students told the *Chronicle of Higher Education,* "We won't compromise on that principle." The BLSA then exercised its own rights by voting to maintain the blacks-only rule, and choosing to move off campus and to forgo university funding. The university's stand was an exception, however, because, despite academic nondiscrimination rules, the national charter of the widespread BLSA restricts membership to blacks only, and the Iowa chapter had been, until 1996, a conspicuous exception.[29]

At the University of California–San Diego, by contrast, the Black Student Union (BSU) in 1995 actively sought nonblack members who shared its sense of black issues. It attracted a sizable minority of such students. One, Colleen Coffey, said that she missed the racial integration of her high school years and profited deeply from her experience in the BSU: "I've learned about what it feels like to not look like everyone else. You don't have to be black to really care about black issues." Some members of the organization encouraged her to run for office in the BSU, and the group elected her as its treasurer. In reporting on Coffey's and the BSU's satisfaction, however, the *Chronicle of Higher Education* noted that this was the exception. At Oberlin College, for example, nonblack students may attend social events hosted by Abusua, the Oberlin black student group, "but are barred from regular meetings." The Oberlin Asian American Alliance opened its social events to non-Asians, but barred them from "political" meetings. At the College of Wooster, the Black Student Alliance prohibited nonblacks from being elected to official positions, an exception to a nondiscrimination policy created by a faculty vote in 1989.[30]

At Macalaster College, the director of multicultural affairs (MCA), Carol Johnson, told *The Mac Weekly* that "all of the functions of MCA are directed at enhancing the academic achievement of students of color—in the classroom, in their relationships with their advisors, and in their activities outside the classroom."[31] Countless students, of a thousand backgrounds, desperately need precisely that assistance. How might one, then, establish "race" and "color" to prevent the unworthy from receiving such benefits? There are precedents. German charts and instruments to measure ethnic identity? A length of nose or set of facial angles? The old Southern categories? A drop of blood, a sixteenth, an eighth, a quartering?

At UCLA, in December 1995, every sophomore and junior received a letter from Pearl Petit, coordinator of the graduate division's "Summer Research Program for Underrepresented Undergraduate Students." It announced a splendid eight-week program, with free room and board, a stipend, a travel allowance, and a rare opportunity for students "to conduct research with prominent faculty members in . . . the arts, humanities, biological, physical and social sciences as well as engineering." Admission would be on "a competitive basis to individuals." Those "individuals," however, had to be American citizens who met the following specifications: "of Alaskan Native (Eskimo or Aleut), American Indian, Black/African American, Chicano/Mexican American, Latino, Native Hawaiian, Pilipino or Puerto Rican heritage." Asian students, it specified, were eligible, but only if they were "currently pursuing degrees in the social sciences, arts and humanities." Women, "regardless of ethnicity," could apply, but only if they were "pursuing degrees in the physical sciences and engineering."[32]

In short, no white men! That would include, of course, any number of groups "historically underrepresented" in graduate studies and the professoriate: the sons of blue-collar families, of war dead, of family farmers, or of day laborers. What about Republicans, orphans, evangelicals, Seventh-Day Adventists, Southern Baptists, New England Portuguese fishermen, Appalachian miners, Hasidim, or Pennsylvania Dutch? Note the stereotyping built into the program as well. Asian-Americans with interests in the sciences were excluded, because there were too many of their kind already. White females in the humanities also were excluded, because there were too many of their kind also. That is the multiculturalism of academe.

These double standards by official group identity exist far beyond race and ethnicity. The UMass School of Education announced, in 1996, a one-credit weekend workshop on "Examining Queer Identities and Creating Queer Communities." The official (indeed, credit-conferring) workshop sought to provide "a safe place" for "Gay, Lesbian, Bisexual and Transgender students."[33] The spokeswoman for the workshop, Dawn Bond, a UMass residence director, told the Daily Collegian: "We want this to be a retreat for Gay, Lesbian, Bisexual and Transgender students only or for those in question."[34] This was at a public university bound by nondiscrimination policies. As usual, this exercise in multiculturalism had a partisan view of issues. Its first goal was to "examine introspectively messages of internalized homophobia and look at how this oppression manifests itself in the lives of GLBT people." Its final goal was to "challenge participants to develop a queer community that fosters a socially just, celebrative, inclusive environment which builds bridges among multiple identity [e.g., race and sexuality]."[35] In the fall of 1992, when UMass opened its gay, lesbian, and bisexual residence, "Two in Twenty," Jennifer Fazzi, a columnist for the campus conservative journal, The Minuteman, asked the Housing Assignments Office if a homosexual couple, or a bisexual couple of different sexes, could be assigned to the same room in the new program. The answer was yes. Could a heterosexual couple be assigned to the same room in other campus dorms? The answer was no: "There's a policy that says it is not allowed." Why the discrepancy? She was told, "To create a comfortable living environment for these people. . . . In most cases, a heterosexual couple is not facing the same issues as a homosexual couple."[36]

If one truly believes in the liberty of gay and lesbian students, of course, the real struggle is not for special privilege, but for equal rights. Legislatures in culturally conservative states frequently attempt to bar the funding of gay and lesbian student organizations on the grounds that these organizations affront the values of most citizens. The answer to that assault on the legal equality of individuals and their voluntary organizations rests upon a civic value that allows all of us to live by and advocate our deeper private values: equal justice under law. Colleges and universities, no less than some legislatures, have shown contempt for precisely that principle. Without a commitment to that value, gay and lesbian students (and faculty) will not be "empowered"; they will be helpless.

At Stephen F. Austin State University in Texas, the student government voted to deny funds to the Gay and Lesbian Student Association on the grounds that "sodomy" was illegal under Texas law. The university, claiming that any violation of equal rights would constitute the illegality, refused to withhold the funds. As Keith Roberts, the president of the Gay and Lesbian Student Association told the *Chronicle of Higher Education,* "You don't realize what you have until someone tries to take it away from you."[37] That is profoundly true, but it is true for everyone. The assault on the core value of American political life—the legal equality of free individuals—if successful, would be fatal not only to individual dignity and freedom, but, as a consequence, to the rights of any unpopular minorities of any kind.

The academic mania for group identity presupposes what free individuals must decide for themselves—the nature and compound of their own individual lives. Blacks are free to be, by their own individual choices, radical, moderate, conservative, or apolitical; separatist or assimilationist; Afrocentric or South Carolinian. They do not need universities to assign them their identities. Women are free to see or not see themselves as members of an oppressed class, to understand themselves primarily as instances of gender or primarily as participants in communities undefined by sex. They do not need universities to assign them those identities. Gays and lesbians are free to make their sexual identity a central or a minimal part of their selves, and, as in fact they do, to move diversely to any part of the political, cultural, intellectual, and lifestyle spectrum that they choose. (David Brudnoy, the popular, conservative, gay talk-radio host, is fond of asking what in the world sexuality has to do with opposition to confiscatory taxation.) The struggle for dignity is about that right to define oneself, and there are few greater oppressions than to deny the reality and the legitimacy of that individuation. Those who understand that truth with particular force, however, are least likely to accept positions in offices of student life as "role models" for specific official groups.

UMass's associate chancellor, Susan Pearson, spoke on Boston radio station WBUR in 1995, defending UMass's proposed new speech code. It was right, she argued, that a heterosexual student should be punished for calling someone a "faggot" whereas a gay student should not be punished for calling someone "a disgusting homophobe." Why? Because gay men were more "vulnerable." On December 6, Robert Chatelle replied on the sexual-minority listserve of the National Writers Union, observing that "gay men are no more or less 'vulnerable' (or 'sensitive' or 'artistic') than any other class of citizens."[38] Indeed, Chatelle noted, Pearson "was engaging in negative stereotyping," which, "ironically enough . . . is forbidden under the speech code she was defending." "Scratch a defender of 'political correctness,'" he observed, "and you'll find some variety of bigot." For Chatelle, "defenders of 'political correctness' subscribe to two myths that are damaging to the rights of minorities: . . . vulnerability and . . . interchangeability."

The "myth of vulnerability," Chatelle observed, is based on the patronizing belief that "members of minority groups are so damaged by discrimination that we become incapable of speaking for ourselves." What is the fate of people so patronized? In Chatelle's words, "We lose agency and thus become something less than fully human. We are thus dependent upon the goodwill of benevolent protectors—usually upper middle-class white heterosexual 'liberals.'" Those opposed to gay exercise of full political rights must love such analyses and notions of group identity, which reinforce the notion "that sexual-minority people are demanding 'special rights.'" Chatelle replied: "We are not. We want equal rights. But it is difficult to make that argument convincing when people like Sue Pearson are going around and stating that gay men are 'vulnerable' people who need 'special' protection."

The "myth of interchangeability," for Chatelle, was equally dangerous. It "holds that there is such a thing as 'the women's viewpoint,' the 'gay/lesbian viewpoint,' [or] 'the African-American viewpoint.'" Such a myth "denies diversity within minority communities by stating that not only do we all look alike, we all think alike," which invited a "demeaning and insulting tokenism."

For Chatelle, these two myths, both embodied in the official group identities and the double standards of our universities, are a route back to the worst days of gay and lesbian oppression, because it is precisely the values of legal equality and individuation that underlie the freedom and dignity of minorities. If "we shall be silenced and imprisoned again," he wrote, "so many of us will have helped forge the chains that will be used to bind us."

———

Universities, thus, when they speak of "multiculturalism" and "diversity" mean, in fact, officially designated ethnic, racial, or sexual groups. The preferred euphemism, at the moment, is "underrepresented minorities" (which implies, of course, that other officially designated groups are overrepresented). The assumption is that the identity of individuals at our universities is inseparable from those official categories that the university recognizes, quite independently of how such individuals view themselves. Diversity means the acceptance of those distinctions by blood and history. Multiculturalism means the acceptance of the view that individual students exist not as individuals, but as instances of group identity useful to some partisan understanding of the history of oppression. The "Mission" of the "Multicultural Resource Center" of Oberlin College is not the study of foreign cultures, but to "advocate on behalf of . . . [and] foster the intellectual, cultural, social, and personal growth of students of color, and lesbian, gay, and bisexual students." Oberlin holds separate first-year orientations for blacks, Hispanics, and Asian Americans, and for gay, lesbian, and bisexual students.[39] At Pennsylvania State University, the "Multicultural Resource Center (MRC)" assists only "African/Black American, Latino/Hispanic American, Asian and Pacific American, and American Indian/Alaskan Native undergraduate students." The center informs such "students who don't think they need . . . an MRC counselor [that] MRC counselors want to meet every student eligible for its services, regardless of a student's present circumstances."[40] At Ohio State University, the Division of Student Affairs announces that it values both differences and similarities, but it has separate offices of student services for each of (and only) the following groups: American blacks; Americans of Asian descent; gays, lesbians, and bisexuals; Hispanics; American Indians; and women.[41]

The fact that this occurs at public as well as private universities appears to shock almost no one. The University of Wyoming, for example, although formally committed not to discriminate by race or ethnicity, holds a separate "orientation and open house for ethnic minority students and faculty" each semester, in order to introduce them to "representatives of various minority clubs" and to the "Minority Affairs Office." That office, in its own mission statement, explicitly exists to "support" only "Asian/Pacific Islander, Black/African American, Hispanic/Mexican American/Chicano, and American Indian/Alaskan Native, or multi-ethnic students [of mixed ethnicities] before they enter and when they are undergraduate and graduate students." Its segregated services include, in its own words, "FREE tutoring and personal guidance, personal support and guidance, [and] student advocacy."[42] The University of Virginia, although it expressly promises not to discriminate by race, gender, or ethnicity, holds special "leadership development seminars" open only to "Asian-American, African-American, Hispanic and women students."[43]

It is with these meanings in mind, then, that one must understand the various offices devoted to multicultural affairs or diversity at our colleges and universities. The promulgation of a politicized group identity is a growth industry in higher education. In 1997, an ever greater number of universities advertised in the *Chronicle of Higher Education* for new or vacant administrative positions with "multicultural" or "diversity" in their names.[44] A common job requirement for deanships, directorships, and countless positions in student life or residence is "a commitment to cultural diversity," with "commitment" often modified by the adjectives "strong," "dedicated," or "proven." Prospective residence directors at UMass–Amherst must be able to promote "diversity-sensitive approaches in all aspects of the position." A student activities position at Weber State in Utah is typical, demanding "sensitivity to issues of diversity and multiculturalism." The vice president for student affairs at Boise State University and residence directors at SUNY–Binghamton must "promote cultural diversity." The dean of student affairs at Southern Oregon University must have "strong values embracing diversity" (which, with a master's degree, will earn him or her seventy to eighty thousand dollars per year). The associate dean of Vermont Law School must have a "demonstrated commitment to fostering diversity." Without understanding the coded language, one might mistake these posts for some commitment to integration, the study of foreign civilizations, or a pluralism that embraced beliefs.

It has been this way for years. Why might a residence hall director at the University of Wisconsin–River Falls have felt obliged to censor a Republican poster? In December 1994, an advertisement for that position in the *Chronicle of Higher Education* asked every applicant to send "a one-page statement" on "The Role of the Residence Hall Director in Developing Diversity Programs for Students on a Predominantly White Campus." If you believed individual differences in race to be morally insignificant, would you have applied?

It is useful, thus, and honest, when such advertisements make explicit what the institution means by multicultural. The University of Connecticut advertised for a vice provost for multicultural affairs, and explained that "the terms multiculturalism, diversity or pluralism" in its notice, "as they apply to the Office of Multicultural Affairs, embrace racial and ethnic minorities, women, people with disabilities, individuals of diverse sexual orientations, and individuals of varying social and economic groups." At the University of

Florida, the assistant dean for student services and director of multicultural affairs would have supervision of only two cultural institutes: one for "Black Culture" and one for "Hispanic/Latino Culture." In a few months' span in 1997 the *Chronicle of Higher Education* ran advertisements for administrative positions in "Multicultural Affairs," "Residence," or "Student Life" that were defined in terms of the following specific constituencies: "minority students" (Southern Illinois University); "underrepresented groups" (University of San Diego); "ethnic minority students" (Indiana University of Pennsylvania); "African American students but with awareness of the needs and concerns of other minority students on campus such as Latino, Native American, Asian/Pacific Islander, and Gay, Lesbian, Bisexual and Transgendered students" (Guilford College); "African American, Asian American, Native American, Latino-and-Hispanic American, and inter-cultural undergraduates" (Cornell University); "students of color" (University of Oregon); "women and minorities" (University of Maine–Farmington); and "students of color" (Princeton University). Sometimes, indeed, an institution simply will state its balkanization of student life directly. Thus, in that same span, the University of Michigan advertised for a "Director, Office of Lesbian, Gay, Bisexual, and Transgender Affairs," Wellesley College for an "Advisor to Students of African Descent," and New York University for a "Coordinator of Gay, Lesbian, Bisexual and Transgender Student Services."

To understand the moral consequence of academic official group identity, consider the appalling predicament of students from multiracial families. At Penn, in 1995, students formed an organization with the sardonic name "Check One." As Kam Santos, president of Check One, wrote to the *DP* in 1996, the group "takes its name from the fact that one is asked literally to check one race or ethnic group when filling out standardized forms." A *DP* columnist had deplored the creation of Check One, calling it a new separatism of people who were "half and half." Santos's reply should burn the conscience of every academic who is perpetuating the system of official classification by blood on almost all of our campuses: "We are largely an ignored people, and segregation, which preserves and reinforces culture, can also serve to exclude us." Members were not "half-and-half," she wrote, because they were not made up "of segmented parts . . . distinct and separate pieces."[45]

In June 1991, the *New York Times* published a major piece of investigative journalism—"For Mixed-Race Americans, Life Isn't Simply Black or White"—about the proliferation of organizations of individuals who did not fit into official academic group identities. The *Times* reported that at the University of Michigan, students with one white parent, expressing their displeasure at the antiwhite attitudes of official campus black groups, formed "the Multiracial Group," declaring the continual "affront" to one of their parents appalling. Similar organizations and sentiments existed all over the country. At Stanford, Carl Hicks, a Korean and black senior, formed, with other students uncomfortable with Stanford's official group identities, an organization called Prism. He understood the immoral and intended consequence of current academic multiculturalism and anti-individualism: "When I got to Stanford I didn't think of myself as black or Korean or white. I thought of myself as Carl Hicks. But everyone kept labeling me."[46] This is a nation, however, whose decent future depends precisely on Carl Hicks being treated "as Carl Hicks," unless he chooses to enter voluntarily into a subcommunity of his own preference. Our colleges and universities justify their assault against individual identity by claiming that they have inherited the unavoidable legacy of the injustices of American history. In fact, the leaders of those institutions are making deliberate choices to betray the birthright bequeathed by that history. As Justice Jackson wrote, the individual's freedom in "the sphere of intellect and spirit" is inseparable from the highest values of American liberty and possibility.

CHAPTER 9

AMERICAN THOUGHT
REFORM

In 1990, Tulane University's administration announced its official new program, "Initiatives for the Race and Gender Enrichment of Tulane University." The introduction to the document, written by Ron Mason, a vice president of the university, spoke plainly: "Racism and sexism are pervasive in America and are fundamentally present in all American institutions. Racism and sexism are subtle and for the most part subconscious." Mason added: "We are all the progeny of a racist and sexist America."[1] Such frankness in public statements is rare (and rarely repeated off-campus). It expresses the worldview of the overseers of university life. It is part of a deeper critique of America.

From this perspective, American history is a tale of the oppression of all "others" by white, heterosexual, Eurocentric males, punctuated by the struggles of the oppressed. "Beneficiaries" see their lives as good and as natural, and falsely view America as a boon to humankind. Worse, most "victims" of "oppression" accept the values of their oppressors. A central task of education, then, is to "demystify" such arbitrary power. Whites, males, and heterosexuals must recognize and renounce the injustice of their "privilege." Nonwhites, women, gays, and lesbians must recognize and reject their victimization, both in their beliefs and in their behaviors.

Such "demystification" has found a welcome home in a large number of courses in the humanities and social sciences (and a growing number of schools even mandate credits in one or two such courses about "diversity" as graduation requirements). For the true believers, however, these curricular changes are insufficient, because most courses remain optional, many profes-

210

sors resist the temptation to proselytize, and students, for the most part, choose majors that take them far from Oppression Studies.

Indeed, students forever disappoint the ideologues. Men and women generally see themselves neither as oppressor nor oppressed and, far from engaging in class warfare, often quite love each other. Most women refuse to identify themselves as "feminists." Group-identity centers—although they can rally support at moments of crisis—attract few students overall, because invitees busily go about the business of learning, making friends, pursuing interests, and seeking love—all the things that eighteen-to-twenty-two-year-olds have done from time immemorial. Attendance at group-identity organizations is often minuscule as a percentage of the intended population, and militant leaders complain endlessly about "apathy." Whites don't feel particularly guilty about being white, and almost no designated "victims" adopt truly radical politics. Most undergraduates unabashedly seek their portion of American freedom, legal equality, and bounty. What to do with such benighted students? Increasingly, the answer to that question is to use the in loco parentis apparatus of the university to reform their private consciences and minds.

Unknown to most faculty—for which administrators and willfully ignorant professors bear equal responsibility—a shadow university has emerged in offices whose mission used to be the delivery of services. Increasingly, offices of student life, residence offices, and residence advisors have become agencies of progressive social work whose mission is to bring students to mandatory political enlightenment.

———

Such practices violate far more than honest education. Recognition of the sanctity of conscience is the single most essential respect given to individual autonomy. There are purely practical arguments for the right to avoid self-incrimination or to choose religious (or other) creeds, but there is none deeper than restraining power from intruding upon the privacy of the self. Universities and colleges that commit the scandal of sentencing students (and faculty) to "sensitivity therapy" do not even permit individuals to choose their therapists. The Christian may not consult his or her chosen counselor, but must follow the regime of the social worker selected by the women's center or by the office of student life.

Judicial settlements are, by rule at most universities, wholly confidential. Critics rarely get a look at them. We possess, however, a settlement offered to a student in April of 1992. The student had rejected the Penn plea bargain, and had taken his chances with the ordeal of a hearing, where he had been acquitted of sexual harassment. It took courage to take that chance when accepting a bargain would have ended the matter. The proposed settlement, typical of what we know to occur at so many universities, seemed in one of its provisions more appropriate to "thought reform" at the University of Beijing during the Cultural Revolution than to a free university in America. It was chilling in its command over time and private conscience, and in its authoritarian and partisan supervision. Although the administration claimed that it was aberrational when it was brought to their attention, an attorney in the office of general counsel confirmed that he had "signed off on scores" of identical settlements.[2] When one reads of "educational" resolutions of judicial matters at universities, it all too often means this:

> You are to participate in a comprehensive program on sexual harassment, except for the time you are attending classes . . . or [at] employment. Said programming shall include . . . assignments . . . each week in which classes are in session through the Spring 1992 term. You [must] present written evidence of completion of assignments, and a satisfactory performance must be documented by Elena DiLapi, Director of the Women's Center, or her representative, before your transcript can be released.[3]

From the Inquisition to Soviet psychiatry, history has taught us the nightmare of violating the ultimate refuges of self-consciousness, conscience, and private beliefs. In Schiller's *Don Carlos,* Alba proclaims to the mighty Phillip his right to keep his opinion from the king, noting that even "a slave can keep his feelings from a king. It is his only right." The final horror of *1984* was the party's goal of changing Winston's consciousness against his will. The song of the "peat bog soldiers" sent by the Nazis to work until they died was, appropriately, "Die Gedanken sind frei"—"Thoughts are free"— for that truly is the final atom of liberty. No moral person would pursue another human being there. Colleges and universities do.

From 1988 to 1990, Penn, borrowing heavily from models in place at other universities, designed and instituted its "Diversity Education" initiatives for first-year orientation and its "Challenge for Change" programs for residential life. The committees to which it assigned the crafting of this thought reform consisted almost exclusively of proponents of the most partisan "multiculturalism," although two students critical of this intrusive agenda made their way onto those committees and passed along the internal reports and memoranda of that enterprise.[4]

Penn simply set about to control the ways its students thought about and valued the world. It viewed incoming students as incapable, on their own, of sorting out their differences and their common humanity, of understanding how to live decently, and of thinking critically about America. Above all, the university viewed its students as ignorant of the real nature of their group identities. One student on the subcommittee on "Diversity Follow-Up Programs" complained in a memo about the planners' contempt for individualism and individual identity, their "desire . . . continually to consider the collective before the individual." Within each official "group," she pleaded, "there are so many diverse and individual experiences that it is impossible to incorporate them into one neat package we might call a group experience." "The desire of this subcommittee to dictate what to think regarding groups or individuals," she wrote, was the antithesis of a critical, analytic education and offered "merely a process of thought homogenization" that destroyed the most educational pluralism, namely, "intellectual diversity."[5]

A fellow committee member, an administrator, underlined the word "individual" on the student's memo, and replied that "This is a 'RED FLAG' phrase today, which is considered by many to be RACIST." "Arguments that champion the INDIVIDUAL over the group," he informed her, "ultimately privileges [sic] the 'INDIVIDUAL' belonging to the dominant group." Indeed, he concluded, "in a pluralistic society, individuals are only as significant as their groups."[6]

The planning documents, which focused on the private thoughts and values of students, embodied remarkable notions of "education," warning that "facilitators" would face transitions from "low risk" to "high risk" emotional discussions that could lead to "threats to safety." The committees, as the student concerned about "intellectual diversity" saw all too clearly, had an agenda of "group identity" at the center of their concerns. They produced a guide for "Programming . . . for Diversity Topics," whose subtitle, "Challenge for Change," embodied its real agenda. It established four required "priority" educational programs in every residence: "gender, multicultural, religious, and sexual preference . . . diversity."

Each of these topics was further divided into subtopics that constituted a veritable wish list of ideologically uniform indoctrination. Gender, for example, would cover "Levels of Sexism," "Sexual Discrimination," "Economics and Women," and "Feminism." The agenda for "multicultural" diversity, was, in its entirety: "prejudice; racism; racist behavior; American racial and ethnic groups; racial supremacy groups; racism at Penn; stereotypes; race as social construct; ethnicity; minority vs. majority." The full pro-

gram for "sexual orientation" was "definitions of heterosexism and homophobia; causes of heterosexism and homophobia; effects of homophobia on
heterosexual people; coming out; internalized homophobia; parenting;
causes of sexual orientation; violence and harassment; personal and institutional discrimination; lesbian/gay/bisexual lives at Penn; stereotypes and
myths; sexual orientation and religion." The administration had delegated
"education" on such matters to the ideologues of the office of student life.

As always, the treatment of religion was tendentious and question-beg-
ging. The full docket for "religious" diversity was "defining religious diversity at Penn; religion and ethnicity; religious freedom of belief and diversity;
religious stereotypes; anti-semitism; the holocaust and its meaning; religious
diversity and public policy: abortion/contraception; lesbian, gay, bisexual
questions; Middle East, Central America and politics; sexuality and religion;
sexism/women clergy; defining a social agenda." Within that, creative re-
dundancy abounded. For example, "public policy" on matters of religion
listed only six areas of concern: "separation of Church and State;
abortion/contraception; AIDS; the sanctuary movement and refugees; gay,
lesbian and bisexual issues; the Middle East, Central America, politics, and
religion." Under "religious freedom and diversity," there were five recommended programs on the "struggles" of "religious communities": "Women
clergy/sexism; homosexuality; liturgy [that is, the struggle against patriarchal
worship]; defining a social agenda; sexuality."

In addition to defining moral agendas and indoctrinating students on all of
these issues, Penn's "Diversity Education" was going to teach undergraduates how to bare their souls. Planning documents and facilitators' guides
instructed the thought reformers on techniques and tricks for "breaking
the ice," getting students to "brainstorm," having students begin their ob-
servations with "I," and participating in "role-playing games" about these
issues.

The 1989 planning committees were instructed to provide Penn students with a "common vocabulary" about "diversity." One handout circulated among the planners, borrowed from the University of Michigan where
it already was in use for freshmen orientation, included a loaded set of definitions. Some were merely political: "PEOPLE OF COLOR. A term of solidarity
referring to [the world's majority of] Asians, Blacks, Latinos, Native Americans and Pacific Islanders. . . . The term 'minority' . . . obscures this global
reality and in effect reinforces racist assumptions." Some were not only polit-

ical, but were also patronizing and intrusive: "INTERNALIZED OPPRESSION AND PSYCHOLOGICAL CAPTIVITY . . . states of mind in which subordinated individuals accept stereotypes and myths of themselves that are perpetuated by the dominant society." Some slipped in the crucial sociological notion of current thought reform, namely, that absent his or her group's domination of institutions, no individual could be a "racist" or "sexist." Thus, "RACISM" and "SEXISM" were, respectively, "racial prejudice [and] sexual prejudice with institutional power." Some offered wholly new "isms," such as "HET-EROSEXISM . . . attitudes, actions, or institutional practices which subordinate individuals whose sexual orientation is not heterosexual." These are not definitions, of course, but political, sociological, moral, and ideological claims, always fit for intensive study and debate, but never fit for mandatory indoctrination. The most revealing "definition," however, was "CULTURE," because that was the unit of diversity: "As [the Italian Communist] Antonio Gramsci has observed, 'Culture can be hegemonic: an order in which a certain way of life and thought is dominant.'"⁷ That, of course, was not a "celebration" of all cultures. The real goal of "diversity education" was the devaluation of the so-called "dominant" culture.

There are core beliefs of current thought reform. An individual is not an autonomous moral being, but a member of a racial and historical group that possesses moral debt or credit. There is only one appropriate set of views about race, gender, sexual preference, and culture, and holding an inappropriate belief, once truth has been offered, is not an intellectual disagreement, but an act of oppression or denial. All behavior and thought are "political," including opposition to politicized "awareness" workshops. The goal of such opposition is the continued oppression of women and of racial or sexual minorities.

To teach a new creed requires a new vocabulary. In fall 1990, the Office of Student Affairs (OSA) at Smith College gave every freshman a guide to "identity" and "oppression." "Oppression [was] discrimination . . . on the basis of certain stereotypes, generalizations, and attributes (conscious or unconscious)," by possessors of "institutional power." (It did not occur to the OSA that at Smith, *it* was the embodiment of institutional power.) The guide explained the need for its new vocabulary: "As groups of people begin the process of realizing that they are oppressed, and why, new words tend to be created to express the concepts that the existing language cannot." The complete vocabulary of "oppression" was as follows:

Smith

ABLEISM: oppression of the differently abled, by the temporarily able.

AGEISM: oppression of the young and the old, by young adults and the middle-aged in the belief that others are "incapable" or unable to take care of themselves.

ANTI-SEMITISM: oppression of Jewish peoples in the belief that they are members of an inferior group because of ethnic identity and religion.

CLASSISM: oppression of the working-class and non-propertied by the upper and middle-class.

ETHNOCENTRISM: oppression of cultures other than the dominant one in the belief that the dominant way of doing things is the superior way.

HETEROSEXISM: oppression of those of sexual orientations other than heterosexual, such as gays, lesbians, and bisexuals; this can take place by not acknowledging their existence. Homophobia is the fear of lesbians, gays, or bisexuals.

LOOKISM: the belief that appearance is an indicator of a person's value; the construction of a standard for beauty/attractiveness; and oppression through stereotypes and generalizations of both those who do not fit that standard and those who do.

RACISM: the belief that one group of people are [sic] superior to another and therefore have the right to dominate, and the power to institute and enforce their prejudices and discriminations.

RELIGIOUS DISCRIMINATION: oppression of religions other than the dominant one in the belief that the dominant way of worship is the only correct way.

SEXISM: stereotyping males and females on the basis of their gender; the oppression of women by society in the belief that gender is an indication of ability.[8]

Smith, thus, provided its students with breathtakingly partisan definitions of oppression in the first week of college. If those students, during four years of critical study, reached different understandings of oppression (such as conservative, liberal, libertarian, or various religious schools of thought might hold), it would only be by resisting the official newspeak.

———

The transformation of freshmen orientation is a significant phenomenon, and the *New York Times* rightly made it front-page news in August 1991, observing that "orientation has evolved into an intense . . . initiation," some of which involved an "academic boot camp." It accurately reported that "these programs . . . are being instituted at hundreds of colleges and universities for the first time," some offering "comprehensive, well-structured" programs "that can last up to a year." Such orientations, the *Times* noted, had moved onto new terrains: "delicate subjects like date rape, drug abuse, race relations, and how freshmen, some from small towns and tiny high schools, are supposed to deal with them."[9]

These orientations create an official moral agenda for students who arrive with a wide variety of personal ethical commitments. In 1992, Heather MacDonald surveyed a range of such programs for the *Wall Street Journal*. She found that orientation at Berkeley addressed "racism, homophobia, statusism, sexism, and ageism." Michele Frasier, assistant director of the New Student Program at Berkeley, said that the goal was "to make students aware [of the] issues they need to think about." (If Frasier had defined those as the loss of faith, the decline of individual responsibility, or the parasitism of the welfare state, faculty would have noticed.) Dartmouth had a mandatory orientation program for freshmen, "Social Issues," which Tony Tillman, assistant dean of freshmen, described as "the various forms of 'isms': sexism, racism, classism," all of which, he insisted, were interrelated. At Duke, President Keith Brodie informed all freshmen by letter that after a keynote speech by Maya Angelou, "You and your classmates will engage in a discussion of questions raised by Ms. Angelou." At Bowdoin, the assistant to the president for multicultural affairs held a program for freshmen entitled "Defining Diversity: Your Role in Racial-Consciousness Raising, and Cross-Cultural Social Enhancers." Oberlin informed its incoming students about "Differences in race, ethnicity, sexuality, gender, and culture," after which there were separate orientation programs for blacks, Hispanics, gays, lesbians, and bisexuals, and Americans of Asian ancestry.[10]

The *New York Times* described Columbia University's 1992 freshmen orientation, observing that the keynote speaker "described the archetypes and stereotypes in American society that support racism and prejudice." Students had the chance " 'to reevaluate, [and] learn things' " so that they could rid themselves of " 'their own social and personal beliefs that foster inequality.' " Incoming students had been sent a reading list of three works that all portrayed America as a land of oppression: *The Autobiography of Malcolm X; Ronald Takaki's Strangers from a Different Shore: A History of Asian Americans;* and Warren Blumenfeld's and Diane Raymond's *Looking at Gay and Lesbian Life.* Gathered in the gymnasium for their introduction to Columbia, they heard a gay student, an undergraduate of Asian ancestry, and a black student all talk about their encounters with bigotry and discrimination. Why did

Columbia choose such an orientation to four years of critical study? It was most certainly not to initiate dissent and debate. Assistant Dean Michael Fenlon, who noted that the program "will continue through their four years here," told the *Times* that "the goal is to initiate an awareness of difference and the implications of difference for the Columbia community." Columbia's administrators simply did not believe that their students could work things out spontaneously. Katherine Balmer, assistant dean for freshmen, said, "You can't bring all these people together and say, 'Now be one big happy community,' without some sort of *training* [emphasis added]."[11]

In the *Wall Street Journal*, MacDonald quoted Greg Ricks, outgoing "Multicultural Educator" at Stanford, who explained why "multicultural" orientations that emphasized difference were essential: "White students need help to understand what it means to be white in a multicultural community." Stanford, he believed, had succeeded relatively well in "trying to help students of color, and women students, and gay and disabled students to figure out what it means for them." However, "for the white heterosexual male who feels disconnected and marginalized by multiculturalism," he explained, "we've got to do a lot of work here."[12]

Schools, of course, must monitor and evaluate the formal academic work of students, and they must explain and enforce appropriate and equally applied behavioral regulations. None of that intrudes upon matters of intimate private belief, value, and identity. It is quite a leap, however, to assemble undergraduates newly and anxiously arrived on campus in order to probe such matters, to define appropriate objects of conscience, and to make them "aware" of how, correctly, they should view complex human, ethical, and social issues.

Such phenomena began, of course, with the ideological reformation of offices of student life themselves, after which few who were not "multicultural" zealots or careerists who feigned such zealotry were permitted (or, indeed, given the atmosphere, chose) to work there. In 1982, for example, the entire Division of University Life at Penn was subjected to mandatory "racism awareness seminars" predicated on the explicit proposition that "all whites are racists," which follows from the formula that prejudice (which all groups might have) plus institutional power (which all and only whites possess) equal "racism." Attendance was mandatory. A follow-up questionnaire to all participants asked: "Now that you have completed the Racism Awareness Workshop, how much consideration have you given to the subject of

American racism? . . . How much are you able to identify the indicators of American racism in the University [and] your department office? . . . How much do you feel that the training helped build a better sense of trust and teaming on the problem of American racism in the University Life Division [and] your office?"[13]

In spring 1982, an administrator who had devoted his life to Penn refused to attend further sessions. "An employer," he wrote to his immediate superior, "does not have the right, no matter how just the cause, to attempt to 'dictate morality.'" "Racial awareness," he urged, was a matter of "individual conscience," and "compulsory awareness seminars" were both "inappropriate" and "counter-productive." Such a view, he knew, would lead to his being labeled a "racist by those . . . running this program . . . who propound the doctrine that 'all whites are racists.'"[14] Describing the embarrassment these sessions had caused to blacks and whites who had worked together for long years, he resigned. The careerists and ideologues stayed.

What does it mean to enforce "correct" understandings of human relations? By 1992, Smith College already administered an official code of behavior, with sweeping notions of harassment. It already instructed its freshmen about "identity" and "oppression." These, however, were insufficient means of dealing with students who might stay within the letter of the law without truly grasping the college's full political meanings. Thus, Smith proudly announced, President Mary Maples Dunn was creating a "Bias Response Panel" to handle bias "that violates Smith's community standards but is not illegal." Its purpose was to "respond to those incidents which dishonor cultural identity." Ideally, it would offer those guilty of dishonoring cultural identity "channels for education, reintegration, and forgiveness." To her own rhetorical question—"What about free speech?"—Dunn replied, "Where insensitive speech (not harassing) is at issue . . . educational strategies will be preferred." If students did not accept that reeducation and reintegration, however, Smith had other means of persuasion at its disposal: "The panel will be able to use a full range of disciplinary actions, including . . . suspension, or permanent separation from the College."[15]

UMass was yet more ambitious, creating a "Multicultural Conflict Resolution Team." The team coordinator, Leah Wing, described this as an effort to "provide culturally-relevant interventions early in disputes." "Resolutions," however, depended upon certain assumptions. The team, Wing explained, "cannot be value free," because its commitment included "the elimination of inequality and oppression, and the creation of a multicultural University . . . in which social diversity is encouraged and valued, and in which social justice exists." Toward that end, the Conflict Resolution Team attended a week's training, for ten hours per day. The "students were trained in oppression issues relating to class, race, sex, sexuality, disability, and Jewish oppression." Further, they learned about "oppression dynamics and theory . . . [and about] themselves and each other in regards to each of these issues." To be able to deal with white students, who were likely to cause conflicts, "the students learned mediation techniques based in the Euro/ Anglo tradition." They faced a difficult task: "the challenge of being both committed to eliminating oppression and discrimination and also desiring to work effectively as mediators."[16]

Ironically, in December 1996, the president of UMass himself, William Bulger, was charged with discrimination by a black, female subordinate. He did not call in the Multicultural Conflict Resolution Team. He did not speak of "social justice." He did not speak of "oppression dynamics." His "spokesman" dismissed the charges as "a massive distortion of the truth," and declared that "the truth will prevail." A suit is pending.[17]

————————

The "dishonoring of cultures," of course, far from being outlawed, dominates academic thought reform. In fall 1994, the University of California–San Diego (UCSD) distributed an essay, "Combating Racism," to all incoming students. It proclaimed: "No individual can be racist in isolation [from power]. . . . Blacks cannot be racists." By contrast, the essay informed each new student, "the majority of white males [among those who have power] make 'power decisions' . . . which benefit white people." Indeed, whites "are consciously making racist decisions in that they realize that their decisions will impact more favorably on white people than on minorities."[18] That was UCSD's welcome to four years of education and the possibility of integration. A student journalist wrote, "The opinions expressed . . . are not the main problem—everyone is entitled to his own opinion. . . . UCSD, however, should not affirm that these opinions are correct. . . . This could not possibly encourage whites to combat racism. Seeing the university support statements such as 'blacks cannot be racists' will anger whites even more."[19]

Universities might introduce students to the life of the mind by discussion of fields of study or, if they wish to stimulate the habit of honest debate, by exposure to conflicting opinions about major issues of public policy and social analysis. Instead, they increasingly teach their canon of oppression by race, gender, and sexuality, converting some, no doubt, but making cynics out of others, and, indeed, enraging no small number who refuse to assume the historical or moral role assigned to them.

Northwestern University, for the planning of its New Student Week in 1989, formed a Cultural Diversity Project Committee. John Kibler, assistant dean of students, solicited program "facilitators" by explaining that the "committee project wants to educate everyone," because "it is important that we be involved in the moral education of our students." According to an enthusiastic (and candid) committee member, John Bremen, president of the Residential College Board, the committee's desire was "changing the world, or at least the way [undergraduates] perceive it." On September 12, one hundred fifty students and faculty members who had responded to this call attended a "facilitator training seminar." One faculty volunteer became so appalled by the political bias and personal intrusiveness of the exercise that he invited a student reporter to attend the otherwise closed meeting, and she reported to the campus on what occurred.[20]

The cofounders of "Self-Evaluation Consultants," Rita Starr and Charles Young, advised the group for four hours. Volunteers had been invited to learn how to aid discussion of "prejudice." Instead, they were lectured on white male oppression and internalized racism. Starr and Young informed them that "people developed racist feelings and thoughts through systematic mistreatment and lack correct information when they are young by the adults closest to them." One pleased committee member told the reporter, "It's basically a white guilt organization." The next day, New Student Week began, and the keynote speaker informed fifteen hundred freshmen that they were not to blame for the "customs and habits of thought" inherited from their parents and communities, but that they now must remake their lives, ridding themselves of "the ugliness, the meanness, . . . [the] narrowness and [the] tribalism." Students next had to discuss the lecture, led by the "facilitators" who had been trained the day before.[21] The faculty member, fascinated, stayed with the program. In 1994, in a letter to a skeptical colleague, he described the "further training sessions for facilitators" organized by Kibler. At one, the thirty trainees were "instructed to strike someone designated by a 'game,' in my case a black female student! I did not." The Cultural Diversity Program, he discovered, also trained the campus activities advisors, who were "at the elbow of" the leaders of almost all organizations and publications, and who conducted further campus "leadership" training.[22]

At Haverford College, in 1993, under the auspices of the dean of the college, upperclassmen made presentations on race relations in freshman dormitories. Ana Maria Garcia, assistant dean of the college, told the *Philadelphia Inquirer,* "There's a reality of having to learn about other people." Students were divided into two groups—the Alphas and the Betas—with different sets of private behavioral rules. They "took turns being visitors to the other culture . . . trying to interact according to their perceptions of the new culture's rules." They generally failed, because the "friendly and happy Alpha community [who only used chips in games] seemed dumbfounded upon entering the next room's world, where unsmiling Beta members seemed interested only in trading and acquiring chips."[23]

The experiment was quite successful: "Students in both groups said the game made them feel excluded, confused, awkward, and foolish." After-wards, Garcia made the analogy to society. "Are there situations in the real world where you don't know the rules?" she asked students at one of the most selective colleges in the United States. The purpose of the exercise, organizers told the *Inquirer,* was "to raise student awareness of racial and eth-nic diversity."[24]

Academic thought reform, however, as Columbia's assistant dean had explained, is no longer a "one shot affair."[25] At Harvard, in 1989, Dean Hilda Hernandez-Gravelle of the Office of Race Relations and Minority Affairs directed a weeklong official offering of speakers, panels, and "work-shops," called AWARE ("Actively Working Against Racism and Ethnocen-trism"). Robert R. Detlefsen, then a postdoctoral fellow in the government department, described the program in an article for *The New Republic.* AWARE's goals, stated on "Workshop Evaluation Forms" given daily to par-ticipants, were, in full, "to address people's denial about racism; to engage people in trying to understand racism and to take responsibility to change it through actions; to give people some new perspectives, ideals, and tools to use." In short, accepting "new perspectives, ideals, and tools" meant "aware-ness." Rejecting these meant "denial." The keynote address, "Racism Among the Well-Intentioned," was by Professor John Dovidio of Colgate University. Dovidio declared the sins of his own white racism, informing the Harvard community that 15 percent of whites were overt racists and 85 per-cent were subtle racists. What most struck Detlefsen was the audience re-sponse: "During the question period that followed the speech, no one rose to challenge his contention that we are all guilty of racism."[26]

The next evening, the speaker was Greg Ricks, formerly a dean at Dart-mouth, then a Senior Fellow of the Campus Opportunity Outreach at Har-vard, and later the "Multicultural Educator" at Stanford who told MacDonald about all the work that universities had to do on whites. Ricks asked, "Are these schools [the elite universities] genocidal in nature?" In reply to his own question, Ricks told of a black Dartmouth student who had come to doubt his own abilities, and of the assurance he had given that student: "They have brought you in, turned you around, and fucked up your mind." Ricks then told the students how to fight racism: "Don't tolerate racist jokes! . . . Don't tolerate any racist, sexist, homophobic discussions at the dining table, or anywhere else! . . . Don't sleep with racist, sexist dogs just because they're cute! . . . Throwing tampons at the male sexist dogs of Dartmouth was educational! . . . Create an environment that will force these institutions to do what is just; why do we have to have a fact-finding commission before we respond to student demands?" On the last day of AWARE, the dean of Harvard College, Fred Jewett, praised the week's events and asked students to keep its spirit alive. One speaker in particular, Lawrence Watson, assistant dean for academic administration of the Graduate School of Design (and cochairman of the Association of Black Faculty and Administrators) caught Detlefsen's attention. The assistant dean offered the following advice to black students: "When you experience racial insensitivity in the classroom, whatever way you choose to deal with it is valid, provided you are willing to accept the consequences." Watson followed this out to its logical conclusion: "Overreacting and being paranoid is the only way we can deal with this system. . . . Never think that you imagined it, because chances are that you didn't."[27]

Lessons such as this not only encourage, intentionally, the sorts of charges brought in the water buffalo prosecution, but also reinforce any hesitancy to interact across racial lines. At one AWARE event, a black student said that he found white students "boring" because "they don't want to contend with me on anything." Detlefsen observed: "But who can blame them? What can one expect from a group of people who have been told incessantly that they are racist, and that they must be highly circumspect in their relations with blacks lest their racism reveal itself in the form of an offensive word or two?"[28]

The University of South Carolina has a "University 101" program for "the freshman-year experience," which also offers national seminars and conferences. Its 1988–89 Conference Series was organized around five "critical issues areas": "promoting moral and character development"; "warming the chilly climate for women"; "learning from historically black colleges"; "promoting leadership training"; and "combating the rising tide of racism." The promotion of "moral and character development" among freshmen may have sounded apolitical, but it was not. American colleges and universities, its description informed participants, either could reflect "the dominant values of our society" or they could take "an alternative stance in attempting to promote individual values clarification and development for students." Institutions of higher education needed to make efforts "to promote specific moral and character development that our society needs," because this was the "1980s, the era of the big deal, the stock market crash, Reaganomics, and freshman love affairs with majors that promise materialistic rewards." The brochure noted that in 1982, two hundred administrators and educators attended the first session of the Freshman Year Experience, but that at the 1988–89 sessions, more than twenty-two hundred were expected.[29] Ironically, such programs invariably reinforce some of the crudest stereotypes about group identity. A workshop for the 1992–93 Freshman Year Experience, for example, discussed the difficulty of helping "Students of Color": "For culturally diverse students, particularly African-American students, seeking help threatens their self-esteem but also reminds them of cultural stereotypes and views which suggest that they have an inferior intelligence."[30]

One of the gospels of offices of student life is the national (and very expensive) publication *Access*, whose editorial board is composed of directors of minority affairs, affirmative action officials, and officers of student life and student affairs. In its issue of March–April 1996, it advised its extensive readership about "conflicts between Asian-American students and western [American] universities." Discussing American students of Asian descent, it advised campus administrators: "In contrast to western philosophy . . . eastern teachings tend to prescribe a structure for family order and encourage hierarchical thinking." To promote the education of Americans of Asian descent, it offered "a primer on how colleges and universities can assist [them] by understanding them." The most important term in that "primer" was "Humility": "This quality is valued above the boisterous, assertive behaviors one might expect from energetic college students on U.S. campuses." It was "humility" that led to "the image of the quiet, shy, and introverted Asian American student, who may have little to add to the fast-paced, action-oriented dynamics of many campus activities."[31] Thus armed, the student affairs officers could break down stereotypes in the minds of the students committed to their charge.

————————

When Penn's "Diversity Education" planning committee sought models, Bryn Mawr College shared the substance (and internal documents) of its "Building Pluralism" program, itself based on a Brown University program.

"Building Pluralism" was a mandatory part of Bryn Mawr's 1988 freshman orientation, leading into three follow-up programs focused on race. To prepare, Bryn Mawr put "facilitators" through a four-day summer workshop, followed by practice sessions with "student leaders" and RAs. Before its students had taken a single course on political or moral subjects, Bryn Mawr sought to change their thinking in these areas. Before those students even had settled in, Bryn Mawr probed their most private experiences. Students were divided into manageable groups, each overseen by a "facilitator." At a series of "exercises," individuals filled out written forms, for discussion, after which the smaller discussion groups were "debriefed" in larger groups. The first exercise, "High School Blues," asked freshmen "What are some of the ways in which you fit? What are some of the ways in which you did not fit? How did you cope with not fitting? What do you think are some of the ways you will fit or not fit at Bryn Mawr?" The third, "Backgrounds," on "race/ethnic origin, class, gender, sexual orientation, religious affiliation, [and] physical ability," asked them, "Coming from your background, what has been a source of difficulty . . . [and] strength for you? How do you anticipate that your background will influence your 'fit' at Bryn Mawr?" The fourth, "Concerns," asked students, "Choose four of the six differences that we have been discussing [in "Backgrounds"] and for each difference brainstorm about situations or scenarios, both academic and extra-curricular, that could arise at Bryn Mawr."[32]

Between "exercises," each group was exposed to a "facilitator's address" or "facilitator's discussion" that addressed, by day's end, "the meaning of difference," "the cycle of oppression: breaking free," "different meanings for different differences," and "the history of difference and inequality in higher education and at Bryn Mawr." At 7:20 P.M., students reported and discussed their "action plans" for "individual and collective action," and for "personal and institutional change." At 8:10 P.M., the "facilitator's closing remarks" covered, in twenty minutes, the day's accomplishments: "new meanings; change and conflict; power and choice; self and/in community; change agents."[33] Thus began their "education."

The University of Michigan has an "Office of Orientation," which presented its program, "Commitment to Diversity," to the 1988 National Conference of the National Orientation Directors Association. Michigan also shared its internal planning documents with Penn. In October 1988, Michigan set the following primary goal for "future diversity programming": "Establish [a] common base for working definitions and understanding of terms and definitions: societal, institutional and individual discrimination; racism;

sexism, homophobia, and heterosexism; religion [sic] intolerance; 'ableism' intolerance; understanding [and] appreciation of differences." It instructed "programmers" to instruct students about both discrimination at Michigan and the significant changes achieved "as a result of student activism." The desired result of this was "recognition that University [sic] is committed to becoming a leader as a multi-cultural institution and that students are expected to commit to contribute to that goal as new members of the community." It further instructed programmers to "engage students personally in the issues," which included getting undergraduates "to look at personal beliefs, values and behaviors that may discriminate against or harm others," and to "make a personal commitment to change."[34]

Michigan provided programmers with written forms that would lead undergraduates to examine, publicly, their private beliefs and values, and to commit to change. There was "A Personal Exploration," which asked participants, among other things, "What is your earliest remembrance of race? . . . Describe one of the first experiences with race that you had in the classroom? . . . Which students do you feel most comfortable with: Black, Chicano, Native American or Asian students? . . . Which students do you feel least comfortable with: Black, Chicano, Native American or Asian students?" What were the goals of such programs? Michigan's Orientation Program Task Force, in its internal documents, stated the "Objectives" of its 1988 Winter Orientation Program for undergraduates: "An understanding of the importance of the issue of diversity, and its applicability to racism and other forms of discrimination, especially sexism and heterosexism; . . . self-assessment regarding their own experiences, background, attitudes, and competencies related to these issues; . . . a heightened awareness to the levels of racism, sexism, and heterosexism and their various impacts."[35]

Wendy Shalit, an undergraduate at Williams College, described her freshman orientation in a 1995 article for Commentary. "This mandatory ritual," she reported, "included a 'Feel-What-It-Is-Like-To-Be-Gay' meeting." Students from the Bisexual, Gay, and Lesbian Union "tour the freshman dorms and require each student to declare, 'Hello, my name is _____ and I'm Gay!'" Next, there was a day-long Community-Building Workshop "in which each freshman is required to join a group and compose a list of insults he or she does not want to be called, as in 'I'm a woman, don't call me a chick!' or 'I'm Hispanic, don't call me a Spic!'" The last session of Williams's "Diversity Sensitivity" orientation was a program on "Race, Gender, Identity, and Community." According to Shalit, the entire freshman class was assembled in a dark auditorium, where, eyes closed, "slurs were hurled at us from all directions." Well, that's one introduction to the life of the human spirit. Shalit, at least, could keep her sense of humor in addition to her sense of outrage: "I humbly offered 'conservative' as my preferred group, and for my insult, 'Don't call me a free-market apologist!' There was considerable uncertainty about whether this counted."[36]

The University of Cincinnati extended "racial sensitivity training" to staff and faculty. William Daniels, a library employee, described his experience at such a session. Attendance was mandatory, and all participants were ordered to have read Barbara Ehrenreich's essay on "cultural diversity." Vice Provost Mary Ellen Ashley called the group's attention to the silence of the white males among them, saying that she would tolerate this for the moment, but that they would have to participate. The vice provost asked all attendees to write an essay on the topic "What I can do to help our department demonstrate our appreciation for diversity," and explicitly stated that anyone who disagreed with the university's policy on diversity should find work elsewhere. When one librarian denied his need for "cultural diversity training," the vice provost asked the entire group to reflect on the "gall" of such a claim.[37]

Abraham H. Miller, professor at Cincinnati, and others described a 1990 "racial sensitivity" session for all faculty at University College. Dean David Hartleb introduced the facilitator, Edwin J. Nichols, from Washington, D.C., as a great teacher. Nichols had the faculty stand and state the source of their undergraduate degrees. Those with the most "prestigious" degrees remained standing, and he repeated the process with their masters and then doctoral degrees. At the end of this process, one young woman remained standing, a white professor who had been at the university for all of three weeks. Nichols kept her standing, and pointed out her blonde hair and blue eyes. Her credentials, he explained, made her the most likely to succeed: "This is a member of the privileged white elite." When the group reconvened after a break, Nichols, opining that this white, blue-eyed blonde would win "a beauty contest" among them, asked her to stand again. She would not, but sat sobbing, enduring Nichols's observation that, a perfect example of the American elite, "she was even wearing her string of pearls." No one challenged Nichols or complained. (Where are the feminists when one needs them?) The university denied this account, but reporters who interviewed the young woman confirmed it.[38]

The "training" of residence advisors (RAs), the university's dormitory agents, is, we already have seen, increasingly partisan and invasive of private conscience. At the University of Cincinnati, Craig Cobane, a political science graduate student, described his experience of a mandatory "Cultural Diversity Workshop" for RAs in 1993. The "sensitivity facilitator" informed them that "all whites were racists," and that no black in any circumstance could be racist. White males, he instructed, held all power in society, and they oppressed ethnic minorities, women, gays, lesbians, and the disabled.[39] In 1995 at Penn, RAs enjoyed an all-day training session directed by Angela Airall, general manager of the firm Diversity Performance and Culture Change and the sister of Zoila Airall, the administrator in charge of Penn's residential multicultural "educational" programming. One RA, J. Christopher Robbins, wrote of the "training" to the administration, threatening, ironically, a "hostile environment" suit of his own. "Ms. Airall's 'diversity workshop' was a racist sham," he complained, for it "created a hostile environment for white men . . . [who] were inexcusably slandered, defamed, humiliated and harassed." Robbins cited several of "the many racist . . . statements which Ms. Airall made": "'White men never have been asked to pick themselves up by their bootstraps'. . . . 'White men . . . go into self-denial about their oppressive propensities.' . . . 'The extent to which you are in the majority is the extent to which you pretend the minority is not oppressed.' . . . 'The merit system has never worked.'" When Robbins and a few other RAs disagreed, Airall said: "'You don't belong in the role you are in and your supervisors should reevaluate things.'"[40]

A university may be able to manage the ideological selection and training of RAs in fine detail, but undergraduates overwhelmingly do not share their would-be reformers' perspectives or agendas. This produces an ironic situation in which RAs receive intensive training about the "multicultural" issues of power, historical injustice, race, gender, sexuality, and "otherness," but actually spend almost all of their time dealing with ordinary roommate conflicts, noise, drunkenness, false fire alarms, broken appliances, petty theft, lost keys, and receptionists who fall asleep on the night shift. One may draw some solace from that, unless one cares about the students barred from RA positions by their politically incorrect political or moral sincerity or, indeed, about what universities are communicating to their students about intellect, spirit, and the open and critical mind.

RAs indeed are expected to carry out the political mission of the university. UMass's Center for Diversity and Development provides RAs with a politicized list of "educational films" to show in their dorms, revealing what counts as "diversity" in academic life. The films are divided into these categories: "disabilities"; "violence against women"; "gender"; "alcohol/health" (many on women's body image); "Jewish"; "gay/lesbian/bisexual"; "cultural/ethnic"; "racism/racial"; "miscellaneous" (some Hollywood films; self-help videos; liberal and radical documentaries; and movies on harassment, sex, power, and Vietnam); "dealing with diversity"; and, count one's blessings, some classic Janus Films. One would not know that conservative, Christian, or free-market perspectives formed any part of the "diversity" of the land. Indeed, under "culture/ethnic issues," only one of twenty-three films deals with any white "ethnicity": *Sacco and Vanzetti,* whose execution as anarchists was "an event that stirred the conscience of the world."[41]

At Montclair State University in New Jersey, RAs attend sensitivity training sessions, one of them on homosexuality. At the 1994 training session, social worker Michael Hunter gave RAs the following "permission slip": "I hereby have permission to be: imperfect with regards to homophobia and heterosexism. It is OK if I do not know all of the answers and if at times my ignorance and misunderstandings become obvious." The slip gave the RAs-in-training "permission to ask questions that appear stupid . . . [and] to struggle with these issues." It even gave them the reason for this leniency: "I am a product of this homophobic/heterosexist culture." There was no need to feel guilty about the residual effect of that culture, they were reassured, so long as they were "struggling to change my false/inaccurate beliefs or oppressive attitudes [and] learning what I can do to make a difference." Hunter informed RAs that black men were more homophobic than white men because of their macho culture.[42] Montclair State has every right to set a *behavioral* code for RAs and to insist that they treat all students equally, without invidious discrimination, but it also wanted their beliefs, their wills, and their consciences.

The commitment to such beliefs and programs increases apace. Between September 1997 and January 1998, hundreds of colleges and universities advertised in the *Chronicle of Higher Education* for positions that required commitments to diversity education. Scores of these administrative jobs called for such education or training in areas of student life. The institutions covered the full spectrum of American higher education and included, among many others, Bard College ("promote awareness of multicultural issues among faculty, staff, and students"); Bloomsburg University ("diversity training skills . . . reports to the Director of Social Equity"); the University of California–Davis ("multicultural education and diversity training practices"); the University of Dayton ("diversity and service-learning programming"); Humboldt State University ("the teaching of multicultural awareness in workshop settings . . . experience with diverse coalitions of students, including ethnicity, religion, gender and sexual orientation"); James Madison University ("working with faculty and other student service offices to provide support and assistance in designing programs related to multicultural issues"); Miami University, Ohio ("development of multicultural awareness programs throughout the College"); Midwestern State University ("multicultural/diversity programming management . . . educational and social programs related to cultural diversity within University Housing"); the University of Nebraska ("to raise awareness of diversity and equity issues among all University students, staff, faculty and administrators"); Northeastern University ("understand the significance of the historical and dynamic agendas in both the affirmative action and diversity arenas, and the relationship between the two"); St. Mary's College of Maryland ("cultural diversity/sensitivity training"); Skidmore College ("campus-wide proactive leadership in matters of diversity . . . educating the campus on issues concerning diversity"); Slippery Rock College ("producing cultural diversity programs that help educate the university . . . on issues that effect [sic] a pluralistic society [and] the continued development of a just and caring community"); Southwestern University ("diversity education . . . [that includes] but [is] not limited to residence life programming; student development programming; . . . recruitment, training, and orientation of residence life staff; and program support to student organizations"); SUNY–Potsdam ("multicultural . . . [and] college-wide diversity programming, and for creating and presenting training programs for students and student groups"); SUNY College of Technology ("diversity programming, training and awareness for the college community" and, a second, "Residence . . . diversity programming and training"); the University of Toledo ("design and implement programs . . . [and] workshops that enhances [sic] the University's understanding of issues that directly and indirectly relate to people of color"); and Wittenberg University ("diversity training for the campus community—students, faculty, and staff").[43]

Some of these advertisements of available positions offer a full ideological agenda. Hampshire College seeks an associate dean for "leading the college's efforts to create an atmosphere in which multiculturalism is a reflected value of the community." This dean "will lead and coordinate staff advisors of students and will co-coordinate a multicultural leadership program." Quinsigamond Community College, in Worcester, Massachusetts, has reopened a search for an "Assistant to the President" who would be "charged with heightening campus sensitivity to multicultural issues in a positive, respectful, and proactive manner in support of an environment in which diversity becomes everybody's business." Xavier University wishes to hire a

"Director of Multicultural Affairs," defined solely in terms of "African American, Asian American, Hispanic American, Native American, and other students of color," who will show them "that we care," and who will "engage and involve the University community in celebrations, discussions, forums, workshops, and interpersonal relationships that help create an awareness, appreciation, and understanding of diversity." Bucknell University hopes to find an administrator who will "offer advocacy to the larger campus community on behalf of students of color," and who will "reduce prejudice, and promote multiculturalism with a global perspective." The University of South Florida seeks a dean of the Sarasota/Manatee campus who "during the review process . . . will be evaluated on commitment to diversity and accomplishments in support of Equal Opportunity/Affirmative Action programs," and a dean of the College of Fine Arts with "an awareness and valuing of multicultural issues . . . and an unquestionable [sic] commitment to principles of affirmative action."[44]

Universities wrongly think that almost no one is watching their efforts at thought reform in the guise of "diversity." In an impassioned article posted on a Christian Webpage, J. Stanley Oakes, Jr., national director of the Christian Leadership Ministries (the faculty ministry of the Campus Crusade for Christ) denounced the intolerance toward evangelical Christians that pervades all facets of campus life, in contradiction of claims of pluralism. He told the well-known story of Timothy Gregory, an RA at Cornell. As part of his "training" and as a condition of employment, he was ordered to watch films of explicit gay and lesbian sexual acts, despite his requests to be excused on grounds of conscience. According to Oakes, when outraged alumni complained, Cornell replied that this was an aberrational occurrence.[45]

Some campus ministries, however, support thought reform with remarkable enthusiasm. On February 8–9, 1991, the United Ministries in Higher Education, Pennsylvania Commission, held a "seminar" on "Racism on Campus" for nine universities in Central and Western Pennsylvania. The goal of the seminar was to send "teams" back to each campus to develop "specific 'next steps' in dealing with issues of racism."[46] On several campuses, offices of student life and student services paid participants' travel and registration fees. The seminar provided a packet of materials from universities around the country. These materials lead us to the logical conclusion of current "multiculturalism," group identity, anti-individualism, and intrusive thought reform.

Participants were given a "Glossary of Terms," which asked, "Who is a racist?" and answered, "All white individuals in our society are racists. Even if whites are totally free from all conscious racial prejudices, they remain racists." Another "term" was "White Racism—Power + Prejudice = Racism. . . . In the United States at present, only whites can be racists." It defined "Personal Racism as: "Lack of support for ethnic minorities who take risks to change an organization. . . . Questioning the need for affirmative action goals. . . . 'Color blind' statements that refuse to see race as a part of an individual's identity." It defined "Organizational Racism" as "Premature negotiation to avoid conflict. . . . Absence of a training program that develops staff attitudes, understanding and skills for combating racism." One crucial document, "adapted from 'Being White at Indiana University,'" gave the following view of student whiteness:

> Not having to think in terms of "what I am not." . . . My culture is the yardstick for what's around me: our history, our music, our society. Never having had to consider that I was part of a race . . . never worrying that when I enter a room of strangers, I will be looked at with hostility . . . never having to doubt that this or that course will have some material in it concerning my race . . . my history, my art, my literature, my national heroes, my race's philosophers, painters, and generals . . . being comfortable . . . going back to the all-white suburb where I grew up . . . being confused by words like "institutional racism."

By contrast, there was "Being Black":

> Being black is to open my textbooks and see pictures of white folk and to read white-washed theory, philosophy and history which are irrelevant to me . . . to go to a white counselor whom I don't trust, and who doesn't know how to handle my presence or my problem . . . worrying about the fact that my roommate will in all probability be white.[47]

We faxed these materials to an administrator of student activities at Indiana University of Pennsylvania, one of the participating schools. She left a message on our answering machine that she believed the documents had originated at Indiana University, Indiana. She was correct, although they had come to Indiana University from the University of Maryland. "They are wonderful," she said. "Feel free to use them however you want."[48] We use them to ask if this model of education is appropriate to a decent society. If you agree that it is not, what can be done?

CHAPTER 10

DOUBLE STANDARDS: SOME ARE MORE EQUAL THAN OTHERS

Speech codes, with their general references to "race, ethnicity, and sexual preference," seem aimed at everyone. They would not last a moment, however, if, in fact, they were. If feminists, multiculturalists, the Left, and various self-proclaimed progressives were forced to censor themselves and worry about "a hostile environment," the speech codes and their equivalents would crumble overnight. Those who throw around the common campus terms "white racist," "homophobe," "potential rapist," "victim of internalized oppression," "Uncle Tom," and "born again bigot" know that *they* never will face hearings and penalties. If unbelievers had to worry that "offense" caused by their denial, criticism, or mockery of sacred Christian beliefs and symbols would subject them to expulsion, termination, or "sensitivity seminars," free speech would be an absolute value on campuses. Pennsylvania State University has a harassment policy criminalizing "verbal conduct" that creates an "offensive" or "hostile" environment of "a sexual nature." In March 1997, a senior there exhibited a quilt, "25 Years of Virginity," with crosses sewn onto the crotches of twenty-five pairs of panties. Catholics protested, and the Catholic League for Religious and Civil Rights asked for the "offense" to be removed. Penn State's president, Graham Spanier, replied, "I can't imagine any circumstances under which this university would want to encourage censorship."[1]

The support for such codes, thus, depends upon the absurd supposition that the potential victims of such selective and biased enforcement will acquiesce indefinitely in the double standards upon which their campus legal inequality depends. In fact, although human patience can be remarkably enduring, no majority in a democratic society will suffer injurious double standards forever. There will be a day of reckoning and, when it comes, where will one find a coalition already formed around the love of liberty, due process, and legal equality to protect those newly out of favor?

On July 19, 1995, groups that care about free expression on the Internet circulated a notice about a "Victory for Free Speech." Originating from libertarians at the University of California–San Diego (UCSD), it informed readers that UCSD voluntarily had withdrawn a restrictive e-mail code forbidding "offensive" communications.[2] Censors, however, almost never make voluntary, moral decisions about freedom, and the events preceding the withdrawal of the UCSD code speak volumes about prevailing double standards, especially because UCSD does not stand out in any way as an offender against rights and legal equality. It is an average place.

On June 1, 1994, June C. Terpstra, of the Sexual Harassment Prevention and Policy Program at UCSD, issued a "Campus Notice," to be posted in all university offices and official bulletin boards. It defined "sexual harassment" for the UCSD community as "unwelcome and unwanted behavior (visual, verbal or physical) of a sexual nature," and informed the university that "complaints regarding letters of a sexually offensive nature via E-Mail at UCSD have recently been reported to the Office of Sexual Harassment Prevention and Policy (SHPP)." "Any use" of campus e-mail "for the purpose of distributing sexually offensive materials," it warned, was "a violation of University policy, [and] persons identified as participating in the creation or distribution of such materials will face disciplinary action." Recipients of such materials were instructed to report this to the SHPP.

On December 9, 1996, one of our research assistants, Lindsey Kaser, interviewed Ms. Terpstra by telephone about what sorts of e-mail had prompted the policy. Terpstra mentioned "quid pro quo" sexual harassment and "child porn," but these, of course, already were illegal under the laws of the United States and, further, it would be rare, to say the least, for someone to put an extortionate sexual demand in writing. On December 11, 1996, she confirmed, by e-mail, that, indeed, "with or without any e-mail policy . . . women already were protected fully from 'quid pro quo' sexual extortion, and from child pornography." In the interview of December 9, 1996, however, she also had mentioned e-mail that would appear more accurately to reflect her ban of "sexually offensive materials" of June 1, 1994, and its warning of disciplinary actions: "creepy messages, dirty jokes, ads from God knows where." Indeed, several administrators at UCSD, including Vice Chancellor Joseph Watson, discussing the policy in January 1996 with

Kors, cited neither illegal obscenity nor illegal quid pro quo extortion, but merely "a few risqué jokes" that had been forwarded by e-mail (by persons whom the university never identified) to individuals whom the posters thought might enjoy them. No one remembered any of the jokes.[3]

Forwards of such jokes—from adolescently misogynistic one-liners to the celebrated feminist "100 Reasons Why Cucumbers Are Better Than Men"—have been circulating electronically for years and show up almost every day at almost every large campus in America. At UCSD, however, a few recipients did not enjoy them, but rather than ask to be removed from someone's mailing list, they complained to June Terpstra, who issued her directive. For the next eight months, there was no visible protest of this vague and manifestly unconstitutional policy at UCSD. According to administrators, one member of the UCSD community—no one will identify her—continued to complain about sexual humor on the Internet.

On February 1, 1995, Richard Atkinson, chancellor of UCSD, wrote to the campus. Aware that "the UCSD computer network has been used to distribute messages that were sexual in nature and may have offended the individuals to whom they were sent," he was promulgating a policy entitled "Improper Use of Electronic Mail": "The use of University resources such as electronic mail to disparage individuals or groups on the basis of gender, race, sex, sexual orientation, age, disability, or religion is strictly prohibited and violates University policy."

Hal Pashler, professor of psychology, and longtime defender of academic freedom at UCSD, wrote to Chancellor Atkinson the next day, asking how the directive could be reconciled "with the principle of academic freedom guaranteed by university policy and applicable law." He asked the chancellor if he would "clarify what you mean by disparaging groups on the basis of gender, race, etc.?" For example, Pashler asked, would a feminist's e-mail praising Andrea Dworkin's view that all men are rapists now "be prohibited conduct"? The directive, with its "bizarre notion" that "faculty, staff and students are not to discuss with each other by email . . . anything that another individual might find offensive" would chill freedom and rights.

Having heard nothing, Pashler wrote again to Chancellor Atkinson on February 6, reiterating that "your notice seems plainly unlawful" and constitutes "an unwarranted infringement on freedoms essential to the nation and the academic enterprise." Three weeks later, Pashler received a reply, not from Atkinson, but from Vice Chancellor Marjorie Caserio, informing him that Atkinson's notice "was in no way intended to abrogate First Amendment rights," but merely to protect individuals from "ad hominem harassment." Pashler replied, copied to Atkinson, that "the purpose of my letter . . . was not to learn more about the intentions of the person who wrote the memo, [but] to point out that the Chancellor's notice in and of itself constitutes a serious and present violation of the principles of academic freedom and free speech."

Pashler reminded the administration of the McCarthy era, when "some administrators trampled on academic freedom," but he noted that even then, to his knowledge, "no Chancellor of [a campus of] the University of California ever went so far as to issue an edict prohibiting speech disparaging the United States of America or free market economics." Atkinson's "edict," he wrote, "is morally and legally equivalent to such a hypothetical prohibition," because all of the "forms of disparagement" it prohibits "have been explicitly recognized by the courts as falling within the bounds of protected free speech."

The Senate–Administration Council formally endorsed Caserio's interpretation of Atkinson's notice in early March. Thus reinforced, Caserio replied to Pashler on March 13 that she would refer the matter to the university general counsel. The faculty's Committee on Academic Freedom, however, took Pashler's view of the matter, and on April 17, it issued a memorandum: "We unanimously support the principle of free and completely uncensored communication on the UCSD campus. We believe that this is essential to the work of the University, its faculty and students." For a full academic quarter, nonetheless, the administration of UCSD did nothing to rescind the directive.

Three months later, on July 19, Chancellor Atkinson issued an official "Campus Notice," distributed electronically to every member of the university, entitled "Replacement Notice on Improper Use of Electronic Mail." Atkinson quoted his message of February 1, and declared that he now was aware that "this statement, however unintentional, is worded so that it has the potential to discourage members of the University from the exercise of their academic freedom and First Amendment Rights." The wording of the "replacement" was remarkably different from that of the original policy, which his administration had defended during the year. In the place of a prohibition, the University now "discourages discourtesy or personal invective in all discussions on the campus, including those conducted through electronic mail." Atkinson committed UCSD to "upholding the principles of academic freedom and free speech." This was the act announced by Internet anticensorship forces as a great victory. What, actually, had happened to rekindle a love of liberty? Enter *Voz Fronteriza* and its editorial on the death, in March, of Luis Santiago.

On March 30, the thirty-year-old Santiago, a border patrol agent of the U.S. Immigration and Naturalization Service (INS), fell to his death while pursuing suspected illegal immigrants, leaving behind a widow and children. *Voz Fronteriza,* which commented editorially on Santiago's death, is the monthly publication of a radical group of students at UCSD that believes, according to its official editorial position, that California and the American Southwest are "occupied Mexico," part of a greater "Aztlan" nation, which also is the view of the organization whose announcements it regularly carried, the Movimiento Estudiantil Chicano de Aztlan (MEChA). *Voz Fronteriza's* lead editorial in March 1995, before Santiago's death, referred to Mexican-Americans as "the Mexican people living on this side of the frontera falsa [false border]."[4] A May 1995 editorial declared: "The odds that the colonizer will give us our land and control of resources peacefully are slim to none. Unless we prepare for armed struggle we will be kept at the level of servitude we find ourselves in today. . . . The revolution has begun, which side are you on?"[5] *Voz Fronteriza* was (and is) an officially recognized publication at UCSD, and in 1994–95, the student government awarded it six thousand dollars in funds from a general mandatory fee collected by the university. The cover of the March 1995 issue had shown Governor Pete Wilson in the crosshairs of a telescopic sight, and he was named "Raza [Race] Enemy #1."[6]

In May 1995, *Voz Fronteriza* published its editorial on the death of Santiago, "this traitor . . . to his race." It was entitled "Death of a Migra Pig," that is, the death of an INS agent. "We're glad this pig died, he deserved to die . . . he is the worst kind of pig there is [one who chases 'his own kind']. . . . As far as we care all the Migra pigs should be killed, every single one . . . the only good one is a dead one . . . The time to fight back is now. It is time to organize an anti-Migra patrol. . . . It is to [*sic*] bad that more Migra pigs didn't die with him."[7]

The editorial should remind us all of the unfettered freedom of the radical campus press of the '60s, a freedom the radical press still enjoys. "Death of a Migra Pig" came in a year when the nation still was reeling from the bombing of the federal building in Oklahoma City, and the president of the United States had implicated conservative talk show hosts as sharing some culpability for spreading contempt for federal officers after Waco and Ruby Ridge. UCSD officials, however, to say the least, did not overreact. Vice Chancellor Watson told the *San Diego Union-Tribune,* "Like most student newspapers, they make an effort to achieve some shock value. Sometimes, it's in very poor taste and lacks sensitivity—particularly in this case, in which there's a death involved."[8] Indeed, "poor taste" and "insensitivity" are not crimes.

How do the phrases "traitor" to his "race," and "all the Migra pigs should be killed," however, compare to the sombrero T-shirts and "south-of-the-border" parties that brought down the wrath of University of California officials upon fraternities? Indeed, if any phrase might send a university into a quandary about the boundaries of free speech, the words "all the Migra pigs should be killed" might be just the phrase to do it. "Offensive"? "Intimidating"? "Hostile"? How does that use of "university resources" compare to the forwarded joke on e-mail that had led Chancellor Atkinson to jettison the United States Constitution?

Throughout June, news of the editorial began to circulate, and by late June, it was the subject of major news stories and editorials in the state and national press. Half a year later, Watson recalled, on the record: "The *Voz* affair began slowly," a few letters, and then press inquiries, and then congressmen, and then "an enormous number of State legislators and senators." The administration engaged in "major discussions" of the crisis.[9]

When the *Washington Times* published an article on the editorial, UCSD's campus director of student activities, Lynn Peterson, reassured the paper that "no way do we endorse it," but added that the university could not control the content of the paper.[10] On that same day, and on the next, Vice Chancellor Watson told the *San Diego Union-Tribune* that the university was not responsible for the article, and that any apology would have to come from the editors of *Voz Fronteriza*.[11] On July 5, UCSD issued a formal response, "University Statement on the *Voz Fronteriza* Article," noting its "derogatory and hate-filled statements about the U.S. Border Patrol and the tragic death of . . . Luis Santiago." Although "the contents of this article are deplorable and offensive," UCSD affirmed, and although "we have strong objections to the contents of . . . any . . . article that advocates hate or violence," UCSD was not free to act: "The University is legally prohibited from censuring [*sic*] the content of student publications." Indeed, UCSD explained, "Previous attempts by universities and other entities to regulate freedom of speech, including hate speech, have all been ruled unconstitutional."

Congressional pressure was now mounting. Representative Brian Bilbray, of California, issued a statement condemning the editorial as "hate speech [that] condones [and] encourages . . . violent actions." More ominously for UCSD, U.S. Representative Duncan Hunter of California, a member of the House Committee on National Security, wrote to Chancellor Atkinson that absent a "retraction and apology" by UCSD, he would introduce legislation "aimed at de-funding institutions whose publications advocate the killing of American officers." Within hours, Vice Chancellor Watson wrote to Representative Hunter "in response to your July 5, 1995 letter to Chancellor Atkinson," reiterating that "whatever strong objections" the administration might have, *Voz Fronteriza* had "the right to publish their views without adverse administrative action." Why? "Student newspapers are protected by the first amendment of the U.S. constitution *as are all other print and Electronic media* [emphasis added]."

For weeks, UCSD officials had been telling congressmen, state legislators, state senators, and the media that despite UCSD's regrets over such immeasurably offensive content, all campus media, including "electronic media," were constitutionally protected. In fact, on July 5, when all those statements about constitutional protection were issued, Chancellor Richard Atkinson's prohibition of speech, defended throughout the year, still was in effect, prompted by e-mail humor so unmemorable that no one at UCSD could recall it. When Watkins wrote to Congressman Hunter that the First Amendment prohibited UCSD from censoring or disciplining any campus media, including electronic media, for calling for the death of Hispanic-American border patrol agents as race traitors, UCSD, in fact, still was bound by Atkinson's own policy specifying precisely that "The use of University resources . . . to disparage individuals or groups on the basis of gender, race, sex, sexual orientation [and so on] . . . is strictly prohibited." Soon after, Atkinson became the chancellor of the entire University of California system.

Academic administrators claim to agonize over the problems posed by faculty-student "power imbalance." (It is the reason why romantic relationships between students and faculty, at all levels, are increasingly prohibited.) This concern, however, is one of the most selectively applied considerations in academic life. It most certainly was not invoked in the case of conservative students at Dartmouth College and Professor of Music William Cole.[12]

The students were editors and writers for *The Dartmouth Review,* a conservative publication highly critical both of the Dartmouth administration and of what it believes to be prevailing campus orthodoxies. Its alumni include many individuals successful in political and public life, journalism, and publishing. Dartmouth's administration has openly loathed the *Review* since the journal's founding in 1981, challenging its use of Dartmouth in its title and its rights of open distribution, and denouncing it both officially and informally innumerable times.

What occurred at Dartmouth in 1988 can be known in detail from a documentary record, and, above all, from the stipulations, uncontested claims, and subpoenaed materials of the court case that followed the event. On February 24, 1988, *The Dartmouth Review* published a caustic criticism of a course taught by a black professor of music, William Cole. Using tapes made by a student in the course, the *Review* quoted Cole's profanities and epithets toward women, whites, and conservatives, and it criticized, in general, what it took to be the politicization of his class.[13]

The *Review* previously had criticized Cole in 1983, and he had instituted a libel suit against it. The suit ended with a settlement that included a public joint statement that Cole continued to believe that the *Review* was racially motivated in its report on his course and that the *Review* continued to believe that its story was accurate and appropriate. In February 1988, the *Review* was advised by its attorney to give Cole a chance, this time around, to respond to its criticisms. On February 25, it sent four of its editors and writers to see the music professor, right after he finished teaching a class. They handed him a letter asking him for a response to their article, and they had a tape recorder and camera, tools of the trade, to document any response. Words occurred. Superior Court Judge Bruce E. Mohl of New Hampshire heard the tape recording of those words, and as he put it in his decision, "Cole became extremely agitated." On February 26, Dartmouth College charged the four students with "harassment," and a hearing date was scheduled for March 5 (although the students' judicial advisor was not available until March 11).

In the time between the formal charge of harassment on February 26 and the supposedly impartial hearing on March 5, much occurred. An assistant dean wrote a memo to the presidents of Dartmouth's fraternities, urging them to "encourage member attendance" at a rally on behalf of Cole organized by the Afro-American Society. The dean of the college, Edward Shanahan, scheduled to preside impartially over the hearing, wrote privately to Cole that he was stepping down from that role in order to be "personally involved in the attempt to develop the case," but then did preside, and made crucial decisions about the inadmissibility of defense evidence. The chairman of the Board of Trustees expressed his concern to Dartmouth president James Freedman: "Get out front . . . to avoid a sit-in or take-over." On February 29, President Freedman, who had not discussed the confrontation or the charges with the accused students, addressed a campus rally against the *Review* at which he expressed his "deep personal concern" about "acts of disrespect, insensitivity and personal attack . . . [and about] racism, sexism, and other forms of ignorance." Again, before the hearing, Freedman told the *Boston Globe* that "I feel dreadful about the attack on Professor Cole."[14] Asked in Superior Court if he hadn't prejudiced the hearing, Freedman testified, "Not for a minute. . . . I had a responsibility to keep the peace and calm of the campus."

Court documents disclosed that the hearing panel judging the case included several individuals who previously had expressed hostility toward the *Review.* One member on the panel, Professor Albert LaValley, had cosigned two prior letters to Freedman calling the *Review* "distorted and slanderous," "sexist and racist," and a "threat" to "the principle of academic freedom on this campus." During their two-day hearing, the defendants were denied their request to cross-examine witnesses. The panel convicted the students of crimes quite remarkable to anyone familiar with radical protests or with the obsession with the faculty's "imbalance of power" over students. One student was disciplined "because he initiated and persisted in a vexatious oral exchange with the professor." Another "because he was repeatedly aggressive, confrontational and particularly vexatious in demanding an apology from Professor Cole in a raised voice." Another "because he repeatedly photographed Professor Cole." "Vexatious oral exchange"? Try telling professors and deans from the '60s about that.

The subsequent Superior Court trial lifted the veil a bit from the confidential Dartmouth judicial system and disclosed interesting details about the comparative gravity of the punishment of the convicted students. In 1986, for example, twenty-nine antiapartheid demonstrators had been convicted of occupying the president's office. They were found guilty, but not punished "in light of how your actions were motivated by strongly held convictions about the educational goals and responsibilities of this College." A student recently convicted of nonconsensual sexual relations had been suspended for one term. The senior editors of *The Dartmouth Review,* by contrast, were suspended for one and a half years. Professor LaValley, a member of the hearing panel, three days after that panel convicted the students, wrote to President Freedman that the *Review*'s "attacks on women, minorities and gays . . . subtly feed into an already somewhat conservative student body— and thus stops [*sic*] the flow of a needful dialogue."

On March 28, Freedman addressed a faculty meeting called to discuss the affair.[15] His address is a window onto contemporary academic life. The *Review,* he declared, "is dangerously affecting—in fact, poisoning—the intellectual environment of our campus." He assured the faculty that he welcomed conservative voices, but of a different kind, "in the high tradition of

Edmund Burke, John Henry Newman, Matthew Arnold, James Madison, and Henry Adams." (Do conservatives get to pick their radical critics, too?) Thus, Freedman continued, he was trying, among other things, to save conservatism, because the *Review* "vulgarizes responsible conservative thought and is, in fact, an affront to it."

Freedman assumed powers that beleaguered administrators of the '60s never dreamed of giving themselves. "I must not stand by silently," he proclaimed, "when a newspaper callously and deliberately impugns the professional reputations of members of this faculty and administration." The *Review*, whose writers were "ideological provocateurs posing as journalists, [had] no right" to judge "the qualifications and standing of members of this faculty."

Finally, Freedman invoked President Eisenhower's 1953 denunciation at Dartmouth of Senator McCarthy, which had urged Dartmouth students "not to join 'the book burners.'" He quoted Eisenhower directly: "Don't be afraid to go in your library and read every book, so long as any document does not offend your own ideas of decency." Freedman, however, picked up only on Eisenhower's second clause, not on his defense of liberty, and he told the campus: "What the *Review* has done on this campus has not been decent. What it has done has been irresponsible, mean-spirited, cruel, and ugly."

The true target of *The Dartmouth Review*, Freedman concluded, "is diversity." What was the diversity that left no room for the *Review?* In Freedman's words: "differences and otherness, in all of their rich dimensions . . . a pluralism of persons and points of view . . . unconventional approaches and unfashionable stances toward enduring and intractable questions . . . different styles of thinking." Surely, the conservative journal added to that, but Freedman really meant only a stereotyped racial, ethnic and gender diversity. Dartmouth, he explained, "must not stand by silently when a newspaper maliciously engages in bullying tactics that seem virtually designed to have the effect of discouraging women and members of minority groups from joining our faculty or enrolling as students." (He did not criticize what the *Review*'s tapes already had revealed, that Cole, in class, had called Dartmouth conservatives "motherfuckers," "cocksuckers," "racist dogs" and "scum of the earth.")

Ironically, however, there were few more racially and ethnically diverse institutions at Dartmouth than the *Review*. From its inception up to that year of 1988, it always had attracted independently minded black, Asian-American, foreign, and female students, many of whom had served as editors. In 1988, Harmeet Dhillon, a Sikh, became the *Review*'s third female editor and second Asian-American editor. The *Review* had had a Jewish editor, and many Jewish writers. In fact, as court documents revealed, at the time of the Cole affair, three staffers of *The Dartmouth Review* were black, and their treatment by the college was striking enough to figure explicitly in the judge's reasoning about the case. No "diversity" for them.[16]

When the students sued that year in New Hampshire Superior Court, K. Christopher Pritchett, a sophomore and black conservative, testified that he and two black staffers on the *Review* were surrounded, in a campus building, by an angry group of black students who called them "Uncle Toms," and that one disabled black *Review* staffer, confined to a wheelchair, had cigarette smoke blown in his face by a black football player. A few nights later, at a candlelight vigil against racism, Pritchett testified, another black student threatened "'to kick your ass.'" Pritchett testified under oath that he told President Freedman about these incidents and the "lynch-mob atmosphere" that black staffers at the *Review* were facing, and that Freedman did nothing, replying, according to Pritchett, that "there are some complex social dynamisms at Dartmouth." Freedman denied making that statement, but acknowledged, under oath, that he could not recall the specific details of his meeting with Pritchett. In January 1989, Justice Bruce E. Mohl ordered the college immediately to reinstate the suspended editors. He appropriately expressed his extreme hesitation to meddle at all in the internal affairs of a private university, but he judged that "Dartmouth is to be held to the standard of fundamental fairness."

Compare Dartmouth's defense of Professor Cole with the treatment of Professor of History Jay Bergman by Central Connecticut State University (CCSU) in a case widely covered by the mainstream media. Bergman is a critic of affirmative action who was particularly upset by what he saw as CCSU's attempts to discredit a colleague, Norton Mezvinsky, who shared the same cause. Bergman posted copies of an article from the national journal *Campus Report* about those efforts. The article quoted from a memo that had come into the author's possession, in which Ronald Fernandez, director of CCSU's Center for Caribbean Affairs, called a Mezvinsky op-ed in the *Hartford Courant* "essentially shit" and outlined a plan to "humiliate Norton."[17]

Bergman was careful to post the article only on "public" bulletin boards not reserved for specific purposes (such as departmental or official announcements). As soon as Bergman posted copies of the article, however, they would be torn down. This happened some twenty-five times in September 1995. Finally, on September 15, he saw a student, Dawn Bliesener, removing the flier. He admonished her for taking down the poster. She refused to stop. They argued loudly. Bliesener claimed that Bergman began screaming at her when he first saw her removing the poster. Bergman claimed that he raised his voice only when she refused to stop and then taunted him. Bergman asked the university to protect his First Amendment rights to post a political flier at a public university. Bliesener, who is black and who had filed complaints about the poster itself before the incident, filed harassment charges against Bergman, saying that she was "extremely offended as a minority student by this flier." According to a reporter from the school newspaper, the *Recorder,* Bliesner said, "I don't care what his rights are. I have a right to tear down anything I find offensive."[18] (She later would deny having made this statement, but the reporter stood by his written notes and said that Bliesener had made no objection to the quotation at the time, despite ongoing communication about the case with the *Recorder.*) Further, on September 18, Bliesener sent an e-mail message to the campus charging that Berman had "harassed [her] over removing one of his NAZI flyers from bulliten [*sic*] board!!!!" She also claimed, though this charge never reappeared, that he had "spit" at her, which Bergman termed "false and slanderous" in reply.

Explicit CCSU policy made it an extremely serious offense to silence someone's expression, so Bliesener's public statement that she had removed his flier should have presented her with grave difficulties. The student handbook listed a set of egregious behaviors that warranted "the maximum penalty of expulsion," among them "interfering with the freedom of any person to express his or her views." Within four days, Bergman had filed a complaint, in a letter to Merle Harris, interim president of CCSU: "I told her that . . . she was violating my right of free expression. . . . Bliesener's response was that she. . . . could tear down anything that offended her." Bergman closed by saying, "I trust that you will do the right thing."

In late September, President Harris wrote an open letter to the "Campus Community," published in the *Recorder.* He announced preparations for a yearlong series "on the theme, 'Civility Builds Community,'" and he announced: "Any act of alleged harrassment [*sic*] or intolerance by any member of the campus community against another member . . . will be promptly investigated and appropriate action will be taken."[19] Meanwhile, as soon as Karen Beyard, CCSU's vice president for academic affairs, heard of the incident, she sought Bliesener out. In fact, Bliesener wrote a letter to the editor of the *Recorder,* thanking Beyard and the CCSU administration for all the help and support they gave her: "The Administration of this University has supported me and helped me beyond what I ever thought them capable of. Among some, V.P. Karen Beyard, who . . . immediately that afternoon . . . came to me. . . . I did not have to seek her out. . . . Thank God for the Angela Davis School of Diplomacy."[20]

Indeed, Vice President Beyard, soon after President Harris had received Bergman's complaint against Bliesener for interfering with his free speech rights at CCSU, informed Bergman that the university was investigating *him*. On October 2, 1995, Beyard sent a "Memorandum" to all faculty on "Campus Civility," warning the faculty of the special responsibility of the university toward students, with reference to "patterns of sexism, racism, and sexual preference harassment." Next, without specific allegations or a hearing in which Bergman could confront Bliesener, let alone cross-examine her, Dean George Clarke issued a written opinion that Bergman's freedom of speech had not been violated. In a memo to Bergman on October 12, Clarke charged him with "conduct unbecoming a faculty member," and informed him: "The University . . . is considering disciplinary action." On November 7, Clarke delivered an official, formal "reprimand" that he ordered remain in Bergman's personnel file for two years, "for verbally assaulting and threatening a member of the university community." Bergman never had been given the chance to rebut any claims about his "conduct."

Bergman's collective bargaining grievance first was heard by Dean Clarke (whose reprimand was the very object of the grievance); Clarke dismissed it. Bergman's second appeal was heard by Vice President Beyard; she dismissed it. On December 8, 1995, Bergman filed a formal complaint against Dawn Bliesener with the university's Student Judicial Office, for violation of his freedom of expression. At this point, and in contrast to what she had reportedly said at the time of the incident, Ms. Bliesener told the judicial office that she merely had taken the poster off the bulletin board in order to read it more clearly. The judicial office, apparently discounting the report of Bliesener's previous statements to the *Recorder,* declared that because the case now was Bergman's word (removal) against Bliesener's word (reading), there was not enough evidence to proceed to a hearing. William J. Cibes, Jr., president of the Connecticut State University system, wrote on April 5, 1996, to Lieutenant Governor Jodi Rell, who had made inquiries on Bergman's behalf, that "the student denied removing the article in question from the bulletin board for any purpose other than to read it," and he cited "the lack of witnesses to the contrary."

In response to growing media interest in the case (and a complaint by the Anti-Defamation League about double standards), CCSU's director of university relations, Peter J. Kilduff, told the press, on December 12: "No one defends that action of taking down the posted article." Why had CCSU punished Bergman for defending his right to post the article? Kilduff explained: "We give more leeway to students . . . because students do not have the empowerment of the professor's knowledge and understanding of these things."[21] The *New York Times* summed up the case: "Instead of the university's looking into whether Bliesener broke a campus rule, Bergman found himself the subject of an administrative investigation . . . and an official reprimand . . . in his personnel file."[22] On January 30, 1996, the ACLU of Connecticut (the Connecticut Civil Liberties Union Foundation) wrote to Harris: "We believe that the University appears to have violated Prof. Bergman's First Amendment rights as enunciated by the U.S. Supreme Court and the U.S. Court of Appeals for this judicial circuit." The ACLU gave the interim president a brief course on public forums, content neutrality, and freedom of expression, and it concluded: "Prof. Bergman is entitled to assert his First Amendment rights."Bergman hired an attorney, who threatened a suit. In the fall of 1996, CCSU's new president, Richard Judd, rescinded the reprimand and removed all reference to it from Bergman's record retroactively and forever. The wrong, of course, remains.

───────────

It has been more than a decade of double standards and generational fraud. Too many members of the generation of the '60s, and their heirs, turned out to have supported the Free Speech movement not because they embraced free speech as a value, but because they believed that movement to be useful to their entire "progressive" agenda. When a majority of Americans—and a significant majority of students—accepted neither that agenda nor its proponents' self-assigned roles as moral gurus, then free speech, for so many academics, became dispensable.

The paradoxes of generational difference, the Marcusean side of "progressive" free speech, and the frequent self-delusions of celebrants of the '60s emerged sharply during the massive four-day reunion marking the thirtieth anniversary of the Berkeley Free Speech movement in the fall of 1994. The *Times* described the participants as "the aging alumni" of a protest that "brought the full range of First Amendment protections to the University of California at Berkeley and changed American campuses everywhere." (The *Times* omitted mentioning that their heirs at Berkeley had adopted a speech code.) Those present at the reunion sang "Those

Were the Days." Jacob Weinberg, credited with uttering the phrase in 1964, "Don't trust anyone over thirty," now was fifty-four and an administrator of Greenpeace. The *Times* noted the far more "conservative" nature of the audience of current students. In the course of the Free Speech reunion, only one person attempted to say a dissident word about contemporary politics, and her case was revealing. As the *Times* noted, "When one alumna tried on Thursday night to defend Proposition 187, which would deny illegal immigrants health and welfare benefits, she was booed, hissed, and eventually silenced. 'Wait a minute!' someone from the audience shouted. 'You're not going to let her speak? Is that a Free Speech Movement?' She was then allowed to continue."[23]

Penn had inherited, from the Free Speech movement, "Guidelines on Open Expression" whose trained "monitors" had the obligation to protect the content neutrality of a full freedom of expression. Only circumstantial restrictions (such as time, place, or noise level), applied equally, could serve to limit the freedom of expression. The guidelines, distributed for decades to all members of the Penn community, stated: "The substance or the nature of the views expressed is not an appropriate basis for the restriction upon or encouragement of an assembly or demonstration."[24]

There has been a double standard in enforcing such guidelines since the early 1980s, when almost the entire student life apparatus at Penn, as at most institutions of higher learning, fell into the hands of partisan ideologues. Fortunately, dissident administrators have made Penn a sieve, so we know what "open expression" came to mean. On April 11, 1986, for example, gay and lesbian students at Penn exercised their own freedom and held a well-advertised event called "Flaunt-In." On April 18, 1986, Claudia Apfelbaum, a university life official and an open expression monitor, wrote a report on an "incident" that occurred at "Flaunt-In" to Charlotte Jacobsen, director of the Office of Student Life (OSL), with copies to various administrators. According to Apfelbaum, "Two young men put an anti-gay poster on a garbage can right beside the students who were participating in the Flaunt-In." Apfelbaum explained why, under content neutrality, that poster was not also "open expression": "The act was experienced as a direct confrontation of and an infringement of [*sic*] the gay/lesbian rights to open expression." Apfelbaum followed the two dissenting students "and tried to get [their] names. . . . [When] they refused to give me their I.D. cards," she called the campus police herself. The officers "took information from the two young men," which Apfelbaum was going to file "with the Judicial Inquiry Officer." The monitor of Penn's supposedly content-neutral guidelines concluded: "I believe that the two young men who put up the poster were harassing the gay and lesbian students. They were interferring [*sic*] with gay and lesbian students' right to express love and affection for one another and were thus infringing on gay men and lesbians' lives."[25]

In 1986, with those same guidelines in place, a Penn fraternity had advertised a "show off your tan party" after winter break. Its poster, in imitation of a Coppertone ad, painted a coed pulling down just a bit of the back of her bikini bottom, revealing a tan line. Some campus feminists were outraged by this "commodification" and "denigration" of women, and Penn announced a new policy. Fraternities would have to submit all posters to the administration for prior approval. Announcing this policy of prior restraint in the *DP* of February 14, an administrator expressed the heart and soul of what the Division of University Life truly believed: "If your poster is on campus, you are limited by community standards. We at the University of Pennsylvania have guaranteed students and the community that they can live in a community free of sexism, racism, and homophobia." If a poster is denied permission for posting, however, fraternities "will be able to appeal the decision to Penn's Women's Center Director" Ellie DiLapi, Penn's designated leading feminist.[26]

A handful of Penn faculty protested to President Sheldon Hackney, reminding him that Penn tolerated feminist and prochoice posters with offensive, even scatalogical, representations of religious figures, signs proclaiming "Keep Your Rosaries Off Our Ovaries," and chants against "born again bigots." "If antiabortion students are offended by feminist posters," they asked him, "must the authors of the latter seek the approval of anyone, and then appeal to the Newman [Catholic] Center?" Under mounting pressure, Penn abandoned the policy.

"Open Expression" worked wonderfully to protect the Left and various "minorities." When Contra leader Adolfo Calero spoke by invitation of a conservative group, during the height of debate over U.S. foreign policy in Central America, open expression monitors rightly permitted radical protesters to pass out leaflets, shout, chant, and stage guerrilla theater "murders" in the aisles during his talk, as long as he eventually could be heard.[27] Compare this, however, to the official report of the open expression monitor on a speech at Du Bois College House, on September 25, 1985, when the Black Student League (BSL) invited a speaker from the Nation of Islam. The open expression report by monitor Rene Abelardo Gonzales, of the Office of Student Life, noted that the speaker was surrounded by bodyguards from the Fruit of Islam who ordered all white students to sit together in one section of the room. The monitor concluded, however, that because someone from the Residence Office told the students that they did not have to comply, this order posed no problem whatsoever.[28]

The talk was on "Black-Jewish Relations," Gonzales reported to Charlotte Jacobsen, director of the OSL, and dealt with, to quote the report's description in its entirety, "The Myth of Jews as God's Chosen People, Blacks as Black Muslims are God's Chosen People, Jews are Wicked, the Pope is a Liar, and the Exploitation of Blacks in the U.S." Gonzales reported that the Open Expression Committee was requested to intervene in a dispute between "two groups of students with different points of view." The "points of view" differed over whether or not the dissident students, members of the InterFaith Council of the University of Pennsylvania, could hand out leaflets on religious tolerance at the meeting "before Mr. Muhammed arrived" to speak. They were prevented from doing so by the BSL, on instruction from the Fruit of Islam bodyguards. Gonzales concluded, as the official monitor, that "this action does not violate any part of the Open Expression guidelines. . . . The Open Expression guidelines are not clear on leaflet distribution." Indeed, how could the distribution of religious leaflets on behalf of tolerance, at a public meeting, be any part of "Open Expression"?

In January 1990, there was a vigorous prochoice rally at Penn, led primarily by the Progressive Student Alliance (PSA). A silent prolife vigil, with students holding religious signs against abortion, was conducted next to it. The group of silent, prolife counterdemonstrators was composed of eight students: five women, two of whom were black; and three men, two of whom were Asian-Americans. The PSA members surrounded them and chanted, "Racist, sexist, antigay, born-again bigots go away." That was not deemed to have created a "hostile," "offensive," or "intimidating" environment.[29] Similarly, on February 19, 1990, State Representative Stephen Freind spoke at Penn against abortion. Student protesters, bearing witness to their prochoice views, displayed a large sign, SPREAD YOUR LEGS FOR CHRIST. That, too, was protected speech.[30]

Compare the SPREAD YOUR LEGS FOR CHRIST sign, however, to the sign declaring homosexuality sinful displayed by the two dissenting students at Flaunt-In. The latter dissidents were held to be "harassing the gay and lesbian students . . . and infringing on gay men and lesbians' lives." Compare the sign SPREAD YOUR LEGS FOR CHRIST also to the sign HETEROSEXUAL FOOTWEAR DAY, the latter having been cited as actionable harassment at mandatory diversity education for incoming freshmen at Penn. Compare that sign to the south-of-the-border poster, deemed to depict "a lazy Mexican," also presented as actionable harassment during diversity education.

———————

In his book *All the Trouble in the World*, P. J. O'Rourke, a hippie leftist in the '60s and a mordant "grunge conservative" now, described a recent return to his alma mater, Miami University (Ohio), where he was struck by the section of the current student handbook called "University Statement Asserting Respect for Human Diversity": "We will strive to educate each other on the existence and effects of racism, sexism, ageism, homophobia, religious intolerance, and other forms of invidious prejudice." It also pronounced "intolerable" any situation where "such prejudice results in," among other things, "psychological abuse, harassment, [or] intimidation." It further warned that "nor will we accept jest, ignorance, or substance abuse as an excuse, reason, or rationale for it." O'Rourke remembered his '60s too well not to be startled ("Jest, ignorance or substance abuse," he wrote, "have been the excuse, reason, or rationale for my entire existence."), and he denounced these regnant formulae as "sanctimoniousness, [an] intellectual offal mixed into virtue stew." For O'Rourke, the illogic and immorality were on the other side: "Invidious prejudice results from categorizing people rather than treating them as individuals. But here people are categorized exhaustively." Further, he noted, while it made perfect sense to treat all races the same, people not only did "differ according to sex," but "this difference is necessarily important sometimes, when making babies." Also, he observed, "ageism is not an evil at all," and, indeed, anyone "who failed to discriminate between a six-year-old and a twenty-six-year old would be insane in all circumstances and jailed in some." Most deeply, he saw immediately what seems beyond the comprehension of almost all universities, the insincerity of calling for the simultaneous "respect" of mutually exclusive worldviews. Despite its call to protect all religions, O'Rourke predicted, Miami will not extend that to creeds with politically incorrect views of women and gays.[31]

He could not have known how right he was. Students who actually take seriously the surface language of the harassment codes, with their obligations to "mutual respect," thinking that these truly apply to all, understand nothing. Thus, in March 1996, the *Cincinnati Enquirer* reported that when Miami University was scheduled to show the movie *Priest*—about a Catholic priest struggling with his homosexuality—the Student Senate, citing the university's "diversity statement," condemned the film as "anti-Catholic," and passed a resolution urging the Program Board not to show the film. *Priest,* the Senate voted, would "serve to create 'a hostile environment' for faithful Catholics at Miami, as well as flagrantly violating the spirit of the University Statement Asserting Respect for Human Diversity." The university, of course, overrode that vote and showed the film.[32] Catholics are not among the protected groups. It never truly meant its policy at all. If it did, it would not have such a policy, because everyone would be silenced. As Orwell noted presciently in *Animal Farm,* describing the process by which the oppressed became the oppressors, "All animals are equal, but some animals are more equal than others."

The academic double standard is nowhere more glaring than in the treatment of Christian belief and value. In 1992, a gay and lesbian student organization, in a campaign for gay rights, gave Penn several blocks' worth of graffiti on its main thoroughfare. Many of the comments were extremely (and crudely) contemptuous of the Catholic Church.[33] In a letter to the *DP,* one of Penn's Catholic students tried to make sense of Penn's double standards: "As a member of Penn's small and normally silent Catholic community, I must express the extreme abhorrence I felt upon viewing the vandalism [of] . . . the homosexual community['s] . . . assault upon the Catholic Church." He asked how the "shameless profanity" of these "anti-Catholic slurs" fit in with Penn's promise of a "supposedly multi-cultural academic environment." He noted that any "frat boy" or racist who had scrawled "the same type of vandalism or graffiti," but with a different content, "would currently be facing serious JIO charges."[34]

Penn's Open Expression Committee ruled that the speech was wholly protected, but the letter-writer was absolutely correct. It is the same almost everywhere. Recall that UCLA had suspended a student editor for publishing a cartoon critical of affirmative action. In 1995, at that same school, Rev. Paul Dechant, associate director of the University Catholic Center, lamented an official Campus Events advertisement that appeared in the *Daily Bruin* unfavorably comparing Jesus Christ—labeled as "some holy guy"—to a rock band. His analysis of the double standard at UCLA was on target: "It is unacceptable at UCLA to degrade anyone because of their Jewish, African, Asian, Muslim or Latino heritage. . . . The exception though, seems to be in regard to the symbols of Christianity."[35]

When Senator Jesse Helms attacked taxpayer funding of Andres Serrano's "Piss Christ," the object of his criticism involved the immersion in urine of the most sacred symbol of America's Christian majority—Christ on the cross. The academic community, in response, rallied behind the content neutrality of liberty. It consistently has agreed with Serrano himself, who replies that even offensive ideas are not dangerous, but that the suppression of ideas always is. Universìties and colleges did not announce that they did not place as high a value on the cross—or the sentiments it evoked—as they placed on other symbols or sentiments. Politically, they couldn't have done that. Instead, they argued that when it came to freedom, it did not matter who was offended. Compare this, however, with the behavior of the School of the Art Institute of Chicago (and the deafening silence of the academic world) in May of 1988, when a student exhibit at the politically correct institute included a whimsical portrait of the late mayor Harold Washington (the first black mayor of Chicago) in a tutu. On May 11, several black aldermen, accompanied by Chicago police officers, stormed into the school's museum and removed the painting from the building. One of the aldermen, Allan Streeter, told the *New York Times* that if the school got a court order to put it back up, " 'I'll be the first one there to take it down again. . . . But the next time, I'll destroy it.' " Students attempted but failed to block the police and aldermen from committing their theft, lying down in their path.[36]

The students spent the next day, according to the *Times*, "passing out petitions and handbills protesting the seizure of the painting." On the same day as the seizure, the Chicago City Council passed a resolution to cut off all public funds to the art institute if the painting were not removed. Alderman Streeter, without irony, told the *Times* that whites never would allow Ronald Reagan to be depicted with disrespect. The response? As the *Times* reported: "Officials of the school and the Art Institute said they . . . would issue a public apology for exhibiting the painting of the former Mayor." Further, "Anthony Jones, the president of the school, said today that 'it would be highly irresponsible for the art institute to reinstate the painting,' adding that its exhibition would be as inflammatory as 'shouting fire' in a crowded theater."[37] Should Christians appalled by the "Piss Christ" learn from this? What would the academic world have done if Jesse Helms had marched into a university art museum, with armed officers no less, and taken down Serrano's work? (Indeed, what would the academic world *not* have done in response?)

This double standard is destroying equal rights to free expression in higher education. As presented in chapter 7, Patrick Mooney had been fired as a residential adviser at Carnegie Mellon University (CMU) for refusing—on grounds of Catholic conscience—to wear a symbol of gay and lesbian causes. Two years later, in March 1994, Mooney, now a senior, passed a bulletin board in the corridors of the university, where he saw a poster with a picture of Roman Catholic Cardinal John O'Connor, in grotesque attire, his forehead stamped "public health menace." Next to

Cardinal O'Connor's face was the inscription "Know Your Scumbags." The poster was titled "Stop the Church."[38]

Mooney, who felt at least as strongly about Cardinal O'Connor as Alderman Streeter did about Mayor Washington, asked some students near the bulletin board how anyone could put up such an anti-Catholic poster, and he found some sympathetic allies. Visiting Professor Tim Saternow passed by. Saternow, as he later would write to a dean, wears a pink triangle on his book bag, a symbol with which Mooney certainly was familiar. Saternow told Mooney that the poster's description of the cardinal was true. According to Saternow, Mooney asked him, "Why are you homosexuals attacking the Church?" Professor Saternow formally charged Mooney with "harassment on the basis of sexual orientation," writing in a formal complaint that he felt harassed by Mooney's "loud denouncements of homosexuals attacking the church" and by his dogmatic assertions of "what real truth was." The story was well documented by the campus, local, and national media.[39]

Mooney had noticed that the poster had failed to meet a formal requirement for "posting" at CMU—it did not include the name of the organization that sponsored it (that space was inscribed, "We're here. We're queer. We're funded by your Student Activities Fee")—and he and several students removed the poster, taking it to the dean of students the next day. They passed scores of other copies of the poster and left them. A gay and lesbian student organization, CMU–Out, later took credit for the poster, and also filed harassment charges against Mooney.[40] In their own view, calling Cardinal O'Connor a "scumbag" did not create a "hostile" or "offensive" environment for Catholics, but offending their own sensibilities did. Why shouldn't they believe that? It's what universities are teaching.

The whole event should have provoked, among those interested, discussions about the Church and homosexuality, and probably should have led the university to abandon its rule against anonymous posters. In terms of campus laws, however, there was the issue of Mooney's wrongful removal of a poster technically in violation of CMU's bulletin-board rules, and the crucial issue of whether or not Mooney had harassed Professor Saternow by the expression of his view of gays and objective moral truth. The university held a formal hearing on Mooney's act of "harassment," during which it questioned him about his sexual life, his religious beliefs, and the intimate details of his conscience and behavior. After a three-hour closed-door hearing on March 24, the tribunal acquitted Mooney of "harassment" for disagreeing with Professor Saternow, but found him guilty of violating the campus's poster policy and of having denied the free-speech rights of

CMU-Out, placing him on "disciplinary probation" until his graduation in May. The letter from Dean Murphy to Mooney announcing the probation forbade Mooney from discussing its contents and, beyond talking with his lawyer, from "discuss[ing] or disclos[ing] matters relating to the decision or the university process." Mooney's lawyer, Peter K. Blume, however, did speak about it. Strongly protesting the nature and secrecy of the hearing, the refusal of the university to give him a transcript of the hearing, and the gag order upon Mooney, Blume told the press: "Given the fact that the punishment that had been requested was expulsion, I'm certainly pleased that the dean saw fit not to grant that demand." He also found "the excessiveness of the discipline . . . curious . . . given the fact that a violation of poster policy calls for a fine of $10."[41]

Mooney had faced expulsion if found guilty of harassing Saternow by disagreement—before a tribunal that operated in total secrecy. Further, his guilt in removing one poster—and the serious penalty of academic probation—now were a permanent part of his transcript and record. The Pittsburgh and national media, however, kept an intense eye on the case, and CMU retreated under criticism. On April 19, the university announced that it was changing the "probation" to a "disciplinary warning," and that the record of that sanction would be expunged from Mooney's record upon his graduation on May 15.[42] In July, it settled Mooney's three-year lawsuit against it for having fired him as a residential advisor in 1991. The terms remained confidential, but Mooney and his lawyer expressed delight about them. Although the university would not discuss it publicly, Dean Michael Murphy did tell the media, at long last, that "it's not appropriate that anybody be asked to declare a belief he doesn't hold. No one should be put in that position." For three years, of course, CMU had argued exactly the contrary. Speaking of both cases, Mooney's father, Vincent, told the *Washington Times,* "There are lots of innocent victims out there who live with hurt and pain and don't know how to fight back."[43] The problem, of course, as we have seen, is that most colleges and universities simply cannot imagine white Catholic males as "innocent victims."

So, there we have Mooney, a Catholic student, threatened with expulsion and a permanent judicial record for his confrontation with a protected professor at CMU. And there we have the conservative students at *The Dartmouth Review,* suspended, officially reviled, and unaided in the face of threats for their "vexatious oral exchange" with a protected professor at Dartmouth. The reverse of these two cases is simply unthinkable. A gay student denounces an antigay poster to other students, is verbally accosted by a Catholic professor who intrudes himself into the discussion, removes an improperly posted antigay screed, is charged by the Catholic professor with harassment, tried on that charge, and, for removing the poster, is punished? Feminist writers for a feminist journal criticize a conservative professor for classroom behavior, are denounced by him vulgarly in class, engage in a heated discussion with him after a class, are charged by him with harassment (upon which the administration joins rallies over his pain and suffering), and are suspended for three semesters? Not in anyone's wildest dream.

———

To understand what it is like to live under an unequal set of rights, let us linger a moment over the case of Professor James Aist at Cornell.[44] Aist is a professor of plant pathology, a born-again evangelical, and very active in the Christian community outside of Cornell. He believes that homosexuality is a sinful behavior that can be "cured." He also advocates equal rights for gays, and he accepts Cornell's policy of nondiscrimination against gays. Wishing homosexuals at Cornell to have at their disposal, if they choose, the full range of views about homosexuality, Aist occasionally places a poster, "Alternative to Homosexuality Anonymous (AHA)," on public bulletin boards and in general purpose, unrestricted brochure racks. All of these spaces at Cornell are subject to rules of content neutrality.

The poster lists two professors, one administrative assistant, two undergraduate students, and one graduate student as names to call if interested in AHA's information, and it promises confidentiality to the caller. It makes the following offer:

> If you, a friend, or a relative would like to find out . . .
> - What most of the scientific research and clinical results have shown about the nature and root causes of homosexuality
> - What the Bible says about homosexual behavior
> - Which reparative therapy programs have achieved success rates of 65%–75% in reversing orientation
> - How ex-gays have walked away from homosexuality
> - Where qualified help is available nationwide for those who want to change
> —You can request a free copy of documented, verifiable literature from any of the co-distributors listed below.

Further, Aist's strict list of guidelines for AHA members permits posting of fliers "only on general-purpose bulletin boards and in accordance with University policy" and limits any provision of "AHA materials only in response to a specific request." Imposing upon AHA restrictions that virtually no advocacy group on any campus would accept, Aist warns his associates explicitly and emphatically not to "initiate a discussion with an inquirer" and not to "counsel an inquirer with reference to homosexuality." The sole purpose of AHA is to provide written information to those who request it. Further, Aist instructs all members of AHA: "Do not use Campus Mail, which is for business purposes only"; "Do not use any Cornell name, emblem, seal or other item that would identify AHA with Cornell or any of its units"; and "Do not use any Cornell materials or supplies." Finally, Aist instructs his members that they must "make your own copies" of fliers "at your own expense."

If inquirers specifically request the information, AHA sends them a summary of what it considers to be scientific, psychological, and Christian conclusions about homosexuality, with an extensive bibliography. For this exercise of his freedom of belief and freedom of expression, Aist endured a veritable inquisition. It is a documentable ordeal, both because Aist keeps extensive records of conversations, memoranda, e-mail, and official letters, and because sympathizers within the University have provided him with a vast array of confidential documents depicting the actual number and circumstances of Cornell's ten investigations of him.

In 1993, Aist posted a flier, "Help for Homosexuals," on general purpose bulletin boards in the Department of Plant Pathology, next to posters that he considered to advocate a gay and lesbian lifestyle. His chairman asked him to cease, but Aist refused. Nonetheless, he agreed to a meeting with his chairman and the ombudsman, where they developed a set of posting regulations in which he agreed to limit his flier simply to two announcements: the sorts of information that he could make available, and how to request the information. (We know of no groups or individuals on the cultural Left with similar restrictions.)

In the winter of 1994–95, a group of gay and lesbian activists complained about the posters to the ombudsman's office at Cornell, and asked that Aist be prohibited from posting them. The ombudsman advised them of the 1993 agreement, but asked the associate vice president for human relations, Joycelyn Hart, and the dean of the faculty to provide formal opinions as to whether or not Aist's flier violated any university policy. (No Catholic Newman Center at a secular American university could succeed in getting the ombudsman, associate vice president, and dean to investigate whether a gay activist flier critical of the Church could be posted. The sky would fall.) They investigated, but they concluded that his fliers were protected speech.

Aist also was investigated by Bruce Chabot, the associate dean of the College of Agriculture and Life Sciences (CALS), in January 1995, for sexual discrimination and harassment. Chabot even sought the opinion of the general counsel, who advised him that the First Amendment protected Aist. The tone of that confidential letter, however, was revealing: "There isn't much we can do without trampling [his] First Amendment rights." On February 8, 1995, some twenty-five gay activists occupied the main office of the Department of Plant Pathology, demanding that Aist be silenced. Jessica Brown, codirector of Direct Action to Stop Homophobia, said, "The posters create a form of sexual harassment as well as the possibility of physical and mental harassment." Another occupier said, "The remedy is to remove [him] from the Cornell community. . . . Aist has chosen between his career and his beliefs; it is time for the University to recognize there is no place for him here."

How did Cornell respond to such claims? Members of Cornell's administration, including Bruce Chabot, the same associate dean of CALS who recently had dismissed the charges on advice of the general counsel, publicly agreed, orally and in writing, to a demand that Aist be reinvestigated. Indeed, the associate dean of CALS and an official Cornell University press release announced to the world that Aist was being investigated for "harassment" and "discrimination." This was, of course, a humiliating piece of news that sounded infinitely more ominous than the only act that underlay those charges, his posting of fliers inviting individuals, if they chose, to consider a point of view. Bruce Chabot issued a press release stating: "Acts of intolerance toward any member of the Cornell community cannot be accepted" (which certainly must have been news to the evangelical Aist). This time, the associate dean, having reopened the investigation, did not dismiss the charges, but forwarded them to Cornell's Office of Equal Opportunity (OEO).

In the first two weeks of April 1995, Aist resumed posting his fliers, and three new complaints were filed against him with the OEO, making four charges pending in total. The OEO was staffed by ideologues, and had a reputation for finding discrimination everywhere. Aist requested that the case be turned over to the regular judicial system, because the *Cornell Policy Notebook* specifically stated: "All violations of the Campus Code of Conduct by a student, faculty member or University employee shall be processed through the judicial system." The OEO claimed and retained jurisdiction, however, on the grounds that, as noted in that same notebook, "The OEO is the central University office for handling complaints and concerns of harassment and discrimination based upon EEO [the U.S. Equal Employment Office] protected class status against faculty and staff." In its view, individuals offended by Aist's beliefs constituted a "protected class" under federal regulation.

The OEO became a frightening arena for Aist. He learned from reputable sources (and documents) that it had solicited secret testimony from the complainants. The OEO refused to specify the exact charges against him, and it refused to provide him with the names of any of the complainants' witnesses or with any description, let alone the transcript, of their testimony. Further, under Cornell's OEO rules, one staff member acts as "impartial fact finder," sets his own procedure, and determines guilt or innocence. The only external constraint upon the OEO's simultaneous investigator-prosecutor-judge-and-jury is that he or she must "talk with the complainant to determine what she or he wants to have done." Finally, "OEO works with the departments involved in the complaint to take appropriate action to restore an environment free of harassment," which, for faculty, includes: "Oral or written warnings; transfers or reassignments; suspensions; demotions; resignation requested; dismissals from the University."

When Aist asked the OEO for its definition of harassment, it clarified the crime for him, adding words (in italics) that do not appear in Cornell's published harassment policy: "verbal, *visual, written,* or physical conduct constitutes harassment when such conduct . . . [creates] an intimidating, hostile, or offensive working or learning environment." Aist was in trouble.

After six months, the complaints still were pending, but Aist, late in the game, had secured legal representation through the Rutherford Institute, an organization devoted primarily to the legal defense of religious exercise. Gregory Hession, the Rutherford Institute's regional coordinator for the Northeast, wrote several letters to the Cornell administration and met personally with Cornell's OEO several times, warning all that Rutherford attorneys were prepared to defend Aist's constitutional rights of religious expression. Threatened with a lawsuit, Cornell's OEO at last delivered a judgment of "No Finding" on all the charges against Aist. Hession said in a press release, "It is shameful that Cornell, an institution which prides itself on tolerance and freedom, should even consider Professor Aist's action harassment."

What is it like when other individuals, but not you, may express beliefs without fear of punishment, defamatory press releases, and Star Chambers? What does the voice of "progressive" repression and censorship sound like? Even after Aist's exoneration by the OEO, Valerie O. Hayes, director of the OEO, denied him access to a general use brochure rack in her office, and changed office policy (and signs) to prohibit his postings. When Aist questioned this, she informed him that "any further issues should be directed to the Office of the University Counsel."

Joel R. Seligman, director of campus information and visitor relations, was more direct. In November 1995, he wrote to Aist: "Please refrain from posting [your] documents in Cornell's Information and Referral Center. They are offensive to me and my staff and contradict the university's widely publicized statement on equal opportunity for sexual minorities." Aist should assist "in ensuring that all of our prospective students and their families feel welcome at Cornell," and he should know that "messages to the contrary are counterproductive to our efforts."

Evangelical Christians, conservatives, and libertarians, however, are clearly not part of Joel R. Seligman's "all," for brochures that would make them feel profoundly "unwelcome"—if disagreement with their beliefs happened to produce that effect—are everywhere in Seligman's center. What would Seligman have done with Saternow's rights at CMU? Calling a cardinal a "scumbag" to a Catholic is protected free speech at our universities, and rightly so . . . but only if everyone has the same right to say what he or she believes. Those who don't understand that truly understand nothing.

On January 4, 1996, Aist wrote to Cornell's president Rawlings. Did the president agree with Seligman, Hayes, and others, that Aist could not place his brochures beside brochures of a differing viewpoint, and, if that were in fact the case, what was the explanation? The general counsel replied that offices reserve the right to restrict brochures to official university business.

The *Cornell University Policy Notebook* explicitly prohibits any "attempt to interfere with the lawful exercise of freedom of speech . . . as protected by the constitution and laws of the United States and the State of New York." Coining the term "Administrative Harassment," Aist wrote a brief memorandum about his case, in which, despite that prohibition, "five offices at Cornell have investigated this project, to one extent or another, a total of ten times." Aist wondered why he had "to invest large amounts of time and energy to defend my First Amendment rights," why the administration "didn't punish the perpetrators of the illegal sit-in, instead of caving in to their demands," and why the OEO "didn't . . . dismiss the charges against me outright, instead of dragging me through a six-month investigation." He posed the essential question: "Could it be that the principle of 'free speech' applies only to the politically correct at Cornell?" If that is the case, then "what are we teaching our students by the handling of controversial issues in such a manner?"

Aist recognized that someone with dissident, unpopular views on campus should expect opposition, but he refused to accept the partisan, unconstitutional, chilling terms offered by the university as the context of that opposition: "I do have a problem with the failure of a university administration to uphold the First Amendment consistently, with its failure to enforce the university's campus code of conduct consistently, with its willingness to participate in the public humiliation of a politically incorrect professor, and with the administrative harassment that is inherent in multiple investigations of a politically incorrect campus activity."

Finally, Aist spoke a truth that everyone who cares about the future of liberty and the rule of law should take to heart. As we have noted, there surely will be a day of reckoning, because it will not happen that this nation accepts these double standards with infinite patience. When that day arrives, will there be a sufficient number of administrators and faculty who can say, "we defended everyone's liberty, and everyone's protections under law"? Aist concluded: "Such official responses are not unique to Cornell University, however, and should serve, therefore, as a wake-up call to everyone in academia who respects and cherishes the free speech and religious liberty that are supposed to be guaranteed by the First Amendment."

That wake-up call is ringing, and academia had better respond to it first. There is nothing encouraging to report on that front. The *Chronicle of Higher Education* has reported yearly surveys of full-time professors at American colleges and universities, conducted by the Higher Education Research Institute at UCLA. The 1994–95 and 1995–96 surveys revealed that a clear majority favored codes that prohibited "racist" and "sexist" speech on their campuses.[45]

If those who subsidize, protect, endow, and send their sons and daughters to our colleges and universities get that wake-up call before the colleges and universities, higher education will face a catastrophe. That call is beginning to penetrate the slumber of free beings. They will not sacrifice their freedom forever to a self-proclaimed "progressive intolerance." One way or another, individuals at universities will have to find ways to talk and argue things out, and it would be better for everyone, but especially for minorities, if that occurs in circumstances of equality before the law. If universities do not reform themselves, society, clumsily, we fear, will do it for them.

The worst catastrophe would be if other Americans actually came to believe what universities believe: that they do not have to tolerate what offends their private and commonly shared values, and that they rightfully and proudly may dispense freedom and justice unequally—the Constitution be damned—according to their sense of <u>decent and indecent beliefs and groups</u>. Where will all our self-proclaimed progressives find shelter when those winds blow, after they themselves have attempted to convince everyone who passes through their portals that the protections of liberty and legal equality are wholly dispensable?

PART IV

THE ASSAULT ON

DUE PROCESS

CHAPTER 11

THE RULES OF CIVILIZATION

Narcotics officers burst into the home of Antonio Rochin on the morning of July 1, 1949, but before they could grab the suspect, he swallowed several capsules of what the officers believed to be illegal narcotics. They rushed Rochin to a hospital, where, in the words of the U.S. Supreme Court that eventually reviewed Rochin's drug conviction, "at the direction of one of the officers a doctor forced an emetic solution through a tube into Rochin's stomach against his will." This "stomach pumping," said the Court, "produced vomiting," and the offending capsules were recovered and used as evidence at his trial.[1] The Supreme Court ruled that the evidence should have been excluded from the trial because the method used to obtain it "shocks the conscience" and hence violates the clause of the Fourteenth Amendment that assures each citizen "due process of law." This test was among the most subjective that a court could devise as a guide to police officers and lower courts. After all, what shocks one person's conscience might be acceptable to another's. However, the Court noted that the test was not entirely subjective, because it "gains technical content" by "the deposit of history." The Court quoted Justice Benjamin Cardozo, who described due process rights as those "so rooted in the traditions and conscience of our people as to be ranked as fundamental [and] implicit in the concept of ordered liberty." Thus, centuries of evolution in the Anglo-American legal system have produced broad standards defining uncivilized conduct forbidden to government. Methods such as forced stomach pumping, said the Court, "are . . . too close to the rack and the screw." States must "respect certain decencies of civilized conduct."

265

Although the "shocks the conscience" test has been largely supplanted by more precise judicial pronouncements, it never has been overruled, and it still has value as an underlying principle. It reminds us that there are certain things that civilized governments simply do not do. After all, the due process clause of the Fifth Amendment, binding on the federal government, is by its very language a broad mandate: "[N]or shall any person . . . be deprived of life, liberty, or property, without due process of law." The Fourteenth Amendment, adopted after the Civil War to protect the blessings of liberty from infringement by state governments, was more expansive in listing broad categories of fundamental rights:

> No State shall make or enforce any law which shall abridge the privileges or immunities of citizens of the United States; nor shall any State deprive any person of life, liberty, or property, without due process of law; nor deny to any person within its jurisdiction the equal protection of the laws.

As the U.S. Supreme Court has elaborated and defined these concepts, two major branches of due process rights have emerged: *substantive* and *procedural*. Substantive rights protect the individual from abusive treatment by government. For example, a merciless police beating of an arrested suspect would be a violation of substantive due process. Procedural due process requires fairness and rationality in the methods by which determinations are made that affect life and liberty. Since the Bill of Rights (that is, the first ten amendments to the Constitution) applies only to the federal government, it does not technically restrain action by the governments of the individual states. However, over the years, the Supreme Court has come to define Fourteenth Amendment due process (which does apply to state governments) to include, or "incorporate," many of the rights enumerated in the Bill of Rights.

Generally, due process requires that as the penalty becomes more extreme, the formality of the procedures followed must increase. Serious crimes and punishments merit formal procedures. They also require clarity of the laws that set out one's legal obligations and duties, the violation of which leads to conviction and punishment.

The Requirement of Clarity

For a scheme of rights and law to function, the rules defining the duties of citizens to the state and to one another must be set out in clear language, readily understood by the average citizen. Governments can be bound by broad and rather vague admonitions to "due process" and "equal protection of the laws." The obligations imposed upon citizens, however, must be precisely and unambiguously defined. This is perhaps the only instance in which constitutional law permits, indeed requires, a double standard. Governments, in exercising broadly defined powers, are bound by due process and other limitations that federal and state constitutions impose to protect citizens from official unfairness, overreaching, or tyranny. This effort protects human liberty by imposing negative restrictions on governmental power. Although some limitations are quite specific, others, such as the due process requirement, are far more general and depend for their definition upon long-established and well-accepted notions of what abuses of governmental power are unacceptable in a decent society. To paraphrase Justice Potter Stewart's famous attempt to define obscenity, it may be impossible to define with precision, but "I know it when I see it."[2] That is sometimes the case with denial of due process.

The rights retained by the nongovernmental sector of the society, however, are deliberately vast and largely undefined. Indeed, the Ninth Amendment makes it clear that while certain rights of citizens are set forth, this does not define the whole of citizens' rights: "The enumeration in the Constitution, of certain rights, shall not be construed to deny or disparage others retained by the people." These rights, both those specifically guaranteed to the people and those "retained" by them, belong to civil society—that vast, largely unregulated world of social intercourse and organization that exists and operates largely outside of governmental hegemony: churches, charities, civic groups, professional associations, political associations, social clubs, athletic teams, private educational academies, friendships, families, and countless human enterprises.

There is, however, a critical reverse side to this essentially undefined and autonomous world within which civil society functions, namely, the highly specific and defined nature of the individual's legal *obligations*. If the citizen's legal obligations were as vague as those of the government, then the potential for tyranny would be frightfully large, for citizens would not have a sufficiently clear understanding of their obligations to the government and to one another. That understanding is essential because it permits them to conform their behavior to known requirements and thus to avoid the penalties imposed by the law, particularly by the criminal law, for violations. To impose vaguely defined legal obligations upon the citizen would delegate overly broad enforcement and penal powers to the government—powers that would likely be enforced arbitrarily, defeating an important goal of liberty.

This requirement of clarity in defining the citizen's legal obligations is imposed upon government by the due process clause. It serves four different, although somewhat related, purposes.

First, clarity puts the citizen on notice as to what types of conduct society requires, accepts, and forbids. There should be no substantial danger that one could commit a crime unintentionally or unwittingly. This ensures that the law does not become a trap for the unwary innocent.

Second, clarity imposes limits on the discretion of law enforcement officers in deciding whether a crime has been committed that justifies an arrest. In contrast, vague criminal laws are an invitation to the arbitrary and capricious enforcement of the law according to the biases, prejudices, and personal predilections of an individual officer. They invite government by whim rather than by equal and deliberated law.

Third, clarity prevents the law from having a "chilling effect" on the citizen as he or she goes about the business of daily life. When a statute is sufficiently vague that it can cover a very wide swath of human activity, it encourages the more cautious citizen "voluntarily" to refrain from engaging in what is, in fact, lawful activity. If we wish to encourage the range and vibrancy of civil society, then we cannot afford to allow vague laws to operate by fear to curtail free activity. This is a particularly important consideration in the area of free speech, where vague statutes will produce self-censorship. In the Supreme Court's words in the 1964 case of *Baggett v. Bullitt,* people who are "sensitive to the perils posed by [vague language], avoid the risk . . . only by restricting their conduct to that which is unquestionably safe."[3]

Fourth, clarity makes it possible for the law to have value as precedent. When a clear statute is enforced by a court in a particular way, other courts and fellow citizens learn with more precision what conduct is prohibited or allowed. The law, as it develops, is thereby given definition and consistency. This accumulation of precedent is a central feature of Anglo-American law. The outcome of a prior case, decided upon a certain set of facts, informs the outcome of a subsequent case presenting similar facts. One's fate should not depend on how a judge got out of bed that morning, nor, of course, on one's race, religion, or other irrelevant factor.

This system of obedience to precedent, known as *stare decisis,* is a necessary adjunct to equality before the law guaranteed by both the due process and equal protection clauses of the Fourteenth Amendment. The imperative that all citizens be treated equally before the law, and that courts develop consistent modes of decision-making, is perhaps the single most important notion in our legal system and the sine qua non of a just, humane, and civilized society. It is a legal "golden rule": give unto others the process to which you feel you are due. It may sound trite, but there is a reason that the Biblical admonition "Do unto others as you would have them do unto you" has become an accepted axiom (approaching a universal truth) in all areas of religious and secular life—it works as a system of human life. If those who make laws, and those who enforce them, are themselves required to live under the regime they impose upon others, then there is a high degree of assurance that laws will be just and enforced with fairness.

The Supreme Court has addressed vagueness in a number of contexts, stressing the vital importance of its impermissibility in a wide array of circumstances. Freedom of speech is the area that has been most zealously protected by the Court from a lack of clarity. In *Smith v. Goguen*,[4] the Court struck down a Massachusetts statute criminalizing the "contemptuous treatment" of the American flag as unconstitutionally vague. The Court noted that the language of the statute effected "a standardless sweep [that] allows policemen, prosecutors, and juries to pursue their personal predilections." Such an invitation to "selective law enforcement," said the Court, "is a denial of due process." What is contempt to one observer might well be patriotism to another. Some exercise their patriotism by praising their country for its virtues, while others do so by criticizing it for its failings. In order to function properly, a society needs both its optimists and its prophets of doom, those who give generous praise and others who deliver stern criticism, those who offer stability with their support for what is nobly done and those who prod their fellow citizens to change by bearing witness to injustice. Unless all are protected and heard from, a free and stable yet dynamic society cannot flourish. In practice, the flag-burner will be more vulnerable to official attack than the flag-waver, but by allocating equal rights to both the system maintains the potential inherent in freedom.

In the context of education, vagueness proved a particular threat during the Red Scare. In 1961, the Supreme Court was faced with a statute compelling education employees to swear that they had never "knowingly lent their aid, support, advice, counsel, or influence to the Communist Party." Those falsely swearing would be subject to a perjury prosecution. In *Cramp v. Board of Public Instruction of Orange County, Florida*,[5] the Court declared the statute violative of due process and void for vagueness because it was not susceptible to reasonably clear definition. "Could a journalist who had ever defended the constitutional rights of the Communist Party conscientiously take an oath that he had never lent the Party his 'support'?," asked the Court.

"The very absurdity of these possibilities brings into focus the extraordinary ambiguity of the statutory language."

The other aspect of due process is that in addition to requiring clear laws setting forth the obligations of citizens, a free and decent human community requires specific substantive and procedural requirements for the enforcement of such laws.

Substantive Due Process Rights

Substantive due process connotes those concepts and rules that are deeply rooted in Western history and sensibility. This includes rights that have been specifically enumerated, such as freedom of speech and of the press, as well as a broad category of unenumerated rights that Professor Laurence Tribe has aptly summed up as "rights of privacy and personhood."[6] Among these are freedom of conscience and of inquiry; freedom from coercive conditioning, "brainwashing," and from physical invasions of the body; the freedom to procreate or refuse to do so; to marry or not (including to marry the person of one's choice, even across racial lines); to decide certain aspects of one's own death; to choose one's vocation and establish one's life; to travel; and to mold one's physical appearance and wear clothes of one's choosing. In addition, free human beings in a decent society enjoy a right to privacy, generally defined as those liberties that allow the individual, in Tribe's words, to "control the mass of information by which the world defines one's identity," as well as liberties connected with intimate and family life, and with sanctuaries of the mind, person, and spirit.

Each of these rights has its own body of law, a full analysis of which would take volumes. Our point is simply that Fourteenth Amendment substantive due process has come to include a variety of those liberties that most free and civilized people consider to be outside the power of government to erode.

Procedural Due Process

Unlike substantive due process, which has become broader as our society's concept of civilized conduct has become more refined (and, some critics would say, too far extended beyond the original intentions of the Constitution's drafters), the jurisprudence of procedural due process is in large measure concerned with identifying specific procedures effective in discovering the truth. These procedures reflect society's view of the solemn importance of obtaining an accurate result when a citizen stands accused. Proceedings against citizens may be either civil or criminal. Civil charges may result in the citizen's being deprived of some benefit or property. Criminal charges may result in the defendant's being tarred with a conviction and deprived of either liberty or property, with the attendant deprivation of certain privileges of citizenship (such as the right to vote). Criminal proceedings, threatening more serious consequences, entail more rigorous procedural protections. It is to some of these rights that we now turn.

The Right and Opportunity to Prepare a Defense with Legal Counsel

In one of the more infamous criminal cases to reach the U.S. Supreme Court, the so-called Scottsboro Boys, a group of illiterate black youngsters passing through Jim Crow Alabama were accused of raping two white girls while hitching a ride on a train in 1931.[7] When the train reached Scottsboro, a county seat, the boys were arrested and charged. The trial commenced a mere six days later, and the boys went without legal counsel until the trial date itself. The defendants were broken up into three groups for purposes of trial, and each trial was completed within a day.

There was neither an attempt by defense counsel to conduct an investigation nor the opportunity granted by the judge to do so. Each defendant, noted the Supreme Court, was "stripped of his right to have sufficient time to advise with counsel and prepare his defense." The Sixth Amendment is unusually clear on the right to counsel and other rights granted criminal defendants, which have become incorporated into the notion of procedural fairness:

> In all criminal prosecutions, the accused shall enjoy the right to a speedy and public trial, by an impartial jury of the State and district wherein the crime shall have been committed . . .; to be confronted with the witnesses against him; to have compulsory process for obtaining witnesses in his favor, and to have the Assistance of Counsel for his defense.

The Supreme Court viewed the lack of time for preparation as equivalent to a deprivation of counsel, and it reversed the convictions and attendant death sentences. The Court explained that in addition to the clarity of the Sixth Amendment, there was another reason to conclude that the right to counsel was so fundamental: "The United States by statute and every state in the Union by express provision of law, or by the determination of its courts, make it the duty of the trial judge, where the accused is unable to employ counsel, to appoint counsel for him. . . . A rule adopted with such unanimous accord reflects . . . the fundamental nature of that right."

The Right of Cross-Examination and Confrontation

The right to counsel is useless if other safeguards are not in place. Perhaps the most important are cross-examination and confrontation of adverse witnesses. The Supreme Court dealt with these in a 1959 case, *Greene v. McElroy*,[8] involving revocation of the security clearance of a government contractor's employee, resulting in his discharge. When the employee attempted to protest, he was not allowed access to the classified Department of Defense file containing the specific evidence on the basis of which his clearance was revoked, largely reports of interviews with witnesses.

The employee sued the Department of Defense, and the Supreme Court ruled that because punishment "depends on fact findings, the evidence used to prove the Government's case must be disclosed to the individual so that he has an opportunity to show that it is untrue." This is particularly important, said the Court, "where the evidence consists of the testimony of individuals whose memory might be faulty or who, in fact, might be perjurers or persons motivated by malice, vindictiveness, intolerance, prejudice, or jealousy." For this reason, "the requirements of confrontation [with] and cross-examination [of witnesses] . . . have ancient roots." Cross-examination is the practice by which witnesses for both sides are subject to being questioned not only by the side presenting them, but also by the opposing lawyer. For more than two hundred years, cross-examination has been considered an essential feature of the process by which truthful testimony is separated from falsehood. "No statement," warned the Court in the *Greene* case, "should be used as testimony until it has been probed and sublimated by that test," a proposition that "has found increasing strength in lengthening experience." It is not all that easy to lie in a trial and carry the perjury through to its conclusion with impunity, provided the witness is subject to skillful cross-examination. The basis of the technique is rooted in a commonsense observation familiar to most people—that it is easier to tell the truth than to lie, since lying requires having to remember what one has said previously. A skilled questioner with a better memory than a witness is often able to catch a perjurer by forcing the witness to contradict himself. Furthermore, truth is not a simple fact. Rather, it is a mosaic composed of many pieces. Any single piece of the mosaic, as testified to by the witness, may be tested by putting it into a larger context of known or conceded truthful facts. If the witness is lying about an important piece of the whole, there is usually a discernible lack of fit. As the testimony unfolds, common-sense jurors can, with surprising frequency, detect the lie.

The Court has displayed a similar attitude toward the right of confrontation, also specified in the Sixth Amendment. Confrontation entails the right to meet an adverse witness face-to-face in the presence of judge and jury. As with cross-examination, confrontation's effectiveness is based upon a commonsense observation recognized by any parent seeking to get the truth from a child—that it is harder to tell a lie while in the presence of one falsely accused, and harder still when looking the victim of that prevarication in the eye. While such a confrontation, the Court observed in *Maryland v. Craig* (1990),[9] "may, unfortunately, upset the truthful rape victim or abused child . . . by the same token it may confound and undo the false accuser, or reveal the child coached by a malevolent adult."

The Court in *Craig* also justified the sometimes painful process of confrontation by praising "the strong symbolic purposes served by requiring adverse witnesses at trial to testify in the accused's presence." "There is something deep in human nature," the Court has said repeatedly, "that regards face-to-face confrontation between accused and accuser as 'essential to a fair trial in a criminal prosecution.'"

The Right to a Public Trial

In 1948, the Supreme Court considered an unprecedented event in American judicial history—a criminal trial held before a judge *in secret*. In a world in which secret trials are scandalously common, the fact that a case involving such a trial did not arise in American jurisprudence until 1948 was in itself a tribute to the rule of law in an open society. In a procedure unique to Michigan, a judge was empowered by statute to conduct investigations, a so-called one man grand jury. This judge had the power to subpoena witnesses and interview them privately while deciding whether to indict a suspect. An adjunct to this investigatory authority was the judge's power, exercised in secret, summarily to convict and punish for "criminal contempt" those witnesses he deemed to be recalcitrant, evasive, or untruthful. The "one man grand jury" in the case of *In re Oliver*[10] claimed not to believe a witness he had interrogated in a closed proceeding, whereupon he found the witness guilty of contempt and immediately sentenced him to sixty days in jail.

The procedure had many defects, the Court noted, including several of the rights discussed earlier in this chapter—"no . . . benefits of counsel, no chance to prepare his defense, and no opportunity either to cross-examine the other grand jury witnesses or to summon witnesses to refute the charge against him." However, the Court focused on the secret trial (a procedure unfortunately common in many parts of the world today). It reported that not only was it "unable to find a single instance of a criminal trial conducted" in secret in all of American history, but also that it had not "found any record of even one such secret criminal trial in England since abolition of the Court of Star Chamber in 1641, and whether that court ever convicted people secretly is in dispute." Secret trials, the Court admonished, are "a menace to liberty."

What is it about a *public* trial, asked the Supreme Court, that makes it so different from one held in secret? Public trials have "always been recognized as a safeguard against any attempt to employ our courts as instruments of persecution. [The] possible abuse of judicial power" is thwarted by "the knowledge that every criminal trial is subject to contemporaneous review in the forum of public opinion." Nor is a secret trial any less a violation of due process when the defendant is acquitted. Society has an equally fundamental interest in both fairness and the appearance of fairness, and hence a right to have trials be held in public. Corruption of the system and abuse of power can promote not only the enhanced risk of conviction of the innocent, but also the acquittal of the guilty. Such corruption and abuse thrive—indeed, fester—in an atmosphere of secrecy.

Thus, in *Richmond Newspapers, Inc. v. Virginia,*[11] the Court considered a 1978 murder trial where the judge acceded to a defense request to conduct the proceedings in private. The judge closed the trial, he said, to avoid having public spectators distract jurors. Despite the Supreme Court's ruling thirty years earlier in *In re Oliver* that secret trials were a violation of a defendant's due process rights, the judge felt he was permitted to close this murder trial since it was the defendant who requested it and, hence, it could not be said that the defendant's rights would be violated by the procedure. Once he closed the trial, the judge, without explanation, excluded all of the prosecution's evidence, removed the case from the hands of the jury, and himself proceeded to acquit the defendant. (It was no wonder that the defendant not only did not complain about a secret trial, but actually had requested it.) The local news media, however, filed suit, seeking a declaration that, in the future, such secret trials would not be held. The Supreme Court, by a 7 to 1 vote, ruled that the First Amendment guarantees the public the right to attend criminal trials.

The practical, commonsense, empirical basis for the historic insistence that justice not only be done, but that it be done in public, was thus revealed by these two complementary cases, decided thirty years apart. Secret trials are the enemy not only of justice, but of democracy. Both corruption and injustice have a harder time surviving in the light of day. Those who administer justice must undertake this task in full view of their fellow citizens. Justice is too important to entrust solely to the judgment of judges and lawyers.

The Right to an Impartial Judge

The right to an open trial is required even if there is no reason to believe that a judge is biased or inclined to corruption or abuse of power. However, when there is cause to believe that the judge is not impartial, due process steps in to guarantee a neutral arbiter. In the 1926 Prohibition-era case of *Tumey v. State of Ohio,*[12] the Supreme Court faced a peculiar Ohio statute that allowed charges for the unlawful possession of alcohol to be tried not only by judges and magistrates, but also by the mayor of the village in which the offense was committed. The proceeds from fines assessed upon conviction were in part turned over to the village treasury, a portion even going to pay the mayor for his judicial service. This statute was aimed, the Court noted, at providing an economic incentive "stimulating the activities of the village officers" to enforce the Prohibition laws, which presumably were not among the most popular, even with police, prosecutors, and judges. Hence, the legislature rewarded Prohibition enforcers with a piece of the action. This system meant that if a defendant were acquitted, the mayor or judge went unpaid.

In seeking to determine whether the procedure violated a fundamental precept, the Court looked as far back into English legal history as the reign of Richard II, noting that "there was at the [ancient English] common law the greatest sensitiveness over the existence of any pecuniary interest however small or infinitesimal in the justices of the peace." By thus looking "to those settled usages and modes of proceeding" as existed in England "before the emigration of our ancestors," the Court voided the Ohio statute.

These rights governing criminal trials and other proceedings that could result in substantial deprivations of a defendant's liberty and property, along with the additional right to subpoena witnesses and compel them to give testimony, the ancient and venerated right of trial by a jury of one's peers, and yet a few others, together constitute the core of what is deemed "due process." There are many variations upon and refinements of these themes, resulting from the ongoing process of enforcement and litigation as well as legislation, but the fundamentals have been maintained with remarkable fidelity even during periods when national crises and public hysteria would have made it easier for courts to turn a blind eye to violations. In recent history, none of these rights has been violated on so flimsy an excuse as the perceived need to "educate" citizens as to their social obligations, or to redress "offensive verbal conduct" that creates "a hostile educational environment."

There is virtually no place left in the United States where kangaroo courts and Star Chambers are the rule rather than the exception—except on college and university campuses. Where instances of gross unfairness are still found in the "real world," they usually result when established rules are evaded or disregarded. Thus, one still hears of rampant injustice in local municipal courts, especially where no verbatim record is made. The failure of police fully and accurately to inform arrestees of their constitutional rights, and the occasional application of undue pressure to obtain confessions, remain significant problems at the lower echelons of the criminal justice system. Employees still lose jobs without being given an opportunity to argue in their own defense. These derelictions, however, when they occur, do so in opposition to the laws, court rulings, union contracts, or other civilized norms that provide otherwise. Such actions by those in positions of authority are violations of law and of accepted notions of fairness in government or industry.

The academy remains the only major sector of civilian life in this country where not only is arbitrariness widespread, but where fair procedure and rational fact-finding mechanisms, with disturbing and surprising frequency, are actually precluded by regulations. (One says "surprising" only because this phenomenon is in such stark contrast to two of the announced missions of most universities—to explore, understand, and expand human sympathy for the place and plight of mankind in the world, and to search for truth wherever it may lead.)

In matters of substantive freedoms, such as free speech, colleges and universities feel obliged to promise one thing even while their codes, as enforced, deliver quite another. This, however, is typically not the case in matters involving procedural fairness. There, what is delivered is, alas, frequently precisely what is promised—scandalously little. Indeed, even when something approaching fairness is promised by disciplinary procedural rules, it is often delivered grudgingly and imperfectly, and, in times of crisis, evaded entirely.

The U.S. Supreme Court historically has been reluctant to interfere with the internal disciplinary proceedings of colleges, and even more reluctant to intrude into matters of academic standing. Nonetheless, a concern for fundamental fairness has driven the Court, along with lower state and federal courts, to intervene in response to patently unjust or irrational administrative maltreatment of students or faculty. Indeed, courts have, from time to time, under a variety of theories, intervened in the affairs even of private universities. By denying due process outrageously and capriciously, universities have sorely tempted—at times virtually forced—courts to effect some semblance of fairness. Such events have created a body of court decisions that restrict to some extent the self-governance of private colleges and public institutions.

Such interference, while posing a threat to autonomy and hence to institutional academic freedom, has nonetheless produced substantial (if involuntary) improvements in the health of individual academic freedom and fundamental fairness on some campuses. Nonetheless, in a free society with a large and vibrant private educational sector, and even at public institutions, academic self-governance should be the norm. While that principle still holds considerable sway, it is weakened every time unbearably indecent injustice forces a court to extend its reach into university disciplinary concerns. One need not approve of this judicial development in order to understand how the colleges have brought it upon themselves.

From the start, a sharp distinction must be made between judicial intervention in disciplinary matters—trial and punishment for infractions of rules of behavior—and intervention in academic affairs. Courts have been more willing to address issues of fairness in disciplinary hearings for misconduct than to question the academic judgment of faculty and administration. Typically, court intervention in nonacademic disciplinary matters has been aimed at procedural unfairness. For example, a college surely has a right to discipline a student who becomes intoxicated and disturbs the peace of the campus. However, if the institution is public and hence bound by the Fourteenth Amendment, or if state legislation or a student-college contract exists assuring procedural fairness in private colleges, courts will often insist that a reasonable level of procedural fairness and rational fact-finding be accorded.

Courts have appeared particularly willing to intervene where free speech has been denied students, at least on campuses where constitutional rights apply. The same courts that tread lightly when intruding upon disciplinary matters, and that show even more hesitation to second-guess a college tribunal that expels a student for inadequate academic performance, have less difficulty insisting that student speech not be silenced.

Several lessons emerge from this hierarchy of circumstances in which courts will intervene in campus life. For one thing, universities have sought to justify speech codes on academic grounds. Unless "harassing" speech is banned, they argue, and a "hostile environment" avoided, it will be difficult for students in "historically disadvantaged" categories to benefit from educational opportunities. The willingness of courts to intervene to protect speech rights, however, indicates that they do not buy the argument that speech restrictions are part and parcel of an administration's oversight of academic life.

In the ever-evolving, delicate, and sometimes contentious area of relations between courts and universities, few rules are absolute. Predictions as to precisely what a court will do, or when a court will see fit to intervene, are perilous, as Princeton University learned in the *Schmid* case. Universities already have lost enough free speech cases to send a signal that only the most obdurate fail to read and heed. This fact alone makes it so remarkable that speech codes persist even at public universities, that they have been adopted as recently as the decade of the 1990s (including at such institutions as the Harvard Law School), and that they are enforced. Though largely discredited in courts, legislatures, news media, and public opinion, codes continue to be de rigueur on campuses.

As surprising as it is that speech codes have survived, indeed proliferated, on campuses, it is equally startling that the vast majority of universities maintain procedural rules that are grossly prejudicial to the rights of accused students and ill-designed for discovering truth. Such rules are justified by administrators and some faculty members, of course, on "educational" grounds. Their mantra is that the student disciplinary process is meant to teach, not merely to punish; hence, such decencies as procedural fairness and rational fact-finding are not required.

As institutions of higher learning have proven stubbornly immune from notions of fairness that long have prevailed in the "real world," courts have come to intervene more frequently in the affairs of the academy. In a 1987 article in *The Yale Law Journal,* James M. Picozzi reported:

In 1980, Edward J. Golden, the Assistant Dean of Students at the University of Virginia, contacted eighty-three different public institutions and asked them what procedural protections were afforded students who faced disciplinary dismissal. Of the fifty-eight institutions that provided data on disciplinary procedures, 36.2% did not allow cross-examination by the accused student, and 37.9% did not allow the student to have legal counsel. Staggeringly, 55.2% did not assure an impartial decision maker, 60.3% did not guarantee a right to confront accusers, and 91.4% provided students with no assistance of any kind—let alone compulsory process—in compelling specific persons to testify.[13]

Under the veneer of an "educational process" lies, on most campuses, a relentless adversarial relationship between the student and the disciplinary authorities. This is a well-kept secret, because most hearings are closed. To make matters worse, disciplinary tribunals frequently take up allegations of student misconduct that, if true, not only would violate campus disciplinary codes, but criminal laws as well. In such cases, some colleges have a practice of postponing their own hearings until the outside prosecutor has completed his or her investigation and (if there is one) prosecution. However, this is not universally true, and a student facing an immediate college hearing while a criminal investigation or prosecution is pending faces an agonizing dilemma. Anything that the student testifies to at the college hearing could be used by the prosecutor in court. If the student does not testify before the college tribunal, he or she is virtually assured of losing the case. Although the Fifth Amendment guarantees all Americans the constitutional right not to testify at one's own criminal investigation or trial, there is generally no such right before the typical college tribunal.

Furthermore, most universities have campus police forces that have close working relationships with municipal law enforcement agencies. Indeed, many campus police are deputized with official police powers and have the authority to carry weapons, obtain and execute search warrants, and make arrests on, and even off, campus. Campus police, aided by lawyers in the office of general counsel, expend considerable resources building a case against accused students and frequently share evidence with outside prosecutors.

Given these realities, the claim that a college disciplinary proceeding, particularly where the conduct alleged is possibly criminal as well, is an opportunity for the student to have an "educational" experience is unrealistic. (The growing number of student sexual liaisons that result in charges of "date rape" in both campus tribunals and criminal courts gives real urgency to the frequent failure of college disciplinary bodies to recognize the inappropriateness of trying rape charges in front of casual or informal college disciplinary committees, particularly before criminal proceedings have been completed.)

One need not be selective in order to get a picture of the one-sidedness, unfairness, and irrational or inadequate mechanisms of fact-finding in college disciplinary procedures. The problem is not confined to any particular kind of institution, public or private, nor to any geographic area. Of course, disciplinary proceedings lacking any semblance of due process protections might be perfectly acceptable on religious, private military, or other such parochial campuses, because students choose to accept such circumstances knowingly. By contrast, students at most colleges are under the dangerous illusion that they are attending liberal educational institutions dedicated to academic freedom, liberty of the mind and spirit, unfettered pursuit of truth, legal equality, and fairness.

We have examined many hundreds of colleges and universities, public and private, and have selected a representative cross section. The selection consists of, among the *private* institutions, Duke, Cornell, Yale, Chicago, MIT, Princeton, Emory, Brown, and Harvard; and, among the *public* institutions, University of California-Berkeley, Florida State University, Iowa State University, Pennsylvania State University, University of Michigan, University of Kansas, and University of Vermont. We have focused on procedural rights widely considered fundamental to a fair procedure followed by a just result.

Open Versus Closed Proceedings: Confidentiality

Closed hearings purportedly to protect "confidentiality" are found throughout academia. At Brown, the University Disciplinary Committee Guidelines provide that "all hearings shall be closed." Exceptions arise only "in special circumstances where the presence of observers is considered beneficial to the University community and where the charged student does not object."[14] In such cases, a student must petition the Office of Student Life to permit a reasonable number of observers (who must, in most cases, be limited to members of the university). The Harvard guidelines state "the College's rules of confidentiality apply" and provide a gag rule—"because a case necessarily involves the confidential affairs of other students, it is not appropriate to discuss it openly with members of this community or beyond, or with those who may be affected directly by the case or its outcome." MIT limits attendance to those directly involved and assigns the chairman of the hearing arbitrary discretion in deciding whether to permit witnesses to attend when they are not testifying. As for "confidentiality," MIT now prohibits tape recording the hearing, a recent "reform." At Princeton, requests for an open hearing are subject to committee ruling, and "in exceptional circumstances, the committee reserves the right to hold a portion of the hearing in closed session." At Berkeley and the University of Michigan, all hearings are closed unless the grievant and respondent agree otherwise (an unlikely scenario in any case involving allegations of rape, sexual misconduct, or harassment of any sort).

Some institutions show a degree of flexibility. The Duke University Judicial Board conducts hearings in private unless the accused requests otherwise. However, any party may object to such a request, in which case the board by majority vote may close it. Duke, however, does mandate tape-recording of hearings.

Cornell, Florida State, Chicago, and Penn State are more open, but all still impose significant restrictions on the right to a public hearing. At Cornell, an accused, on forty-eight hours' notice, has a right to open the proceedings, although the board reserves the right to limit the number of public attendees. Nevertheless, Cornell also specifies that "all hearings in cases of sexual harassment, abuse or assault, or of rape shall be private and the defendant shall not have the option of requesting an open hearing." Florida State requires five days notice of a request to open proceedings and specifies, moreover, that "charges involving alleged sexual misconduct will not be heard in public without the prior written consent of the alleged victim." At Chicago, an accused may have "a few observers of his own choosing" present to watch an otherwise closed hearing, or, with the assent of the University Disciplinary Committee, a hearing open to the public. Penn State offers a similar provision whereby an accused can request an open hearing but the chairperson determines how many may attend.

The question of open versus closed hearings is neither minor nor merely technical. Open trials, fundamental to liberty, do not guarantee fairness or justice, but they make them more likely. At the least, they allow a person wrongly convicted to demonstrate his or her plight to peers and the world. An accumulation of unjust outcomes, widely known, ultimately can force reform, but even if not, one still bears in mind the observation of Justice Felix Frankfurter in his remarkable 1953 dissenting opinion, published after the hasty execution of convicted atomic spies Julius and Ethel Rosenberg, when the Supreme Court, called into emergency session, vacated a temporary stay of execution issued by Justice William Douglas.[15] Frankfurter believed that the case merited unhurried consideration, and he issued a full legal opinion, detailing his reasons for believing the death penalty in that case was unlawful. Explaining why he was bothering to elaborate publicly his views in a case where the defendants had already been executed, he wrote that even though publishing "an opinion in a case affecting two lives after the curtain has been rung down upon them has the appearance of pathetic futility," nonetheless "history also has its claims . . . in the long and unending effort to develop and enforce justice according to law."

Composition of Board: Faculty, Students, Administrators

Some disciplinary boards are controlled by administrators answerable to the corporation and its general counsel, while others have representation by faculty and students. Brown's, although of mixed membership, favors administrators and faculty over students, as does Chicago's. Cornell ranks among the best in terms of balanced representation, as does Emory. MIT differs slightly from Emory, Cornell, and Yale in that faculty members are elected by their colleagues rather than appointed by the dean or president. Its numbers are comparable, with six faculty members, three undergraduates and two graduate students. Of this group of elite private colleges, Harvard stands alone in its unwillingness to have *any* undergraduate representation, its Administrative Board being heavily weighted to administrators, with a smattering of senior faculty. Notwithstanding a 1992 report by the student-run Civil Liberties Union of Harvard that criticized "judicial determinations [made] in a non-judicial manner," the administration remained adamant about its control.[16]

The school of law at the University of Kansas provides unusually specific guidelines for Judicial Board members, including the requirement that a jury of "peers" must take race and sex into account. At least one member must belong to the same race and sex as the complainant. Florida State, by contrast, provides a range of possible hearing bodies and allows the defendant some say in their composition.

The prevalence of administrative control of the student disciplinary process raises a troublesome issue. Administrative officers of a college or university by law have an obligation of undivided loyalty and duty to their respective institutions. Not only is it their natural inclination to take the institution's side, but it is their legal duty to do so. In the larger sense, of course, it is surely in the long-term interests of the university to dispense justice fairly. However, in the short term, on a case by case basis, an administrator and the general counsel advising him or her is likely to interpret that duty as one of avoiding institutional notoriety or financial exposure. Of the entire campus community, administrators and in-house lawyers are in the worst position to be entrusted with an obligation of neutrality in a dispute between the institution and a student.

The Right to Have an Adviser or Lawyer

Although most universities grant that students have a right to some form of adviser, definitions vary. Universities commonly restrict the choice to nonlawyer members of the campus community. At Harvard and Duke, the administration plays a key role in both advising and decision making. At Duke, the dean of student development assigns an adviser, although the accused may decline the choice and select another member of the community. Advisers may not directly address the hearing panel nor act as advocates. Similarly, a Harvard student receives an assigned adviser who is a member of the Administrative Board, usually a senior tutor or resident dean (but other Board members are acceptable if the student prefers). During the initial investigation, a student may seek "personal support and advice" from an adviser outside the board. At one administrative board hearing for two students who were also under criminal investigation, the board excluded the students' lawyers from the room and, remarkably, was resistant (but eventually acquiesced) even to having the students represented by Harvard Law School faculty members.[17]

At the University of Vermont, a defendant may choose an adviser from within the university community, but this adviser "is not permitted to speak or otherwise represent" the student. Advisers may not be lawyers, although, unlike at Harvard, exceptions are made "when related criminal charges are pending." Yale specifies that all advisers must belong to the Yale community, and that they may not act as advocates, but rather as "a source of personal and moral support." At most, advisers may "unobtrusively suggest questions" to the student during the hearing. In cases involving charges against persons or property, it allows attorneys to be "consulted." An attorney, once admitted, may "request the Chairman to pursue a particular direction of questioning," although this is ultimately left to the chair's sole discretion.

Among the slightly more enlightened policies with regard to counsel are those of Cornell, Iowa State, Princeton, MIT, and Brown. At Cornell and Iowa, advisers may be selected from either the university or the general public. These policies are not without severe trade-offs, however, because neither institution permits advisers to present the case, directly examine witnesses, or present a summary argument. At MIT, both the respondent and the complainant may bring a nonfamily, nonattorney member of the MIT community to the hearing. (This was a modification of a less restrictive earlier practice, under which one accused student, Adam Dershowitz, was able to bring his uncle, Harvard law professor Alan Dershowitz, into the hearing, under a rule excluding lawyers but allowing family members to attend. MIT plugged this loophole by changing the rule.)

Princeton offers a different bargain. Advisers must belong to the university but may "participate in the same manner as the student in the hearing."

Brown specifies that advisers (chosen from within the university) may make statements on behalf of students as well as cross-examine witnesses. It also permits attorneys to act as advisers "for the purpose of safeguarding the charged student's rights at any subsequent criminal proceeding" in the sole case of "allegations that could constitute a capital life offense under Rhode Island criminal law." Even in those instances, the attorney's role is curbed.

There is, in our society, a vigorous debate over whether lawyers play too great a role in civic life. Indeed, the extent to which general counsels sometimes dictate policy at the academy is more than troublesome. However, one place where lawyers are essential is in our courts. As long as universities insist upon trying serious cases in institutional tribunals, there should be no resistance to having lawyers present. Their skills, after all, are honed in techniques for sifting truth from falsity. Few laymen can approach the cross-examination skills of a moderately good trial lawyer. Colleges cannot have it both ways, combining cozy informality with adversarial hearings, an "educational" experience with ruinous penalties. The stakes at college tribunals are grave. A student may be forever labeled a harasser or rapist or might be expelled, with permanent effects on his life and career. To force an inexperienced young person (or anyone) to undergo such a process without skilled advice and independent representation is something our legal system, for good reason, abandoned centuries ago. It is a practice still found in authoritarian countries and on college campuses.

The Right to Challenge the Hearing Panel

Cornell does not specify a right to challenge the hearing panel, but notes that a panel member's prior knowledge of events related to the allegation would be a disqualification. Students at Vermont, Brown, and Florida State fare somewhat better; they possess the right to challenge a panel member by filing a written complaint of specific bias. Yale permits challenges restricted to ties of kinship or close personal or professional relationship, whereas at Kansas, Iowa, and Penn State either party may challenge for conflict of interest or previous involvement. Duke offers one of the most liberal policies. A student may challenge any member(s) of the Judicial Board, either on grounds of cause or prejudice, or merely as a peremptory challenge (that is, requiring no justification or explanation).

In the real world outside the campus, the right to an impartial judge and jury is never questioned. Procedural rules require that a judge be removed from a case not only if he is in fact biased, but even if he appears so. Justice must not only be done but must appear to be done. Even after trials lasting months, verdicts are vacated should it be discovered that a single juror, out of twelve, bears a relationship to the case, the issue, or one of the parties that could lead a reasonable person to question the juror's impartiality. On some campuses, panel members with actual and apparent biases and conflicts of interest judge cases with impunity.

The Right to Question and Call Witnesses

Most campus regulations provide, in theory, a right to call and question witnesses, but this is severely limited in practice. Harvard represents an extreme. There, a hearing subcommittee of the Administrative Board meets separately with each witness, in keeping with its policy on "confidentiality," and then summarizes each witness's testimony in a report to the full board. The report also contains the subcommittee's "assessment and recommendation." Only a complaining or defending student may appear in person before the board. The full board thus does not see or hear live witnesses, except for the opposing students, much less hear the defendant question witnesses. At Yale, both parties may ordinarily be present during the questioning of witnesses, but the committee can vote to "enter into closed session with or without one or both parties." Yale limits witnesses to those "deemed relevant by the Committee."

At Michigan, a student may not call witnesses unless both parties agree. Other schools limit this right by admitting only certain categories of witnesses. At Vermont, for instance, the respondent must submit a list (including names and summaries of expected testimony). Although issues of credibility might be crucial, students are warned that "character witnesses generally are considered irrelevant and will not be permitted to testify." Student access to witnesses is severely curtailed. An accused at Vermont may hear all testimony but must submit questions to the hearing officer and judicial council, "who will decide which, if any, of the questions to ask witnesses." At Iowa and Kansas the hearing board and the accused may call witnesses, but neither school explicitly enumerates a right to cross-examine. Princeton students may request the presence of, and may question, "a reasonable number of persons, all of whom normally must be current members of the resident University community, and whose only role is to provide information about the character and qualities of the student." Cornell gives students the right to call and cross-examine witnesses. Brown permits witnesses and cross-examination and even allows advisers to participate, but it specifies that "individuals who are not members of the University community will generally be permitted to testify at a hearing only if they have direct knowledge or information regarding the actions of the involved parties relating to the incident." Penn State's policy allows good access to witnesses, and at Berkeley both parties have the right to examine all witnesses. Duke assures the right of the accused to confront accusers and hostile witnesses, although the student must submit questions in writing to the chairman, who "must ask such question(s) so submitted unless they are unfair and/or irrelevant and/or purely capricious."

Many of these limited procedures serve to evade the truth rather than to discover it. The reason that the right to confront witnesses is fundamental in our judicial system is that thousands of years of experience teach that a false accuser is less likely to repeat a lie comfortably when looking the falsely accused directly in the eye. (These universal truths, taught in college psychology courses, often do not escape the classroom into the tribunals.) Those persons who actually know something about an event are the ones most likely to wish to avoid having to appear and testify, yet it is rare for an accused student to have the unfettered power to compel the appearance and testimony of students, much less faculty and administrators. On many campuses, an administrator wishing to appear as a witness for a student must obtain permission, or at least "advice," from the general counsel—this, in a nation where, in 1807, the great Chief Justice John Marshall declared in *United States v. Burr* "That the president of the United States may be subpoenaed, and examined as a witness, . . . cannot be controverted."[18]

On campuses, character witnesses are typically not allowed, as at Vermont, because they are considered "irrelevant." Thus, the accused faces a credibility contest with accusers, without being allowed to establish a history and reputation of truth-telling. Harvard allows a subcommittee to "summarize" testimony for the tribunal. Yale "ordinarily" allows the accused to be in the same room as witnesses who testify against him. Vermont allows the accused to submit questions that the panel then poses. Such rules can be maddeningly frustrating to a falsely accused student. They make a mockery of the notion that the process is "educational." If it is an education in anything, it is an education in helplessness.

Deferral for Criminal Investigation/Prosecution

Most universities make little or no mention of deferral of college hearings until criminal (and sometimes civil) investigations and trials are completed. Iowa makes deferral an option for the college, but not a requirement. Harvard similarly specifies that "if legal or civil action is contemplated in relation to a disciplinary case, the College *ordinarily* will not take up the case until court action is resolved" (emphasis added), but exceptions are not unknown. Yale does little better, specifying that "the Executive Committee *may* decide to defer its consideration of the complaint until after the matter has been adjudicated by the courts" (emphasis added)—a decision made by secret ballot.

Michigan acknowledges that while "resolution and appeal processes are administrative functions and are not subject to the same rules of civil or criminal proceedings, . . . students may be accountable to both the legal system and the University." It does not specify, however, a deferral policy. At Princeton, when the outside charge "is more serious than a disorderly person offense, the student will be granted permission not to speak or to answer questions without prejudicing the committee's decision," and the dean has discretion to postpone the hearing altogether and to suspend the student until it can reconvene.

The rush to try student disciplinary cases has still other consequences. Passions and publicity following the suspected commission of a heinous crime are intense, and courts typically postpone trials until the furor dies down. In its most famous pronouncement on this point, the Supreme Court in 1966 overturned the spousal murder conviction of Dr. Samuel Sheppard (*Sheppard v. Maxwell*[19]) because of the "reasonable likelihood" that a prejudicial atmosphere prevented a fair trial. When the case was retried in calmer circumstances, Sheppard was acquitted, and recent DNA evidence supported that verdict. Yet college tribunals routinely try the most highly politicized cases in the midst of campus candlelight vigils and other demonstrations.

Variation in disciplinary procedures from campus to campus is substantial, although not a single college we have examined provides a tribunal and set of rules that remotely approach the due process accorded a defendant in any real court. The fairest schools' procedures, at best, might permit a true and just verdict in a case involving a minor, nonpoliticized violation not involving either constitutional rights, criminal conduct, or the campus's latest *crime du jour*. The least fair, such as Harvard's, are weighted against producing a just result in even the inconsequential case. Moreover, none of the procedural codes we have seen would be appropriate for deciding, on campus, a charge of violation of the criminal law. Campus tribunals nowhere are capable of fairly and accurately judging a charge so serious, for example, as rape, yet they routinely decide such cases even in atmospheres of political crisis.

CHAPTER 12

THE COURTS OF
STAR CHAMBER

It was not much better for students in the old days: A dean sized
you up, and he forgave, admonished, punished, or expelled you
as he wished. At best, you went before an honor board that often treated athletes, the rich, and the prestigious with kid gloves, but took off those gloves
in dealing with the rest. There were individual schools, then as now, that
tried to be more fair than others, but, to say the least, there was no "golden
age" of academic due process.

When we were undergraduates at Princeton in the early '60s, some athletes and senior-class officers vandalized the room of two gay socialists, destroying a library of Marxist books and pouring ink over graduate school
applications. Princeton let the offenders off with barely a slap on the wrist.
Our goal is not to fabricate and glorify a past that never was, but to call the
present to account.

The generation of the '60s promised much to universities: openness,
justice, and procedural fairness, even for unpopular persons and views. Living through that age, one had the sense that, perhaps, when the dust settled,
universities would learn to achieve both a certain order and a deep respect
for rights and due process. That promise has not been fulfilled. The lack of
due process remains with us, now entwined with issues of intense controversy and passion.

The attempt to compensate for historical wrongs and to eradicate perceived evils leaves little patience for procedural fairness and consistency. As
part of that effort, colleges and universities criminalize behaviors (including
verbal behaviors) that the criminal and civil laws do not always see as crimes

at all. "Harassment" and, most dramatically, "tacit consent" to sexual relations often have profoundly different meanings as used in our schools and as used in the larger world.

We wish neither to appeal to prurient interest nor to publicize the names of students caught up in the erotic politics of this age, so let us offer just one example, without the names or place, although it is a case that we have studied closely, and it is increasingly typical. A young woman brought marijuana to a young man's dormitory at a large university, smoked with him, and went to his bedroom. To the annoyance of other students in the living room, they engaged in loud oral sex, on and off, for hours. They slept naked in his bed. She awoke to find him touching her face and entering her. She told him no. He stopped. The next day, friends with whom she discussed what had happened told her that she had been raped, and referred her to the university office that dealt with crimes against women. The university charged the young man with rape, found him guilty, and expelled him. The district attorney was pressed by campus activists to bring a criminal charge of rape against the young man, and he did. It took a real jury about half an hour to acquit him on the grounds that the woman had given tacit consent to intimate sexual relations.

Universities prefer not to leave such decisions to public courts, where such cases belong. "Harassment" and "date rape," when they reflect the legal meaning of those terms, are terrible things. Universities, however, often assign these names to actions that few others would so describe. The stain of conviction, however, especially when the entire judicial record is confidential but the verdict is public, is indelible. In civilized societies, the more serious the accusation, the more formidable the safeguards of fairness, but campuses want simultaneously to define a larger and larger number of acts as grave, and to do so without providing those due protections. There are ways to think about due process in good faith: What protects the innocent? What procedures should be in place to ensure justice for you or someone you love?

Would the cases and codes discussed in this book meet your criteria? Vague statutes, selective enforcement, and no rule of guiding precedent? The admissibility of unsworn and hearsay evidence, at secret hearings, with no subpoena power, and under rules that change according to the passions of one's accusers? No right to confront and cross-examine one's accusers and their witnesses? Counsel unequal in training or experience to the prosecutor? Judgment by a biased panel in an environment heated by hostility? These are simultaneously the very abuses against which the efforts of civilization have struggled and, we will see, a description of the state of judicial process, in part or even in whole, in most of academic life.

The antithesis of due process would be the presumption of guilt and the contrivance of sure means of gaining a conviction. The precondition of due process is the separation of the accusation from the issue of procedural propriety. That is not difficult, however. It is what ordinary citizens in a lawful society swear under oath to do on juries. Colleges and universities appear to find it impossible. Let us begin with their treatment of faculty, because if they may deny due process to members of their faculties, who have so many contractual and traditional protections, what student can feel secure in the expectation of fairness?

Leroy Young was a tenured professor of graphic arts at Plymouth State College in New Hampshire. He had founded the department, was its guiding spirit, and was much beloved as a teacher.[1] When his troubles occurred, forty-three students at the college who had taken courses with him signed a petition about his integrity, character, and nurturing dedication. Young, however, faced three potential difficulties in the gender pathologies of academic life. First, he and his wife often became friends with students, inviting them to their home, meeting them at restaurants, talking late with them about art and life. Second, he taught the photography of the nude, which involved discussions of the body and the aesthetics of nude photography. Third (and of equal danger), he was charismatic, warm, and inspired great affection.

There is an extensive documentary history of Leroy Young's case. In 1993, a student who had shown him marks of appropriate friendship accused him of sexual harassment, namely, hugging her in public, giving her a kiss, and touching her leg in a restaurant. The Sexual Harassment Hearing Panel (SHHP) found him guilty of sexual harassment on November 12, and the president of Plymouth State, Donald Wharton, sentenced him to two months' suspension without pay or benefits. Young appealed, as appropriate, to the college Appeals Board, which, on February 6, 1994, reviewed all the evidence and dismissed every single count against Young except the innocuous charge of a public hug (which Young never had denied, except to assert its innocence).

The Appeals Board was openly astonished and appalled by the special harassment panel's adjudication of the case, which it repeatedly labeled "unreasonable." Its review of the SHHP hearing opens a window onto current academic judicial proceedings. Concerning his conviction for kissing the student on the lips: "There were no witnesses to the alleged event, and by her own testimony [the student] acknowledged that it was 'a long while' before she 'realized' that the alleged kiss was on the lips rather than on the cheek as she testified that she had believed initially." Concerning his conviction on touching the student's leg at a dinner with students, with Young's wife Tatum, and with the Youngs' visiting son: "As testified by [one student present at the dinner] and confirmed by [the accuser], the individuals in the group were seated close to each other around the table making accidental touching under the table likely, and [the accuser] became highly inebriated during the course of the gathering." The Appeals Board review also noted that the accuser had testified to the SHHP that there were willing witnesses to certain events, but she had not produced even one, either then or at the Appeals Board hearing.

The SHHP, it ruled, had accepted wholly insufficient evidence, belated changes in the accusations, and contradictions: "Had a diligent investigation occurred before the Hearing Panel convened, or if a diligent investigation had been conducted by the Hearing Panel, it is highly unlikely that the unsustainable findings against [Professor Young] would have resulted." It ordered Young's immediate reinstatement, the full payment of any lost salary and benefits, and the removal of President Wharton's letter of reprimand from Young's personnel file.

Wharton, however, did not follow the ruling of the Appeals Board, despite the fact that the college's Sexual Harassment Policy and Procedures explicitly state that "the written ruling of the Appeals Board shall constitute a final decision." There were no internal procedures, however, for enforcing that rule. When Young asked the Appeals Board to deal with the president's refusal to follow its "final decision," the board ruled that a professor could appeal only substantive findings, which in this case had been favorable to Young. As for President Wharton, not only did he not reinstate Young, but he now pursued the exonerated professor in a manner that circumvented all possible protections.

While these unsustained charges were being rejected, a second young woman came forward and charged that the graphic arts professor had harassed her also. The former student had graduated from Plymouth State the year before, and under explicit college guidelines, no harassment charges could be filed more than sixty days after a student's graduation. Thus, the judicial offices refused to act on her accusations. President Wharton, however, initiated a personal investigation of this second set of charges. Starting in December 1993, he held informal meetings with the Youngs and their attorney. As soon as Young heard of the new charges against him, he took and passed a polygraph test with a celebrated New Hampshire expert who regularly performed lie-detector tests for the New Hampshire State Patrol, George Tetreault, who reported that Young was telling the truth in all of his denials of the new charges. Young presented the polygraph results and analyses to President Wharton and the college's in-house attorney.

To the Youngs' lawyer, the charges, verbally described by President Wharton, seemed so preposterous, the Youngs' accounts so consistent with the facts, and the polygraph test so compelling, that in January 1994, he told Leroy and Tatum not to waste their money paying him to attend further university meetings, but to wrap things up themselves. On March 15, 1994, however, President Wharton summoned Young by letter to be in his office on March 21 to "respond to" these charges. According to Young, Wharton now sprung new accusations against him, including the "charge" that he and the student had exchanged gifts at Christmas. Young replied whimsically, "That doesn't ring a bell." At a later college hearing, Wharton would say that at that moment, he was certain that Young was guilty.

Young knew that his accuser also was suing the college. He knew that the president had believed—or purported to believe—charges against him that an impartial panel had found to be totally without foundation. Now, however, it was simply the president weighing whether he found Young or his second accuser more credible. A thirty-year vocation in teaching hung in the balance, and Young had no *procedural* protections. The accusations occurred after the college's statute of limitations had expired; there were no written charges; there was no hearing; there was no accuser to be cross-examined; there were, in fact, no witnesses to be deposed and cross-examined; there were no rules; there was no panel or impartial judge.

The circumstances surely demanded due process and impartiality. The student had been a close friend of Leroy and Tatum Young for several years, but the relationship had soured. Young disputed every charge against him. It was, at the least, a complex charge of sexual harassment that demanded the fullest, fairest evidentiary hearing. Instead, Wharton decided to intuit a truth about the case.

Invoking a clause of the Plymouth State College faculty personnel policies that asked the president, in charges involving a faculty member, "to conduct a frank review of the problem and seek a mutually agreeable resolution," Wharton conducted his own "review." According to Young, Wharton generally ignored Young's supporters, and forgot about the "mutually agreeable resolution" that was a formal requirement of such informal procedure. On March 28, 1994, without a single evidentiary hearing or a single chance for

Young to cross-examine, let alone confront, his accuser, President Wharton summarily stripped him of tenure and fired him. Wharton announced, in a press release, that Young's dismissal was for "flagrant neglect of duty and moral delinquency of a grave order." It made the accuser's allegations public, but not Young's replies to her specific allegations. The press release also made very clear the "process" by which the tenured professor was dismissed: "Professor Young again issued a blanket denial of having done any of the things. . . . I reviewed again for myself the entire matter and concluded that [the accuser's] testimony was well-founded and that Professor Young was not telling the truth." In addition, Wharton's press release let slip that "on January 14, USNH General Counsel Ron Rodgers and I met with [Young's accuser] and her attorney in my office for two and a half hours." Perhaps the accused and his attorney should have been there too.

Young now had the right to appear before the Faculty Review Committee, but that body created a hopeless catch-22. It ruled that it could not accept Young's appeal of the president's actions because the accuser "is no longer a student." Thus, she was someone "over whom the jurisdiction of the Faculty Review Committee may not extend." Further, it ruled that it could not deal with Young's case because "the Review Committee is not privy to all the information which might have formed the basis of the President's decision, nor does it have the means or resources to examine parties which do not belong to the college community." Indeed.

Young appealed this decision to the five-member College Appeal Committee, which did not hear the case until May 1995, by which time Leroy and Tatum were back in their native North Carolina, working odd jobs. The issues before the committee were procedural: Did President Wharton have the right to fire Young unilaterally, without a hearing? If it were appropriate to hear the charges against Young, what would constitute a due process disposition of the case? On November 27, 1995, the committee found that Young had been improperly dismissed, that the president's behavior had been inappropriate, and that the president had not had a sufficient basis for dismissing Young. However, by a 3 to 2 vote, without formal charges against which Young could defend himself, without cross-examination, and without calling a host of relevant witnesses, the committee ruled that the evidence before it sufficed to recommend dismissal for cause. In one day, President Wharton, following the committee's recommendation, rehired Leroy Young, restored his lost pay and benefits, and dismissed him immediately for cause.

The two dissenting members concluded that "the proceedings in this case have not produced answers to a number of [in fact, seventy] questions

germane to the truth of the matter." The questions that the dissenters declared to remain unanswered shed much light on the procedures used in
Young's appeal: a lack of "direct evidence" on crucial issues; essential factual
discrepancies in the allegations of Young's accuser, discrepancies that grew
more elaborate over time; major differences between the accuser's testimony
and that of her supposedly supportive "hearsay" witnesses; failure to call a
witness whose "testimony is potentially crucial"; mysteriously missing vital
evidence; failure to compare the force of Young's polygraph test, on the most
crucial issues in contention, to the accuser's otherwise unconfirmed and
often "vacillating" accusations. They noted also that the accuser, during a
period that she had described as "hostile" because of Young's alleged harassment, had sent Young an inscribed book of love poetry and a copy of the
novel *The Thorn Birds* (about a young woman in love with a priest who
chooses to be faithful to his vows). For the minority, "the totality of the evidence brought before the Committee does indicate a relationship beyond
the normal student/teacher relationship," but that never was the issue, and
"it is just as likely as not that [the] . . . allegations constitute a distorted account of what, if anything, actually occurred." To them, it was obvious "that
President Wharton did not meet the burden of proof . . . for recommending
dismissal for cause."

Nonetheless, Young was dismissed, and he and his wife, together, have
filed suit in federal court against President Wharton, Plymouth State College, and the New Hampshire University system for, among other things, violation of their civil rights and libel, a case that is pending. One impartial
tribunal, however, had heard the college's case against Leroy Young. In the
spring of 1994, after his dismissal, Leroy Young filed for unemployment benefits in New Hampshire. His benefits were denied when the NHUS objected, arguing that he had been fired for just cause. Young appealed to the
Appeal Tribunal of the New Hampshire Department of Employment Security, which ruled: "The employer provided no credible evidence to support
its position." After a review "of all the records and testimony," the tribunal
found "that the claimant was discharged by the University of NH [system]
on March 25, 1994 for a reason other than misconduct connected with his
work." Indeed, "the Appeal Chairman finds the University's behavior in this
case," the ruling concluded, "reprehensible."[2]

———————

Colleges and universities have good reason to fear both the judicial system
and civil society. Civil society likewise has good reason to fear our colleges

and universities. The genuine victims of real and demonstrable harassment—stalking, sexual assault, quid pro quo extortion, and unlawful deprivation of the ability to work—also should fear what is occurring, because strong and rightful cases become confused with capricious and unjust persecutions. The number of cases is growing now in which professors convicted of "harassment" by academic tribunals, at both public and private universities, have taken their cases to state and federal courts, and where judges and juries, often quickly, have found their persecutions substantively and procedurally "reprehensible." Even in the case of self-governing private schools, courts recognize that individuals may not be treated as if they were citizens of a nation without protection of common, tort, and contract law.

In one of the first court cases to articulate a full principle of due process for private universities, a New York state court, in *Starishevsky v. Hofstra,* examined the procedures by which Hofstra University had fired a professor for alleged harassment. These included the interview of a hostile witness after the disciplinary hearing officially had ended, without the defendant's knowledge, and without his chance, obviously, for either cross-examination or rebuttal. The Court ordered the professor's reinstatement. By adopting a process to determine if someone should be fired for "harassment," Hofstra had committed itself to due process. Someone faced with such charges must be judged by procedures that are "fair and reasonable and which lend themselves to a reliable determination." If that principle—long accepted in constitutional and common law jurisprudence, but foreign to the academy—should succeed, then the view that "sexual harassment" is a crime too heinous to be adjudicated by "fair and reasonable" procedures will have to give way on our campuses to a more civilized approach.[3]

Faced by the subpoena of their internal documents, more and more universities now choose to settle with faculty who sue them for denial of due process. These settlements usually are confidential, but academics are not very good at matters of confidentiality, and we know that, recently, some of those settlements have ranged from hundreds of thousands to two million dollars. If campuses cannot provide due process—clear and reasonable regulations, uniform enforcement, and fair, impartial procedures—they will continue to pay a price. Their victims, of course, most of whom never seek nor receive their day in a real court, pay a worse price.

———————

James B. Maas is an eminent professor of psychology and one of the most admired teachers at Cornell University.[4] In the year that his travails began,

Cornell students voted his Psychology 101, which attracted eighteen hundred students, the best course at the university, and voted Maas Cornell's best professor. In spring 1994, however, four of Maas's former students charged him, long after the alleged incidents supposedly occurred, with sexual harassment, including inappropriate touching, grabbing a student's breast, and kissing someone with his tongue. They also charged him with verbal sexual "innuendo," and with giving jewelry and clothing as gifts. Three of the women worked in his Cornell filmmaking lab, and one, his teaching assistant, also was his family's nanny. The last one, now accusing him of coercion and harassment, had written the following letter to him on the date of her graduation from Cornell in 1993: "I can't thank you enough for everything you have done (and continue to do) for me over the years. You have made my Cornell experience an invaluable treasure. Knowing that you will always be a source of encouragement and support for me is the only thing that makes leaving Cornell bearable." She noted that "I am especially flattered to have been 'adopted' by you, Nancy and the boys. You are such a special family and I am thrilled that I have gotten to know you all so well." The next year, she charged him with harassment during those years at Cornell. One of her accusations was that Nancy "made her push the boys' luggage at an airport when she accompanied them on a vacation."

After more than one year, Cornell found Maas guilty of sexual harassment, but it imposed curious penalties, given the charges: no increase in salary, and a requirement to obtain various permissions before he could hire student film crew employees or advise students. The sentence was particularly incomprehensible given the judgment of the Faculty Ethics Committee that tried the case. The committee concluded that Maas "was not found to have either had, or sought, an intimate sexual relationship with any of his students nor to have engaged in the physically abusive behaviors often associated with the term sexual harassment." Nonetheless, the panel convicted Maas of sexual harassment because it "felt that his actions made the women feel very uncomfortable and 'constituted a pattern of sexual harassment.'"[5]

The committee clearly had not believed the most serious allegations of the complainants, but it had apparently sought to placate them with a guilty verdict and some sort of penalty. Maas refused to accept any such verdict. He secured the help of the Center for Individual Rights, the champion of the due process and legal equality of so many faculty members in the current climate, and he sued Cornell in state court for $1.5 million.

The procedures in the Maas case were new. The Cornell Code of Conduct specifies that all alleged violations of its regulations are to be adjudicated by Cornell's Judicial System, which provides a wide array of due process protections. We have seen, however, in the Aist case, how a separate office obtained jurisdiction over cases of "discrimination." In 1991, similarly, Cornell's Arts and Sciences College established a separate Professional Ethics Committee uniquely to hear charges of sexual misconduct against its faculty members. This committee offered almost no procedural protections.

This separation of due process from the most serious charges is now a pattern at hundreds of colleges and universities that have established special tribunals, with fewer protections and presumptions of innocence, to hear cases of alleged harassment. As Jordan E. Kurland of the AAUP told the *Chronicle of Higher Education*, on many campuses, officials who investigate complaints serve as "judge, jury, and coach [of the complainants]." He concluded: "There is little doubt that much of this has gotten out of control." Kurland identified the heart of what colleges and universities had done: "Over the past two years, sexual harassment has been singled out as a very special sort of offense that requires a different kind of due process. We [the AAUP] have always been opposed to that."[6]

We all should have learned from witchcraft trials, courts of Star Chamber, and various inquisitions that justice suffers under tribunals with special moral missions. Such tribunals, established to deal with alleged offenses so awful that regular procedures are inadequate to resolve them, receive a message that invites overzealous persecution: They have a transcendent duty to redress a singular evil. At universities, one begins with flawed procedures and goes downhill from there.

Where, for example, the Cornell Judicial Code had strict statutes of limitations, Maas's accusers brought charges stemming from up to six years earlier. Where the code permitted legal counsel, the Ethics Committee hearing sexual harassment cases did not, and it even barred Maas's choice of "advisor," a professor of law at Cornell, on the singular ground that he was "too much of an expert." Where the code limited judicial actions at Cornell to complaints brought only by current members of the Cornell community, two of Maas's accusers had graduated at least a year before filing their complaints, and some of their complaints alleged incidents that occurred after their graduation. Under the code, they would have had to pursue Maas, appropriately, in civil or criminal courts; under the sexual harassment provisions, they could use the closed ethics committee without being subject to cross-examination. Indeed, the committee barred Maas or his adviser from even being in the room when the women testified (they had to listen on earphones in a room two floors away), because their presence might upset their accusers. Further, the ethics committee has no guidelines concerning the conduct of a hearing. During Maas's trial, its chair said, "We have to make the rules as we go along." Although created because of the belief that there was an epidemic of harassment, the committee had tried only one prior case since its inception in 1991.

The "Acting Senior Sexual Harassment Counselor," Professor of Government Isaac Kramnick, was supposed to determine if the case "had merit," and, if so, to forward it to the ethics committee. According to Maas's complaint in his suit against the school, however, Kramnick's investigation consisted solely of speaking to Maas's accusers. He interviewed no witnesses to the events alleged in the women's complaints, and he made no effort to examine any physical evidence that might corroborate or disprove the allegations. Despite that, Kramnick forwarded the complaints to the ethics committee on May 31, 1994, with a cover letter (also sent to the complainants) asserting not only that the accusers' claims "have merit," but that "[Maas] has engaged in unethical behavior." He called on the ethics committee to recommend to the dean appropriate sanctions. For Maas and his attorneys, "Kramnick's letter . . . infected and prejudiced the subsequent hearings." The university responded to Maas's lawsuit with a motion to dismiss it on legal grounds and has not yet answered his factual claims.

In real trials, witnesses usually are not permitted to hear one another testify. At the ethics committee hearing, the four complainants were all heard at the same time. According to Maas's complaint, the committee had no rules for the admission of evidence, permitted as many as four cross-examinations of Maas and his witnesses to occur simultaneously, and made factual findings and determinations based upon evidence not presented before it and which Maas never had the opportunity to rebut. Even though the ethics committee had apparently rejected all of the most serious claims of physical sexual harassment, it nevertheless found Maas guilty, without citing any specific incident to support that finding, and without indicating what burden of proof (if any) it had applied. Whatever the truth of this case, sexual harassment in general had become a charge so heinous that even innocence is no longer a viable defense. Cornell itself, having promised Maas confidentiality for his participation in this system (although it was not voluntary participation) even issued a press release, on June 23, 1995, describing the allegations against Maas and the findings of the ethics committee. The administration formally accepted those findings.

As noted, Maas sued Cornell, and Cornell filed a motion to dismiss the entire suit against it—irrespective of the truth of Maas's allegations of Cornell's procedural improprieties—which would have prevented both discovery and the need to defend its procedures in open court. On November 15, 1996, New York State trial court judge Phillip R. Rumsey denied Cornell's motion to dismiss Maas's lawsuit entirely, allowing two essential negligence claims to stand. The Center for Individual Rights stated in a press release that day, "Cornell Now Must Answer." In March 1998, however, Rumsey dismissed the two remaining charges. Maas vowed to appeal. Perhaps Cornell will have to answer, perhaps not.[7]

Many universities, nonetheless, will have to answer. To appreciate fully both the reckless disregard at universities for due process and the current craze of preposterous academic sexual harassment charges, readers should study the full sworn testimony and documents disclosed in the case of *Gretzinger v. Lamb . . . and Lamb v. Gretzinger.* This case, decided in August 1996 by a jury of the U.S. District Court for the District of Hawaii, is a King Tut's tomb of political correctness.[8]

Ramdas Lamb, in February 1993, was a professor of anthropology and religion at the University of Hawaii. His courses were extremely popular, above all because they had a reputation for airing all sides of controversial issues. When discussion that year touched on "sexual harassment," however, three women were particularly offended when classmates and Lamb (who always offered counterarguments to speakers' claims) presented challenges to their views. Indeed, other students complained that the three prevented an open discussion.

The three aggrieved women, however, went to a University Sexual Harassment officer and formally complained that Lamb had created a "hostile environment." In addition to the claims based on the recent classroom incident, the women also charged Lamb with sexual extortion throughout the entire prior year—scholarships for sexual favors. Two months later, one of the three students, Michelle Gretzinger, added another claim. Lamb, she now charged, six months before the classroom incident, had forced her to have sexual relations with him over the course of several weeks, including multiple rapes within a few days.

These were dreadful charges that Lamb was now facing. University statutes require the Affirmative Action Office to complete a preliminary inquiry within a month; the office took half a year. In the course of that inquiry, hearings were held, but Lamb was not permitted to cross-examine his accusers or to call witnesses. According to university statutes, the Affirmative Action Office reports its findings to the senior vice president, who issues a ruling within ten days. The senior vice president, however, initiated his own investigation, which lasted months. According to the university's own rules, the adjudication of the case, from beginning to end, must not take longer than eighty days. Ramdas Lamb had to live through this nightmare for thirteen months, during which time he was relieved of the right to advise students and grade papers. A set of offices worked to aid his accusers. He also was the object of virulent campus demonstrations.

Finally, the vice president ruled that Lamb's classroom behavior was appropriate, and that the charges of sexual extortion, sexual relations, and rape were internally inconsistent and unsupported by any corroborating witnesses or evidence. Michelle Gretzinger now sued both Lamb and the university. The university reached an out-of-court settlement with her (a total abandonment of the exonerated Lamb), and Lamb countersued Gretzinger. The case went to a jury trial in federal district court.

The transcript reveals the kinds of charges and testimony that led to Lamb's enduring thirteen months of hearings and personal suffering at the university. Under cross-examination, Gretzinger stated that night after night she had admitted Lamb to her building by a security entrance that could be opened only from the inside (she had to explain why no one ever saw Lamb in the lobbied, monitored building), and that night after night she took him to her apartment, and that night after night he raped her. Then she decided to take his class, was offended by the "hostile environment" of his course, and brought charges against him.

Gretzinger reported more rapes after classes than there had been classes. She claimed that one rape occurred after class on September 7, 1992, but that was Labor Day, and there was no class. She claimed that another rape occurred after class on September 11, but that was the day that Hurricane Iniki had closed the campus. Her story was a tissue of inconsistencies and absurdities; Lamb's account was consistent and corroborated, as it always had been. The trial lasted two weeks (compared to the thirteen months at the university). A jury of four men and four women decided the case in about fifteen minutes, in favor of Lamb and against Gretzinger.

Lamb's attorney, Tony Gill, talked to the jurors afterward. They said they were unanimous on the first poll, and could have reached their verdict in one minute. The jury formally ruled that Gretzinger had defamed Lamb and placed him in a false light before the public; that she had abused the legal process by prosecuting such a flimsy, unbelievable lawsuit; that she had knowingly inflicted emotional distress on Lamb; that she had engaged in "wanton . . . willful misconduct . . . with reckless indifference to the consequences of her misconduct." It awarded Lamb one hundred thirty-three thousand dollars in general, special, and—above all—punitive damages.

(Gretzinger made out well enough, however, because the university had set-tled its case with her for one hundred seventy-five thousand dollars.[9]) Lamb currently is suing the University of Hawaii itself for deprivation of due process. At least it finally did acquit Lamb. Not every academic wrongly ac-cused of sexual harassment is so fortunate.

With faculty routinely denied even minimal due process, students expect yet less, and as the codes and cases in this book testify, that is what they receive. It is bad enough when students must confront campus judicial systems that lack adequate due process. Sometimes, however, they do not come under the protection of even that very leaky umbrella. Thus, residence advisers (RAs) almost invariably are subject to purely administrative sanctions by the often partisan residence offices for which they work. Recall the firing of RAs for failure to endorse "multicultural" opinions to which they had religious ob-jections. When faced with solely administrative proceedings, students truly have almost nowhere to turn for justice. There are many cases of this sort, but we know one of them intimately, because the student turned to us for help. It is illustrative of what can pass for "due process" at our colleges and universities.

Tim Monaco was a political science graduate student at Penn.[10] As an undergraduate at Case Western Reserve, he had risen from RA to head RA for an entire dorm. Admitted to Penn in the late 1980s, he interviewed for a position as head RA of a high-rise dormitory. The only question asked of a private nature concerned his attitude toward homosexuals, and he replied that he took all people as they were. Given his ideal prior experience, he got the position.

Tim was a conservative Republican, perhaps the only head RA of such a stripe. He found Penn's RA training intrusive and politically partisan, but he enjoyed working with students, liked the job and its benefits, and gener-ally kept his conservative personal beliefs to himself. Tim had first sought Kors's advice in the spring of 1992. One of his desk workers had cursed at him when he criticized her. He had flung her curse back at her, and she had complained. The Division of Residential Life wanted him to apologize to her. Convinced that in his position of authority he was bound to a higher standard, he apologized.

In January 1993, Tim had gone to what should have been a routine, weekly one-on-one meeting with his immediate supervisor, Tomas Leal. In-stead, Gigi Simeone, the director of residential living, also was waiting for him, and she informed him orally that he was under investigation for sexual harassment of an undergraduate coworker. Tim was flabbergasted. If anything, he believed, he had been the object of unwanted attention from this undergraduate assistant, to which he had responded with professional behavior. He had saved, for his protection, giant hearts pinned to his door, flattering notes, and diverse offbeat messages. He immediately thought of a large number of eyewitnesses to her invitations to drinks or dinner and to their interactions at these. Indeed, she had left many messages on his answering machine, and since he also saved answering machine tapes (a record, for a head RA, of emergency calls and appropriate or inappropriate responses from staff), he had those as well.

A charge of sexual harassment could have been referred to the Judicial Office, which at least requires written charges and specified rules of procedure. Simeone, however, had decided to handle this as an administrative matter within the Office of Residential Living. She declined to put any charges in writing. She asked for evidence "of his innocence" so that she could decide.

Tim's problems with the Residence Office had been foreshadowed by events at the training session for head RAs that fall. Seated around a table, they had to state what made them "different," and "how that made them feel." Tim was the last to speak, by which time everyone had carved out remarkable minority niches for themselves. He emerged from the conservative closet for the first time: "My name is Tim. I'm a white, male, heterosexual, and a Republican, and oddly enough, I provide a large degree of diversity to this group." Everyone else's self-presentation had led to lively discussion, but Tim's produced silence and a quick "OK, let's move on to the next item" from the "facilitator." Tim did not believe that he now would be treated fairly. Further, a friend in the Residential Living Office told him that they already were making plans to replace him.

Tim decided not to turn over any evidence until Simeone put specific charges in writing, because, otherwise, Penn could change dates and charges in light of his evidence. On January 18, Tim wrote to Simeone, with copies to Penn's highest administrators, expressing his concern that "a charge of sexual harassment has been made against me" in front of a third party, and requesting "either a letter of apology or the specifics of these false and malicious charges in writing . . . [and] a copy of the procedures under which [they] will be adjudicated."

This letter unanswered, he wrote again to Simeone on January 25 (with the same copies), repeating his requests, and adding that "sources in residence, all of them subject to subpoena and testimony under oath . . . have heard you speak of this matter." On January 26, Simeone replied. She charged now that his employee of the prior spring never had received a letter of apology, and she reiterated the general sexual harassment charge that she had presented orally to him. No specific charges were put in writing. As for the means of adjudicating the case, she informed him that "Tomas Leal [assistance dean of residence] and I will be conducting an investigation of these charges, and will determine an appropriate resolution. Please provide me with the names of any witnesses on your behalf who have direct knowledge of your interactions with the staff member in question." In short, Monaco had to prove himself innocent, without a hearing, of unspecified acts.

A few days later, Tim's father suddenly died. He wrote again to Simeone (copied once more to the officers of a university that proclaimed its great sensitivity), begging for the chance to resolve this case fairly. He expressed concern that his accuser continued to contact him: "I have preserved the recent, warm message left on my answering machine by my alleged accuser." He requested, yet again, specification of charges and procedures. Indicating more knowledge of residential living than Simeone knew he had, he specifically asked about "when Zoila Airall . . . met with my alleged accuser," the role of other residential officers in his case, and meetings that had been held to deal with his situation. In conclusion, Tim informed them of his father's death: "I am leaving now for the funeral of my father. Human life . . . is not a game. I expect decency and fairness from you and your office."

Seventeen days later, Simeone replied, without a single word of condolence or sympathy. She repeated that she had said everything that she was going to say at the unexpected meeting of early January. Tim should give them all of his "evidence." As for procedures, "Tomas and I are conducting our investigation. . . . We will meet with you to discuss our findings thereafter."

Tim wrote back to Simeone on March 4, begging for a set of specific charges and evidence to be used against him, "so that I can proceed to defend myself and get a step closer to bringing this outrageous—indeed debilitating—nightmare to a speedy close." He told her that there had been no clear specification of charges during her rambling talk with him on January 15, but continued, "If you know what the charges and evidence are, and if indeed you gave me the information orally, surely it is not beyond your ability to put them in writing." He requested "a public forum" in which to adjudicate all of these "libelous claims" and to try his own counterclaims as well. He received no reply.

Shortly after, Tim indirectly informed the Office of General Counsel and President Hackney that he would sue, not the university, but all individuals involved in the case, including high administrators. He communicated that he had no thought of a constitutional case, but of simple tort charges filed in local court, such as "intentional infliction of emotional distress," "libel and slander" if he were found guilty by a "kangaroo court," and "intentional interference with advantageous business relationships." Indeed, Tim let the attorney who had vetted all of Simeone's letters know, by showing how unfair Penn's procedures were and by showing the response to his father's death, he even could prove malice. All he wanted were charges in writing and a set of appropriate procedures.

The next day, Stephen Steinberg, Hackney's assistant, instructed another assistant to the president to look into the case, writing to Kors that "I have alerted her to the concern for due process." One week later, without ever having submitted one piece of evidence to this Star Chamber, Monaco received a letter from Simeone: "Tomas Leal and I have completed an investigation into performance issues referred to in our letter dated 22 January 1993." On his alleged failure to apologize to an employee the prior spring, they found that the letter of apology indeed had been sent and received. On the charge of sexual harassment, she wrote, "We conclude that there is no reasonable cause to believe you violated our sexual harassment policy," and she warned him to be "mindful of the University's policy prohibiting unlawful retaliation." The attorney from the general counsel's office called Kors to say, "See, the system works." The system most assuredly does not work for most students—only for some of those, it seems, who threaten to sue.

Under "administrative" action, a university may not only avoid having to specify charges, but it even may refuse to receive evidence. Julia Spragg is an outspoken conservative student at San Diego State University (SDSU) and an activist in the Republican Party.[11] She outraged many students at this politicized campus by her participation in the campaign to ban preferences in university admissions in California. She had debated frequently with students in her dormitory, including members of La Raza, a militant group with views similar to those of *Voz Fronteriza,* some of whom denounced her (for she was of Hispanic descent) as a "race traitor."

As reported by the *California Review,* in December 1996 Spragg received a phone call at 2:00 A.M. from her RA, who said that he wanted to discuss her "drug use," having received a complaint against her from a dormitory resident. Spragg asked for any specific charges that she ever had used drugs, for a hearing, and for specification of what due process she would enjoy. According to Spragg, she was told that her conversation with her RA constituted her "due process." The next day, Spragg spoke with Susan Shuckett, SDSU's co-ordinator for residential education, who reportedly said that *their* conversation constituted "due process," and that she should enroll in a drug counseling program. Spragg was scheduled to be evicted from SDSU housing.

Spragg immediately went to the SDSU Corning Clinical Laboratories, received a wholly negative drug test, and submitted the laboratory's finding to all of the relevant administrative staff, which changed nothing. She ap-pealed to the SDSU administration for a genuine hearing and informed the media of her plight. Rick Moore, director of university communication, re-assured inquirers that she would not be evicted immediately. "This is an ad-ministrative fact-finding process," he explained. "There is to be no hearing until later." The hearing itself, however, will be held not by any judicial sys-tem, but by the Housing Office itself, in a closed session. SDSU will not have to prove any charges against Spragg; Spragg must show why she should not be evicted.

How does this lack of due process affect lives? Wherever possible, we will try to shield the names of students, but we have documentary evidence for all of the cases described. At Bates College, in Maine, in the spring of 1994, a white male student, whose two closest friends on campus were black, was charged with sexual harassment, racial harassment, and diversion of secu-rity.[12] He and a black friend played frequent practical jokes on each other, the goal of which was to get the other in hot water. The white student, alone in his black friend's room, knew that all calls to the dormitory's front desk in-dicated the room from which the call occurred. He called downstairs, cursed at the receptionist, and left his friend's room. The incident seems to have been an innocent if foolish prank, involving no malice whatsoever. It could have been settled with an apology, which the student repeatedly tried to offer. The receptionist, however, a black female student, did not find the in-cident at all amusing, and she let people know that. Faced with demonstra-tions by about one hundred angry students from three minority organizations, the college decided to try the offender. Let us focus solely on issues of procedure.

The day after the incident that led to the charges, there was a previously scheduled meeting to deal with prejudice on campus. The student and his two black friends went to the meeting, to explain the incident and its lack of racism and to apologize for any offense given. However, many members of a black organization (AMANDLA!) bitterly denounced the student's racism and his black friends' "sell out." Within days, AMANDLA! demanded the student's expulsion.

Twelve days later, the student faced the Conduct Committee, composed of five students, five faculty, and a faculty chair. Two of the students were members of AMANDLA!. One of those had denounced him at that rally, and now served on the committee for the first two-and-a-half hours of the hearing before resigning in response to the student's protest. According to a chronology of events prepared by the accused student, between the incident and the hearing two public forums were held at which the school's policy toward sexual harassment was discussed, and where his case (although not his name) was mentioned. The first forum was held by the president of Bates, Donald Harward—the person to whom the student would have to appeal any verdict and punishment. The second forum was held by the dean of students and the dean of admissions—the individuals who had to present "information," impartially, to the Conduct Committee. (In a later letter to President Harward, the student diplomatically noted his certainty that the forums were intended only to lessen tension on campus, but he also contended that they influenced the panel's ultimate decision.)

The hearing was held on the night of March 23. The student could not have a lawyer present, and there was neither tape nor transcript of the proceedings. He pleaded guilty to the act, and was permitted to present two material witnesses and one character witness. After convening privately to find him guilty, the committee summoned him for sentencing and asked if he had anything else in his "record." In fact, an earlier, minor flap with another student had led the dean of students to send him a letter of advice in response to the incident. This was distinct from what is known at Bates as an official "Letter of Censure." At sentencing, however, without any chance for the student to present evidence or witnesses about this event, another dean testified, "It's a letter; it can be taken as Letter of Censure. It's a letter." The student was expelled.

He appealed to a five-person administrative and faculty committee (that included the president and the dean of faculty). They reduced his sentence to three semesters of suspension, after which he could reapply for admission, if, as President Harward notified him on April 1, 1994, he also provided "evidence that his behavior and attitudes are altered."

In a real court of law, what reliefs are available to someone who believes himself or herself the victim of unjust deprivations of due process? First, the legal proceeding is public; in this case, however, the hearing was closed. Second, there is a transcript, a public record, to present to the world and to higher courts; in this case, there was no public record. Third, there is the right of appeal to an impartial tribunal; in this case, as so often at universities, the appeal was to a committee that included an individual who, in response to the crisis, had reiterated his opposition to what the student was alleged to have done. As the student wrote to President Harward in his appeal, whatever definition the college gave to "due process," surely it meant "that judgments be rendered by fact finders and judges who are not parties to the dispute, have no vested interest in its outcome, and who assess the issues of liability and penalty objectively."

Due process is absent from most student judicial proceedings, whether in harassment or other cases. The Student Judiciary Board at Wesleyan University is typical: it deliberates in secret, provides no explanation of why or how it reached its decision, and assigns punishments without any regard to uniform sentencing. In 1992, a professor accused a Wesleyan student of stealing her wallet. Since her only evidence was that the student had been seen in the women's locker room, the local police dropped the investigation. Before the Student Judiciary Board, however, the student was convicted on such nonevidence alone, and, just a few weeks before graduation, was suspended for one full academic year. The professor, upon reflection, recanted her testimony, however, and the sentence was overturned.[13] After this story was reported in the *Wall Street Journal,* Krishna Winston, acting dean of the college at Wesleyan, protested in a letter to the editor that the safeguards in the judicial system were, in fact, many: the Student Judicial Board "meets with the dean of the college and a faculty adviser present, and members of the faculty and administration often serve as counselors to both the accused and the complainant." In addition, "The President retains final authority."[14] For whom is that reassuring?

In spring 1993, the Yale Executive Committee expelled a student for rape. Rape is as serious a charge, short of murder, as can be made, and the adjudication of such an accusation requires the fullest legal protections. The Yale defendant, however, could not question his accuser, nor even hear her testimony. This student and many in his situation now are suing universities, on the ground that it is unthinkable that someone should be tried for rape by tribunals that do not provide even the most minimal safeguards of due process.[15]

This scandal is slowly attracting national attention, but not enough to make academics actually mend their ways. In 1994, the *New York Times* reported on a series of abuses of due process. A student at Vassar, accused of leaving a vicious message on a fellow student's answering machine, was tried by the college's Judicial Board. He was not permitted an attorney; he was not allowed to present evidence that his accuser had accused someone else of the act; two witnesses against him were never identified, a third witness having presented their "testimony" (in the law, "unreliable hearsay"). Vassar would not even permit a voice analysis of the answering-machine tape. He told the *Times:* "It's like something from the Middle Ages."[16]

Deborah Leavy, of the Pennsylvania ACLU, told the *Times* that "these boards have a potential to turn into 'Lord of the Flies.'" She said of due process: "These are not nice formalities we're talking about. They were developed over hundreds of years because they get at the truth." Administrators refused to discuss any specific cases with the *Times,* but, in a bit of understatement, "they confirmed that their judicial systems did not always abide by due process." Sue Wise, a New Haven lawyer, represented a Wesleyan student expelled by campus tribunals for a crime of which he was acquitted in a criminal court under appropriate rules of evidence. She noted: "The people running these [campus] hearings often don't weed out what's irrelevant from the real evidence, and they don't discern innuendo and rumor from knowledge." Stephen Blum, then the JIO at Penn, told the *Times,* "The rules of evidence and courtroom procedures often favor gamesmanship more than an impartial finding of fact."[17] That is the prevailing campus attitude toward "rules of evidence" and "due process."

In May 1996, Nina Bernstein wrote a series for the *New York Times* called "Offstage Justice," about the moral cost of closed hearings and the lack of due process at academic tribunals. She surveyed "confidential case files, police records, civil litigation," and conducted more than two hundred interviews at a range of institutions across the spectrum of higher education. She noted that plaintiffs and defendants alike were seriously harmed by cases that "vanished into a separate judicial world so secret that many Americans are unaware that it operates behind closed doors at most of the nation's 3,600 colleges and universities." She detected "a pattern of campus injustice" in this "parallel judicial universe where offenses as serious as arson and rape can be disposed of discreetly under the same student conduct codes that forbid sneaking into a university dance without a ticket." She noted that so many cases "are directly funneled to college judicial administrators by student resident assistants, who get free rooms or tuition discounts for serving as the enforcers of dormitory life." For Bernstein, this unaccountable and irrational "fourth judicial branch" was destructive for both plaintiffs and defendants.[18]

In one instance, at Salem State College, "a recent student rape trial ran for 11 hours, until 1:00 A.M., with no rules of evidence." She wrote of "prosecutors and police officers" for whom "campus proceedings . . . have destroyed viable cases." When she asked a Harvard Medical School administrator why an allegation of rape had not been referred to the police and the criminal justice system for proper adjudication, the former dean of students, "astonished," replied to her: "Oh, no, absolutely not. This was an in-house sort of an accusation." Zealots who approve the current results of flawed procedures should think beyond the cases closest to their hearts. Bernstein understood the matter full well: the same system that sacrifices a defendant to ideology today will sacrifice a plaintiff to the public relations needs of a football team tomorrow.[19]

Even before a hearing, students frequently are denied due process. In November 1996, a student at the University of Pennsylvania Medical School was charged by a classmate with "acquaintance rape." Before a hearing date was set, the plaintiff spoke of the case to a meeting of the Women's Medical Student Association, whose members held a sit-in at an academic building. The medical school resolved the confrontation by barring the accused student from all classes, to prevent, in its words, "a potential crisis of order." Penn Medical School spokeswoman Rebecca Harmon told the *Philadelphia Inquirer* that the ban from classes "implies no judgment of guilt," but was made "to restore a sense of normalcy." Gail Morrisson, the medical school's vice dean for education, broke all written policy by addressing the sit-in about the particular case. "Under normal circumstances we would not discuss an individual case," she explained to them, "but order has been disrupted." She informed them that "the accused student has not admitted guilt" (in fact, he denied the charge categorically), but explained that Penn would make crisis counselors and psychiatrists available to students experiencing stress. Ilene Rosenstein, one of the counselors thus assigned, said, "When someone is harmed or feels pain it sometimes trickles out to all of us."[20]

Attorneys who experience these kinds of proceedings are dumbfounded by what passes for "fairness" on our campuses. In January 1994, Allentown lawyer Donald P. Russo wrote an op-ed in the *Philadelphia Inquirer* about his experience representing a student prosecuted by a local private university for saying of his girlfriend, "She gets me so mad, I could strangle her." The university's Judicial Inquiry Board found him guilty of "verbal abuse," and he was placed on two years of disciplinary probation. What astonished the attorney (beyond the criminalization of such common hyperbole) were what he discovered to be the commonplace procedures of academic life: no legal counsel; no confrontation with one's accuser; no cross-examination; the admission of hearsay evidence; and appeal only to a college president. As he noted, any first-year law student would reject such procedures as fatally flawed in the pursuit of justice, and faculty defending such procedures, "who undoubtedly view themselves as enlightened progressives, are engendering a roughshod style of 'kangaroo-court' justice that would make a 1950s Southern sheriff blush."[21] The problem, of course, is that the universities of today and the stereotypic Southern sheriffs of the 1950s indeed have something essential in common. They both believe that what Penn's Blum called "rules of evidence" and "courtroom procedure" interfere with their more important social goals.

CHAPTER 13

"NOT ON MY WATCH"

At first glance, one might think that the war against liberty on our campuses is led by ideological fanatics. In some instances, this is doubtless the case, particularly when faculty members take up the charge. However, it is often not true of administrators. Real zealots, after all, do not leave their institutions at the mere drop of a better offer to work elsewhere for higher compensation or greater prestige. Testifying before Congress in confirmation hearings, they do not abandon their prior principles merely to get a governmental job. They do not devote their waking hours to pursuing and maintaining high corporate salaries and perquisites, and the image, above all else, of managerial competence.

In the mid-1980s, Thomas Erlich, the provost of the University of Pennsylvania, certainly appeared to be an ideological zealot. His moral commitments looked passionate, and both faculty and students seemed afraid of him. He applied for and won the post of chancellor of Indiana University. His basketball coach, Bobby Knight, said, in a wretched observation, that stress was like rape—one could only lie back and try to enjoy it. If someone at Penn had said that, Erlich would have been the wrath of justice and the spirit of reeducation personified. At Indiana, Erlich began to call Bobby Knight to task. Knight, however, was a revered figure at Indiana, the man who delivered championships and glory. Alumni organized in Knight's defense, and state legislators rushed to defend him. Erlich, whose career suddenly was in peril, backed down. Careerism triumphed.[1]

Do most administrators actually believe that speech codes, unequal rights, selective enforcement, denial of due process, and intrusion upon private conscience serve progressive causes? Perhaps, or perhaps some simply believe that peace and quiet on their campuses depend upon curtailing unrestrained dialogue among feisty students. In any event, it is doubtful that many administrators, whether they support such intrusions upon liberty for ideological or for practical reasons, would sacrifice their careers for such principles. The ideology of administrators does not account for what has occurred on American campuses. It certainly helps the authentic ideological zealots, greatly, to have the sympathy of administrators. Such sympathy, however, is not necessary. Self-serving spinelessness, not ideology, is what has led to the current catastrophe in our universities. Authentic campus zealots naturally bear witness to their values—as is their right. The question is: Why will administrators do almost anything to appease them?

The primary goal of modern academic administrators is to buy peace during their tenure and to preserve the appearance of competence *on their watch*—an appearance essential to their careers. Administrators ask one question above all: Who can disrupt my campus and tarnish my reputation? Two things have made the threat to their careers primary to administrators (until scrutiny of recent absurdities made them marginally more sensitive to public perceptions): the memory of the 1960s, and the willingness of militants of the cultural Left to disrupt a university.

The '60s left one haunting image in the memory of academics: angry groups shut down or paralyzed universities, revealing high administrators as weak, afraid, and, the worst of all sins, incompetent. Paralyzing general strikes occurred. Administrators knew themselves to be no longer the masters of events. Students may have changed categorically since then, but the pictures and recollections of those days remain etched in the souls of universities and of the individuals who run them. Administrators acutely sense potentially disruptive anger, and are pathologically phobic about militant radicals. There is a phrase of the '60s, once used with passion, that still surfaces rhetorically at moments of crisis: "by any means necessary." It strikes a deep chord, and its explicit, implicit, or imagined threat rivets and moves presidents, provosts, deans, general counsels, and the legion of associate-and-vice-everythings.

It is not a complex formula. Republicans, moderates, evangelicals, assimilationist blacks or Hispanics, and devout Catholics don't occupy buildings or cause disruptions that will bring the media to campus. The improbable cry "the Lutherans are really mad" will not send administrators into panic. Administrative attention, thus, goes to the grievances of those who might occupy buildings, disrupt the campus, and attract the media. Individualists do not frighten administrators. The self-appointed militants who claim to speak on behalf of all blacks, Hispanics, gays, lesbians, and feminist women do frighten them. Thus, the administrative imperative: appease the militant leaders of potentially disruptive groups. Indeed, anticipate their needs. Give control over the entire apparatus of the symbolic and judicial university in loco parentis to individuals and groups acceptable to those militants, and hope that it increases the chances of their leaving the rest of your domain alone. It has been, until now, the safest course to follow.

In 1984—a mere coincidence, to be sure—the Massachusetts Institute of Technology (MIT) proposed a systematic prior censorship of movies in an effort to mold the sexual attitudes of its undergraduates. Such censorship, the administration argued, would make the campus a more genial place for women. In contrast to more traditional censorship, which establishes broad categories of prohibited speech (e.g., "obscenity") and punishes offenders after the fact, "prior restraint" prohibits material *in advance* of its expression or distribution. With traditional censorship, the public has an opportunity to hear (or see) the banned expression, even though the speaker may be subject to later punishment. With prior restraint, the offending speech never sees the light of day. It is considered, therefore, the most serious form of censorship, and the Supreme Court has deemed government use of it presumptively unconstitutional.

The year 1984, however, was a time when there was great acclaim and job security to be had by innovations in the struggle against sexism. The MIT administration jumped on that bandwagon by forbidding all forms of expression perceived to be "demeaning" to women. After a two-year delay, the administration's first attack was on the student MIT Lecture Series Committee's tacky (but popular) tradition of showing a sexually explicit movie on registration day each semester. MIT promulgated the following policy in 1986: "No x-rated or unrated sexually explicit film can be shown without prior review by [a] committee [composed of students, faculty and staff], except as described below." The policy explained, "If any group or individual decides to show a film which the Screening Committee finds does not meet its criteria, . . . the film may not be shown on Registration Day . . . [and] may not be shown in Kresge Auditorium [because it] is in close proximity to many of the dormitories." Further, it said, "Any group or individual planning to show a sexually explicit film must notify the Office of the Dean for Student Affairs (ODSA) of this intent at least six weeks prior to the proposed showing date."

The policy implemented "review guidelines" to distinguish art from smut and reflected a remarkable attempt to define and govern the most intimate human expressions for MIT students:

1) The film should reflect believable reality or normalcy in the relationships and sexuality displayed;

2) The sexuality portrayed should not be objectified as being separate from the individuals involved;

3) The sexually explicit content and the emotional content should not unfairly reflect the viewpoint and the sexual feelings of men and/or women; and

4) The films should generally promote a positive attitude toward sexuality.[2]

As should have been obvious to anyone familiar with American, much less many foreign films, a huge swath of cinematic fare was excluded, particularly by points 3 and 4. More fundamental, perhaps, was the obvious and clumsy attempt to mold "positive attitudes."

In order to test the validity of these regulations, Adam Dershowitz (the nephew of Harvard law professor Alan Dershowitz) posted an open invitation to attend a screening of *Deep Throat* on registration day, spring 1987. He chose the film, he assured MIT, precisely because it already had been judicially determined to be nonobscene under the city of Cambridge's "contemporary community standards." He was testing whether a movie that could be shown in any movie house in the city would be banned from an academic campus within that city.

In direct violation of the MIT policy, Dershowitz showed the film on registration day without giving the required prior notification to the Screening Committee. In response, Associate Dean for Student Affairs James Tewhey formally charged him with violation of MIT's prior censorship rule. This brought Dershowitz before the Committee on Discipline (COD), a student-faculty body that was the highest disciplinary authority on campus.

Almost nine months after the showing of *Deep Throat,* the COD tried Dershowitz for violation of the "Policy Statement on Sexually Explicit Films." He defended himself with the guidance of noted civil libertarian (and MIT faculty member) Louis Menand, and he was further advised by three attorneys experienced in free speech law, including his uncle from Harvard Law School, and Harvey Silverglate, who was counsel from the Massachusetts ACLU in this case. Dershowitz requested a public hearing, which was refused, but an official tape-recording was made of the closed hearing (a practice that MIT soon would change).[3] Dean Tewhey testified as the prosecution witness. Asked for the basis of his view that *Deep Throat* violated MIT's film censorship policy, Tewhey stated that he was totally opposed to movies "where women are used as objects to be exploited." Films that are "degrading [to] other human beings" are forbidden, he said. Peppered with questions about the free speech aspects of the case, he responded that this was not an issue of freedom of speech, but, rather, one "of power," namely, the power that pornography gave men over women.

Adam's uncle, Alan Dershowitz, testified as an "expert witness" about free speech. A student reporter for the *Tech* testified that only willing students had attended the screening. A female student, the president of East Campus, testified that she had attended the screening, felt neither offended nor degraded, saw no one at the screening who was under coercion to be there, and heard not a single complaint about the screening from anyone. The unanimous faculty-student COD's decision, issued on November 18, 1987, was a rude awakening for the administration:

> The MIT Policy Statement on Sexually Explicit Films constitutes an excessive restraint on freedom of expression at MIT. This freedom is fundamental to the broader principle of academic freedom and cannot be unduly abridged by administrative action. The Policy is, therefore, inappropriate for MIT. . . . By unanimous vote, the Committee thereby dismisses the charges against you. As to the concerns that led to the formulation of the Policy Statement on Sexually Explicit Films, the Committee urges the MIT community to engage in a renewed vigorous debate to address these concerns.[4]

The COD sent a copy of this decision to MIT's then-president, Paul E. Gray and to Associate Dean Tewhey. This decision was the institutional equivalent of the U.S. Supreme Court's declaring a statute unconstitutional on free speech grounds. At MIT, however, the executive authority treated its own formally recognized judicial system with contempt, despite a unanimous decision by the very faculty-student committee to which the administration itself had referred the case. The COD had called for an appropriate educational response: "a renewed vigorous debate" about the substantive issue, the treatment of women in film. Convinced, however, that to get at "sexism" and other evils, MIT should be governed, censored, and disciplined by administrators, whatever its stated procedures, the administration would not rescind its policy. Students with strong beliefs about their right to make their own aesthetic decisions do not cause problems; accusations of "sexism" do.

In the fall of his senior year, Adam Dershowitz wrote to Associate Dean Tewhey and others about MIT's failure to rescind the policy. If the policy

were over, so were his film-showing days, he told them, but if the administration still intended to enforce it, he would be showing *Deep Throat* once
again on registration day without consulting the Screening Committee.
Shirley McBay, dean for student affairs, replied by letter: "The current Institute Policy on Sexually Explicit Films remains in effect unless and until the
Academic Council decides to revise it."[5] This asserted full administrative
control. The policy had been drafted by the Office of the Dean of Student
Affairs, and the Academic Council, which promulgated it, was composed
entirely of administrators and deans. Samuel Jay Keyser, associate provost for
educational policy and programs wrote to the *Tech,* with complete disregard
for MIT's own judicial system: "This matter does not have to do with academic freedom or free speech, but with decent conduct within a diverse, pluralistic university community."[6] After unsuccessfully offering, again, not to
show the film if Keyser would recognize the COD's ruling, Dershowitz
screened it a second time.

The administration surely knew the COD would acquit Dershowitz
again, so it evaded its own judicial system and took the matter arbitrarily into
its own hands, inflicting summary punishment. Keyser wrote to Dershowitz:

> I am writing directly to you in my capacity as Associate Provost to repri-
> mand you for having violated Institute policy with respect to pornographic
> films and to inform you that this letter of reprimand will be made a part of
> your educational records at the Institute and will remain there for at least
> two years or until you graduate from the Institute, whichever occurs first.
> Placing this letter into your file is a serious matter.[7]

Dershowitz soon learned that there was no official body at MIT capable of
reviewing either the administrations's arbitrary (but presumably official) reprimand or its refusal to abide by an earlier acquittal in its own judicial system.
Silverglate, on behalf of the ACLU, wrote Keyser protesting Dershowitz's inability to present his case directly to the faculty and citing faculty rules and
regulations that gave that body the authority to formulate "educational policies and other policies" at MIT.[8] He sent copies of his letter to President
Gray, as well as to MIT's provost, John Deutch (who later became director of
the CIA). The reply, however, came not from MIT's administration, but
from MIT's outside legal counsel, Jerome N. Weinstein. By this time, Adam
had graduated, and Weinstein reported that Dean Keyser had removed the
letter, "so MIT, at least, considers the case closed."[9]

Dershowitz now sought to complain directly to MIT's governing Board
of Trustees, which presumably knew nothing of Tewhey's and Kaiser's ac-

tions. Silverglate, as Dershowitz's ACLU attorney, wrote to the new MIT president, Charles M. Vest, with copies to all of the trustees.[10] This action brought another response from Weinstein, indicating that "the subject matter of your letter will not be placed on the Corporation's agenda," and admonishing Silverglate that "as counsel to M.I.T., you [sic] should address any further communications concerning this matter to me."[11] In short, MIT invoked the rule of legal ethics that when one party is represented by legal counsel, the other party's lawyer is obliged to communicate only with the opposing party's lawyer.

This remarkable assertion—that *all* of MIT, including the trustees as individuals, was Weinstein's "client," hence unapproachable by Dershowitz's legal counsel—ensured that MIT's trustees would not receive any information about this embarrassment except what Weinstein shared with them. Combined with the secrecy of disciplinary proceedings, it permitted the administration to keep both trustees and faculty in the dark. Administrators had found an effective means of retaining unaccountability.

Shortly after being been stung by some publicity given to Dershowitz's case (and acquittal), MIT revised its judicial procedures. It removed the COD's discretion to permit student press attendance at its hearings, banned the future representation of a student by a family member (presumably in case Adam's younger sister decided to attend MIT), and forbade the tape-recording of judicial proceedings. If the administration were going to have another such battle, it would conduct it wholly secretly, and entirely on its own terms.

Life sometimes being stranger than fiction, however, the real cause of sexual scandal to MIT turned out to be not Adam Dershowitz, but, ironically, Dean Tewhey himself. Tewhey had sought the feminist moral high ground against Dershowitz before the COD. In fall 1993, however, amidst charges of sexual harassment lodged against Tewhey, MIT asked for his resignation. There ensued a circus of leaked letters, widespread press coverage, civil suits, and desperate attempts by MIT to contain the damage.[12]

Normally, Dean Tewhey's private life would be no one's legitimate concern. Indeed, the private, consensual lives of adults, including college students' lives, should be no one's business but their own. In this public case, however, watching Dean Tewhey was like watching Senator Joseph McCarthy call for due process and fairness upon being labeled a Communist spy.

As associate dean for residence and campus activities in the office of the dean for undergraduate education and student affairs, the sanctimonious Tewhey had considerable authority over sexual harassment charges at

MIT. When his own troubles became notorious in fall 1993, letters to the *Tech,* written in varying degrees of either glee or anger (or both) by those he had pursued with charges, described his high-handedness in the exercise of that power. On November 1993, alumnus Michael Miles, '90, recalled his own run-in with Tewhey.[13] A woman who frequently had trouble with neighbors had charged him and his roommate with excessive noise, a matter adjudicated by the graduate resident tutor. The woman, however, appealed to a higher administrative authority, Tewhey, who accused Miles and his roommate of "sexual harassment," although the complainant herself never had made such a charge. Tewhey threatened them with expulsion from campus housing and, Miles recalled, "was not interested in facts, he was interested in power." Tewhey attempted "to make us repeat rumors about others living in our dorm so that the dean could continue his witch hunt. . . . He refused to listen to our side no matter how hard we tried to explain it." The writer said that the administrator "has for years abused his position in knee-jerk reactions to complaints filed by women [and] called sexual harassment any complaint filed by a woman against a man." Tewhey, exclaimed Miles, was "the same man who now expects the MIT community to cry for his plight." Another alumnus, Art Mellor, '85, wrote that "I felt I had to add my . . . disgust at Tewhey's double standard of 'justice' at MIT (that he shouldn't be treated by MIT as he treated students)."[14] There were several other letters to the same effect.

Court proceedings and public documents revealed that Tewhey, who objected so vehemently to the objectification or use of women, had engaged in an eighteen-month affair with a woman who worked in the Office of Student Financial Aid. When the relationship ended in 1992, each charged the other with sexual harassment, and each eventually obtained court restraining orders against the other.[15] MIT asked for Tewhey's resignation. In his lawsuit against MIT, Tewhey publicly charged that female staffers at MIT had accused him of, among other things, having multiple affairs with undergraduate women.[16] Tewhey, in a published open letter to the MIT community, now complained: "In its effort to be 'politically correct' and to react without hesitation to any allegation that any woman makes, MIT has fostered an environment where no male is protected from the damage of a fabricated charge."[17] Tewhey had just learned about those who live by the sword.

In his open letter, this same dean, who had refused to abide by the judicial verdict in favor of Adam Dershowitz or to return the subsequent charge to the system that had earlier acquitted the accused, lashed out against arbitrary administrative power and called for fair, impartial hearings on his own

case. "I have found both the harassment policy and the grievance procedure," he noted, "to be no more than 'smoke and mirrors.'" As the MIT
Student Association for Freedom of Expression posted: "[This] has local
civil-libertarians . . . rolling on the floor, pounding the carpet through tears
of laughter, saying, 'WE TOLD YOU SO!' It's been a long-standing position
that the vague definitions of harassment and secret investigation with no accountability or due process leads [sic] to extreme politicization."[18]

One should, however, give Tewhey the same credit one gives Dershowitz
(if not the same marks for consistency). The MIT administration was willing
to sweep it all under the rug if only Tewhey would resign. Tewhey refused
and fought the matter on what he believed to be principle, although he eventually either left or was forced out, depending on whom one believes. "Not
on my watch" has a far different sound if it is oneself who is being thrown
overboard. The governance issues presented by the Dershowitz case—the administration's summary punishment of an acquitted undergraduate, and its
enforcement of a policy that an authorized faculty-student committee had
declared a violation of academic freedom—never were formally resolved.
Nonetheless, administrators do listen for the source of noise. Despite their efforts to keep the case from gaining too much attention, it had caused a minor
furor. When the movie censorship policy came up for renewal, it was quietly
abandoned.

The immeasurably better known hypocrisy of Rutgers University President
Francis L. Lawrence, however, makes Dean Tewhey's seem small potatoes.
Lawrence was the soul of political correctness. Upon becoming president of
Rutgers in 1990, he threw himself behind every "multicultural" cause in the
university system, appointing group-identity administrators and opening vast
group-identity centers. In particular, as the New York Times reported in February 1995, he was "instrumental in the passage of an anti-hate 'speech code'
on the university's three major campuses."[19] He was caught in his own web
when, in November 1994, addressing the faculty at the university's Camden
campus, he said, "Let's look at SATs. The average SAT for African-Americans is 750. Do we . . . not admit anybody with the national test? Or do we
deal with a disadvantaged population that doesn't have that genetic, hereditary background to have a higher average?"[20] The Rutgers AAUP made a
transcript of his remarks public during an impasse in union negotiations,
causing an uproar. They led to months of intense, angry, and public demonstrations; demands for his dismissal, and a headline-making protest during a
nationally televised basketball game. Lawrence, whose own code would have

come down very hard on any member of his university who had uttered those words, issued an apology that concluded, "I cannot explain a remark that said precisely the opposite of my deeply held beliefs."[21] He courted the Board of Governors and weathered the storm. On February 8, he ordered that protests cease. Reuters reported that he said of those demonstrating against him: "They've made their statements, and now no further disruptions will be appropriate."[22] The author of the speech code and all the rules proclaimed himself innocent.

A proposed harassment policy and speech code were released by the UMass administration in September 1995. When unexpected press coverage and sharp criticism from liberal sources made the administration aware that it had pushed the envelope of vagueness and oppression too far, those who had drafted the policy sought to avoid public ridicule by shifting the blame. The administration now claimed that its own nightmarish proposal was in fact the result of nearly two years of "contract negotiations" between the university and the collective-bargaining unit of its teaching graduate students, the Graduate Employee Organization (GEO). The truth, as best gleaned from press releases and public statements, media interviews of graduate student union leaders, and our own exchanges with active participants, is as follows.[23] The GEO had been organized by the United Auto Workers (UAW) as a collective-bargaining agent. When, during contract negotiations, the UMass administration chose to consult the GEO about speech provisions of its proposed harassment code, it intersected two distinct sets of graduate student interests. First, there were teaching assistants who, without reference to "harassment," long had been concerned about their authority in the classroom and were calling for means to impose limits on what they saw as challenges to that authority. Second, as often happens with organizations, the most militant members came to dominate the negotiating committee, and once the administration put its proposed harassment policy on the table, these more radical graduate students proposed to make the policy yet broader. Thus, the written negotiating position presented by the GEO in the spring of 1995 asked UMass to expand the terms of the administration's proposed policy beyond race, gender, and sexual preference, to include "citizenship, culture, HIV status, language, parental status, political affiliation or belief, and pregnancy status."[24]

When the administration presented its own policy, it included, in brackets, a modified version of the GEO's proposed broadening of the harassment policy, indicating explicitly that it believed the GEO's additions redundant. The inclusion of those brackets, however, was tactically useful, because it made the administration appear to occupy a middle ground between a militant GEO and free speech absolutists. The strategy was initially successful, and the GEO became the object of campus ridicule. The administration, at the beginning of the controversy, managed to appear above the fray, emphasizing how the proposed policy had emerged from union negotiations, and casting the GEO as the would-be censors. The GEO, however, could not escape a severe union backlash. Its parent union, the UAW, is also home to the National Writers Union, whose then-political issues committee cochair, Robert Chatelle, is the mortal enemy of all censorship. He, union activist Steve Simurda, and their union allies engaged the leadership of the GEO in intensive discussions about free speech. Before the fall semester of 1996 was over, they won over the GEO.[25] The GEO was chagrined, aware that it wrongly had been made the villain, and convinced that UMass had used it to deflect criticism of the administration's own proposed censorship.

In a press release in December 1996, the GEO stated that during contract negotiations the organization had asked for adoption of a policy protecting its members from real harassment in the workplace. The administration had responded that a university wide harassment policy was already in the works and would be in place within the next year. In turn, the GEO included in its contract a clause that if such a policy had not yet been implemented by that time, the organization would negotiate with the administration a harassment policy to cover GEO members. The GEO now expressed dismay that the discussion of this clause had become the focus of debate and that the GEO was being tarred as the initiator of a demand for punishment of student and faculty speech. James Delle, a former GEO negotiator, explained, perhaps a bit disingenuously:

> There is a widespread perception that GEO supports a comprehensive speech code. We do not and would not support a policy that limits the content of expression. However, when the time, place, and manner of that expression severely or pervasively affect an individual's ability to participate in campus life, particularly their [sic] employment, something should be done about it.[26]

Chatelle had been persuasive. The GEO, committing itself to content neutrality, apologized for the narrow-mindedness of its initial document and expressed its appreciation for and agreement with the many criticisms of that "first draft." Delle further explained that the administration now had asked the GEO to be the sole authors of any new harassment policy, but that the GEO had demurred, calling for discussion among faculty, other graduate students, and a wide array of undergraduates. As embattled Chancellor David K. Scott quipped at the beginning of the spring 1996 term: "Stay tuned."[27] However the speech code wars at UMass turn out, the events of 1995–96 ensure that the administration will have to take public responsibility for its own actions. The spotlight of publicity, and the GEO's revealing public denunciation of its scapegoating by the administration, seem likely to assist the forces of liberty on the campus. In short, the administration's calculation of how best to prevent "trouble on my watch," having failed, would have to be revised.

———

Harvard College, in 1993, was in the early stage of a massive $2.1 billion capital fund-raising campaign, its most ambitious ever. In addition, its Office of the General Counsel, which controlled the Harvard University Police Department (HUPD), was locked in contentious contract negotiations with an unruly police union that was taking advantage of every opportunity to publicize every event, particularly crimes on campus, that might embarrass the university. It was in this potent mix that Inati Ntshanga found himself.

Ntshanga, a member of the Harvard class of 1995 who came from a modest but proud South African black family, was planning to return to his country after graduation in order to participate in rejuvenating South Africa under its newly installed democratic government. He was an idealistic and courageous young man who had stood up to South Africa's racist police, which had harassed him during civil rights demonstrations.

Ntshanga had a run-in with the Harvard University Police Department one day in November 1992 when he claimed he had been picked on without cause, while the police overlooked a transgression by some white students in the vicinity. According to Ntshanga and two other witnesses, the incident resulted in his having an argument with one HUPD officer, Sgt. Kathleen Stanford, whom Ntshanga accused of harboring racist attitudes. The argument took place at HUPD headquarters, where Ntshanga had an on-campus job of dispatching vehicles operated by a campus shuttle service.

While the memory of that event still simmered on both sides, Ntshanga found himself the following month face-to-face with four HUPD officers who happened upon him while he was performing his second campus job of collecting dirty linen in a dorm basement during the Christmas vacation period. To Ntshanga's surprise, the officers asked him to produce Harvard student identification or be arrested for trespass. Ntshanga did not have his Harvard student ID card on him, but when he explained this to the officers one of them outraged him by asking if he had "a welfare card." Ntshanga's ire just began to rise over what he viewed as a racist slur when Sgt. Stanford arrived on the scene. "*She* knows me," Ntshanga told the officers, assuming that her identification of him as a student would end the incident. He reported, however, that Stanford denied that she knew he was a Harvard student and allowed the trespass arrest to proceed. He was booked on a complaint charging breaking and entering, trespass, and possession of burglary tools (the keys that he used legitimately to gain entrance to the building).

After the charges were dismissed by a county prosecutor who was startled to learn that HUPD had arrested a Harvard student for trespassing while carrying out his on-campus job, Harvey Silverglate, Ntshanga's lawyer, wrote a complaint to General Counsel Margaret H. Marshall, who coincidentally was a native of South Africa who had been active in the anti-apartheid movement during her student years and who since had made a considerable splash in Boston's legal community. (She later was appointed to the highest court in Massachusetts by Massachusetts's then-governor William Weld.) Marshall assigned the investigation to University Attorney Allan Ryan, who issued a ruling ten months later that cleared the officers, finding that none of them, including Sgt. Stanford, knew that Ntshanga was a Harvard student when they arrested him. Ryan, who found that HUPD's asking for a welfare card "is standard procedure when a person says he has no identification,"[28] cleared the officers while refusing to interview two witnesses named by Ntshanga who would have confirmed the Ntshanga-Stanford argument of a month before the arrest.

When Silverglate complained to Marshall that Ryan's "independent" investigation was a whitewash and that Ryan had refused even to speak to witnesses who would have confirmed Ntshanga's claim that the HUPD well knew he was a Harvard student and not a trespasser, Marshall brushed it off and urged Ntshanga to just "let go" of his grievance.[29] She was attentive, gracious, and respectful to Ntshanga, agreeing even to an extraordinary personal meeting with the student, but in the end she was adamantly supportive of Ryan's investigation and conclusion. A subsequent complaint to Harvard president Neil Rudenstine produced no response. An April 1995 letter to Dean John B. Fox, secretary to the faculty of arts and sciences and the Faculty Council, asking him to bring the matter to the council's attention so that an independent investigation could be conducted by the body charged with governance over student life, went unheeded.[30]

The Office of the General Counsel successfully concluded its contract negotiations with the HUPD, avoiding a strike as well as a continuation of the highly publicized tactical criticisms that the police were directing toward Harvard and the safety of the campus. Harvard's largest fund-raising campaign proceeded successfully into high gear. Marshall was confirmed for her position as a justice of the Supreme Judicial Court of Massachusetts. Ryan remained in his post at the general counsel's office. Ntshanga returned to his country with a bitter taste of what happens on an American college campus when institutional and individual agendas clash with the ideal of justice and fairness for students. Harvard's speech code, which claimed to protect blacks, among others, from offensive, demeaning, and stereotyping language, obviously was not going to be applied to the HUPD's demand that Ntshanga produce his welfare card, an insult that University Attorney Allan Ryan deemed "standard procedure" under the circumstances.

Harvard Law School Dean Robert Clark, having appointed a committee to look into the drafting of proposed "Sexual Harassment Guidelines" in the wake of the Mary Jo Frug parody episode (discussed in chapter 7), submitted the drafting committee's work product to the entire faculty for debate and, ultimately, adoption. Harvey Silverglate, having been sent a copy of the draft by a faculty member who was disturbed at the proposed guidelines' implications for academic freedom, wrote to Dean Clark to urge him to use his influence and authority to scuttle the project.[31] In response, the dean made clear that he believed himself in no position and was not disposed to take such a stand:

> Your sentiments [opposing the Guidelines] have been echoed in the faculty chambers along with many others. This discussion is a sign of the times, as is the need perceived among students that we have to discuss this or be seen as uncaring of their concerns.[32]

Suddenly, Clark's instincts as administrator appeared to have overtaken his sense of his moral responsibility to the academic freedom of his institution. When named dean in 1989, Clark brought with him a conservative reputation that led observers to believe he would seek to preserve academic integrity and freedom at an institution then rent by fierce ideological struggles and factionalism within the faculty. *The National Law Journal,* for example, reported one professor's comment calling Harvard Law School "the Beirut of legal education." It was bad enough having this image appear in the legal press, but even worse to see it picked up by *Vanity Fair* in October 1992,[33] during Clark's deanship, and then to have the image spread to other nonacademic publications.

The faculty disputes centered primarily around a split between the traditionalists and the adherents to the Critical Legal Studies school of thought (known as the "Crits"). The Crits believed that the doctrines, structures, and institutions of the legal system did not operate in an objective manner, but, rather, were manipulated by the wealthy and powerful to maintain their exalted positions at the expense of the poor and powerless. They believed that to understand how the legal system functioned, one had to examine and understand power, not rights. Their proposals to redress these imbalances cast aside traditional notions of rights and instead sought openly to reallocate power.

The Traditionalists and the Crits had been at loggerheads for years, resulting in an embarrassing interruption in faculty hiring and tenuring. Clark was determined to get the system moving again and, in general, to moderate the law school's image as a battleground. Moreover, he had launched a mammoth, $175 million law school capital fund-raising campaign, and it was not a good time to have the vicious faculty contentiousness and student demonstrations that had characterized the early years of his deanship. Clark's remark was as close as he came to confessing that "the times" required him and the faculty to do something that he, and many of his faculty colleagues, might privately have considered distasteful, maybe unprincipled, but politically expedient.

On October 25, 1995, Dean Clark notified the law school community that the Sexual Harassment Guidelines were "now officially in force." It was a little-noticed event locally or nationally. Everyone seemed content to keep it that way. However, Silverglate wrote an op-ed column about the guidelines, which was published in the *Wall Street Journal* in January 1996 and made the policy public. This column, headlined HARVARD LAW CAVES IN TO THE CENSORS,[34] provoked a blizzard of letters to the editor by faculty members, pro and con, as well as a letter by Clark himself. Mentioning nothing about the Frug parody that had certainly appeared to occasion the move to adopt a speech code, Clark attributed the need for such guidelines to the case of a student who allegedly was pressured to have sexual relations by a prospective employer. The dean did not explain why restrictions on the speech of students and faculty members were necessary to redress that kind of extortionate conduct by an outside prospective employer. He also made vague references to instances of alleged sexual harassment of students by their peers—again, without specifying whether these instances were anything more than speech deemed offensive by the listener.

However, what was most interesting about Clark's letter to the editor was his paradoxical defense of the speech restrictions. Clark claimed that the guidelines, taking up "nearly 20 single-spaced pages of text, analysis and il-lustrative examples, [were] as clear as humanly possible about what is for-bidden and what is protected" and that "they strive for clarity *in order to protect speech, not limit it.*"[35] [emphasis added] There is "ample latitude" in the guidelines, continued Clark, to permit mere "boisterousness and insen-sitivity." The notion that free speech was such an endangered species at Har-vard Law School that the choice was between official, lengthy restrictions and unpredictable censorship arising on a case-by-case basis spoke volumes about the sad state of liberty on campuses. As another faculty member, Pro-fessor David Rosenberg, somberly reminded everyone in his letter, also published in the *Journal:*

> [This] strategy of controlled self-censorship to ward off something worse . . . is depressingly familiar. In the 1950s it took the form of "red-baiting" by unions, organizations such as the ACLU, and many universities. Counted among those leading the resistance to McCarthyism in academia were Harvard Law School's Dean Erwin Griswold and former professor, then Justice Felix Frankfurter.[36]

Robert Clark was no Erwin Griswold and no Felix Frankfurter. Indeed, the whole Sexual Harassment Guidelines history might cause one to ques-tion whether, if a Griswold or a Frankfurter were to come along today, he would have the dubious qualifications needed for the deanship of Harvard Law School—a moral flexibility suitable for what Clark referred to, ruefully, as "the times."

In earlier times, college presidents and deans most often were chosen from the faculty by colleagues who admired them, and they frequently returned to the faculty after serving a five- or ten-year term. Today, higher education is burdened with a large permanent class of professional academic administra-tors who bide their time at their institutions, consult "headhunters," and await the announcement of a national presidential search conducted by a more prestigious college or university. They move interchangeably from in-stitution to institution, performing their jobs with one eye on their current campus and another on the next rung of the ladder. When they have reached a career apex in academia, they look to the leadership of some foundation or to retirement as consultant to the university.

In short, at all levels, including academic administration, our colleges and universities have taken on many of the trappings—without the accountability—of large corporations. Yet if a university is in some respects like the corporate world—large, complex, facing competition, and searching to finance increasingly more expensive undertakings—it is a very special kind of enterprise. It has at its core a sacred obligation to sponsor and encourage research, to support and nurture scholars, to effect the education of new generations of individual minds and critical spirits, to pursue knowledge and truth wherever they might lead, and to speak honestly to power. The contemporary academic administrator steps onto a delicate balance of this mission of the university, on the one hand, and the corrupting influences of career, on the other. The need for deep guiding principles is great. The motto of many academic administrators, however, is the motto of careerists everywhere—"no trouble on my watch." There is all too frequently more interest in avoiding high-profile problems than in achieving academic and intellectual greatness. One view of happiness is that it is achieved more by the presence of positive events than by the absence of negative ones. If that is true, modern-day college presidents are willing to settle merely for the absence of unhappiness, and, above all, for the absence of the discomforts that put an end to the mobility of careers.

The president of Santa Rosa Junior College, for example, could have instructed his ample legal staff to resist, in court if necessary, any effort by the Office of Civil Rights (OCR) of the U.S. Department of Education to impose a clearly unconstitutional speech code on the college's computer communications system. A court fight, however, would have entailed publicity, and the college administration would have had to explain that it was not in favor of vulgar speech but was simply honoring its obligation to preserve free speech and academic freedom. Capitulation was less risky to the careers of Santa Rosa's administrators, though far more perilous to the cause of liberty. Thus, Dean Robert Clark of Harvard Law School could have persisted in his early opposition to the calls from some members of his faculty and student body to punish political speech. National publicity, however, began to throw a spotlight on the faculty's culture wars and on the racial and gender politics of its struggles over hiring and tenure. Rather than deal with those issues courageously and in principled fashion, Clark abandoned his duty to protect the legacy of free speech that Harvard had fought so heroically to preserve during the McCarthy era. Academic freedom at Harvard Law School appears to have been sacrificed in order to avoid "trouble on my watch" as a $175 million capital fund-raising campaign commenced.

The shame is that it does not require deep courage to resist the sacrifice of liberty and legal equality for peace. There are nations in the world where a college president indeed would risk his life by standing up for academic freedom. That is not the situation in the United States today. What is required is not so much courage as dedication to liberty and legal equality supported by just a bit of backbone. The fact that our academic leaders are not up to this task is alarming. The fear of disruption, of causing offense, of being associated with controversy, linked to careerism, has produced a hollow, unprincipled cowardice.

Where are the faculties in all of this? Even on the rare occasions when a faculty momentarily says "enough" and asserts its moral authority on behalf of academic freedom and individual equality, there is no follow-up. Administrators are able to isolate, outlast, and disengage their faculties (just as they do their trustees, who get most of their information from the administration). Indeed, when faculties, or even, on occasion, administrators, do attempt to assert themselves, they are told by the omnipresent lawyers—both in the offices of general counsels and in outside law firms—that prudent "risk management" outweighs the perils of freedom. The extent to which lawyers now serve as policy officers in higher education is an untold scandal of the modern academic age. To understand better the lawyers' contribution to UMass's sorry record on academic freedom, for example, one need only examine the May 1991 article in the *Student Rights Advocate* entitled, "The First Amendment's Clash With University and College Disciplinary Codes."[37] The authors, Charles J. DiMare and Thomas Coish, are both attorneys in the administrative Student Legal Services Office at UMass–Amherst. They express their nominal loyalty "to the protection of all people's right to free speech," but they seek to repress "the use of racial, ethnic or sexual slurs, particularly when aimed at specific individuals or groups." They offer a tendentious and superficial analysis of U.S. Supreme Court precedents on speech, and they advance the doctrine that free speech principles "may in some situations appear to be in conflict with other constitutional notions." They conclude that it would be wholly constitutional to devise a "narrowly tailored" prohibition of speech. That narrow tailoring would punish speech that "is intended to insult or stigmatize an individual or small group of individuals on the basis of their race, national or ethnic origin, color, religion, gender, disability (and perhaps sexual orientation)"; that "amounts to 'fighting words' or their equivalent"; or that "increases a

'hostile (education or employment) environment' for such individuals."
They recommend "remedial education" about proper speech, holding the
adopted disciplinary policy in reserve for cases where students are resistant
to such instruction.

The acquiescence of top academic leaders to the regime of speech
codes, secret kangaroo courts, and mandatory attitude and sensitivity training, all under the close eyes of lawyers seeking to avoid legal or economic
risks and of public relations offices seeking to avoid adverse publicity, has
led to the creation of vast middle-level bureaucracies. These bureaucracies
are charged with implementation of the new world of Student Life—a
world in which selected students, if among the political elect, are to live
with neither stress, nor insult, nor unpleasantness. That world, however,
can only be achieved by police-state control, injustice, and double standards. That is what actually is happening on the watch of most of our current academic leaders.

———————

Sheldon Hackney's career is perhaps the embodiment of the "not on my
watch" concept and its resulting double standards. Hackney was heroic
against Senator Jesse Helms, who wanted to remove "offensive" art from the
public trough; that defense of "unfettered freedom" served Hackney wonderfully well in academic life. At Penn, he imposed speech codes, double
standards, and thought reform. Senator Helms could not harm Hackney's
career. Pennsylvania state legislators, however, could do much to wreck it,
because even though it is a private school, Penn is uncomfortably dependent
upon major appropriations from the Commonwealth of Pennsylvania.

In fall 1989, Professor Carolyn Marvin, a scholar who has defended
everyone's freedom and equality at Penn, was teaching a course on freedom
of expression. The Supreme Court recently had declared laws against flag
burning unconstitutional. Professor Marvin led her class into a courtyard and
burned a small American flag, after which they all engaged in critical discussion of the issues and of the views on both sides. When word of this reached
the public, the Pennsylvania State Assembly formally voted to condemn her,
and there was talk of cutting the state's subsidy to Penn. On March 20, 1990,
the *Daily Pennsylvanian* informed the campus that Penn administrators had
written to a state legislator that they "very much regret that this incident
happened."[38] There were queries from a few concerned faculty about that
communication. Two wrote an open letter published in *The Pennsylvania Almanac*, urging Hackney and Provost Michael Aiken to "stand by the right of

Professor Marvin to say whatever she pleases, even if it offends, and, indeed, even if it offends those who may threaten to cut the university's state subsidy."[39] In fact, on October 23, 1989, Hackney did write a letter to scores of members of the state House of Representatives, affirming Marvin's rights and Penn's devotion to free expression.[40] He emphasized, however, that Marvin's act was not political, but merely pedagogical: "Let me say first that Professor Marvin's action was not meant as a political statement or demonstration." He added: "Her destruction of the flag was done not as protest but as part of an academic exercise." He most certainly had not written Senator Helms similarly about the display of "Piss Christ" at Penn. Nor, in this letter, did he sound the theme he had sounded against Helms, that the mere threat of a loss of public funding categorically chilled essential freedom.

More revealing than Hackney's letter, however, which he made public to the university community, was the private letter written on his behalf to Representative Jerry L. Nailor by James E. Shada, assistant vice president for Commonwealth relations. Representative Nailor had written to Penn, on September 26, expressing his outrage over Marvin's "public flag burning." The provost's statement, he wrote, that "she 'was within her academic rights' . . . only adds to the indignity of the incident." On behalf of those killed in battle, their loved ones, and wounded veterans, he demanded "more respect than Professor Marvin's inalienable right to 'prompt a class discussion.'"[41] Universities are not often impressed by patriotic passion, but they pay attention to it when it comes from individuals whose hands control the purse strings. How did Penn respond? First, there were Nailor's views of the provost's apparent assertion of the rights of academic freedom. Shada, writing officially for the Penn administration, replied that Provost Michael Aiken was "quite disturbed" by news accounts claiming that he had said "that Marvin was within her academic rights to burn the flag." Rather, Shada explained, Aiken had said that the recent Supreme Court decision "appears" to have made Marvin's act "legal," but that "he [Aiken] personally supports laws protecting the flag." He assured "Jerry" that "the Provost was not supporting Marvin's act." Then, there was the issue of the administration's views. Shada wrote that he had met no one in the Penn administration "who does not share many of your feelings with respect to the situation." Hackney, he wrote, "is a Navy veteran, . . . Aiken . . . an Army veteran," and "we very much regret that this incident happened, and we hope that you understand our feelings about it."[42]

When Sheldon Hackney faced the U.S. Senate Committee on Labor and Human Resources on June 25, 1993, for confirmation hearings as chairman of the National Endowment for the Humanities, he faced two immediate problems, both of which had prompted diverse editorials calling for his rejection. There was the water buffalo case, and there was his equivocal response to the unpunished theft of issues of the *DP.* Now, the audience was neither Penn nor the academic world, but, rather, the U.S. Senate, the media, and the American public. At Penn, Hackney had spoken and acted repeatedly on the basis of one of his apparently deepest beliefs, namely that the nation, and Penn in particular, owed a special solicitude to historically oppressed minorities. When Senator Nancy Kassebaum asked him about political correctness on campuses, however, he replied:

> Senator, . . . it would be a serious problem if it were to capture a campus, if it were to become the orthodoxy. . . . There are various forms of political correctness . . . but I think in general one can think of it as a term that refers to being overly solicitous of the rights of minority groups and of fashionable and trendy concerns in the present. I think that is one form that could be quite worrisome because you want to have a very balanced and fair approach to things on the campus.[43]

Hackney's Penn had seen a flowering of the recent deconstructionist and postmodern schools of literary and critical analysis. Once confirmed at the NEH, Hackney would continue the NEH's tradition of funding work done from those perspectives. No one at Penn could recall a critical word that he had said about these academic outlooks. To Senator Kassebaum, however, Hackney testified: "The other form I frankly worry about a bit more is . . . an intellectual form of political correctness . . . deconstructionism and post-structuralism, a rather radical form of relativism, if you will, with the notion that every thought is a political thought and that every statement is a political statement, so there can be no objective test for truth."[44]

Senator Hatch asked Hackney about the remarkable case of Murray Dolfman. The Dolfman affair had been widely covered, in the press, in books, and even in a television documentary on PBS. Any senator or aide doing even minimal research about Hackney would have known about it, and a *Wall Street Journal* editorial of that morning had begged the Republican senators to pose questions to him about it.[45] Murray Dolfman, in fall 1984, was an adjunct professor of business law in the Wharton School at Penn. He was an idiosyncratic, eccentric, and brash teacher, of a sort quite common in a previous generation. He joked with students, corrected their grammar and pronunciation, and embarrassed them, indiscriminately, when they didn't know what he thought they should know. He taught by the Socratic method, with a string of questions trained on an individual or a set of individuals. Nat Hentoff, who wrote several articles on Dolfman and who devoted a portion of his book on free speech to him, described him accurately: "He makes demands of his students. He challenges them. He will single out a student—of whatever color or creed—and drill him in a point of law or a section of the Constitution. If you come unprepared to Dolfman's class, you are in peril."[46] On November 12, 1984, Dolfman asked his contract class why not even a signed contract in the United States could force an individual to work against his will. The class could not answer. Dolfman explained that the reason arose from the Thirteenth Amendment and asked his class to recite its terms. No one could. Exasperated, Dolfman said that Jews, "as ex-slaves," began Passover each year by celebrating their release from slavery in Egypt. "We have ex-slaves in this class," he said, pointing to four black students, "who should know about and celebrate the Thirteenth Amendment." This was terrible teaching. Students in classes are individuals, not members of a group, but it was from the heart, and it certainly was Dolfman's style. Dolfman compounded his error, exponentially, by calling on a black student to stand and read the amendment aloud several times. Almost immediately, three of the four black students came to see Dolfman in his office. They said that they had been humiliated by being singled out, called "ex-slaves," and told that they should be grateful for the end of slavery in America. Dolfman agreed with them, and he apologized. He explained that he had meant no offense and that he regretted what he had done. He acknowledged that the phrase "ex-slaves" was inappropriate, and that, at worst, he should have said "descendants of slaves." The students were not particularly mollified, but there the incident stood. Dolfman had learned a painful lesson.

Three months later, Penn was celebrating "Black History Month," and there was a major effort, from various black organizations, to encourage the university to enact a promised racial harassment policy. At a meeting, someone told the story of Dolfman's class as an example of the abuse faced by black students at Penn. Suddenly, the Dolfman affair was reborn. There were angry demonstrations in front of Hackney's campus home, calling for Dolfman's dismissal. On February 13, ninety days after the incident and his apology to the students, a group of black students (not in his course) disrupted Dolfman's class, calling for his resignation and denouncing him as a racist. Dolfman publicly apologized to the campus, but nothing appeased the sentiment against him. On March 13, the University Council, including a majority of the faculty members present, voted 15 to 4 that Dolfman should be suspended, prior to any hearing, as a clear and present danger to his students.

In this heated atmosphere, the Wharton Committee on Academic Freedom and Responsibility met, decided that Dolfman should not be renewed the next year, and set his undergoing "racial sensitivity training" as a precondition of rehiring.

Asked about the case, Hackney testified that it was the faculty, not he, who had dealt with it. Asked by Senator Hatch if Dolfman's teaching technique might not have been appropriate as a way to get students to think, Hackney replied, "I think it is very difficult to know exactly what went on." Hatch asked him if he meant "how he [Dolfman] handled it [the class]"? Hackney replied, "How he handled it, yes." Hatch pressed Hackney, who explained that he had left the matter of Dolfman wholly to the discretion of the Wharton faculty:

> *Hatch:* So your approach, since that was the procedure at the University of Pennsylvania, [was] to allow the faculty to make these determinations. Your approach was not to overrule the faculty.
>
> *Hackney:* Yes, absolutely.
>
> *Hatch:* Without somebody bringing better facts to your attention?
>
> *Hackney:* That's right.[47]

Hackney's testimony, before senators in the spring of 1993, thus distanced him from the Dolfman case, taking neither credit nor blame for its handling.

In February of 1984, however, Hackney had a somewhat different constituency to satisfy, and a somewhat different voice. In addition to its rally before the president's home, the Black Student League (BSL) issued a series of communiques to the campus and its media. One warned that the disruption of Dolfman's class and the demonstration on Hackney's lawn were just the beginning. Doubters "should brace yourselves for a very rude awakening." Penn was being offered "a final chance." It would be folly to "believe that our fury will subside," they warned, adding that they had communicated this to Hackney and to Erlich: "You will learn as did the President and Provost of this University on yesterday that we are DEAD SERIOUS." The BSL warned the administration not to delay its action: "Mr. President, Mr. Provost, you must ask yourselves the question of what price?" They answered: "THE FIRE NEXT TIME!!!!!!!!!!!!!" In another statement, the BSL declared itself "empowered . . . to seize our dignity and personhood immediately and by any means necessary!"[48] Consequently, on February 18, 1985, before the Wharton Committee even had been convened to investigate the incident, Sheldon Hackney sent a personal memorandum to the Black Student League membership. It was marked, with underlining, "Confidential," and it did not seek to distance himself from the resolution of the case:

> I met with Mr. Murray Dolfman at 11:00 a.m. this morning and empha-sized the seriousness with which I regarded the incidents in his class and that a public apology was in order. Professor Dolfman issued a public apology. A letter [of apology] is being sent to the Daily Pennsylvanian and The Voice. Dean Russell Palmer is asking the Wharton School's Committee on Acade-mic Freedom and Responsibility to review the entire situation with regard to Mr. Dolfman and to advise the Dean about what further steps may be ap-propriate.[49]

In 1989, Dolfman's case was taught to students as an "Incident of Ha-rassment" in "Diversity Education" for incoming students.[50] The facts were so distorted that the university publicly admitted that the mischaracterization of his behavior arose from a "composite" rather than literal account.[51] Mur-ray Dolfman finally commented:

> It's been a little over five years since I uttered that famous hyphenated word [ex-slave] which has caused quite a furor. Up until today I have not said one word in my defense publicly, because of a pledge that I gave to President Hackney five years ago that I would do nothing to increase the tensions on this campus, and the pledge by Dr. Hackney that this would remain a cam-pus matter.[52]

Hackney survived both the fury of 1985 and the confirmation hearing of 1993. Administrators know how to land on their feet.

PART V

RESTORING LIBERTY

CHAPTER 14

SUE THE BASTARDS?

The courts with some frequency have utilized constitutional doctrines, as we have seen throughout this book, to restrict serious incursions by colleges and universities into student (and faculty) liberties. These doctrines have been particularly effective in controlling the authoritarian proclivities of administrators of public colleges. In addition, however, lesser known nonconstitutional avenues have been developed that apply equally to private institutions. While legal protections, available through resort to the courts, are not always predictable or reliable, they are sufficiently potent to cause most administrators and their general counsels to think twice before taking on an aggrieved student who makes a credible threat of legal action. While the student cannot always predict victory, given the somewhat malleable state of the law in this area, neither can the university, especially since, in the more egregious situations, courts frequently will intervene.

In 1961, the legendary civil rights attorneys Jack Greenberg and Thurgood Marshall sued in the U.S. District Court in Alabama, contesting the right of Alabama State College, a black teachers college in Montgomery, to expel six students on grounds of misconduct. The students had been shown no detailed charges and, indeed, no evidence. The college president, in letters to the students, referred to their case merely as "this problem of Alabama State College."

When the court refused the students any relief, Greenberg and Marshall appealed to the U.S. Court of Appeals for the Fifth Circuit, which had jurisdiction over much of the South. By a vote of 2 to 1, the circuit court ruled in the students' favor in *Dixon v. Alabama State Board of Education,*[1] affirming the students' rights to due process at a public college, answering the specific question of "whether due process requires notice and some opportunity for hearing before students at a tax-supported college are expelled for misconduct."

At first glance, the outcome of the *Dixon* appeal was a surprise. Federal courts had been reluctant to interfere with such decisions by college administrators, even when penalties as severe as expulsion were imposed, and even where no questions of academic competence were involved. This was not an ordinary case, however, and the president of Alabama State College (and the members of the Alabama State Board of Education) had not expelled ordinary college students for ordinary reasons. The circuit court's impetus for applying Fourteenth Amendment due-process standards to this expulsion became obvious in the questioning of Harry Ayers, a member of the state board, set out in the trial record:

> Q. Mr. Ayers, did you vote to expel these negro students because they went to the Court House and asked to be served at the white lunch counter?
> A. No, I voted because they violated a law of Alabama.
> Q. What law of Alabama had they violated?
> A. That separating of [*sic*] the races in public places of that kind.

The governor, John Patterson, gave a somewhat more sophisticated reason, but the bottom line remained clear enough:

> Q. There is an allegation . . . that . . . the . . . action of expulsion was taken [to punish and] intimidate [the students] for having lawfully sought service in a publicly owned lunch room with service; is that statement true or false?
> A. Well, that is not true; the action taken by the State Board of Education was . . . to prevent incidents happening by students at the College that would bring . . . discredit upon the School and be prejudicial to the School . . . and would have resulted in violence and disorder, . . . and we felt that we had a duty to the . . . parents . . . and to the State to require that the students behave themselves while they are attending a State College.

Further, the state superintendent of education testified that he had cast his vote for expulsion because the students broke a college rule, that is, they held "demonstrations without the consent of the president of [the college]."[2]

The authorities did not seek to justify the expulsions on the ground that the students merely advocated desegregation of lunch counter facilities. They obviously understood that the federal courts would not allow a public college to punish core political speech. Instead, they cast their justification in

terms of the students' conduct: The students had violated Alabama's segregation laws; they had demonstrated without the college president's consent;
and their presence on campus was likely to provoke "violence and disorder."
(Likewise, college administrators today claim never to be punishing students
for unpopular, out-of-favor, politically incorrect speech, but for "verbal conduct" that either constitutes "fighting words" likely to provoke violence or
that creates "a hostile environment.")

Thus, it took an outrageous action by Alabama officials to force the federal courts to overcome the deference historically accorded even public colleges. Significantly, because the issue raised directly in *Dixon* was not the
First Amendment right of students to demonstrate against segregation, the
circuit court decided the case *on a procedural due process ground:* the students
were entitled to hearings. "Whenever a governmental body acts so as to injure an individual," the court held, "the Constitution requires that the act be
consonant with due process of law." In arriving at its conclusion, the circuit
court, chiding both the college administration and the district court that had
refused to intervene, cited what it termed "the eloquent comment" by Professor Warren A. Seavey in the *Harvard Law Review* on the subject of due
process rights for expelled students: "It is shocking that the officials of a state
educational institution, which can function properly only if our freedoms are
preserved, should not understand the elementary principles of fair play. It is
equally shocking to find that a court supports them in denying to a student
the protection given to a pickpocket." Thus did Professor Seavey and the
Fifth Circuit begin to bridge the gap between due process in civil society and
in state colleges and universities.

The circuit court went further. It pointed out that since the charge was
"misconduct, as opposed to a failure to meet the scholastic standards of the
college," it was particularly deserving of determination by a hearing with
procedural rights necessary to find the truth. The court noted, "This is not
to imply that a full-dress judicial hearing . . . is required." However, the court
continued, "the rudiments of an adversary proceeding may be preserved
without encroaching upon the interests of the college." The court set out
these "rudiments": "The student should be given the names of the witnesses
against him and an oral or written report on the facts to which each witness
testifies" and should have "the opportunity to present to the Board, . . . his
own defense . . . and to produce either oral testimony or written affidavits of
witnesses in his behalf."

Dixon remains an influential precedent for due process standards in public college disciplinary hearings, because the U.S. Supreme Court, which declined Alabama's request that it review the circuit's opinion, has not had occasion to rule otherwise. However, fourteen years later the Supreme Court finally did accept for review a case that raised a question related to *Dixon*. The issue in *Goss v. Lopez*[3] (1975) arose out of a public high school. The Court ruled that ten-day suspensions for high school students constituted a deprivation of liberty or property sufficient to require procedural due process before punishment could be inflicted. Although the Court recognized that school officials were having difficulty keeping order at that time of unrest, it said that was no excuse for the failure to give "some kind of notice" and "some kind of hearing." "Fairness," said the Court, "can rarely be obtained by secret, one-sided determination of facts decisive of rights." Even with considerable deference given to the discretion of school officials, "discretion will be more informed and . . . the risk of error substantially reduced" if the student may present his side.

Although *Goss* was not a college case, it obviously extended at least the same level of due process protection, if not more, to public higher education. First, as in the free speech area, the Court has made it clear that administrators in primary and secondary schools have more authority to restrict students than in higher education. Second, the Court in *Goss* explicitly referred to *Dixon* as a "landmark decision of the Court of Appeals for the Fifth Circuit." It noted, too, that lower federal courts uniformly had applied the doctrine of *Dixon*. In *Goss,* the Supreme Court indicated its own approval of *Dixon,* and even hinted at future implementation of further safeguards in proceedings where a student's penalty might be more serious.

Lower federal courts discerned in *Goss* a sea change in the Supreme Court's attitude, and they proceeded to apply this interventionist doctrine more expansively in, for our purposes, higher education. In *Gaspar v. Bruton* (1975), a federal court of appeals ruled that a nursing student at a public vocational school had to be given advance warning that she was failing and was on the verge of being expelled. Thus, without becoming involved in purely academic judgments, the federal courts insisted that, procedurally, even in the academic area, where the courts are most loath to intervene, students be dealt with fairly. Likewise, that same year another federal court ruled that a state medical school had violated a student's due process rights by notifying an association of medical schools that the student was not equipped to practice medicine. Before taking a step with such a devastating impact on the student's future, the school should have given the student notice "in writing of the alleged deficiency in his intellectual ability" and should likewise have "accorded [him] an opportunity to appear personally to contest such allegation."[4]

Then, in 1978, the Supreme Court spoke again. In *Board of Curators of the University of Missouri v. Horowitz,*[5] a student had been dismissed from medical school for *academic* reasons. The Court ruled that while the student was entitled to some level of notice and an opportunity to respond, she had received as much fair process in this situation as was due her. The school had informed her of the faculty's judgment about her poor educational progress, and, the Court said, when a state college was "careful and deliberate" in its academic decision-making, courts would not second-guess those judgments. Significantly, the Court made clear it would grant great deference to the institution and would require "far less stringent procedural requirements *in the case of an academic dismissal*" than in a purely disciplinary matter. [emphasis added] The Court recognized that, realistically, colleges in disciplinary matters take an adversarial stance toward the student and that special procedural protections were therefore in order, but that "the same conclusion does not follow in the academic context."

Thus, the Supreme Court set out the two poles—disciplinary cases in which courts would intervene on due process grounds *(Goss),* and academic cases in which judicial deference more often would govern *(Horowitz).* It did not take long for the Supreme Court's distinction to filter down. Later that year, the Court of Appeals for the First Circuit, with jurisdiction over most of New England, intervened when the University of Rhode Island (URI) denied a student, accused of assault with intent to rape, the right to have legal counsel in a campus disciplinary case while he awaited trial on criminal charges. In *Gabrilowitz v. Newman,*[6] the alleged rape victim, also a student at URI, charged Steven Gabrilowitz with assault with intent to rape, lodging charges both with the police department and the university. When URI insisted that he appear without his lawyer at a campus tribunal held before his criminal trial, he went to federal court. The First Circuit took the extraordinary step of ordering the university to allow the student to have his lawyer present at the disciplinary hearing, even though counsel would not be allowed to examine witnesses. Where "the specter of a criminal case hovers over the hearing," wrote the court, forcing the student to attend the college hearing without legal counsel would violate due process. The student's "need for an attorney at the hearing seems obvious."

Nonetheless, the most striking characteristic of the Supreme Court's approach to due process standards in public colleges and universities is its lack of clarity. The Court has been careful not to define precisely the limits of such procedural rights. This ambiguity likely indicates that while the Court is unwilling to intervene with too heavy a hand, it is equally unwilling to send a message to administrators that they are free to trample students' rights at will. This approach has allowed the lower federal courts, and state courts as well, to experiment with various levels of oversight and intervention, and to deal with the most outrageous administrative misconduct at public colleges.

Protections for students at private colleges are less favorable, but the extent of judicial relief available at such institutions is considerably greater than is commonly imagined. The bravado and high-handedness demonstrated by private college administrators often betrays an exaggerated sense of legal invulnerability. True, private colleges are not bound by the Bill of Rights. Hence, neither the First Amendment's free speech guarantee, nor "due process of law" requirements, nor "the equal protection of the laws" assured by the Fourteenth Amendment directly affect private campuses that have contempt for those values. This is good news for institutional autonomy, however bad for students and faculty who live under academic despots.

Nonetheless, despots are not quite immune, because the Bill of Rights is not the only legal constraint available. Private colleges, after all, are bound by the same laws and rules that apply to other private entities, and there is a body of law that has been developed to constrain outrageous private conduct that is older, in fact, than the Bill of Rights. For example, if a college contracts with a food delivery service, it is bound to pay and may be sued for failure to do so. Private agreements are as enforceable against private colleges as they are against private companies. Private institutions, academic and commercial, all must honor their legal obligations.

This elementary fact of civil life has led to the development of legal precedents that have taken the assurances given by colleges to students, in student handbooks and other official school literature, as the foundation of an enforceable contract between college and student. Thus, if a college has indicated that accused students will be given certain procedural rights at disciplinary hearings, this may be construed as a term of a binding contract between the two parties, enforceable in court, when a student is charged.

The contractual basis of enforceable student rights was demonstrated in 1983, when third-year law student Leevonn Cloud sued private Boston University for expelling him.[7] The U.S. Court of Appeals in Boston heard the case, analyzed the claim as an alleged breach of contract, and concluded that the generally accepted standard governing such contract cases was one of "reasonable expectation." Had there been a more precise Massachusetts state standard defining the nature of the university-student contract, the federal court said, it would have followed that, rather than the normally accepted standard. This did not help Mr. Cloud, in this particular case, because the court concluded that the school officials had in fact acted reasonably, treated him fairly, given him an adequate hearing, and proceeded in good faith to expel him. The court's having taken jurisdiction and decided the case on its merits, however, was a vital sign—and an important legal precedent—of the judiciary's increasing willingness to insist upon civilized procedures even in purely disciplinary matters at private institutions.

While Massachusetts state law was not specific as to what constitutes a student-college contract (forcing the federal court to use a commonly accepted definition), the state's highest court did have occasion that same year, in *Coveney v. Holy Cross College,* to give its view on what kinds of hearings must be held by colleges and universities, public and private, before a student may be seriously disciplined: "If school officials act in good faith and on reasonable grounds . . . their decision to suspend or expel a student will not be subject to successful challenge in the courts."[8] While this standard is fairly deferential to administrators, it is not a carte blanche.

Elsewhere, state courts have concluded that students have a variety of contractual rights that may be enforced against colleges, including with respect to such purely academic matters as promised remedial tutorials, arbitrary cancellation of courses, and programs where reasonable student expectations had been created by the college's prior statements. Student handbooks contain a variety of assurances that courts are willing to view as contractual promises, the violation of which, in egregious cases, call for a remedy. The essential lesson is that many states have determined a minimal level of fair dealing that colleges owe students, either on the basis of common law or statutory contract doctrine, other state doctrines, or state court interpretations of state constitutional provisions. While the New Jersey Supreme Court in the *Schmid* (Princeton) case was more "activist" than most state courts in applying state constitutional free speech rights, other state courts are far from hands-off. When administrators act reasonably, courts typically demur, but judges have demonstrated time and again that traditional constraints on outrageous conduct have teeth and that judicial tolerance has limitations.

Those limitations were reached in the 1994 Vermont case of *Fellheimer v. Middlebury College.*[9] Ethan Fellheimer had sexual intercourse with a fellow student. She filed rape charges with both the district attorney and the college. The DA decided not to prosecute, but the college proceeded. The dean of students, Ann Craig Hanson, brought the charge and announced that she herself would hear and decide the case, rather than refer it to the Student Judicial Council, because, as she wrote the accused student, "of the seriousness of these charges, the sexual and personal nature of the entire matter, and the issues of privacy." Fellheimer, obviously fearing a stacked deck, sued under the traditional state legal doctrines of breach of contract and "intentional infliction of emotional distress."

The "intentional infliction" claim demonstrates yet another route by which aggrieved students and faculty have sought court redress against private colleges. There is a branch of civil law known as tort law that comprehends a wide range of legal standards, the breach of which entitles the victim to seek compensation for damages in a civil action against the perpetrator. These civil wrongs, or torts, are part of the common law legal tradition bequeathed to the United States when the colonies became independent of England. The typical civil complaint that alleges damages resulting from negligent or intentional misconduct is a tort suit. (Certain misconduct can be both civil and criminal. As a rule of thumb, just about all criminal violations can lead to suits for civil damages, although only intentional misconduct can lead to criminal charges as well.)

A number of states have recognized, either by legislation or court decision, the intentional infliction of emotional distress as a tort. This tort is not uncontroversial. To critics of the legal system, it is an example of a society obsessed with litigation, focused on turning the ordinary hurts of daily life into legal causes of action and on classifying every person who has suffered inconvenience or minor injury, real or imagined, a "victim" entitled to compensation. To others, the development of this tort is evidence that we are becoming more civilized. The state of Vermont defines this tort as "outrageous conduct, done intentionally or with reckless disregard of the probability of causing emotional distress." Indeed, legal causes of action of this nature are a fact of law and life in many states in these litigious times. While this tort has been alleged against private and public colleges with only limited success, it does give judges and juries considerable leeway to determine the limits of what constitutes uncivilized conduct.

In *Fellheimer*, the court found that Middlebury's conduct did not reach this level of outrageousness, but it did hold, based on the college handbook, that Middlebury had violated a contract between student and college. While recognizing the need "to keep the unique educational setting in mind when interpreting university-student contracts," the court said, "a College is nonetheless contractually bound to provide students with the procedural safeguards that it has promised." As the court analyzed the case, Fellheimer was deprived of one important right that was promised but not delivered. When Dean Hanson realized that Fellheimer was not, in fact, guilty of rape (presumably for the same reasons that led the district attorney not to prosecute), she nonetheless found him guilty of the offense of "disrespect for persons." Since Dean Hanson had earlier written to Fellheimer that "you are being charged with rape," he defended against a rape charge, not an allegation of "disrespect." The student handbook required that the college "shall state the nature of the charges with sufficient particularity to permit the accused party to prepare to meet the charges." It was fundamentally unfair, and a violation of Middlebury's contractual promise, for the student to be found guilty of "disrespect for persons," an offense not charged, simply because the evidence of rape turned out to be wanting.

In 1994, the U.S. District Court in Manhattan was asked by a student, who maintained a pseudonym throughout the litigation, to declare his college in violation of state law for the manner in which it proposed to handle a disciplinary matter growing out of what the judge called "a spree involving alcohol abuse" leading to "sexual misconduct."[10] Judge Vincent L. Broderick, uncomfortable with having the case in court, noted that "lawsuits of this type may be extremely harmful to the ability of an educational institution to maintain discipline." On the other hand, he noted, New York law plainly prohibits "arbitrary" action in violation of "a supposed contract between university and student, or simply as a matter of essential fairness in the somewhat one-sided relationship between the institution and the individual . . . where discipline imposed by a private educational institution results in suspension or expulsion." Judge Broderick listed several aspects of what he deemed fair procedure: an impartial decision maker; notice of the charges; an opportunity to appear and defend; presentation of names of witnesses to be interviewed by the decision maker; and no penalty for a student's refusal to testify. Uncomfortable with the task of commanding the college, the judge urged the administration to use fairness and commonsense in treating students, so as not to tempt or force courts to intervene. It is a message seen over and over again in these cases—a lesson that educational institutions rarely seem to learn.

In various jurisdictions, there are yet other potential causes of action that aggrieved students have available against abusive universities. No one loses status as the free citizen of a nation of law by becoming a student. For example, defamation laws exist to redress written (libelous) and spoken (slanderous) falsehoods. Such lawsuits are more easily won by complainants who are private persons rather than public figures, on the theory that a well-known person, who is in the public eye, has many avenues available to respond effectively to falsehoods. Nearly any student, however, would have an argument that he was a private figure in a suit against a university. To win a defamation lawsuit, he or she would simply have to prove falsity, some level of fault by the university, and actual damage to his or her reputation, career, or livelihood. As with other causes of action, a university would fare worse in a defamation suit if a court concluded that it acted outrageously toward a student to whom it owed a duty of decent treatment.

These same themes are sounded in judicial opinions throughout the country. Faculty members who invoke the law to contest the infliction of discipline sometimes have a harder road than students, because administrators have been accorded, in some instances, a certain amount of control over the conduct of their "employees" in the interests of institutional efficiency. Students, however, are not employees and hence do not surrender rights that might be limited by employment.

It is not the purpose of this book to examine the current state of the law in any particular jurisdiction, nor indeed to offer legal advice to aggrieved students or faculty. However, we note that there are many morally compelling—and binding—legal foundations upon which a victim of abusive power may base a claim of intolerable mistreatment, procedural or substantive, by a college or university, public or private, with precise legal theories differing from state to state.

Consider, for example, what occurred when Eden Jacobowitz, the accused student in the Penn "water buffalo" case, sued the university for its treatment of him. Penn, of course, is a private university and hence not bound by constitutional free speech and procedural due process restrictions. Jacobowitz's lawyer, Edward H. Rubenstone, therefore framed his court complaint in terms of Penn's negligence, breach of contract, intentional infliction of emotional distress, invasion of privacy, and defamation. At the heart of his claim were Penn's failure to investigate the case competently, and its unfair treatment of Jacobowitz, including false accusations, adherence to double standards, and the institution's "failing to disclose exculpatory evidence to Jacobowitz."[11]

In their response to the complaint, Penn's lawyers raised every technical objection imaginable. Ordinarily, it is expected that a defendant in a lawsuit will pull out all stops and raise every conceivably available defense. However, some eyebrows were raised by Penn's reply to Jacobowitz's claim that the university's published policies were to be taken seriously as a binding obligation:

[Penn] denies that there was or is a "contractual relationship" between the University and Jacobowitz and that the University owed to Jacobowitz a contractual "duty" to conduct its judicial proceedings with fundamental fairness and to follow the Charter [of the University Student Judicial System].[12]

Equally curious was Penn's position, taken by the attorneys in the name of "the Trustees of the University of Pennsylvania" (the named defendant in the lawsuit), in response to Jacobowitz's allegation that Penn proceeded to prosecute him despite its possession, from the start, of evidence that would have exonerated him and given him public vindication, had it been disclosed: "Contrary to [Jacobowitz's] suggestions, moreover, he was not entitled under any University rule to disclosure of 'exculpatory evidence,' or to an opportunity for 'public vindication.' "

The judge allowed the allegations of negligence to stand and ordered the lawsuit to proceed. (It has since been settled upon payment of Jacobowitz's legal fees, without an admission of wrongdoing by Penn. Jacobowitz explained that he simply could not afford the time consumed by the litigation.) It is no wonder that Penn failed to achieve dismissal of Jacobowitz's charges under state law. The U.S. Supreme Court, in the 1963 case of *Brady v. Maryland*,[13] held that due process requires a prosecutor to disclose to the defense lawyer any exculpatory evidence that would tend to negate the defendant's culpability. To return to Professor Seavey's formulation, Penn was unwilling to grant its student the same rights accorded an accused pickpocket and should not have been surprised that the judge did not react favorably.

The precise contours of a private university's obligations to its students have not been spelled out by courts. Indeed, given the necessarily vague definition of the concepts involved and the hesitation of courts to become involved in fine-tuned supervision of campus life, it is not likely (nor, indeed, necessarily desirable) that precise contours in fact will be established judicially. This hardly means, however, that even a private institution should feel free to treat its students arbitrarily, unfairly, or with a degree of contempt that would be considered beyond the pale in civil society. For universities to exercise powers and take positions patently outrageous to moral sense is a virtual invitation to courts to assert jurisdiction. As the U.S. District Court in Rhode Island stated in the 1986 case of *Russell v. Salve Regina College*,[14] involving expulsion of a student from a private nursing school, the "boundaries" in this area of the law, while they grant "broad freedom [to] academic administrators," nonetheless give a student the right "to be sheltered from gratuitous debasement or intrusiveness (or worse, from malicious conduct which offends fundamental notions of human decency)." There are, said the court, "standards of behavior which a university and an undergraduate can reasonably expect from each other."

In short, administrators at private as well as public institutions would be foolish to assume immunity from legal challenge when they act at their arrogant and tyrannical worst. Students and faculty who have been subjected to treatment that society would consider outrageous, but who have been unable to obtain redress through other channels, might well have the option of going to court. Litigation is never a pleasant option (except, perhaps, for some attorneys). It is expensive, lengthy, messy, aggravating, uncertain of result, and a sometimes frustratingly blunt instrument, and it can become all-consuming of time, energy, and spirit. However, the law concerning substantive rights of academic freedom and procedural or contractual rights in disciplinary matters is real and hardly insulates administrators. If one does not have a philosophical objection to all judicial intervention in campus affairs regardless of how outrageous the provocation, then litigation is an option of last resort.

Potential civil lawsuits have become a sufficiently potent threat so that some general counsels and private lawyers have been advising their university employers and clients to use extreme care when making representations in publicly available student handbooks, catalogs, and bulletins concerning the school's policies and procedures. The cautious among them now advise that colleges would do well to protect themselves by not making too ringing a set of representations concerning devotion to free speech and the rights of students to procedural fairness. They warn administrators to avoid describing highly specific procedural protections (that students might later claim constituted contractual undertakings), or, indeed, to include a clause that no contractual obligation nor promise is intended. In short, university bulletins, catalogs, and student handbooks are now reviewed by lawyers, lest the school make a representation that it later might be required to honor.

The tension thus escalates between the desire of administrators to present a glowing self-image to the public (including potential students) and the warning of general counsel that institutions not promise what they do not intend to deliver. Colleges increasingly will face the question of whether, at long last, they should conform their actual practices to their professed ideals of liberty and academic freedom, equality before the law, and procedural fairness. The alternative choice, which likewise would be in keeping with truth-in-advertising, would be for them simply to cease professing institutional fealty to such values. One way or the other, the currently vast and indecent gap between appearance and reality, between what is promised and what is delivered, is likely to close substantially. It is not clear that most universities will in the end opt to return to a devotion to true liberty and equality, but it is likely that, at the least, the courts' increasing insistence on truth-in-advertising will enable students and parents, before choosing a school, to have a better idea of what awaits them.

Further, colleges and universities should not think that only courts are feeling increasingly pressed to intervene in outrageous institutional treatment of students and faculty. Legislatures, too, have taken note of current academic phenomena and, in particular, of the fact that more pervasive censorship exists on our campuses, public and private, than exists elsewhere in civil society.

In 1991, for example, in an extraordinary example of the adage that "politics make strange bedfellows," conservative Republican Congressman Henry Hyde, who became chair of the House Judiciary Committee in 1994, joined with the American Civil Liberties Union and its president, Nadine Strossen, a vocal opponent of speech codes, to introduce the Collegiate Speech Protection Act of 1991. This bill provided that students at nonsectarian private colleges that receive federal funds (which is to say, almost all private colleges) would have a right to go to court to obtain redress from institutions with unconstitutional speech codes. At a press conference introducing the bill, Rep. Hyde charged that "free speech is under siege in our country today in places where it ought to be nurtured, protected and enhanced, namely at our universities." ACLU president Strossen added that "students must be able to express whatever ideas they choose, even if others are offended by those expressions."[15] These two representatives of very different parts of the political spectrum had good reason to be concerned, because just two years earlier a study by the Carnegie Foundation for the Advancement of Teaching revealed that 60 percent of the colleges and universities surveyed had adopted conduct codes prohibiting speech, and that an additional 11 percent were considering adopting them.

In the end, the Hyde proposal did not attract sufficient support to be enacted. It was not well-received by the academic Left, nor, of course, by college and university administrations. The bill also drew sharp and deeply principled opposition from libertarian and other constituencies for academic freedom, that believed that imposing a governmental, particularly a federal, solution for such problems would constitute undue meddling in private universities. The Hyde bill did contain an exception for colleges operated by religious groups, which still would be allowed to enforce speech restrictions with bona fide religious purposes. Nonetheless, the autonomy of private, secular educational institutions would have been compromised by such a statute. It would have established a precedent, its sympathetic critics feared, that, in the long run, would come back to haunt its supporters. Thus, the academy was spared the sharp federal sword, but it was a close call, and a signal that universities had best put their house in order before an impatient Congress did it for them.

State legislatures, too, took notice of the move toward oppression on private campuses. In the most notable instance, the California legislature adopted a statute that essentially accomplished in that state what the Hyde bill would have established nationally. It provided that the free speech rights binding on public universities apply equally to private educational institutions. Section 94367 of the California Education Code, popularly known as "the Leonard Law" (after its chief sponsor), gives a student at a private college the same right of free speech on campus that he or she enjoys off campus—that is to say, the right protected by the U.S. and state Constitutions. Indeed, it was the Leonard Law that allowed the Superior Court of Santa Clara County, California, to declare the Stanford University speech code unconstitutional. Stanford argued in court that the law restricted the university's speech rights by forbidding it from expressing, via speech restrictions on its students, its own institutional opinions on racial and other epithets and harassing speech. As the judge noted, Stanford argues "that there is no way for Stanford to express that view and mean it, except by prohibiting discriminatory harassment and epithets and disciplining students who use them on campus." The court easily disposed of that defense by noting, first, that the Leonard Law, unlike Stanford's speech code, actually was "viewpoint neutral," and, second, that Stanford very easily could "ardently and effectively express [its] intolerance for intolerance through wholly constitutional means." Stanford's "inability to punish a student under the Speech Code," concluded the judge, "would not interfere with [its] ability to express [its] disapproval of any speech."

Apart from the question of whether other state legislatures will be tempted to emulate California's Leonard Law, some states already have more general civil rights legislation that well might offer private as well as public college students some degree of substantive and procedural protection. These state civil rights statutes vary considerably in their provisions and coverage, but to one extent or another they protect citizens from overreaching that results in violation of civil liberty. California, in addition to its Leonard Law, has passed such a state civil rights statute, as have Alaska, Florida, Maine, and Massachusetts.

Students who sue have one additional advantage. Universities are notoriously hesitant to engage in protracted litigation once a student's or professor's case has gotten beyond the initial stage. That "initial stage" is the preliminary moment in any civil lawsuit where the defendant asks the court to dismiss the complainant's case on the ground that, even if all of the factual assertions alleged were true, the law does not provide a legal remedy. Colleges—particularly private colleges—typically respond, when sued, with a claim, for example, that institutional academic freedom insulates them from judicial scrutiny, or that the assurances set forth in the student handbook do not constitute a legally enforceable contract, or that the administrator's action was not *so* outrageous as to constitute the tort of intentional infliction of emotional distress.

However, once the plaintiff survives this dismissal stage, he or she is allowed to begin the extraordinary process of "discovery." Discovery is the nightmare of administrators and their general counsel. In discovery, the student may compel administrators and other college employees (including secretaries, who frequently know the things that walls would testify to if they could talk) to answer questions under oath. Documents otherwise hidden securely in university files, even those marked "confidential," are subject to disclosure by subpoena. Minutes and recollections of the proceedings of secret meetings and hearings, and even e-mail, become producible evidence. In short, the discovery process instantly rips down the veil of secrecy and lays bare the machinations of college administrations. Few academic institutions that persecute their politically incorrect students and professors can withstand this searching, profoundly invasive inquiry. Engaging in litigation is quite risky for most institutions, not only because of the possible verdict, but because of the discovery that long precedes a verdict and that occurs even in a case where the plaintiff eventually loses. With their dirty linen spread on the public record and hence available to the news media and other interested parties, administrators suddenly have questions to answer. Normally, the parties may release documents and transcripts produced during discovery, unless the opposing side obtains a "protective order" from the court keeping those items confidential. Such protective orders, however, are the exception rather than the rule, because courts usually take the position that there is a public interest in litigation being open to public scrutiny, an interest strengthened by the First Amendment.

In short, while the outcome of litigation against a college may be uncertain, the process can be counted upon to produce at least a substantial amount of "sunlight" which, as we shall argue in our concluding chapter, is "the most powerful disinfectant" of all.

———————

There is a terrible dissonance between what universities profess and what they practice. It is a dissonance that the greater society, including judges and juries, would be loath to tolerate once the facts are known. For all its faults, the judicial system remains a potent threat of last resort to the continued maintenance of the authoritarian fixtures plaguing campuses, in part because of the enormous discretionary power (and limited patience) of judges and jurors, and in part because of the power of litigation to draw the curtain back and expose the secrets of academic despots. A truly aggrieved student is able to "tell truth to power" in a way unimagined in closed societies.

There is a certain majesty to a system where a student may force a college dean or president to respond under oath to the student's questions and allegations. After all, as the Supreme Court has noted repeatedly much to the chagrin (and worse) of several of our nation's chief executives, even the president of the United States must respond to a subpoena. The university may be an enclave, but it is not a sovereign nation. Ultimately it will have to answer for its betrayal of the nation's and its own traditions.

CHAPTER 15

"SUNLIGHT IS
THE BEST DISINFECTANT"

In the fall of 1996, in response to a growing number of troubling cases decided in secrecy by Harvard's judicial system, many voices—including the *Harvard Crimson,* the *Harvard Law School Record,* and the Civil Liberties Union of Harvard—called for reform of the judicial Administrative Board and its mysterious procedures. Even outgoing Harvard College dean L. Fred Jewett, who had defended the board for so long, called for greater openness and accountability. The new dean, Harry Lewis, however, refused to make any of its procedures, findings, or patterns subject to inspection. The openness that students wanted, he explained to the *Crimson,* "would be a violation of the Buckley Amendment."[1]

Lewis's invocation of the Buckley Amendment stopped the argument in its tracks. Formally known as the Family Educational Rights and Privacy Act of 1974, the Buckley Amendment revised federal education laws to strengthen Congress's prior (and unsuccessful) efforts to protect student privacy and to prevent administrative misuse of confidential student records. Named after its chief legislative sponsor, Senator James Buckley of New York, the law governs the disclosure of certain academic records by any educational institution, public or private, that receives any federal funding (that is, nearly every college and university in the country). Congress's threat to the colleges was simple: Continue to ignore our insistence upon student privacies, and you lose your federal dollars.[2]

The Buckley Amendment gave students (and, in the case of minors, their parents) the right to inspect their college records, and it created an executive branch authority to terminate federal funding to any school that violated the act's provisions. It also prohibited a college or university from disseminating students' records without their permission.

Universities, however, have attempted to convert this law into a means to insulate administrators from accountability for their treatment of students by claiming that they have a legal obligation to engage in covert justice (and injustice). Indeed, almost every college and university cites the Buckley Amendment as grounds for not commenting on alleged injustices and uses it as a protective wall around student disciplinary proceedings. Power loves secrecy.

At Penn, in 1995–96, the administration sought to prevent forever a repeat of the scrutiny brought about by the water buffalo affair. What had made that scrutiny possible was the right of a defendant, guaranteed by Penn's judicial charter, to discuss his or her own case. In the wake of that searing scrutiny, the outgoing administration had appointed a blue-ribbon committee to advise the incoming administration about what had gone wrong. The panel concluded that the judicial system was not constituted to withstand public examination. What was the incoming administration's response to that? It decided to forbid any disclosure about the system.

Thus, in 1995–96, Provost Stanley Chodorow proposed and defended a new "confidentiality" clause banning any discussion of any aspect of any case. If such a clause had been in place in 1993, Eden Jacobowitz's public exposure of Penn's prosecution of him would have been a separate offense subject to further university punishment. According to Chodorow, "after reconsidering the University's obligations under the Buckley Amendment," Penn had no choice but to gag the participants in its tribunals. He therefore issued a new policy on confidentiality:

> All disciplinary proceedings, the identity of individuals involved in particular disciplinary matters, and all disciplinary files, testimony, and findings are confidential. . . . No member of the University community (including complainants, respondents [defendants], witnesses, [or] advisors) . . . may disclose or cause to be disclosed or participate in the disclosure of confidential disciplinary matters in violation of the Charter or University policies on confidentiality. . . . Failure to observe the requirement of confidentiality by any member of the University constitutes a violation of University rules and may subject the individual to the appropriate procedures for dealing with such violations.[3]

There was one single exception, behind which one could see a last-minute gasp by the general counsel: The policy would not prevent "a student from seeking legal advice."[4] The new policy was scheduled to go into effect on July 1, 1996. Under this policy, defendants could not tell parents, spouses, lovers, best friends, pastors, or therapists that they had been charged, mistreated, acquitted, or convicted. If the world were assuming their "guilt" on the basis of things said prior to a formal charge at Penn, they could not respond to or satisfy the world by disclosing the verdict or the facts of the case. Sentenced to "community service" or "counseling"— two options of the judicial system—they could not answer either the agency director's or the therapist's questions about why they were there. No defendants could describe—or appeal to public opinion against—malice, selective prosecution, discrimination, lack of due process, or indecency. If they told the only person they could tell, their lawyers, the latter could not talk to the media without the defendant being guilty of having "caused to be disclosed."

Students began a furious assault upon a gag rule that would have left them silenced once they were involved, in any manner, with a disciplinary hearing. At a University Council meeting on February 21, 1996, when the administration sought to put the matter to rest, Lance Rogers, the chairman of the Undergraduate Assembly, pressed the administration to continue discussion of the gag rule. The president of the university, Judith Rodin, replied to him, "Get a life!"[5] (She since has convened a national panel on "incivility" in public discourse.)[6]

The Undergraduate Assembly and an undergraduate First Amendment Task Force, however, continued their theoretical and detailed criticisms of the policy. Student editorialists reiterated that under the policy, suspended defendants could not even tell their parents why they suddenly were home. Above all, students focused on Penn's self-serving use of censorship to remove any possibility of a future public embarrassment. Chodorow told the University Council that if a student disclosed anything about a judicial case, the university would be sued. This was simply absurd, as students were quick to point out. The Buckley Amendment forbade the university from publishing a student's record, including his or her grades, to the world. By the provost's logic, this meant that no student could talk about his or her own grades, or another student's, let alone complain about discriminatory grading, without the university being legally liable.[7]

On March 2, 1996, a *Daily Pennsylvanian* reporter, Andrea Ahles, gave the campus the facts. She had called the Department of Education itself, whose spokesman, Jim Bradshaw, let all the air out of Chodorow's balloon. According to Bradshaw, the Buckley Amendment applied only to the uni-

versity as a corporate institution, and in no way prohibited students from discussing their own academic or judicial records. As he told the *DP*, the Buckley Amendment "does not cover a situation where a college would try to
prevent a student from talking about disciplinary proceedings outside of the
hearing."[8] On March 4, Chodorow, having previously assured Penn that he
had secured the best possible legal advice in imposing his rule of silence, announced that the confidentiality clause would be lifted from the charter.[9] In
less than a month of struggle, the undergraduates had overturned the gag
rule. For the first time, Penn students had refused to accept the generational
swindle of the '60s. They had taken President Rodin's mocking (and uncivil)
words quite literally, and they had gotten a life.

The widespread assertion by academic administrators and their general
counsels that federal law requires the kind of secrecy routinely practiced on
campuses throughout the country is incorrect. Indeed, Senator Buckley
himself declared that the purpose of the 1974 legislation was to remedy the
growing abuse of students by academic institutions that collected and dis-
seminated personal information without a student's "informed consent," including details about a student's social attitudes, ethical beliefs, personal
tastes, family life, moral values, and social development. Buckley decried
such invasions of privacy, and, in particular, the inclusion of prejudicial anec-
dotal comments in a student's school record. "When parents and students are
not allowed to inspect such school records and make corrections," the senator said in a 1974 speech to the legislative conference of the National Congress of Parents and Teachers, "such material can have a devastatingly
negative effect on the academic future and job prospects of an innocent, unaware student. A simple inaccuracy or a comment by a spiteful, neurotic
teacher can potentially ruin a student's future."[10]

To remedy this, the statute threatened a loss of federal funds to schools
that have "a policy of denying, or which effectively prevents, the parents of
students [or students eighteen or older] who are or have been in attendance
at a school . . . the right to inspect and review the educational records of
their children." (The law exempted parental financial statements, letters of
recommendation where the student explicitly had waived access, and reports
done for law enforcement purposes.)[11]

In a later addition to the law, Congress expanded its protection of the
dignity of students from institutional abuse by means of prohibitions that al-

most every mandatory "diversity" and "sensitivity" session—and almost every campus judicial system—violate:

> No student shall be required, as part of any applicable program, to submit to a survey, analysis, or evaluation that reveals information concerning: (1) political affiliations; (2) mental and psychological problems potentially embarrassing to the student or his family; (3) sex behavior and attitudes; (4) illegal, anti-social, self-incriminating and demeaning behavior; (5) critical appraisals of other individuals with whom respondents have close family relationships; (6) legally recognized privileged or analogous relationships, such as those of lawyers, physicians, and ministers; or (7) income, . . . without the prior consent of the student . . . or . . . parent.[12]

In short, the Buckley Amendment gives students protection against a range of intrusive acts by colleges and universities. There is nothing in the legislation that prevents students from having access to their own academic and disciplinary records. Indeed, precisely to the contrary, the law assures students and their parents free access to those records. If one student's records were entangled with another's, of course, the university could edit them appropriately. The statute in no way prohibits students from disclosing to anyone—including the news media—the institution's treatment of them. Indeed, what the expanded Buckley Amendment would most affect of the things discussed in this book are the practices of politically correct student life bureaucracies. The law makes current intrusions upon individual privacy clear grounds for shutting off the flow of federal dollars to colleges and universities.

Finally, neither the Buckley Amendment nor any other provision of law prohibits a college or university from conducting open disciplinary hearings, especially if a defendant requests such openness. Even the broadest possible interpretation of the Buckley Amendment cannot be stretched to defend the secrecy of the hearings themselves. Indeed, the Buckley Amendment itself clearly authorizes the release of the records of such proceedings with the student's permission.

Academic administrators, thus, are contemptuous both of ordinary standards of decency and of the actual law. Students who are confronted by abusive campus power may challenge confidentiality rules either by going to court or by disclosing their cases regardless of threats. They should do this loudly and publicly, raising the stakes for careerists or ideologues determined to punish them for seeking to apply Justice Brandeis's profound insight, that "sunlight is the most powerful of all disinfectants."[13]

Sunlight is a powerful threat. Recall the *Wabash Commentary* and its defunding. Its editors took their case public and received great publicity in national and local media. Stung by criticism from alumni and donors, and embarrassed by the glare of sunlight, Wabash, within a month, ended its prosecution of the critical content of the journal.[14] In the spring of 1997, a diverse group of faculty members at West Virginia University learned from public discussion outside their university that they and their students were governed by repressive "verbal conduct" provisions of harassment policies and by the definition of crimes of belief and expression promulgated by their campus Office of Social Justice. Embarrassed to have slept on their watch, and fearful for the liberties of their students and colleagues, they organized a group to expose such policies to criticism and debate and to communicate their outrage to the administration. The university denied that there was any problem. The group reappeared in the fall with the ACLU at its side and indicated its determination to go for relief both to federal court and, more important, to the court of statewide public opinion; shortly afterward, the administration began to have a change of heart. In January 1998, the administration thanked the group for calling these problems to its attention, proclaimed its devotion to the First Amendment, and announced that it was withdrawing these policies from the university's Website. As we write, the group of faculty is working to make certain that these policies are withdrawn from the university's life.[15]

What can sunlight accomplish? The best answer may be found at Penn, where our story began, and where exposure had been most intense. Nothing happened immediately after the dismissal of charges against Eden Jacobowitz, and much did not change at all. Indeed, the university's first response—in the report of its investigative committee on the water buffalo incident—was to blame and seek to block off sunlight itself.[16] In 1996, Penn's legal position in seeking to dismiss a lawsuit by Eden Jacobowitz was that its judicial charter (with its promise of "substantive justice") created no contractual obligations on its part, and that it never had been and was still under no obligation whatsoever even to provide "exculpatory evidence" to a student whom it accused of a university crime.[17] The Office of General Counsel still stands, a Mount Everest of administrative self-protection between Penn's claims of judicial impartiality and the reality of its administrative self-interest. As we write, the partisan director of Penn's "Women's Center" still sits ex-officio on university committees as the voice of Penn's "women," appropriating their true diversity and individuality.

Nonetheless, sunlight changed a great deal, above all the moral perspective and resolve of individuals. Recall, from chapter 9, the Penn residence advisers (RAs) who in August 1995 finally found the courage to speak their minds about the use of their job training as an exercise in political reeducation and vitriolic denunciation of whites. By then, the provost and the acting vice provost for university life already were in the process of reexamining the "educational programming" in the residences, the training of RAs, and first-year orientation. The administration responded apologetically and with concern to the protest of the policies that Penn had sponsored for years. A powerful administrator replied to a memorandum on the RAs' complaint: "I also deeply admire our students' right to dissent, . . . to free speech, and . . . to equality as individuals. . . . I also do not support any agenda that is inane, divisive, or hateful."[18] Within a year, Zoila Airall, associate director of residence, in charge of partisan "educational" programming, and Gigi Simeone, the director of residence, were gone.

Even a few students at the law school found their moral courage. In February 1995, the student *Penn Law Forum* published a "Top Ten List" that vulgarly poked fun at a female professor who was also a dean. The politically correct at Penn now forgot all about "the imbalance of power" between faculty and students. The dean of the law school, Colin Diver, and twenty-three professors, including the great majority of the most influential members of that faculty, sent an open letter to the editors and staff of the *Penn Law Forum,* expressing their outrage at the "insulting and sexist terms" of the "schoolboy" satire. Hinting at actionable offenses that might disqualify someone from admission to the bar, they accused the *Forum* of "completely [failing] to grasp the legal and moral obligations of each of us to maintain a work environment that is not hostile to women." The open letter then got to its coercive purpose: "Those of you who have not yet either resigned [from the journal] or in some other way publicly disclaimed authorship or approval of this article, should do so now. Not to do so is to condone what is condemnable, and shall be so construed by us." In short, the students' dean and twenty-three of their professors had informed them that their character and fitness for the bar would be determined by whether or not they followed this directive. The students were to resign from the *Forum,* or, at the very least, to disclaim not only authorship, but inward approval of the article, and to do so immediately, whether editors or merely staff.[19]

This time, however, as with the RAs, there were those who had had enough of double standards and abuse of power. Fifteen courageous law students wrote an open response to the dean and faculty. They agreed that the "satirical piece" reflected "poor editorial judgment," although they were nearer the critical mark when they termed it merely "ridiculous" and "sophomoric." They pointed out the obvious: "Nobody at Penn Law would dispute the faculty's opinion of Professor Hurd. Her popularity and prominent stature are exactly the reasons why she was the subject of the controversial satire." Then, they addressed the core issue of "the faculty's response [which was] its disregard for the basic principles of free speech": "The faculty's response . . . erodes the liberal foundation that an academic institution needs to prosper." Students "are already afraid" to criticize the faculty's letter, and "chilling free speech on any issue . . . has a stifling effect on the exchange of ideas within the law school community." Law students should be free "to express their opinions—no matter how offensive— without fear of reprisal by the faculty." The letter writers struck the bull's-eye: "The faculty who signed the open letter should be embarrassed by their veiled threats and the consequences of those threats to the student body."[20]

The student reprimand was understated, of course, because the threats had been anything but "veiled." Something had changed at Penn, however, and being labeled a censor with contempt for freedom of expression had become almost as unacceptable as being labeled insensitive. On February 27, 1995, Dean Diver sent a memorandum to every law student, announcing that the faculty of the law school unanimously had adopted a new resolution. Although the dean and faculty reiterated their condemnation of the column's "altogether unacceptable and offensive comments," they expressed their "regret that some have read the letter . . . as containing a threat of retaliation, [because] the signers of that letter did not intend to convey any such threat." "The faculty," it assured the law students, "would not engage in or tolerate any reprisal or retaliation. We are committed to free speech and open dialogue."[21]

Exposure, from 1993 on, indeed has worked its magic at Penn. It has changed the perspective and resolve—for the long moment, at least—of both the wielders and the victims of power. It produced a transformation that should give hope to anyone who has become fatalistic about the loss of liberty, legal equality, and respect for individual dignity on our campuses.

Penn was deeply embarrassed by the national exposure of 1993. What seemed so right to administrators in their clubby, insulated private precincts had been exposed, and to the rest of the world, it seemed bizarre, absurd, and abusive. Penn had become worse than notorious; it had become a symbol of silliness. Hundreds of national stories and references continued to appear throughout 1993–94 about both the water buffalo case and the unpunished theft of the *Daily Pennsylvanian*.[22] The fall 1993 cover of *Campus,* a national student publication, showed a gagged student next to a statue of Ben Franklin, with the caption "U. Penn: The Most Poisoned Ivy?"[23] When, as late as the winter of 1994–95, the media picked up the story of Penn Women's Center director Elena DiLapi barring a tearful black woman from a meeting of "White Women Against Racism" at Penn (they needed to work out their guilt in safety, DiLapi explained), a beleaguered Penn spokeswoman asked the *Chronicle of Higher Education,* "Why is it always Penn?"[24]

It wasn't always Penn, of course, but given how much sunlight was shining its way, the university was clearly in public view. Penn, in response, began to change, for two principal reasons. First, anyone at Penn who cared about liberty, equality, and individual dignity no longer could remain in denial. Fear of being labeled by the self-righteous had led many to persuade themselves to wait it all out; they convinced themselves that prevailing wickedness, which they preferred to call prevailing nonsense, would not endure. Having no way of denying the reality of evils on their campus after the events of 1993, such individuals faced a moment of truth. Many found courage, voice, and the necessity of acting consistently with their principles. Second, the embarrassment of Penn by public exposure had led careerists to identify with the need to change Penn's public image. It still might be damaging to alienate the most militant groups, but, for the first time, it would be yet more damaging to their careers to defile liberty and fairness.

Throughout the water buffalo affair, various Penn trustees privately had voiced their outrage over Eden Jacobowitz's plight. In its aftermath, the executive committee of the trustees chose to act. At long last assuming the most essential of its fiduciary obligations—passing on a free university to posterity—the Board of Trustees announced that it expected Penn's students to enjoy the protections of the Bill of Rights and that it would hold administrations to that standard. Administrators, wielding arrogant power for so long, always had claimed to speak in the name of "the Corporation," asserting their legal prerogatives to govern the institution. The trustees, however, *were* "the Corporation," and from the moment that their executive committee spoke on behalf of liberty in 1993, the die was cast.[25] Administrators are good at keeping trustees in the dark and securing desired authorizations from them. They are not good at defying informed trustees, however, because, quite simply, administrators work for them.

The trustees of Penn had called for freedom, and they meant it, passionately. No one who favored speech codes and the apparatus of oppressive inequalities any longer had a bright administrative future at Penn. It gave some administrators the courage of their secret convictions, sent others scurrying to rediscover the principles of liberty, and drove still others into the same state of hypocrisy into which they themselves had driven people for a decade. Fiduciary obligation—the moral and legal responsibility of individuals and groups toward what is in their trust—has its root in the Latin word *fides,* meaning "faith." The trustees of the University of Pennsylvania finally had acted in full good faith. The leaders of the faculty at Penn were now beside themselves at this "mischievous," "inappropriate," and "uncollegial" intrusion upon the university.[26] The speech codes, though few understood it clearly at the time, were doomed.

On February 1, 1994, the Commission on Strengthening the Community, appointed in the wake of the water buffalo affair, and including among its members trustees, administrators, faculty, students, and prominent Philadelphians, reported to the university. It offered many suggestions to be acted on within a year, but it called for the immediate abolition of the speech codes.[27] In fits and starts, the new interim president of Penn, Claire Fagin, chipped away at the speech codes, but in the midst of various uproars, she could not quite bring herself to do it categorically, writing instead an equivocal document that encouraged freedom of expression but left "community standards" as the final arbiter.[28]

Anyone who knew the leading trustees, however, knew that the person whom they hired as Penn's next president would not get the position without a commitment to honor the trustees' earlier proclamation by dismantling the central engine of oppression. By 1994–95, almost everyone seemed to know that abolition was both inevitable and appropriate. The voices that for so many years had insisted so passionately upon progressive intolerance at Penn fell silent. The rhetoric of righteous wrath and redistributive justice abandoned them. There was no real debate. The abolition that should have come about by moral argument now would occur simply in response to public awareness of the idiocy and shame to which political correctness had led the university. When Penn's new president, Judith Rodin, was installed, she did her duty, writing a letter to Penn parents and alumni that reassured them about steps being taken to ensure physical safety at Penn and informed them of the initiatives of her administration. Among other things, she wrote:

For a university to succeed in its mission as an open forum where competing ideas, beliefs, and values can contend, it must also promote a different kind of security: that necessary to intellectual risk-taking. It must encourage the free exchange of opposing ideas and viewpoints, even when some may find those viewpoints disturbing. Today at Penn, the content of student speech is no longer a basis for disciplinary action.[29]

It took only one simple clause: "the content of student speech is no longer a basis for disciplinary action." The use of the phrase "no longer" was an act of gracious integrity. Most administrators simply would have said "is not," leaving the issue at that. The "no longer" was a statement that Penn needed to hear: A wrong had existed and now it was being set right. The speech codes were abolished.

———————

The changed climate also emboldened an exemplary administrator at Penn, Valarie Swain-Cade McCoullum. McCoullum, better known as Valarie Cade, proceeded not only to speak dangerous but vital, exhilarating truths to an entire university, but to do so from the previous inner sanctum of oppression, the office of vice provost for university life, replacing Kim Morrisson, who, not surprisingly, moved out of that office shortly after the water buffalo fiasco.

Cade was an obvious choice for such a position, although her nomination was bitterly opposed by conservative student voices. She had served in various capacities in the university life area under Hackney and Morrisson; she had been housemaster of Penn's Du Bois College House for black culture; she had shown a strong commitment to many causes at the core of the office's prior missions. She was beloved by minority students, who knew full well how much she cared about the quality of their Penn experience. She felt a special affinity, empathy, and sympathy for the difficulties that many of them faced entering this new institution, and for their diverse ambivalences. She also was outspoken in her efforts to make the campus more welcoming of gays, lesbians, feminists, and foreign students.

Above all, however, Cade treated each student as an individual, not as the embodiment of an abstract group. She was a demonstrative, compassionate person, open and emotive in her expressions, and her kindness was legendary. When news of her appointment became public, however, the campus conservative journal, *The Red and Blue,* sharply challenged her impartiality.

For Valarie Cade, the water buffalo incident at Penn had been painful, and she was deeply troubled by widespread perceptions—by conservatives, moderates, libertarians, and religious students—of partisan unfairness of Kim Morrisson's officers, especially in the Residence Office, and in various divisions of the Office of Student Life. Such perceptions mattered to Cade, not for careerist reasons—she does not compromise her principles for reward—but because she had been perfectly sincere when she claimed that she wanted to make all students at Penn feel welcome and part of a larger academic community. The events of 1993 had touched her far more than anyone realized, and once she assumed her permanent office, she brought a moral presence and voice to Penn that had not been heard from any administrator for decades.

One of Cade's first surprises was to seek an interview with *The Red and Blue.* This was an act of both substantive and symbolic importance, because *The Red and Blue* had been demonized the year before by self-proclaimed campus progressives, and had been treated scandalously by the Office of Student Life. The interview was conducted by Thor Halvorssen, an encounter of no small interest.

Halvorssen was a student from Venezuela (of Norwegian ancestry on one side, two generations back), and the scales had fallen from his eyes during the events of 1993 and 1994 at Penn. He had defended students, as an adviser, before the judicial system, and he was appalled by its partisanship and its procedural flaws. He had observed closely the university's efforts to foster "Hispanic" identity, and he found it patronizing, paternalistic, and, generally, absurd. For Halvorssen, Penn's Hispanic community was an impressively diverse set of individuals who varied profoundly, among themselves, by nationality, culture, politics, interests, and values. For Penn, in his eyes, Hispanics were caricatured as Sandinistas, and university "celebrations" of Hispanic culture slighted its rich diversity, its Catholicism, its traditions of European culture, its cultural conservatism, its links to Bolivar's "Enlightenment" and his classical liberalism, its actual national problems, and its deeply complex and vital relationship to the United States.

As a high-ranking staff member of *The Red and Blue* during the prior year, when it fought defunding because of its conservative content (from monies collected by the university in a mandatory general fee), Halvorssen had encountered firsthand the partisan hostility of student life officials. Fervently prolife, Halvorssen was particularly dismayed by the Women's Center's equation of "women" with abortion rights and radical feminism. He had fought against Cade's appointment. The interview, however, turned out to be a remarkable meeting of minds and sensibilities. Halvorssen asked tough questions, and Cade gave answers that changed the whole dynamic of the Division of University Life at Penn.[30] On "freedom of speech," Cade said:

> I truly believe very strongly in freedom of speech. In my own personal history, I have had family members who have been persecuted when they attempted to have their voices heard. . . . My parents raised all of us to support that freedom, to be able to be heard and to take rebuttal as a responsibility. People must hold fiercely to their right to express themselves, and others who hear that expression [and disagree with it] have the responsibility to rebut avidly whatever that expression is. It is in that dialogue, I think, that progress occurs. Even without that dialogue . . . the search for truth and the expression of one's individual truth, however one finds it, is essential.[31]

This "seems to be a radical change in the administration's view of freedom of speech," Halvorssen said, because in the past "only some students were allowed . . . in this 'dialogue.'" In terms of rights, Penn had divided "individuals into groups [and] many times these individuals feel that the group identities have nothing to do with their own souls." Cade replied: "I think that it is essential for any individual to come to her or his own definition of self. . . . It is important to have the individual freedom to determine one's self." "Some institutional labels," she added, were appropriate, such as "first-year students," and some were required by law, for the purpose of providing demographic data. Nonetheless, she insisted, "the best case is for students to come in as individuals and to define themselves."[32]

Halvorssen reminded her that "the University Life Division was seen by moderate and assimilationist students as hostile," and asked how she could implement such a redefinition of the office "among employees who do not believe in individuality and are simply not tolerant of some views?" She replied, "The President, the Provost, and I believe strongly in these rights and responsibilities," and she promised to do whatever was appropriate to bring the University Life Division and its programs into "concert with these principles." She vowed that university life would offer services that respected all students' "definition of self."[33]

Halvorssen pressed her on the Women's Center, where "women who are pro-life are not fully supported . . . [and] devout Muslim and Roman Catholic women who disagree with homosexuality are not welcome." Describing it as "a bastion of radical [feminism]," he asked how it was "going to become more inclusionary." She replied that the Women's Center would have to be "in concert with" her "inclusionary principles," and that she would work "to assure that all community members will feel welcome." "Whatever individuals choose to believe," she reiterated, "is their personal choice."[34]

Finally, Halvorssen spoke of the previous August's RA training, where "there was an ideological requirement for RAs," and he argued that "the political climate discouraged Evangelicals, Muslims, Orthodox Jewish students, and conservative students from becoming RAs." Cade was categorical: Ideology would not be a factor. Indeed, the complaining RAs were now among the group who would plan future training, "so that we can assure that all of those people feel both welcome and nurtured as well as prepared. We will be modifying RA training over the next months for next year." She acknowledged that "some people do not feel that [way]," but that she would move "very quickly to reinforce those principles."[35] The Old Regime had fallen.

Even more striking, Cade soon published a set of "University Life Principles" that she insisted must guide all of the divisions that reported to her. In the place of the principles of political correctness and thought reform, Cade articulated essential moral and educational truths. In the place of the usual preface about building a therapeutic community of mutual celebration, Cade reminded Penn of its actual mission: "The essential role of the university," the principles began, "is to produce educated, critical, and open minds." When she spoke of Penn's diversity, she referred to it as "racial, ethnic, religious, intellectual, political, ideological, sexual, and geographic." Most essentially, she described that diversity as the province not of Penn as an institution, but of the individuals themselves:

> These citizens of Penn are free to individuate according to their private conscience. They are equal in their rights, dignities, and responsibilities. They freely make deeply-held personal choices as to how they define themselves as members of voluntary larger communities. All individual members of our University community may have their own particular political or ideological agendas, but . . . we must work to make all students who follow the policies and the regulations of the university feel equally welcome and equally respected as individuals free to differ in the private choices they make about their lives and values. I also believe, absolutely and resolutely, in both freedom of expression and the individual's moral responsibility [to rebut] views that he or she might find abhorrent.[36]

The exercise of her leadership, she announced, would be "toward the end of making all students know that they are equal members of the University in their rights, dignities, and responsibilities . . . building a University of trust and of both real and perceived fairness."[37]

Valarie Cade has met opposition from entrenched ideological warriors who nominally serve her, but she has refused to be moved from her principles. In 1996–97, a student who worked for a division that reported to university life, tutoring underprivileged students, wrote a letter to the *Philadelphia Inquirer* critical of the moral principles of affirmative action. The administrator who supervised him declared that such views rendered him unfit to continue as a tutor. When word of this disciplinary action reached Cade, she patiently but firmly explained to her officer both the First Amendment and the indispensability of intellectual freedom. The two of them apologized to the student, expressing their full respect for his independence and for his rights.[38]

In three years, Cade has worked tirelessly to end in loco parentis indoctrination at Penn, opened up the offices that report to her to the full spectrum of Penn's students, honored individualism, and ended every double standard that she could find. She has demanded that employees cease abusing their positions as fiefdoms from which they undertake the partisan moral reformation of students and begin to deliver the services for which they are paid.

Vigilance always will be necessary. In the fall of 1997, administrators and faculty on the University Council outvoted the students and overrode the Undergraduate Assembly (UA), assigning a separate undergraduate seat on the University Council to the United Minority Council. The action undid a reform that had been undertaken by the UA itself in the wake of the events of 1993 (and a reform that had not decreased, at all, the place of "minorities" among the UA representatives).[39] It was a dreary act both symbolically and in terms of its restoration of apartheid representation. Nonetheless, if the dismantling of so much of an oppressive regime could happen at Penn, it could happen anywhere. It requires leaders such as Valarie Cade, who have the courage to articulate an academic vision of individual dignity, legal equality, and liberty, and it requires defenders of that vision, across many spectrums, to sustain the effort.

In the early '70s at Penn, before the oppression began, a unique institution flourished. It was called Van Pelt College House, an educational residence with a reputation as a good place to be whoever you were, with no governance in loco parentis, and certainly no speech codes. It housed four faculty fellows, eight graduate fellows, and 180 undergraduates, and the fellows' role was educational, cultural, and social, not therapeutic or political. In its first eight years, it attracted and had living together evangelicals and gay activists, Catholic Newman Center members and radical feminists, conservatives and revolutionaries, blacks and whites of all persuasions, including the first few presidents of the militant Black Student League and blacks majoring in finance at the Wharton School. At a time when Penn was only 2 or 3 percent "minority," Van Pelt's remarkably diverse black population was, after its first year, never less than 20 percent of the house, by sheer force of the appeal of its individualistic atmosphere. It was refreshing for students to be in a community where they were not "representatives" of larger, officially designated groups.

Van Pelt lived the real discovery of difference. Its members moved each year from distance to conversation, and from mutual suspicions to various degrees of understanding and, usually, to touchingly kind relationships. People offended each other all the time, but then they learned to talk to each other and to understand each other.[40] We are paying a terrible price by denying students that experience in the '90s.

At our nation's universities today, the great potential allies of liberty, equal justice under law, and the dignity of the free and responsible individual are not careerist administrators seeking quiet on their watch; nor craven, intimidated faculties that gave up years ago on their responsibility to preserve free institutions; nor indifferent trustees who feel civic by serving without any regard for deeper fiduciary obligation; nor parents who invest in a degree rather than in a critical education; nor uncomprehending alumni who often celebrate a golden age that never was. Rather, the great potential allies of liberty on our campuses are the undergraduates themselves, who at last are beginning to understand their bondage to social engineering, indoctrination, censorship, and double standards. The great cause at American universities should be nothing less than the emancipation of students from the partisan and authoritarian regimes under which they live.

This requires that colleges and universities come to accept two deep and fundamental truths: first, that all students are individuals, free to associate voluntarily, but too dignified, as emancipated human beings, to have identities assigned to them by partisan academics and administrators; second, that undergraduates should have at least the same rights as their peers in the larger society. At a minimum, students at private universities that advertise themselves as committed to free inquiry and human equality should have the same rights that students theoretically enjoy by law at constitutionally obligated state universities.

Private universities, of course, as voluntary associations, have the right to define themselves, but truth-in-advertising has a moral dimension as well as a legal one. Let the current centers of politically correct governance of student lives in loco parentis have the courage, if they truly stand by their policies and ideologies, to put this most essential information on page one of their catalogs. Let them say to their public what they say to themselves: "This University believes that your sons and daughters are the racist, sexist, homophobic progeny—or the innocent victims—of a racist, sexist, homophobic, oppressive America. For $30,000 per year, we shall assign them rights on an unequal and compensatory basis and undertake by coercion their moral and political enlightenment." Let them advertise themselves honestly and then see who comes.

If the American experiment in human liberty is to survive, citizens must work to keep alive the honest and unfettered pursuit of critical truth and the free exchange of ideas, values, and convictions; to preserve due process; to secure the rule of law, not of arbitrary, individual will; and to guarantee the equality of all individuals before the law. The alternative has a name, tyranny.

It is appalling but true that the academic world needs a lesson in freedom and dignity from the larger society. In such a context, all who care about higher education need to separate their particular, partisan politics from their obligation to liberty and to the life of the mind and spirit. Universities at which politically incorrect students and faculty are punished and officially marginalized for expressing their beliefs will play no role in the society's larger debate about freedom and legal equality, except to erode the sincere commitment to both. Everyone who cherishes liberty, however, must understand that it is indivisible. No one enjoys in safety more than the least of us enjoys.

To cherish freedom and equality before the law is not to approve of all or even most of the uses individuals make of that freedom. That is an absurd notion, and it has become a form of moral blackmail. Rather, it is to cherish freedom itself as a way of being human, and to understand the right to respond to speech with speech, not force, and to argue, debate, and even, at times, to change individuals and persuade them, not by coercion, but by appeal to their free and equal human minds and souls. There is a terrible and stultifying oppression and double standard in American academic culture. In some future, as in our coming to terms with the period of McCarthyism, people will ask: What did individuals of goodwill do? Each should be able to answer: I fought to keep alive the spirit of open-minded inquiry. I fought to keep alive the full rights of criticism and debate. I fought to give to others the same rights to free expression, including angry or sharp free expression, that I desired or demanded for myself. I fought to preserve persuasion and education against coercion and indoctrination. I fought to permit students to individuate—within the fullest possible freedom allowed by law—according to the lights of private conscience and critical mind—the ultimate precondition of human dignity and liberation. How many trustees, administrators, faculty members, so-called student leaders, parents, donors, and alumni can say that now?

It is our liberty, above all else, that defines us as human beings, capable of ethics and responsibility. The struggle for liberty on American campuses is one of the defining struggles of the age in which we find ourselves. A nation that does not educate in freedom will not survive in freedom, and will not even know when it has lost it. Individuals too often convince themselves that they are caught up in moments of history that they cannot affect. That history, however, is made by their will and moral choices. There is a moral crisis in higher education. It will not be resolved unless we choose and act to resolve it.

In Robert Bolt's *A Man for All Seasons,* Richard Rich offers the perjured testimony that would send Sir Thomas More to the executioner. As Rich passed by the defendant's dock, More noticed a new chain of office around Rich's neck, and asked what it was. Thomas Cromwell answered that Rich was now attorney general for Wales. Looking at his false accuser with a mixture of pain and amusement, More said: "For Wales? Why, Richard, it profits a man nothing to give his soul for the whole world. . . . But for Wales!"[41] Indeed. For an unmerited trusteeship? For administrative salary and perquisites? For tenure? For promotion? For shelter from partisan charges? For a sterile peace and quiet? Our universities acutely need more men and women for all seasons, and if they cannot produce them, then a moral society should cease to provide them with gilded chains and offices. There should be no rewards for infamy.

Let us all keep our wits about us, for Marcuse's heirs almost all and always think tactically. The theory of "repressive tolerance," or, more precisely, its practice of "progressive intolerance," still governs the extracurricular lives of nearly all of our students. It is easy, however, to identify the vulnerabilities of the bearers of this worst and, at the time, most marginal legacy of the '60s:

They loathe the society that they believe should support them generously in their authority over its offspring; they are detached from the values of individual liberty, legal equality, privacy, and the sanctity of conscience toward which Americans essentially are drawn; and, for both those reasons, they cannot bear the light of public scrutiny. Let the sunlight in.

NOTES

Chapter 1. The Water Buffalo Affair

1. From late March of 1993, Kors was Eden Jacobowitz's judicial advisor at Penn. He possesses all of the official documents, correspondence, and e-mail referred to in this chapter. He interviewed scores of witnesses, administrators, and University of Pennsylvania police officers. He retains all relevant messages left on his telephone answering machine.
2. University of Pennsylvania, *Policies and Procedures, 1987–1988.*
3. University of Pennsylvania, 1989 New Student Orientation Program, "Incidents of Harassment."
4. University of Pennsylvania, *Almanac,* April 12, 1988.
5. Sheldon Hackney, "The Helms Amendment Imperils the Basis of Intellectual Freedom," *Chronicle of Higher Education,* September 6, 1989; Sheldon Hackney, "Freedom of Ideas and the NEA/Funding Controversy," *Almanac,* September 5, 1989; Sheldon Hackney, "The Arts Battle: Our Soul as University at Stake," *Almanac,* September 12, 1989.
6. University of Pennsylvania, *Policies and Procedures, 1990–1991.*
7. Oral exchange between Kors and Hackney, Spring 1989.
8. Letter from JIO Robin Read to Eden Jacobowitz, March 22, 1993.
9. Conversations on the Judicial Office's verbal stipulation of charges held between Kors and Fran Walker, director of student life (and Eden's first adviser), during April 1993 and May 13, 1993; confidential University of Pennsylvania Police report on its follow-up investigation, January–February 1993; testimony of eyewitnesses and interviews by Kors of witnesses; testimony of Sheldon Hackney during his nomination hearing for the chairmanship of the National Endowment for the Humanities, U.S. Senate, Committee on Labor and Human Resources, June 25, 1993.
10. Ibid.
11. Uncontested letter and public statements of Eden Jacobowitz from January 13, 1993 on. Also, see note 9 above.
12. Letter from Eden Jacobowitz to Robin Read, April 5, 1993.
13. Letter from Robin Read to Eden Jacobowitz, May 8, 1993.

14. Letter from professor of English Daniel Hoffman (University of Pennsylvania Poet in Residence and director of the writing program) to Kors, April 22, 1993.

15. Written affidavit from Duke University Professor of English Kenny Jackson Williams to Kors, May 10, 1993.

16. Testimony of Sheldon Hackney, nomination hearing, U.S. Senate, Committee on Labor and Human Resources, June 25, 1993.

17. Ibid.

18. Telephone conversation, John Brobeck and Kors, April 12, 1993.

19. Message relayed "from Sheldon" to Kors by Assistant to the President Stephen Steinberg in phone call placed by Steinberg, April 14, 1993.

20. Court testimony reported in *Daily Pennsylvanian,* May 11, 1990.

21. *Daily Pennsylvanian,* April 20, 1990 and May 3, 1990.

22. *Daily Pennsylvanian,* January and February 1993.

23. *Daily Pennsylvanian,* January 14, 1993.

24. *Daily Pennsylvanian,* February 25, 1993.

25. *Daily Pennsylvanian,* March 19, 1993.

26. Interviews with Greg Pavlik; copies of correspondence in possession of authors; telephone call between Kors and President Sheldon Hackney, March 9, 1993; telephone call between Kors and Provost Michael Aiken, March 9, 1993.

27. Reprinted for the whole university community as a letter from Hackney to the editor of the *Daily Pennsylvanian,* March 18, 1993.

28. Interviews with members of *Daily Pennsylvanian* staff; discussion between Kors and the special faculty JIO appointed by Hackney in this case, who explained that he wanted an "educational" settlement of this matter, not "punishment."

29. See the *Daily Pennsylvanian's* frequent coverage from April to September 1993; *Almanac,* April 20, 1993; *Philadelphia Inquirer,* April 18, 1993; *Editor and Publisher,* May 22, 1993; *Almanac,* July 13, 1993; *Daily Pennsylvanian,* July 15, 1993; *Daily Pennsylvanian,* July 22, 1993; official documents exonerating students but condemning guard published by *Wall Street Journal,* July 26, 1993; *Philadelphia Inquirer,* July 30, 1993; *Chronicle of Higher Education,* August 2, 1993; on the dropping of the charges against all students, see University of Pennsylvania press release, September 14, 1993, *Almanac,* September 14, 1993, and *Daily Pennsylvanian,* September 15, 1993.

30. *Daily Pennsylvanian,* April 16, 1993.

31. Sheldon Hackney, press release, April 17, 1993, printed in *Almanac,* April 20, 1993.

32. Sheldon Hackney, press release, April 2, 1981.

33. *Philadelphia Inquirer,* April 18, 1993.

34. *Village Voice,* May 4, 1993.

35. Letter in possession of authors.

36. University of Pennsylvania, "Judicial Charter," in *Policies and Procedures, 1992–1993.*

37. *Forward,* April 23 [April 22], 1993.

38. Interview of Dorothy Rabinowitz.

39. *Wall Street Journal,* April 26, 1993.

40. *Washington Post,* April 29, 1993.

41. Interview by Kors.
42. *NBC Nightly News,* May 14, 1993.
43. *Washington Times,* April 27, 1993.
44. *Philadelphia Daily News,* April 27, 1993.
45. *Financial Times,* May 8, 1993.
46. *New York Times,* May 30, 1993.
47. *NBC Nightly News,* May 13, 1993.
48. Gary Trudeau, *Doonesbury,* July 11, 1993.
49. Copy of letter in possession of authors.
50. *Daily Pennsylvanian,* September 9, 1993.
51. Telephone conversation between Kors and Fran Walker, May 18, 1993.
52. *Almanac,* April 5, 1994.

Chapter 2. Free Speech in a Free Society

1. *Gitlow v. New York,* 268 U.S. 652 (1925).
2. *Hague v. Committee for Industrial Organization,* 307 U.S. 496 (1939).
3. Nat Hentoff, *Free Speech for Me—But Not for Thee* (New York: Harper Collins, 1992), p. 1.
4. *Schenck v. United States,* 249 U.S. 47 (1919).
5. *Brandenburg v. Ohio,* 395 U.S. 444 (1969).
6. *Near v. Minnesota,* 283 U.S. 697 (1931).
7. *Snepp v. United States,* 444 U.S. 507 (1980).
8. *Miller v. California,* 413 U.S. 15, 25 (1973).
9. *Jenkins v. Georgia,* 418 U.S. 153 (1974).
10. *Chaplinsky v. New Hampshire,* 315 U.S. 568 (1942).
11. *Abrams v. United States,* 250 U.S. 616 (1919).
12. Ibid., 630.
13. *Beauharnais v. Illinois,* 343 U.S. 250 (1952).
14. *Cafeteria Employees Local 302 v. Angelos,* 320 U.S. 293 (1943).
15. *Terminiello v. Chicago,* 337 U.S. 1 (1949).
16. *Street v. New York,* 394 U.S. 576 (1969).
17. *Cohen v. California,* 403 U.S. 15 (1971).
18. *United States v. Eichman,* 496 U.S. 310, 318 (1990).
19. *Feiner v. New York,* 340 U.S. 315 (1951).
20. *Gooding v. Wilson,* 405 U.S. 518 (1972).
21. *Papish v. Board of Curators of the University of Missouri,* 410 U.S. 667 (1973).
22. *United States v. Schwimmer,* 279 U.S. 644 (1929).
23. Laurence H. Tribe, *American Constitutional Law,* 2d ed. (Mineola, N.Y.: The Foundation Press, 1988), 838, n.17.
24. *R.A.V. v. City of St. Paul,* 505 U.S. 377 (1992).
25. Nadine Strossen, "Regulating Racist Speech on Campus: A Modest Proposal?" 1990 *Duke Law Journal* 484.

Chapter 3. What Is Academic Freedom?

1. "General Report of the Committee on Academic Freedom and Tenure," 1 *AAUP Bulletin* 17 (December 1915), as reproduced in William W. Van Alstyne, ed., *Freedom and Tenure in the Academy* (Durham: Duke University Press, 1993), pp. 393–406.
2. Ibid., pp. 397–98.
3. Ibid., p. 402.
4. Ibid., p. 394.
5. Ibid., pp. 405–406.
6. Walter P. Metzger, "The 1940 Statement of Principles on Academic Freedom and Tenure," in *Freedom and Tenure in the Academy,* pp. 3–77.
7. Ibid.
8. "1940 Statement of Principles on Academic Freedom and Tenure," in *Freedom and Tenure in the Academy,* Appendix B, pp. 407–409.
9. Ibid., p. 407.
10. "Joint Statement on Rights and Freedoms of Students," as reproduced in *Freedom and Tenure in the Academy,* Appendix C, pp. 411–18.
11. Ibid., pp. 411–12.
12. Ibid., pp. 413–15.
13. Ibid., pp. 416–17.
14. Ibid., pp. 417–18.
15. *Adler v. Board of Education,* 342 U.S. 485 (1952); "Academic Freedom and the First Amendment in the Supreme Court of the United States: An Unhurried Historical Review," in *Freedom and Tenure in the Academy,* p. 105.
16. *Wieman v. Updegraff,* 344 U.S. 183 (1952).
17. *Sweezy v. New Hampshire,* 354 U.S. 234 (1957).
18. *Keyishian v. Board of Regents of the University of the State of New York,* 385 U.S. 589 (1967).
19. *Tinker v. Des Moines Independent Community School District,* 393 U.S. 503 (1969).
20. *Bethel School District No. 403 v. Fraser,* 478 U.S. 675 (1986).
21. *Hazelwood School District v. Kuhlmeier,* 484 U.S. 260 (1988).
22. *Healy v. James,* 408 U.S. 169 (1972).
23. *Regents of the University of Michigan v. Ewing,* 474 U.S. 214 (1985).
24. *State v. Schmid,* 84 N.J. 535 (1980).
25. William G. Bowen, "The Role of the University as an Institution in Confronting External Issues," as excerpted in *State v. Schmid,* ibid. at p. 631.
26. *Harvard Crimson,* November 20, 1996.
27. Judge Learned Hand, "Spirit of Liberty" speech given at "I Am an American Day" ceremony in New York, 1944 as excerpted in William Safire, *Lend Me Your Ears* (New York: W.W. Norton & Company, 1992), p. 63.

Chapter 4. Marcuse's Revenge

1. Herbert Marcuse, "Repressive Tolerance," in Robert Paul Wolff et al., *A Critique of Pure Tolerance* (Boston: Beacon Press, 1969), pp. 81–123 (originally published 1965).

2. Richard Delgado, "Words That Wound: A Tort Action for Racial Insults, Epithets, and Name Calling," 17 *Harvard Civil Rights–Civil Liberties Law Review* (1982) 133.

3. Mari Matsuda, "Public Response to Racist Speech: Considering the Victim's Story," 87 *University of Michigan Law Review* (1989) 2320.

4. Charles R. Lawrence III, "If He Hollers Let Him Go: When Racism Dresses in Speech's Clothing," *Duke University Law Journal* (1990) 431.

5. Mari Matsuda et al., *Words That Wound* (Boulder: Westview Press, 1993), pp. 1, 5.

6. Charles R. Lawrence III, "If He Hollers, Let Him Go: Regulating Racist Speech on Campus," in Matsuda et al., eds. *Words That Wound,* pp. 62, 68.

7. Richard Delgado, "Words That Wound: A Tort Action for Racial Insults, Epithets, and Name Calling," in *Words That Wound,* pp. 108, 109.

8. Mari Matsuda, "Public Response to Racist Speech: Considering the Victim's Story," in *Words That Wound,* p. 35.

9. Ibid., pp. 44, 45.

10. Matsuda et al., pp. 9, 14–15.

11. Matsuda, "Public Response to Racist Speech," pp. 39, 43.

12. Catharine A. MacKinnon, *Only Words* (Cambridge: Harvard University Press, 1993), pp. 72–73.

13. Ibid., p. 71.

14. *Brandenburg v. Ohio,* 395 U.S. 444 (1969).

15. *Claiborne Hardware Company v. National Association for the Advancement of Colored People,* 458 U.S. 886 (1982).

16. MacKinnon, *Only Words,* p. 86.

17. Stanley Fish, *There's No Such Thing as Free Speech, and It's a Good Thing Too* (New York: Oxford University Press, 1994).

18. Ibid., pp. viii–ix.

19. Ibid., p. 91.

20. Ibid., p. 115.

21. Ibid., p. 111.

22. Ibid., pp. 111, 118.

23. Thomas C. Grey, "Discriminatory Harassment and Free Speech," 14 *Harvard Journal of Law and Public Policy* (1991) 157, 158.

24. Ibid., p. 162.

25. Ibid., pp. 159–60.

26. Bill Bell, "Re: ACLU and constitutionally mandated speech restrictions," September 11, 1995 electronic posting to free speech discussion (quoting Thomas Grey), electronic listserve amend1-L@uafsys.uark.edu

27. Grey, *Discriminatory Harassment,* pp. 162–63.

28. *Plessy v. Ferguson,* 163 U.S. 537, 554 (1896).

29. Ibid., pp. 554, 559.

30. Marcuse, "Repressive Tolerance," p. 107.

31. All policies on "harassment" and "verbal behavior" have been taken from the Web-pages and handbooks of the colleges and universities discussed during the period 1994–97, unless otherwise indicated.

32. *The UWM Post, Inc., et al. v. Board of Regents of the University of Wisconsin,* 774 F.Supp. 1163 (1991).

33. *Robert J. Corry, et al. v. The Leland Stanford Junior University, et al.,* Case No. 740309, Superior Court, State of California, County of Santa Clara, Order on Preliminary Injunction, February 27, 1995.
34. Pub. L. 88-352 (Title VII), as amended 42 USC sec. 2000e (1964).
35. 29 CFR Ch. XIV (7 July 1994 ed.) Sec. 1604.11.
36. *Meritor Savings Bank, FSB v. Vinson,* 477 U.S. 57 (1986).
37. 20 U.S.C. §§ 1681–88.
38. *Franklin v. Gwinnett County Public Schools,* 503 U.S. 60 (1992).
39. Ibid. p. 75.
40. *UWM Post Inc., et al. v. Board of Regents of the University of Wisconsin,* 774 F.Supp. 1163, 1177 (1991).
41. Robert J. Henry letter to John E. Palomino, September 20, 1994; Anthony Lewis, *New York Times,* November 27, 1995; Norma V. Cantu, letter to editor, *New York Times,* December 8, 1995.
42. *Cohen v. California,* 403 U.S. 15 (1971).
43. *R.A.V. v. City of St. Paul, Minnesota,* 505 U.S. 377 (1992).
44. Henry Louis Gates, Jr., "Let Them Talk," *The New Republic,* September 20 and 27, 1993.
45. George Orwell, *Animal Farm* (San Diego: Harcourt Brace Jovanovich, 1990 [© 1974]).
46. *Rolling Stone,* March 21, 1991.

Chapter 5. The Moral Reality of Political Correctness

1. *Academe,* September–October, 1991.
2. *Regina v. Butler* (70 C.C.C. 3d 129, 1992 CCC LEXIS 60, Supreme Court of Canada, February 1992).
3. The policy and guide were introduced as evidence and analyzed at length by Judge Avern Cohen in *Doe v. University of Michigan,* 721 F. Supp. 852 (E.D. Mich. 1989).
4. All relevant documents and citations in the *Boston Globe,* August 26, 1994, and January 29, 1994.
5. *Boston Globe,* January 29, 1994.
6. Ibid.
7. *Gambit,* July 23, 1996. Copies of the original letter and cover letter are in the possession of the authors.
8. Copy of letter in possession of the authors.
9. *Times–Picayune,* September 17, 1996.
10. *Driftwood,* August 22, 1996.
11. Six-page letter, single-spaced, from Chatelle to Copping, September 30, 1996; letter from Chatelle to O'Brien, November 18, 1996. Copies of originals in possession of the authors.
12. Chatelle to Copping, September 30, 1996.
13. *Now Notes,* March 3, 1997.
14. Letter from Chatelle to University of New Orleans administration, July 24, 1997. Copy of original in possession of authors.

Chapter 6. The Assault on Faculty Speech

1. *Boston Globe,* December 20, 1990.
2. Copies of the seven negative ballots, in redacted form without the signatures of the faculty members.
3. Hampshire College, Faculty Meeting Attachment, December 7, 1993, Item No. 3.
4. Hampshire College, Faculty Meeting Minutes, December 7, 1993, contemporaneous notes by atendees (copies in possession of the authors).
5. Authors' interviews with participants.
6. For the essential materials pertaining to the Dean Cohen case, see, above all, the briefs and decision in *Cohen v. San Bernardino Valley College,* 92 F.3d 968 (9th Cir. 1996). See also, *Washington Post,* August 23, 1996; *Chronicle of Higher Education,* September 6, 1996.
7. For the essential materials pertaining to the Donald Silva case, see, above all, the briefs and decision in *Silva v. the University of New Hampshire,* 888 F. Supp. 293 (D.N.H. 1994). See also, *New York Times,* September 17, October 12, and December 4, 1994; *Chronicle of Higher Education,* September 28, 1994.
8. Center for Individual Rights, *Docket Report,* First Quarter, 1995; *New York Times* December 4, 1994.
9. Richard Bernstein, "Guilty If Charged," *New York Review of Books,* January 13, 1994, 11–14.
10. Ibid.
11. The Toni Blake case was reported and documented by Nat Hentoff, "Fear and Deliverance at the University of Nebraska," *Village Voice,* January 18, 1994.
12. Moshman's report to the Academic Senate, as quoted in Hentoff, "Fear and Deliverance."
13. Ibid.
14. The Ayers case was reported and documented by Joseph S. Salemi, "Political Correctness at Dallas Baptist University: The Firing of David Ayers and John Jeffrey," *Measure,* no. 108 (August–September 1992), 1–13. See also the *Baptist Press,* May 29, 1992; the *Texas Baptist Conservative Newsletter,* May 30, 1992; the *Dallas Morning News,* June 3, 1992; the *Fort Worth Star–Telegram,* June 6, 1992; the *Baptist Standard* (August 5, 1992); *Washington Times,* November 30, 1992.
15. See the briefs in *Snyder v. the Chicago Theological Seminary,* 94 1423 (Cir. Ct. Cook Co., Ill.); see also *Boston Sunday Globe,* March 27, 1994; *Washington Post,* May 13, 1994; *Wall Street Journal,* May 9, 1994; Associated Press, January 13, 1995; Nat Hentoff, "Assaulted By the Talmud," *The Progressive,* August 1994.
16. *Washington Post,* May 13, 1994.
17. *Boston Globe,* March 29, 1994.
18. *Washington Post,* May 13, 1994.
19. For the essential materials of the Osborne case, see the court papers in *Osborne v. Braxton-Brown,* Docket No. 5-94-Civ 42 (U.S. District Court, District of Minnesota). See also letter dated October 11, 1994, from Greg Braxton-Brown, President, Arrowhead Community Colleges, to Richard Osborne, sent pursuant to the settlement of the case, rescinding the earlier letter of reprimand and making other assurances consistent with the settlement.

20. Ibid.

21. For the essential facts of the Kleinfeld case, see the papers in the proceeding concerning the University of Alaska-Fairbanks, U.S. Department of Education, Office for Civil Rights, Region X (Seattle, WA), Case No. 10922034, decided by letter of August 7, 1992, addressed to Dr. Joan K. Wadlow, Chancellor.

22. Ibid. See also Ward Parks, "Witch Hunt in Alaska," *Point of View* (The Heritage Foundation), May 13, 1993; Cornell Clayton, "Frank Discussion Needed on UAF Controversy," *Fairbanks Daily News Miner,* December 4, 1991; "Affidavit of James W. Paul" [Superintendent of the Railbelt School District, Alaska, 1979–91], State of Alaska, Fourth Judicial District, subscribed and sworn March 6, 1992. Also, personal signed communications from Judith Kleinfeld to the authors, March 26, 1998, as well as a signed legal Declaration by Kleinfeld, and communications from Kleinfeld's lawyers (Winston Burbank, Fairbanks, Alaska, and the Center for Individual Rights, Washington, D.C.), April 14–15, 1998.

23. For the essential materials of the Gee case, see the court papers and decisions in *Gee v. Humphries,* Civil Action No. 95-40031-RH, U.S. District Court, N.D. Florida; summarily affirmed on appeal by unpublished order dated April 3, 1998, Docket No. 97-2265, U. S. Court of Appeals for the 11th Circuit (per curiam). The decision in *Gee* appears to be in conflict with *Cohen v. San Bernardino Valley College,* 92 F.3d 968 (9th Cir. 1996), cert. denied, 117 S.Ct. 1290 (1997).

24. *Wall Street Journal,* September 26, 1994.

25. *Jet,* November 28, 1994.

26. *Chronicle of Higher Education,* October 10, 1997.

27. Reuters, "University of Florida President Will Keep Job," January 27, 1998; *Chronicle of Higher Education,* February 6, 1998.

28. The essential materials of the Levin case are found in the briefs and decisions in *Levin v. Harleston,* 770 F.Supp. 895 (S.D.N.Y. 1991); 966 F.2d 85 (2nd Cir. 1992).

29. The essential materials of the Jeffries case are found in the briefs and decisions of *Jeffries v. Harleston,* 828 F.Supp. 1066 (S.D.N.Y. 1993); 21 F.3d 1238 (2nd Cir. 1994).

30. *Jeffries v. Harleston,* 52 F.3d 9 (2nd Cir. 1995); see also, *Chronicle of Higher Education,* November 23, 1994.

31. The essential materials in the Gottfredson case are found in the case documents in *University of Delaware Chapter of the American Association of University Professors and the University of Delaware: Pioneer Fund Grievance,* Case No.14-390-1935-90-A, American Arbitration Association. All documents described and quoted are in the possession of the authors. Kors interviewed several parties to this affair.

32. "Report of the Faculty Senate Committee on Research on the Issue of the University of Delaware's Relationship with the Pioneer Fund," April 19, 1990.

33. University of Delaware press release, "U.D. Takes Action on Pioneer Fund."

34. University of Delaware Arbitration Decision.

35. Copies of all memos are in the authors' possession.

36. *Delaware State News,* May 2, 1990.

37. "Report of the Faculty Senate Committee on Research," April 19, 1990.

38. "Memorandum of Professors Linda S. Gottfredson and Jan H. Blits in Support of their Grievance Against the University of Delaware," in *AAUP and the University of Delaware;* see note 31 above.

39. Copies of all memos are in the authors' possession.
40. *The Review* (the campus newspaper), November 15, 1991.
41. Copy of the memo is in the authors' possession.
42. Copy of the memo is in the authors' possession.
43. Copy of the letter is in the authors' possession.
44. *Delaware State News,* March 8, 1994.
45. *Wilmington News Journal,* November 2, 1975.
46. *Philadelphia Inquirer,* October 16, 1977, reporting on the details of Aumiller's successful suit against the university and against Trabant in federal district court. See also, *Wilmington News Journal,* September 15, 17, 1976.
47. *Wilmington News Journal,* October 30, 1977.
48. Ibid.

Chapter 7. *"Shut Up," They Reasoned: Silencing Students*

1. All policies on "harassment" and "verbal behavior" have been taken from the Webpages and handbooks of the colleges and universities discussed during the period 1994–97, unless otherwise indicated.
2. Yale University, "Report of the Committee on Freedom of Expression at Yale" (the "Woodward Committee" report), January 1975; Yale University, "Free Expression, Peaceful Dissent, and Demonstrations," in Yale's published policies and procedures, still in force.
3. For the details of the Wayne Dick case, see Nat Hentoff, "An Unspeakable Crime at Yale," *Village Voice,* July 15, 1986; Nat Hentoff, "The Trial of a Notorious Yale Student," *Village Voice,* July 22, 1986; and John Hechinger, "Civil Liberties, Battle Lines Set at Yale. Student's Antigay Poster Raises Free Speech Issue," *Boston Globe,* July 29, 1986.
4. *Boston Globe,* July 29, 1986.
5. Copy of letter in possession of authors.
6. *Columbia Journalism Review,* October 1994.
7. *Boston Phoenix,* October 27, 1995; *Boston Herald,* November 1, 1995; *The ROC: The Voice of Rock Out Censorship,* December 1995/January 1996.
8. Copy of letter in possession of authors.
9. On the details of the T-shirt and speech code episode at Tufts, see Tufts University, "Freedom of Speech Versus Freedom From Harassment," a policy adopted in spring 1989 and published by the university in "Policies and Responsibilities," 1989–1990; *Tufts Daily,* "Commencement Issue" (May 21, 1989), and all issues throughout September and October 1989; *Boston Phoenix,* October 13, 1989.
10. *Tufts Daily,* September, October 1989, passim.
11. *Boston Globe,* March 17, 1996.
12. Commonwealth of Massachusetts Board of Regents of Higher Education, "Policy Against Racism. Guidelines for Campus Policies Against Racism," adopted June 13, 1989. A copy of these guidelines, which were distributed to high administrators, is in the possession of the authors.

13. On the turmoil surrounding the newspaper takeover, see Gary Crosby Brasor, "Turmoil and Tension at the University of Massachusetts at Amherst: History, Analysis, and Recommended Solutions," a seventy-nine-page report issued by the Massachusetts Association of Scholars in November 1994, and the report's fifty-three-page "Update," issued in March 1996. See also, Massachusetts Advisory Committee to the U.S. Commission on Civil Rights, "Campus Tensions in Massachusetts: Searching for Solutions in the Nineties," October 1992.

14. *Boston Globe,* May 7, 1992.

15. *Daily Hampshire Gazette,* May 7, 1992.

16. Associated Press, May 7, 1992.

17. *Boston Globe,* May 7, 1992.

18. *Daily Hampshire Gazette,* May 9, 1992.

19. Letter from Chancellor David K. Scott to Gary Brasor, April 7, 1994 (copy in possession of the authors).

20. Office of the Chancellor, University of Massachusetts, "Letter from Chancellor Scott to campus community," October 11, 1995, sent with letter from Susan Pearson, Associate Chancellor, September 20, 1995, with attached "Proposed Harassment Policy."

21. *New York Times,* November 27, 1995.

22. Memorandum from Harvard Law School dean Robert C. Clark announcing the enforcement of HLS sexual harassment guidelines, October 25, 1995.

23. *UWM Post v. Board of Regents of the University of Wisconsin,* 774 F. Supp. 1163 (E.D. Wis. 1991); *Doe v. University of Michigan,* 721 F.Supp. 852 (E.D. Mich. 1989).

24. See Mary Joe Frug, "A Postmodern Feminist Legal Manifesto," 105 *Harvard Law Review* (1992) 1045 and parody, "He-Manifesto of Post-Mortem Legal Feminism," 105 *Harvard Law Revue* (1992), pp. 61–62.

25. The Harvard Law School Administrative Board's ruling is dated May 21, 1992, and is in the possession of the authors, along with other papers and reports concerning Professor Kennedy's efforts to discipline the parodists.

26. *The Progressive,* May 1989.

27. Syracuse University, "Policies."

28. *New York Times,* March 17, 1991.

29. *Binghamton Review,* May 1996.

30. On the Marlin Lask case, Kors has interviewed participants, and the authors have copies in their possession of all documents cited or described. Of particular value is the memorandum from Professors William Park and Francis Randall to the faculty of Sarah Lawrence College, September 1, 1993, and fifty-one-page account of the affair, with appendices, by Francis Randall, "The Great Sarah Lawrence Laughter Case; A Tragi-Comedy Without Villains." See also, "Student Guilty of Laughing," *Forward,* May 28, 1993, and "Free Speech Woes at Sarah Lawrence," *New York Times,* December 13, 1993.

31. *New York Times,* December 13, 1993.

32. Memorandum and flier in possession of authors.

33. *Rocky Mountain News,* November 25, 1994; *Record* (Bergen County, N.J.) April 28, 1995; *Providence Journal–Bulletin,* December 16, 1994.

34. Georgetown University, policies and procedures on the Webpage and published, 1996–97.

35. Rutgers University, policies and procedures on the Webpage and published, 1996–97.

36. University of Maryland, College Park, *Sexual Harassment Policy,* introduced on August 22, 1990, by President William E. Kirwan and still in effect as of publication.

37. The authors possess full documentation of the incidents at Carnegie Mellon University from Declan McCullagh, and these documents also are preserved at many Websites concerned with free expression and due process, including the Justice on Campus Website at MIT, in its subsection, "CMU Discplinary Charges," and at the Fight-Censorship Website. In particular, see the full documentation of abuses of CMU preserved at www.joc.mit.edu/charges.html. See also the full documentation, including e-mail among the parties cited here, provided in Declan McCullagh, "The Death of Free Speech at Carnegie Mellon University: A Two-Year History of Politically Correct Campus Discipline," August 4, 1995, unpublished manuscript. See also, *Washington Times,* April 7, 1993, and July 7, 1994; *Tartan,* April 10, 1994; *Pittsburgh Post–Gazette,* April 6, 1994; *Pittsburgh Tribune–Review,* April 6, 1994.

38. On events at George Mason University, see the briefs and decision in *Iota Xi Chapter of Sigma Chi Fraternity v. George Mason University,* 773 F.Supp. 792 (E.D.V.A. 1991); 993 F.2d 386 (4th Cir. 1993); see also, *Washington Post,* May 12, 1993.

39. See West Virginia University Webpages, 1996–97, for the harassment policies, the *Mountaineer Creed,* and the policies of the Office of Social Justice. The OSJ policies were given to new faculty in the fall of 1996. In February 1998, in response to threats from a small group of faculty to publicize the policies and sue the university, West Virginia removed the OSJ policies from the Website, but has not rescinded them.

40. Copies of all the forms and correspondence cited from Vanderbilt are in the possession of the authors. Kors interviewed participants in this affair.

41. Emory University Website "EMORY_REPORT," May 1, 1995.

42. Emory University Website "EMORY_REPORT," April 24, 1995.

43. University of Tennessee, policies and procedures from Website, 1996–97.

44. Auburn University, policies and procedures from Website, 1996–97.

45. *New York Times,* November 11, 1995; *Chapel Hill News,* November 17, 1995; *Charlotte News and Observer,* November 17, 18, 1995.

46. *New York Times,* December 24, 1989.

47. *News and Observer,* September 28, 29, 1993; *Herald-Sun,* September 23, 1993; *Chronicle,* September 28, 1993, March 3, 14, 1994; Dickerson's report published in the university's *Dialogue,* March 4, 1994.

48. *SPLC Report,* issues from 1993–98. See, in particular, the *SPLC Report* (Spring 1997). Documentation was also provided to the authors by the Intercollegiate Studies Institute concerning the unpunished theft of the informal network of conservative and libertarian alternative student publications that it assists.

49. Associated Press, February 11, 1996.

50. Copy of e-mail in the possession of the authors.

51. Websites of *Alligator Online* (University of Florida) and of the Electronic Frontier Foundation.

52. Copies of all e-mail, postings, and correspondence cited in this case at the University of Memphis are in the possession of the authors.

53. University of Chicago, *Student Information Manual,* 1996–97.

54. University of Illinois at Chicago, policies and procedures on Website.

55. On the Wabash College case, see *Chronicle of Higher Education,* September 22, 1995; *Washington Times,* September 25, 1995, October 11, 1995.

56. Department of Human Relations, Michigan State University, "Fact Sheet on Bias-Free Communication," September 1985.

57. On University of Wisconsin speech code—the events surrounding it, its development, and its substance—see the briefs and decision in *UMW Post v. Board of Regents of the University of Wisconsin,* 774 F.Supp. 1163, 1167, 1179 (E.D. Wis. 1991). The code itself, promulgated on September 1, 1989, was part of "Discriminatory Harassment: Prohibited Conduct . . . Revisions" to the University of Wisconsin System Administrative Code, Section 17. See also the history of the 1989 code presented by Patricia Hodulik, "Prohibiting Discriminatory Harassment by Regulating Student Speech: A Balancing of First-Amendment and University Interests," *Journal of College and University Law,* vol. 16., no. 4 (1990). All other university documents cited or referred to are in the possession of the authors.

58. American Civil Liberties Union of Wisconsin Foundation, "Media Release," March 29, 1990.

59. University of Wisconsin System, *Wisconsin Administrative Code,* UWS 17 (1992).

60. *Washington Post,* September 18, 1992. See also, *New York Times,* June 25, 1992, September 14, 1992.

61. On the Central Michigan University case, see the briefs and decision in *Dambrot v. Central Michigan University,* 839 F.Supp. 477, 481 (E.D. Mich. 1993).

62. Copies of all documents cited or described concerning the UW–River Falls case are in the possession of the authors.

63. *Student Voice,* April 13, 1995.

64. *Student Voice,* April 6, 1995.

65. People for the American Way, *Artistic Freedom Under Attack* (1994).

66. Ibid.

67. Ibid.

68. Ibid.

69. *Chronicle of Higher Education,* February 16, 1996.

70. *New York Times,* August 13, 1989.

71. *U. Magazine,* May 1996.

72. *Chronicle of Higher Education,* May 10, 1996. Also see the wonderfully named court case, *Loving v. Boren,* Docket No 97-6086, U.S. Court of Appeals for the Tenth Circuit, January 7, 1998.

73. Electronic Frontier Foundation, Website 1996; Fight-Censorship, Website 1996.

74. *Oklahoma Daily,* May 2, 1996.

75. Minutes and contemporaneous notes are in the possession of the authors.

76. Copy of memorandum is in the possession of the authors.

77. On the events involving the suppression of the College Republicans fliers at the University of Minnesota, see the frequent coverage in *Minneapolis Star–Tribune* and *Pioneer Press* throughout September 1993, particularly the *Star–Tribune's* articles on

September 16 and September 22. The fliers, UM press releases, and memoranda cited or described are in the possession of the authors.

78. *Minneapolis Star–Tribune,* September 22, 1993.

79. *Minneapolis Star–Tribune,* September 16, 1993.

80. *Chronicle of Higher Education,* May 25, 1994.

81. *Chronicle of Higher Education,* April 12, 1996.

82. On the UM–Duluth/History Club case, see the briefs and decisions in *Burnham v. Ianni,* 899 F.Supp. 395 (D.Minn. 1995); 98 F.3d 1007 (8th Cir. 1996); 119 F.3d 668 (8th Cir. 1997).

83. Photographs of the photographs are in the possession of the authors.

84. *Chronicle of Higher Education,* July 25, 1997.

85. *The Montana Professor* (Spring 1994).

86. University of Southern California, *Policies and Procedures, 1994–95*; Leonard Law, Calif. Education Code §94.367, statutes 1993 ch. 1363.

87. Student Press Law Center, *SPLC Report* (Fall 1997).

88. University of North Dakota, *Policies and Procedures, 1995–96.*

89. Full documentation provided by the Websites of the Electronic Frontier Foundation and of Fight-Censorship, March 1996.

90. *Hazelwood School District v. Kuhlmeier,* 479 U.S. 1053 (1986).

91. Student Press Law Center, *SPLC Report* (Fall 1996).

92. Student Press Law Center, *SPLC Report* (January 1998).

93. *Daily Evergreen,* October 31, November 1, 7, and 13, 1996; *Lewiston Tribune,* November 6, 1996.

94. ACLU Press Conference, May 16, 1989; *Los Angeles Times,* May 17, 1989; *Orange County Register,* May 17, 1989; *Record,* May 17, 1989; United Press International, May 16, 1989.

95. Documents in possession of the authors. See also, Linda Seebach, "Condemn Violence as well as Bad Taste," *Los Angeles Daily News,* March 18, 1993.

96. On the University of California–Riverside case, see *Wall Street Journal,* December 22, 1993; press releases, the Individual Rights Foundation, December 1993; *Kalorama Extra,* January 13, 1994; *U. Magazine,* May 1994.

97. *Wall Street Journal,* December 22, 1993.

98. All documents, e-mail, and correspondence cited and described in the discussion of the Smith case at the University of California–Santa Cruz are in the possession of the authors.

Chapter 8. Individual Identity: The Heart of Liberty

1. *Minersville School District v. Gobitis,* 310 U.S. 586 (1940).

2. Ibid., p. 596; Abraham Lincoln: Message to Congress, July 4, 1861. (This also appears in a speech delivered at Washington, November 10, 1864.)

3. *West Virginia State Board of Education v. Barnette,* 319 U.S. 624 (1943).

4. *Stanley v. Georgia,* 394 U.S. 557 (1969).

5. *Wooley v. Maynard,* 430 U.S. 705 (1977).

6. *Sobell v. Reed,* 327 F.Supp. 1294, 1304 (S.D.N.Y. 1971).

7. *American Booksellers Association, Inc. v. Hudnut,* 771 F.2d 323 (7th Cir. 1985).

8. *Hudnut v. American Booksellers Association, Inc., et al.,* 475 U.S. 1001 (1986).

9. *Wallace v. Jaffree,* 472 U.S. 38 (1985).

10. Princeton's letter to minorities is in the possession of the authors.

11. *Washington Times,* September 1, 1994.

12. Office of Multicultural Affairs, University of South Carolina, Website, 1996.

13. Office of Student Affairs, Smith College, handout to each freshman, September 1990. The document is in the possession of the authors.

14. Swarthmore College, "Student Life . . . Black at Swarthmore," Website, 1996.

15. University of Iowa, Website, 1996.

16. Franklin and Marshall College, "Activities of the Associate Dean for Advisement and Multicultural Affairs," Website, 1996.

17. University of Maryland, "Diversity_Resources/Race_Ethnicity," Website, 1996.

18. Occidental College, "Administration . . . Office of Student Life . . . Cultural Resource Center," Website, 1997.

19. Office of Student Affairs, University of Nebraska–Lincoln, "Multicultural Affairs," Website, 1996.

20. University of Massachusetts Amherst, *The Multicultural Experience* [n.d.].

21. *New York Times,* October 8, 1989.

22. Middlebury College, "Palana," Website, 1996.

23. *New York Times,* March 16, 1995; Kenneth B. Clark and Michael Meyers, "Separate Is Never Equal," *New York Times,* April 1, 1995; *Chronicle of Higher Education,* April 14, 1995; *Wall Street Journal,* July 25, 1995; Michael Meyers, letter to the editor, *Chronicle of Higher Education,* August 11, 1995; Brent Staples, "Jim Crow at Cornell?" *New York Times,* May 19, 1996; *Chronicle of Higher Education,* June 17, 1996.

24. Interview of Meyers by Kors and Silverglate.

25. *New York Times,* March 16, 1995. See also the sources cited in note 23.

26. Confidential telephone and e-mail interviews by Kors and Silverglate of residence personnel and faculty.

27. *Wall Street Journal,* July 25, 1995, editorial page; *Chronicle of Higher Education,* May 10, 1996.

28. *Chronicle of Higher Education,* November 24, 1995; *New York Times,* November 19, 1995; Associated Press, November 15, 16, 1995.

29. *Chronicle of Higher Education,* May 3, 1996.

30. *Chronicle of Higher Education,* December 8, 1995.

31. *Mac Weekly,* October 19, 1995.

32. "Dear Student" letter from Pearl Petit, December 12, 1995 (copy in possession of authors).

33. School of Education, University of Massachusetts, announcement of EDUC 392Z, "Examining Queer Identities & Creating Queer Communities" (in possession of authors).

34. *Massachusetts Daily Collegian,* January 31, 1996.

35. Announcement, EDUC 392Z.

36. *Minuteman,* November 1992.

37. *Chronicle of Higher Education,* January 27, 1995.

38. Robert Chatelle, "Political Correctness=Bigotry," National Writers Union Sexual-Minority listserve, December 6, 1996.

39. Student Life and Services, Oberlin College, Multicultural Resource Center Website, 1997.

40. Pennsylvania State University, Multicultural Resource Center Website, 1997.

41. Ohio State University, Division of Student Affairs Website, 1997.

42. University of Wyoming, Minority Affairs Office Website, 1997.

43. University of Virginia, Office of the Dean of Students Website, 1997.

44. The job advertisements that follow all appeared in *Chronicle of Higher Education,* September–December 1997.

45. *Daily Pennsylvanian,* May 1, 1996.

46. *New York Times,* June 5, 1991.

Chapter 9. American Thought Reform

1. Affirmative Action Committee, Tulane University, "Initiatives for the Race and Gender Enrichment of Tulane University of Louisiana," June 4, 1990. In response to a very public outcry occasioned by a small but determined group of faculty, widely reported in the media, a second draft was released on March 21, 1991, a third draft on May 20, 1991, and a fourth draft on November 18, 1991.

2. March 1993 discussions between Kors and Neil Hamburg, in no manner confidential or off the record. Told by Kors that President Hackney had denied in writing what Hamburg just claimed—"What's wrong with this settlement? I've signed off on scores of them"—Hamburg replied, "That's just politics. But if you repeat what I said, I will deny it."

3. Document is in the possession of the authors.

4. All documents cited or described in the discussion of Penn's planning for and implementation of "diversity education" are in the possession of the authors, including the charge of President Sheldon Hackney, and all circulated minutes, internal memoranda, interim and final reports, shared materials from other colleges and universities, and the actual documents produced for use at Penn, from the 1989 "Diversity Education (Oversight) Committee," "Diversity Education Subcommittee on Follow-Up Programs," the "Diversity Education Labor Day [Freshman Orientation] Program Committee," and the 1988 Office of the Vice Provost for University Life, "Behavioral Expectations Subcommittee of the Educational Programs Committee."

5. Memo from Kelly Mulroney to the Diversity Education Subcommittee on Follow-Up Programs, July 13, 1989.

6. Document is in possession of the authors.

7. Office of Orientation, University of Michigan, "Resources for Diversity Programming," also circulated at the 1988 NODA National Conference.

8. Office of Student Affairs, Smith College, handout to each freshman, September 1990. The document is in the possession of the authors.

9. *New York Times,* August 28, 1991.

10. *Wall Street Journal,* September 29, 1992.

11. *New York Times,* September 9, 1992.
12. *Wall Street Journal,* September 9, 1992.
13. University Life Division, University of Pennsylvania, "Racism Awareness Training Goals and Objectives" and "Racism Awareness Questionnaire," 1982; Janis Somerville, memorandum to University Life Staff, "Racism Awareness Training Questionnaire," July 6, 1982. These documents are in the possession of the authors.
14. Copy of letter is in the possession of the authors.
15. Mary Maples Dunn, "College Response to Bias Incidents," a memorandum to all Smith students, November 30, 1992 (the document is in the possession of the authors); Smith College, *AcaMEDIA,* December 19, 1992.
16. Leah Wing, "Multicultural Conflict Resolution Team," *The Fourth R,* December 1993–January 1994.
17. *Boston Globe,* January 3, 1997. The complaint was made with the Massachusetts Commission Against Discrimination. The pending lawsuit is *Nethersole v. Karam, et al.,* Docket No. 97-CV-12478 (U.S. District Court, Dist. of Mass.).
18. UCSD handout is in the possession of the authors.
19. *UCSD Guardian,* October 12, 1994.
20. *Weekly Northwestern Review,* September 29, 1989.
21. Ibid.
22. Copy of letter is in the possession of the authors.
23. *Philadelphia Inquirer,* October 18, 1993.
24. Ibid.
25. *New York Times,* September 9, 1992.
26. *The New Republic,* April 10, 1989.
27. Ibid.
28. Ibid.
29. Division of Continuing Education, University of South Carolina, University 101 Program, the National Center for the Study of the Freshman Year Experience, "Eighth Annual Conference Series: The Freshman Year Experience. The Freshman Year Experience and Beyond: Foundations for Improving the Undergraduate Experience," 1988–89.
30. Ibid., 1992–93.
31. *Access, Improving Diversity in Student Recruiting and Retention,* March–April 1996.
32. Bryn Mawr College, "Building Pluralism at Bryn Mawr College," August 31 and September 2, 1988, the "Glossary of Terms." The full "Building Pluralism" document is in the possession of the authors.
33. Ibid.
34. Orientation Program Task Force, University of Michigan, "Objectives" approved on November 19, 1987; "Winter Orientation Program," January 3, 1988; "Commitment to Diversity"; memorandum from Pam Horne, assistant director, Student Information Services, "Future Diversity Programming," October 9, 1988; Office of Orientation, "Commitment to Diversity," presented to the 1988 National Orientation Directors Association, 1988 National Conference, Sacramento, California. All documents are in the possession of the authors.
35. Ibid.
36. *Commentary,* August 1995.
37. *News Record,* May 10, 1991.

38. Abraham M. Miller, "Inside the Sensitivity Session," *The Intercollegiate Review* (Fall 1992); Walter Williams, "Gestapo Tactics Used to Crush Campus Dissent," *Cincinnati Enquirer,* February 21, 1993, and "Elite Obfuscation and Lies," *New Pittsburgh Courier,* April 10, 1993; Lloyd Billingsley, "Sensitivity Police Brutality," *Heterodoxy,* September 1992; and the definitive study by Nicholas and James Damask, "Inside Room 101: Anatomy of a Sensitivity Training Cover-up," *The World & I,* November 1994. See also Walter Williams, letter to the editor, *Cincinnati Enquirer,* February 28, 1993.

39. Nicholas A. Damask and Craig T. Cobane, "Our Little Workshop in Thought Control on Campus in Ohio," *Washington Times,* October 20, 1993. Craig T. Cobane, "Notes of a Sensitivity Training Survivor," *Heterodoxy,* March 1994.

40. Copies of e-mail both by the participants and by administrators acknowledging and apologizing for the event are in the possession of the authors.

41. Center for Diversity and Development, University of Massachusetts at Amherst, "Educational Films" (packet for RAs). The document is in the possession of the authors.

42. *Washington Times,* November 14, 1994. This material, including the pamphlet "Working With Gay, Lesbian and Bisexual Students in the Residence Halls" is in the possession of the authors. See also *Insight,* November 14, 1994.

43. *Chronicle of Higher Education,* September–December 1997.

44. Ibid.

45. See Oakes's posting at www.iclnet.org/clm. For more on the Timothy Gregory case at Cornell, see John Miller, "Bed Checks and Behavior Mod. PC Dorm," in *Heterodoxy,* November 1992.

46. All of the documents cited and described in the discussion of the United Ministries in Higher Education, Pennsylvania Commission, "Racism on Campus" seminar are in the possession of the authors. They were sent to official contacts at California University of Pennsylvania; Clarion University of Pennsylvania; Edinboro University of Pennsylvania; Indiana University of Pennsylvania; Slippery Rock University of Pennsylvania; Pennsylvania State University at Erie, Behrend College; University of Pittsburgh; Carnegie Mellon University; and Shippensburg University of Pennsylvania, by David C. Rich, United Ministries in Higher Education, Pennsylvania Commission, on December 1, 1990.

47. Ibid.

48. Phone conversation between Kors and Dr. Sherry Kuckuk, Indiana University of Pennsylvania, and message from Dr. Kuckuk left on Kors's answering machine tape. On the genesis of the documents, see Conley and Davidoff, "Being White at the University of Maryland" (1971), and Department of Resident Life, Indiana University–Bloomington, "Being White at Indiana University," c. 1973. See also Department of Residence Life, Indiana University–Bloomington, "Being Black at a Predominantly White University," two-page handout based on Frederick D. Harper, "Black Student Revolt on the White Campus," *Journal of College Student Personnel,* September 1969, p. 29.

Chapter 10. Double Standards: Some Are More Equal than Others

1. *Chronicle of Higher Education,* April 4, 1997.

2. Copies of all e-mail, correspondence, memoranda, notices, UCSD press releases and statements, congressional statements, and correspondence cited and described in the

following account of the UCSD case are in the possession of the authors. Also, on-the-record interviews by Kors, in January 1996, at UCSD, of Joseph Watson and Hal Pashler, and on-the-record telephone interview of June Terpstra by Lindsey Kaser, research assistant to Silverglate, and e-mail exchanges between Terpstra and Kaser.

3. Interview by Kors of Vice Chancellor Joseph Watson and interviews by Kors of computer system personnel at UCSD, January 1996.

4. *Voz Fronteriza,* March 1995.

5. *Voz Fronteriza,* May 1995.

6. *Voz Fronteriza,* March 1995.

7. *Voz Fronteriza,* May 1995.

8. *San Diego Union–Tribune,* July 6, 1995.

9. Interview by Kors.

10. K. L. Billingsley, "Campus Paper Endorses Killing," *Washington Times,* July 6, 1995.

11. *San Diego Union–Tribune,* July 6, 1995.

12. The details of *The Dartmouth Review* affair are drawn, except where otherwise specified, from the briefs and decision in *Dartmouth Review v. Dartmouth College,* New Hampshire Superior Court, January 3, 1989.

13. *The Dartmouth Review,* February 24, 1988.

14. *Boston Globe,* March 2, 1988.

15. The speech was distributed in printed form also, and a copy is in the possession of the authors.

16. See also, L. Gordon Crovitz, "Blacks on the Review," *Wall Street Journal,* December 28, 1988.

17. Copies of all documents, e-mail, memoranda, codes, and correspondence cited and described in the Jay Bergman case discussed below are in the possession of the authors. Interviews of various participants by Kors.

18. Richard E. Hill, Jr., "Justice Eludes Connecticut Professor," *Campus Report,* January–February, 1996.

19. *Recorder,* September 27, 1995.

20. *Recorder,* October 25, 1995.

21. *Washington Times,* December 13, 1995.

22. *New York Times,* January 16, 1996.

23. *New York Times,* December 5, 1994.

24. University of Pennsylvania, *Guidelines on Open Expression.*

25. A copy of the open expression monitor's report is in the possession of the authors.

26. *Daily Pennsylvanian,* February 14, 1986. Kors saw the poster and participated in the successful protest against the policy of censorship and prior restraint.

27. Kors was an eyewitness, and he reported favorably on the behavior of the open expression monitors to the Faculty Senate Executive Committee.

28. A copy of the open expression monitor's report is in the possession of the authors.

29. *Daily Pennsylvanian,* January 23, 1990; Kors was an eyewitness.

30. Kors was an eyewitness.

31. P. J. O'Rourke, *All the Trouble in the World* (New York: Atlantic Monthly Press, 1994), pp. 228–36.

32. *Cincinnati Enquirer,* March 2, 1996.

33. Kors was an eyewitness.

34. *Daily Pennsylvanian,* April 15, 1992.
35. *Daily Bruin,* January 25, 1995, undated press release, Rev. Paul Dechant, CSP, Associate Director, University Catholic Center at UCLA.
36. *New York Times,* May 13, 1988.
37. Ibid.
38. *Washington Times,* April 7, 1994. Interviews with personnel at Carnegie Mellon University. The case struck Catholic Pittsburgh deeply and was widely covered in the Pittsburgh press and in the campus press.
39. Ibid. *Washington Times,* March 30, 1994; *Washington Times,* April 2, 1994; *Pittsburgh Post–Gazette,* April 6, 1994; *Charleston Daily Mail,* March 29, 1994.
40. Ibid.
41. Ibid. *Washington Times,* May 22, 1995.
42. Carnegie Mellon University, press release, April 19, 1994. See also, *Pittsburgh Post–Gazette,* April 23, 1994.
43. *Washington Times,* July 7, 1994, and May 22, 1995. See also UPI, June 10, 1994; www.joc.mit.edu/charges.html.
44. Copies of all fliers, posters, e-mail, records, memoranda, documents, and correspondence cited or described in the Aist case discussed following are in the possession of the authors.
45. *Chronicle of Higher Education,* September 13, 1996, August 29, 1997.

Chapter 11. The Rules of Civilization

1. *Rochin v. California,* 342 U.S. 165 (1952).
2. *Jacobellis v. Ohio,* 378 U.S. 184, 197 (1964) (concurring).
3. *Baggett v. Bullitt,* 377 U.S. 360 (1964).
4. *Smith v. Goguen,* 415 U.S. 566 (1974).
5. *Cramp v. Board of Public Instruction of Orange County, Florida,* 368 U.S. 278 (1961).
6. Laurence H. Tribe, *American Constitutional Law,* 2d ed. (Mineola, N.Y.: The Foundation Press), p. 1302.
7. *Powell v. State of Alabama,* 287 U.S. 45 (1932).
8. *Greene v. McElroy,* 360 U.S. 474 (1959).
9. *Maryland v. Craig,* 497 U.S. 836 (1990).
10. *In re Oliver,* 333 U.S. 257 (1948).
11. *Richmond Newspapers, Inc. v. Virginia,* 448 U.S. 555 (1980).
12. *Tumey v. State of Ohio,* 273 U.S. 510 (1927).
13. James M. Picozzi, "University Disciplinary Process: What's Fair, What's Due, and What You Don't Get," 96 *Yale Law Journal* (1987) 2132.
14. The disciplinary policies and procedures described in this chapter are from the Websites and handbooks of the colleges and universities discussed during the period 1994–97, unless otherwise indicated.
15. *Rosenberg v. United States,* 346 U.S. 273 (1953).
16. Civil Liberties Union of Harvard, "The Need for Reform of Disciplinary Hearings at Harvard College," October 26, 1992.
17. This hearing involved charges of violation of privacy and potential charges of sexual harassment against male undergraduates who were represented generally by

Harvey Silverglate but represented before the Administrative Board by Professors Randall Kennedy and David Rosenberg, both tenured professors at Harvard Law School. The actual details of what transpired in the hearing remain closed per Harvard's rules and procedures, but correspondence and memoranda relating to the students' representation are in the possession of Silverglate.

18. *United States v. Burr,* 8 U.S. 470 (1807).
19. *Sheppard v. Maxwell,* 384 U.S. 333 (1966).

Chapter 12. The Courts of Star Chamber

1. Copies of all documents, correspondence, press releases, decisions, memoranda, and official reports and findings cited or described below in the discussion of the Leroy Young case are in the possession of the authors. There also is a partial public record established by the complaint (and documents appended to the complaint) in *Leroy S. Young and Tatum Young v. University System of New Hampshire, Plymouth State College and Donald P. Wharton,* Civil Action No. 96-75-M, before the U.S. District Court for the District of New Hampshire. The defendants reportedly offered an eighty-thousand-dollar settlement of this suit, raising the due process issues, but the Youngs refused, and, as we write, the case is pending.

2. State of New Hampshire Department of Employment Security, Decision of Appeal Tribunal, Docket No. 94-1486, October 25, 1994.

3. *Starishevsky v. Hofstra* (1994) 161 Misc. 2d 137, 612 N.Y.S. 2d 794 (Supreme Court of New York, Suffolk County).

4. On the Maas case, see the briefs, memoranda, and decisions thus far in *James B. Maas v. Cornell University,* Supreme Court of the State of New York (Third Department), 95-829. See also, *Chronicle of Higher Education,* February 10, September 8, 1995, August 27, 1996; Center for Individual Rights, press release, "Cornell Prof Sues Over 'Harassment' Conviction," August 1, 1995; and Center for Individual Rights, *Docket Report,* March 1997.

5. *Chronicle of Higher Education,* September 8, 1995.

6. *Chronicle of Higher Education,* March 16, 1994.

7. Center for Individual Rights, press release, November 15, 1996; *Chronicle of Higher Education,* March 10, 1998.

8. On the Ramdas Lamb case, see the briefs, exhibits, testimony, and decisions in *Michelle M. Gretzinger v. Ramdas Lamb . . . and . . . Ramdas Lamb v. Michelle M. Gretzinger,* U.S. District Court for the District of Hawaii, 94-00684, and the briefs in *Lamb v. University of Hawaii,* U.S. District Court for the District of Hawaii, 96-00884.

9. Interview by Kors of Tony Gill, attorney for Ramdas Lamb. On the university's settlement with Gretzinger, see *USA Today,* October 10, 1995.

10. Copies of all documents, evidence, memoranda, and correspondence cited or described in the Tim Monaco case are in the possession of the authors. Also, Kors interviewed Monaco, Neil Hamburg, then of the Office of the General Counsel, and other university officials who request anonymity concerning the Monaco case.

11. On the Spragg case, see the informative Goon Pattanumotana, "Injustice at SDSU," in *California Review,* March 1997.

12. Full documentation of this case, including briefs, correspondence between the college and both the students and the parents of the students, official statements, and campus coverage of the events are in the possession of the authors. In addition, Kors conducted confidential interviews with participants in this case.

13. *Wall Street Journal,* September 27, 1993.

14. Krishna Winston, Letter to the Editor, *Wall Street Journal,* October 20, 1993.

15. *Wall Street Journal,* April 12, 1994.

16. *New York Times,* June 1, 1994.

17. Ibid.

18. Nina Bernstein, "Offstage Justice," *New York Times,* May 5, 6, 1996.

19. Ibid.

20. *Philadelphia Inquirer,* November 27, 1996. See also *Chronicle of Higher Education,* December 13, 1996.

21. Donald P. Russo, "Campus 'Courts' Deny Basic Rights to Students," *Philadelphia Inquirer,* January 3, 1994.

Chapter 13. "Not on My Watch"

1. Among extensive press coverage of this incident, see the Associated Press, May 16, 1988; *Orange County Register,* May 15, 1988; *New York Times,* May 14, 1988.

2. Policy Statement on Sexually Explicit Films, MIT, April 1986.

3. Audiotape of MIT Committee on Discipline Hearing re: Adam Dershowitz's charge of sexual harassment, November 17, 1987, in possession of the authors.

4. Letter from Paul C. Joss to Adam Dershowitz, November 18, 1987.

5. Letter from Shirley McBay to Adam Dershowitz, August 4, 1988.

6. Letter to the Editor of *The Tech* from Samuel J. Keyser, September 9, 1988.

7. Letter from Keyser to Dershowitz, October 7, 1988.

8. Letter from Harvey A. Silverglate to Samuel Jay Keyser, March 12, 1990.

9. Letter from Jerome N. Weinstein to Harvey A. Silverglate, April 11, 1990.

10. Letter from Harvey A. Silverglate to Charles M. Vest, January 21, 1991.

11. Letter from Jerome N. Weinstein to Harvey A. Silverglate, February 7, 1991.

12. For extensive press coverage on this incident, see the MIT Student Association for Freedom of Expression's Website (www.mit.edu/safe/home.html).

13. Michael Miles, "Tewey Deserves What He is Receiving," *The Tech,* Massachusetts Institute of Technology, November 30, 1993.

14. Art Mellor, "Tewhey Issued Charges on False Claims," *The Tech,* December 7, 1993.

15. Josh Hartmann, "One Complaint Filed Against Tewhey, Provost Says," *The Tech,* April 27, 1993.

16. *James Tewhey v. MIT,* Massachusetts Superior Court, County of Middlesex, No. 95-2130. Complaint filed April 11, 1995.

17. "MIT Should Investigate Tewhey's Charges," *The Tech,* November 16, 1993.

18. See SAFE Website (www.mit.edu/safe/cases/mit-tewhey/summary.html).

19. *New York Times,* February 1, 1995.

20. Associated Press, February 8, 1995.

21. Reuters, February 8, 1995.

22. Ibid.

23. See Sean Glennon, "Speaking of the First Amendment," *Valley Advocate* (MA), December 14–20, 1995; Anthony Lewis, "Living in a Cocoon," *New York Times,* November 27, 1995; Kevin Cullen, "Codified Tolerance Criticized at Umass," *Boston Globe,* November 4, 1994; Laurie Loisel, "Umass Tries to Define Harassment," *Daily Hampshire Gazette,* November 20, 1995.

24. Proposed harassment policy sent to UMass community with letter from James Delle and Associate Chancellor Sue Pearson on September 20, 1995.

25. Letter from Robert Chatelle on behalf of the National Writers Union to GEO members at UMass, November 13, 1995.

26. GEO Press Release, December 8, 1995; see also *Boston Globe,* December 12, 1995.

27. University of Massachusetts-Amherst, Faculty Senate meeting, March 14, 1996 (contemporaneous faculty notes and tape recording).

28. Letter from Allan A. Ryan to Harvey A. Silverglate, January 6, 1994.

29. Letter from Margaret H. Marshall to Harvey A. Silverglate, November 15, 1994.

30. Letter from Harvey A. Silverglate to John B. Fox, Jr. April 12, 1995.

31. Letter from Harvey A. Silverglate to Robert Clark, March 2, 1995.

32. Letter from Robert Clark to Harvey A. Silverglate, April 3, 1995.

33. "Battle at Harvard Law Over Tenure; So-Called Crits v. Traditionalists," *The National Law Journal,* June 22, 1987; Peter Collier, "Blood on the Charles," *Vanity Fair,* October 1992, p. 144.

34. Harvey A. Silverglate, "Harvard Law Caves in to the Censors," *Wall Street Journal,* January 8, 1996.

35. Robert Clark, letter to the editor, *Wall Street Journal,* January 19, 1996.

36. David Rosenberg, letter to the editor, *Wall Street Journal,* January 31, 1996.

37. The article was updated and appeared in the newsletter of the Massachusetts Bar Association in November 1996.

38. *Daily Pennsylvanian,* March 20, 1990.

39. Copy of the letter published in the *Almanac* is in the possession of the authors.

40. Copy of letter is in the possession of the authors.

41. Copy of letter is in the possession of the authors.

42. Copy of letter is in the possession of the authors.

43. Testimony of Sheldon Hackney, U.S. Senate, Committee on Labor and National Resources, nomination hearing, June 25, 1993.

44. Ibid.

45. *Wall Street Journal,* June 25, 1993.

46. Nat Hentoff, *Free Speech for Me—But Not For Thee* (New York: HarperCollins, 1992), p. 189.

47. Testimony of Sheldon Hackney, June 25, 1993.

48. The documents are in the possession of the authors.

49. A copy of the memorandum is in the possession of the authors.

50. University of Pennsylvania, "Incidents of Harassment," *Diversity Education Labor Day Facilitators Guide,* 1989. The document is in the possession of the authors.

51. *Daily Pennsylvanian,* October 2, 1989; *Almanac,* December 19, 1989.

52. *Almanac,* December 19, 1989.

Chapter 14. Sue the Bastards?

1. *Dixon v. Alabama State Board of Education,* 294 F.2d 150 (5th Cir. 1961).
2. Ibid., 153–54.
3. *Goss v. Lopez,* 419 U.S. 565 (1975).
4. *Gaspar v. Bruton,* 513 F.2d 843 (10th Cir. 1975); *Greenhill v. Bailey,* 519 F.2d 5, 9 (8th Cir. 1975).
5. *Board of Curators of the University of Missouri v. Horowitz,* 435 U.S. 78 (1978).
6. *Gabrilowitz v. Newman,* 582 F.2d 100 (1st Cir. 1978).
7. *Cloud v. Trustees of Boston University,* 720 F.2d 721 (1st Cir. 1983).
8. *Coveney v. President & Trustees of Holy Cross College,* 388 Mass. 16, 19 (1983).
9. *Fellheimer v. Middlebury College,* 869 F. Supp. 238 (DVT 1994).
10. *A. and B., Plaintiffs, v. C. College and D. Defendants,* 863 F. Supp. 156 (SDNY 1994).
11. Complaint for Plaintiff, *Jacobowitz v. Trustees of the University of Pennsylvania* (Philadelphia Ct. of Common Pleas 1994) (No. 2457).
12. Preliminary Objections of Defendant at 7–8, *Jacobowitz v. Trustees of the University of Pennsylvania* (Philadelphia Ct. of Common Pleas 1994) (No. 2457).
13. *Brady v. Maryland,* 373 U.S. 83 (1963).
14. *Russell v. Salve Regina College,* 649 F.Supp. 391 (D.R.I. 1986).
15. The press conference was held March 12, 1991.
16. See chapter 4, note 33.

Chapter 15. "Sunlight Is the Best Disinfectant"

1. "Lewis Opposes Listing Ad Board Case Records," *Harvard Crimson,* November 22, 1996.
2. Federal Educational Rights and Privacy Act, 20 U.S.C. §1232g (b)(1).
3. University of Pennsylvania, *Almanac,* February 13, 1996.
4. Ibid.
5. *Daily Pennsylvanian,* February 22, 1996; University of Pennsylvania, University Council, minutes of February 21, 1996; Kors interviews with over a score of participants at the University Council meeting. See also, *Almanac,* February 27, 1996.
6. She announced this convocation on "civility" in December of 1996. According to the *New York Times,* February 28, 1998, the forty-eight-member national commission on civility, "made up heavily of academics," is "in the midst of a three-to-five-year study." (Let us hope they started very close to home.)
7. University Council, February 21, 1996; postings on the newsgroups upenn.talk and upenn.free-speech throughout February and early March 1996; *Daily Pennsylvanian,* February–March 4, 1996.
8. *Daily Pennsylvanian,* March 2, 1996.
9. *Daily Pennsylvanian,* March 4, 5, 1996; *Almanac,* March 5, 1996.
10. See Speech to Legislative Conference of the National Congress of Parents and Teachers, reprinted in 120 *Congressional Record* 36532 (Dec. 13, 1974) as recounted in *Bauer v. Kincaid,* 759 F.Supp. 575, 590 (1991).
11. 20 U.S.C. §1232g (a) *et. seq.*
12. 20 U.S.C. §1232h(b).

13. Justice Arthur Goldberg concurring in *New York Times Co. v. Sullivan,* 84 S.Ct. 710, 739 (1964).
14. Kors interview of current editors of the *Wabash Commentary,* February 21, 1998.
15. Copies of all correspondence and e-mails are in the possession of the authors.
16. *Almanac,* April 5, 1994.
17. The university's brief is in the possession of the authors.
18. The memorandum and administrative exchange of e-mail are in the possession of the authors.
19. The letter, an undated "Open Letter to the Editors and Staff of the *Penn Law Forum,*" with written signatures, is in the possession of the authors. See Lily Eng, "Spoof in Penn's Law School Student Paper Sparks Outrage," *Philadelphia Inquirer,* February 23, 1995. Kors interviewed the professor and dean who was the object of the vulgar satire—she is a strong civil libertarian and wanted no censorship, explicit or implicit, of the students—three years later, on February 28, 1998.
20. "A Response to the Faculty's Open Letter," with handwritten signatures, February 21, 1995. A copy is in the possession of the authors.
21. The February 27 memorandum to "Penn Law Students," with a copy of the faculty resolution, passed that day, is in the possession of the authors.
22. A Nexis search disclosed over six hundred articles and news program transcripts on the water buffalo affair during those two years.
23. *Campus* (Fall 1993).
24. *Chronicle of Higher Education,* March 24, 1995.
25. University of Pennsylvania, Board of Trustees, resolution of September 19, 1993. The resolution insisted that Penn students from this time forward "must be treated equally" and guaranteed that the trustees would ensure policies that reflected the "fundamental importance of freedom of speech."
26. *Almanac,* September 28, 1993.
27. University of Pennsylvania, "Final Report of the Commission on Strengthening the Community," February 1, 1994. See also, *Daily Pennsylvanian,* February 1, 1994.
28. The documents, including voluminous e-mail exchanges between Fagin and Kors, are in the possession of the authors.
29. Letter from Judith Rodin to "Penn Parents and Alumni," June 30, 1995.
30. Kors interviewed both Cade and Halvorssen after this interview.
31. Thor Halvorssen, "An Interview with Valarie," *Red and Blue,* November 1995.
32. Ibid.
33. Ibid.
34. Ibid.
35. Ibid.
36. Valarie Swain-Cade McCoullum, vice provost, Division of University Life, "A Strategic Plan for University Life," April 1996.
37. Ibid.
38. Copies of all materials pertaining to this case are in the possession of the authors through the kindness of the student involved. Kors also interviewed several administrators and students close to the affair.
39. *Almanac,* October 14, November 18, 1997.

40. Kors was cofounder and an eight-year resident of Van Pelt College House. Over the years, he has interviewed scores of its residents, across all spectrums, about their experiences there.

41. Robert Bolt, *A Man for All Seasons* (New York: Vintage, 1960), p. 92.

INDEX

ABOUT THE AUTHORS

Alan Charles Kors is professor of history at the University of Pennsylvania, where he teaches the intellectual history of the seventeenth and eighteenth centuries. He has written extensively on early-modern French thought and is currently the editor-in-chief of the Oxford University Press *Encyclopedia of the Enlightenment*. He lives with his wife, Erika, and their children in Wallingford, Pennsylvania. His daughter, Samantha, is an undergraduate at Princeton University, and his son, Brian, is a student at Strath Haven High School.

Harvey A. Silverglate practices criminal defense and civil liberties law with the firm of Silverglate & Good in Boston, and is the civil liberties columnist for the *Boston Phoenix* and the *National Law Journal,* both weeklies. He has litigated and written extensively on freedom of speech and freedom of religion issues. He has been active for his entire professional life in the American Civil Liberties Union and is a former president and current member of the Board of Directors of the Massachusetts state affiliate. He taught at the Harvard Law School during a sabbatical in 1987. He lives with his wife, Elsa Dorfman, in Cambridge, Massachusetts. His son, Isaac, is an undergraduate at Columbia University.

Kors and Silverglate have been the closest friends—indeed, brothers—since they met as undergraduates at Princeton University in 1960. Despite their extensive and long-running political, intellectual, and personal differences, they agree passionately with John Stuart Mill's *On Liberty,* that individual freedom and voluntary association are the path to all human dignity and all possibility of progress. They undertook this book as a result of their informal collaboration over many years in defense of students threatened with the new tyrannies.